Feast Days for the Contemporary Mind

By Craig Martin Barnes

"Thy way, O God, is in the sanctuary: who is so great a God as our God?"
Psalm 77:13

World rights reserved. This book or any portion thereof may not be copied or reproduced in any form or manner whatever, except as provided by law, without the written permission of the publisher, except by a reviewer who may quote brief passages in a review.

The author assumes full responsibility for the accuracy of all facts and quotations as cited in this book. The opinions expressed in this book are the author's personal views and interpretations, and do not necessarily reflect those of the publisher.

This book is provided with the understanding that the publisher is not engaged in giving spiritual, legal, medical, or other professional advice. If authoritative advice is needed, the reader should seek the counsel of a competent professional.

Copyright © 2014 Craig Martin Barnes
ISBN-13: 978-1-4796-0138-7 (Paperback)
ISBN-13: 978-1-4796-0141-7 (Hardback)
ISBN-13: 978-1-4796-0139-4 (ePub)
ISBN-13: 978-1-4796-0140-0 (Mobi)
Library of Congress Control Number: 2013956411

Published by

www.TEACHServices.com • (800) 367-1844

All Scripture quotations, unless otherwise noted, are taken from the King James Version. Public domain.

Scripture quotations marked (Good News) are from Good News For Modern Man. Copyright © 1966 American Bible Society. All rights reserved. Used by permission.

Scripture quotations marked (NEB) are from The New English Bible. Copyright © 1961, 1970 by Oxford University Press and Cambridge University Press. All rights reserved. Used by permission.

Scripture quotations marked (NIV) are from The Holy Bible, New International Version®, NIV®, Copyright © 1973, 1978, 1984, 2011 by Biblica, Inc.® Used by permission. All rights reserved worldwide.

Scripture quotations marked (RSV) are from the Revised Standard Version of the Bible, copyright 1952 [2nd edition, 1971] by the Division of Christian Education of the National Council of the Churches of Christ in the United States of America. Used by permission. All rights reserved.

Scripture quotations marked (RV) are from the Revised Version. Public domain.

Throughout this book all emphasis within the references is supplied by the author, unless stated that the emphasis is original.

Table of Contents

Acknowledgments		vi
Foreword		vii
Preface		viii
Introduction		x
Prologue	"Why was Sin Permitted?"	xi
Chapter 1	Feast of Firstfruits: Christ, Our Representative—The Firstfruits Concept	19
Chapter 2	Feast of the Passover: Christ, Our Salvation	32
Chapter 3	Feast of Unleavened Bread: New Life	43
Chapter 4	Feast of Unleavened Bread: Under Control	53
Chapter 5	Feast of Unleavened Bread: Who God Is	67
Chapter 6	Feast of Firstfruits: Christ, Our Harvest—The Fruit of Representation	77
Chapter 7	Feast of Weeks—Pentecost: A Transition	86
Chapter 8	Feast of Trumpets: The History	93
Chapter 9	Feast of Trumpets: The Prophecy	105
Chapter 10	Feast of Trumpets: The Event	111
Chapter 11	Feast of the Day of Atonement: The Coverage	115
Chapter 12	Feast of the Day of Atonement: The Affliction	127
Chapter 13	Feast of the Day of Atonement: Offering by Fire	133
Chapter 14	Feast of the Day of Atonement: A Call to Rest	153
Chapter 15	Feast of Tabernacles	173
Epilogue	"It Is Finished"	192
Appendices		198
Appendix A	The Loom of Heaven	199
Appendix B	Studies in Galatians 2:20	200
Appendix C	Every Man Is in Christ When Entering the World	202
Appendix D	The Cleansing of the Sanctuary	203
Appendix E	Setting the date of "The End of the World"	204
Appendix F	Will There be a Modern-day Prophet?	208
Appendix G	Health	218
Appendix H	Apparel	229
Appendix I	The Daniel 8 and 9 Timeline	236
Appendix J	The Hebrew Religious Calendar	241
Appendix K	The Godhead	245
Appendix L	Are the Feasts to be Observed Literally Today?	257
Appendix M	Christ, Our Representative: Treatise Relating to Arminianism/Calvinism	268
Appendix N	When All Earthly Hope Is Gone	276
Bibliography		277
Index		281

Acknowledgments

To my two fathers who gave me life. First, to my heavenly Father, who is my inspiration and strength. Without Him and His Son, there would be nothing of me, and there would be no book, nor would there be any reason for one.

And secondly, to my earthly father and mother, "the strictest mom in town," who raised me in a Christian home and taught me by precept and example the principles of Christian living. I have never forgotten your wise words of advice:

- "You are not so-and-so, and I am not so-and-so's mom."
- "If it isn't any fun without using money, it isn't a game."
- "Too much of any good thing, is still too much!"
- "The most important asset you have is your health."
- "Don't be a gunslinger, because sooner or later someone will come around who is faster than you."
- "You should always be ready to walk away from affluence without saying 'Goodbye.'"
- "Your actions speak so loudly, I cannot hear what you are saying."
- And my favorite: "Church is not a club."

To my wife, my best friend, my first book critic, and the most precious earthly gift from God I could ever possibly have. She is my Joy.

And to all who have assisted in preparing this book for publication, your contributions have been invaluable, without which this book would not be what it is.

Thank you to all of you for allowing God to use you.

Foreword

I groaned! I had promised Craig that I would look at his manuscript on "feast days" and wondered why he would write on this subject with so many books already on the market! One of them being my own!

How could I be so wrong! As soon as I scanned his introduction, I was hooked! Craig wrapped me in his literary arms and opened my eyes as if I were being awakened from a coma!

He quoted a line from my favorite author that said the "entire system of Judaism was a compacted prophecy of the gospel" [see the preface for the entire quote and reference]. Frankly, I had read those words many times through the years, but Craig turned the lights on for me.

With the skill of a professional auditor, he led me by the hand through the seven feast days of the Israelite year, and I saw for the first time, all over again, why a caring God would explain the "greatest story ever told" through the annual feasts every Jew looked forward to throughout the year.

This book is not a dusty examination of Jewish life thousands of years ago. I felt God talking to me in 2012 as if I were that target for which the Feast of Tabernacles and the Feast of the Day of Atonement were especially given. Now, that does not happen with every book manuscript I have ever read!

Craig skillfully uses illustrations that only an auditor could think of. I feel instructed and freshened! Look for his illustration that illuminated how cleaning a sink is similar to preparing us to reflect the image of our Savior. Or for how an auditor selects his "population sample" as he prepares his auditing statement for the world to see and understand!

Our author realizes how the average reader does not want to be loaded down with "heavy detail" so he prepared dozens of appendices on very important aspects of God's great instruction lessons. Like a good auditor, he wants his readers to get the "full" story, nothing hidden. Some of those appendices are worth the price of this book!

When I finished this manuscript, I felt like I had been given a seminary course on why God took so much time on getting the Israelites to understand and appreciate the good news in their feast days. Just like any proper seminary course, the reader will read each section carefully and pause. Get the message of the first "lecture" clearly, then proceed, like climbing a mountain, always keeping one eye on the summit. When you get "there," the whole world looks different and more glorious.

That is what awaits the reader who owns every word of this awesome book.

Herbert Edgar Douglass, Th.D.
Lincoln, CA
December 7, 2012

Preface

Why study a set of dusty, old feast days? After all, are they not a figment of the Old Testament dating back thousands of years? What could such ancient festivals have to do with the fast-paced frenzy of this modern communication era with its cell phones, televisions, and computers, not to mention pods and blackberries that you don't eat?

To answer this question, I refer to another author, for she writes before computers were available to help her, during an age when the zipper was still on the drawing board. However, even her writings speak to us who are living in the postmodern era. Listen:

> In every page, whether history, or precept, or prophecy, the Old Testament Scriptures are irradiated with the glory of the Son of God. *So far as it was of divine institution, the entire system of Judaism was a compacted prophecy of the gospel.* To Christ "give all the prophets witness." Acts 10:43. From the promise given to Adam, down through the patriarchal line and the legal economy, heaven's glorious light made plain the footsteps of the Redeemer. Seers beheld the Star of Bethlehem, the Shiloh to come, as future things swept before them in mysterious procession. In every sacrifice Christ's death was shown. In every cloud of incense His righteousness ascended. By every jubilee trumpet His name was sounded. In the awful mystery of the holy of holies His glory dwelt.[1]

Through my studies, I have discovered that the seven Jewish feast days by themselves are a "compacted prophecy of the gospel" and resounding good news, for they speak to us especially about Christ's closing work during the last days of earth's history. Each feast says something about Jesus Christ: who He is, what He is doing (even today), and what He is about to do in the future. Speaking of trumpets, there is a whole feast named after *them*, for God is sending to this world a resounding warning so that all may be enlightened and no one will lose out or be lost by accident.

The seven feasts are as follows:

1. **Feast of the Passover,** representing Christ's sacrificial death for the human race.
2. **Feast of Unleavened Bread**, representing Christ's perfect life as our heritage.
3. **Feast of Firstfruits,** representing that Christ is the representative of the human race, who in that capacity took us, corporately and individually (in title), to the harvest of the earth, that is,

---

[1] Ellen G. White, *The Desire of Ages*, pp. 211, 212.

heaven and the new earth to be created.
4. **Feast of Weeks or Pentecost**, representing the early rain of the Holy Spirit.
5. **Feast of Trumpets**, representing the announcement of the convocation Day of Atonement soon to take place.
6. **Feast of the Day of Atonement**, representing a "meeting" of God's people, preparing for the second coming of Christ.
7. **Feast of Tabernacles**, representing the experiential completion of the harvest of the earth, that is, the antitypical fulfillment of the Feast of Firstfruits.

Antitypically, the first five have already been fulfilled. We are currently living in feast number six, and feast number seven is soon to happen. So, wipe off the dust, sharpen your knife, and pick up your fork and spoon. Enjoy a scrumptious, delectable, luscious, even ambrosial, seven-course meal, already prepared and ready to eat—fresh from the garden of God's soul.

The opinions expressed in the book are my own and have been derived from years of study. They may or may not express the opinions or official position of any specific church or denomination. Since each chapter of the book is built on the ones that come before it, I suggest you digest this multi-course meal one course at a time in the order they appear.

I pray that all might hear this invitation and that you, dear reader, will let it ring in your ears and take it to heart. May you receive the unspeakable joy that is yours, joy that you may never have known or experienced, until now.

Introduction

You don't have to read the prologue if you don't want to.[1] After all, I didn't write it. However, the prologue sets the stage for the book.

You also don't have to read the epilogue if you don't want to.[2] I didn't write that, either. But the epilogue sets the stage for the rest of your life.

I will introduce the author of these two sections later in the book, but my book is not about authors, although I invite you to review the bibliography if you are interested in other titles that I have been blessed by reading. Neither is it about just writing another book. It is about introducing you to an Author who deserves the utmost respect and admiration. If nothing else is accomplished by this book, I would consider all my work to be a success if you would become intimately acquainted with the Author of the Bible. The feast days, being a biblical concept, provide an excellent framework through which to do this. They bring a fresh approach to an old subject. I am infinitely grateful to the Author of the Bible for providing this teaching aid.

I introduce to you my best friend, Jesus Christ.

> Accordingly, I encourage first of all, that petitions, prayers, intercessions, and giving of thanks, be made in behalf of all people; For kings, and for all that are in authority; that we may lead a quiet and tranquil life in all godliness and reverence. For this is noble and acceptable before the One who delivers us, Jesus Christ our Savior; who desires all people to receive the experience of salvation, and to come to a precise and correct knowledge of the truth. For God is one, and there is one mediator between God and men, the man Christ Jesus. (1 Tim. 2:1–5, author's paraphrase)

---

1 The prologue is the first chapter of Ellen G. White's flagship masterpiece *Patriarchs and Prophets*, the first volume in *The Conflict of the Ages* series.

2 The epilogue is chapter 79 of *The Desire of Ages*, the central book, volume 3, of Ellen G. White's *The Conflict of the Ages* series.

Prologue

"Why was Sin Permitted?"[1]

"God is love." 1 John 4:16. His nature, His law, is love. It ever has been; it ever will be. "The high and lofty One that inhabiteth eternity," whose "ways are everlasting," changeth not. With Him "is no variableness, neither shadow of turning." Isaiah 57:15; Habakkuk 3:6; James 1:17.

Every manifestation of creative power is an expression of infinite love. The sovereignty of God involves fullness of blessing to all created beings. The psalmist says:

> "Strong is Thy hand, and high is Thy right hand.
> Righteousness and judgment are the foundation of Thy throne:
> Mercy and truth go before Thy face.
> Blessed is the people that know the joyful sound:
> They walk, O Lord, in the light of Thy countenance.
> In Thy name do they rejoice all the day:
> And in Thy righteousness are they exalted.
> For Thou art the glory of their strength: …
> For our shield belongeth unto Jehovah,
> And our king to the Holy One." Psalm 89:13-18, R.V.

The history of the great conflict between good and evil, from the time it first began in heaven to the final overthrow of rebellion and the total eradication of sin, is also a demonstration of God's unchanging love.

The Sovereign of the universe was not alone in His work of beneficence. He had an associate—a co-worker who could appreciate His purposes, and could share His joy in giving happiness to created beings. "In the beginning was the Word, and the Word was with God, and the Word was God. The same was in the beginning with God." John 1:1, 2. Christ, the Word, the only begotten of God, was one with the eternal Father—one in nature, in character, in purpose—the only being that could enter into all the counsels and purposes of God. "His name shall be called Wonderful, Counselor, The mighty God, The everlasting Father, The Prince of Peace." Isaiah 9:6. His "goings forth have been from of old, from everlasting." Micah 5:2. And the Son of God declares concerning Himself: "The Lord possessed Me in the beginning of His way, before His works of old. I was set up from everlasting…. When He appointed the foundations of the earth: then I was by Him, as one brought up with Him: and I was daily His delight,

---

1 Ellen G. White, *Patriarchs and Prophets*, pp. 33-43. This first chapter of *Patriarchs and Prophets* is reprinted in the prologue in its entirety.

rejoicing always before Him." Proverbs 8:22–30.

The Father wrought by His Son in the creation of all heavenly beings. "By Him were all things created, … whether they be thrones, or dominions, or principalities, or powers: all things were created by Him, and for Him." Colossians 1:16. Angels are God's ministers, radiant with the light ever flowing from His presence and speeding on rapid wing to execute His will. But the Son, the anointed of God, the "express image of His person," "the brightness of His glory," "upholding all things by the word of His power," holds supremacy over them all. Hebrews 1:3. "A glorious high throne from the beginning," was the place of His sanctuary (Jeremiah 17:12); "a scepter of righteousness," the scepter of His kingdom. Hebrews 1:8. "Honor and majesty are before Him: strength and beauty are in His sanctuary." Psalm 96:6. Mercy and truth go before His face. Psalm 89:14.

The law of love being the foundation of the government of God, the happiness of all intelligent beings depends upon their perfect accord with its great principles of righteousness. God desires from all His creatures the service of love—service that springs from an appreciation of His character. He takes no pleasure in a forced obedience; and to all He grants freedom of will, that they may render Him voluntary service.

So long as all created beings acknowledged the allegiance of love, there was perfect harmony throughout the universe of God. It was the joy of the heavenly host to fulfill the purpose of their Creator. They delighted in reflecting His glory and showing forth His praise. And while love to God was supreme, love for one another was confiding and unselfish. There was no note of discord to mar the celestial harmonies. But a change came over this happy state. There was one who perverted the freedom that God had granted to His creatures. Sin originated with him who, next to Christ, had been most honored of God and was highest in power and glory among the inhabitants of heaven. Lucifer, "son of the morning," was first of the covering cherubs, holy and undefiled. He stood in the presence of the great Creator, and the ceaseless beams of glory enshrouding the eternal God rested upon him. "Thus saith the Lord God; Thou sealest up the sum, full of wisdom, and perfect in beauty. Thou hast been in Eden the garden of God; every precious stone was thy covering…. Thou art the anointed cherub that covereth; and I have set thee so: thou wast upon the holy mountain of God; thou hast walked up and down in the midst of the stones of fire. Thou wast perfect in thy ways from the day that thou wast created, till iniquity was found in thee." Ezekiel 28:12–15.

Little by little Lucifer came to indulge the desire for self-exaltation. The Scripture says, "Thine heart was lifted up because of thy beauty, thou hast corrupted thy wisdom by reason of thy brightness." Ezekiel 28:17. "Thou hast said in thine heart, … I will exalt my throne above the stars of God…. I will be like the Most High." Isaiah 14:13, 14. Though all his glory was from God, this mighty angel came to regard it as pertaining to himself. Not content with his position, though honored above the heavenly host, he ventured to covet homage due alone to the Creator. Instead of seeking to make God supreme in the affections and allegiance of all created beings, it was his endeavor to secure their service and loyalty to himself. And coveting the glory with which the infinite Father had invested His Son, this prince of angels aspired to power that was the prerogative of Christ alone.

Now the perfect harmony of heaven was broken. Lucifer's disposition to serve himself instead of his Creator aroused a feeling of apprehension when observed by those who considered that the glory of God should be supreme. In heavenly council the angels pleaded with Lucifer. The Son of God presented before him the greatness, the goodness, and the justice of the Creator, and the sacred, unchanging nature of His law. God Himself had established the order of heaven; and in departing from it, Lucifer would dishonor his Maker and bring ruin upon himself. But the warning, given in infinite love and mercy, only aroused a spirit of resistance. Lucifer allowed his jealousy of Christ to prevail, and became the more determined.

To dispute the supremacy of the Son of God, thus impeaching the wisdom and love of the Creator, had become the purpose of this prince of angels. To this object he was about to bend the energies of that master mind, which, next to Christ's, was first among the hosts of God. But He who would have the will of all His creatures free, left none unguarded to the bewildering sophistry by which rebellion would seek to justify itself. Before the great contest should open, all were to have a clear presentation of His will, whose wisdom and goodness were the spring of all their joy.

The King of the universe summoned the heavenly hosts before Him, that in their presence He might set forth the true position of His Son and show the relation He sustained to all created beings. The Son of God shared the Father's throne, and the glory of the eternal, self-existent One encircled both. About the throne gathered the holy angels, a vast, unnumbered throng—"ten thousand times ten thousand, and thousands of thousands" (Revelation 5:11.), the most exalted angels, as ministers and subjects, rejoicing in the light that fell upon them from the presence of the Deity. Before the assembled inhabitants of heaven the King declared that none but Christ, the Only Begotten of God, could fully enter into His purposes, and to Him it was committed to execute the mighty counsels of His will. The Son of God had wrought the Father's will in the creation of all the hosts of heaven; and to Him, as well as to God, their homage and allegiance were due. Christ was still to exercise divine power, in the creation of the earth and its inhabitants. But in all this He would not seek power or exaltation for Himself contrary to God's plan, but would exalt the Father's glory and execute His purposes of beneficence and love.

The angels joyfully acknowledged the supremacy of Christ, and prostrating themselves before Him, poured out their love and adoration. Lucifer bowed with them, but in his heart there was a strange, fierce conflict. Truth, justice, and loyalty were struggling against envy and jealousy. The influence of the holy angels seemed for a time to carry him with them. As songs of praise ascended in melodious strains, swelled by thousands of glad voices, the spirit of evil seemed vanquished; unutterable love thrilled his entire being; his soul went out, in harmony with the sinless worshippers, in love to the Father and the Son. But again he was filled with pride in his own glory. His desire for supremacy returned, and envy of Christ was once more indulged. The high honors conferred upon Lucifer were not appreciated as God's special gift, and therefore, called forth no gratitude to his Creator. He glorified in his brightness and exaltation and aspired to be equal with God. He was beloved and reverenced by the heavenly host, angels delighted to execute his commands, and he was clothed with wisdom and glory above them all. Yet the Son of God was exalted above him, as one in power and authority with the Father. He shared the Father's counsels, while Lucifer did not thus enter into the purposes of God. "Why," questioned this mighty angel, "should Christ have the supremacy? Why is He honored above Lucifer?"

Leaving his place in the immediate presence of the Father, Lucifer went forth to diffuse the spirit of discontent among the angels. He worked with mysterious secrecy, and for a time concealed his real purpose under an appearance of reverence for God. He began to insinuate doubts concerning the laws that governed heavenly beings, intimating that though laws might be necessary for the inhabitants of the worlds, angels, being more exalted, needed no such restraint, for their own wisdom was a sufficient guide. They were not beings that could bring dishonor to God; all their thoughts were holy; it was no more possible for them than for God Himself to err. The exaltation of the Son of God as equal with the Father was represented as an injustice to Lucifer, who, it was claimed, was also entitled to reverence and honor. If this prince of angels could but attain to his true, exalted position, great good would accrue to the entire host of heaven; for it was his object to secure freedom for all. But now even the liberty which they had hitherto enjoyed was at an end; for an absolute Ruler had been appointed them, and to His authority all must pay homage. Such were the subtle deceptions that through the wiles of Lucifer were fast obtaining in the heavenly courts.

There had been no change in the position or authority of Christ. Lucifer's envy and misrepresentation and his claims to equality with Christ had made necessary a statement of the true position of the Son of God; but this had been the same from the beginning. Many of the angels were, however, blinded by Lucifer's deceptions.

Taking advantage of the loving, loyal trust reposed in him by the holy beings under his command, he had so artfully instilled into their minds his own distrust and discontent that his agency was not discerned. Lucifer had presented the purposes of God in a false light—misconstruing and distorting them to excite dissent and dissatisfaction. He cunningly drew his hearers on to give utterance to their feelings; then these expressions were repeated by him when it would serve his purpose, as evidence that the angels were not fully in harmony with the government of God. While claiming for himself perfect loyalty to God, he urged that changes in the order and laws of heaven were necessary for the stability of the divine government. Thus while working to excite opposition to the law of God and to instill his own discontent into the minds of the angels under him, he was ostensibly seeking to remove dissatisfaction and to reconcile disaffected angels to the order of heaven. While secretly fomenting discord and rebellion, he with consummate craft caused it to appear as his sole purpose to promote loyalty and to preserve harmony and peace.

The spirit of dissatisfaction thus kindled was doing its baleful work. While there was no open outbreak, division of feeling imperceptibly grew up among the angels. There were some who looked with favor upon Lucifer's insinuations against the government of God. Although they had heretofore been in perfect harmony with the order which God had established, they were now discontented and unhappy because they could not penetrate His unsearchable counsels; they were dissatisfied with His purpose in exalting Christ. These stood ready to second Lucifer's demand for equal authority with the Son of God. But angels who were loyal and true maintained the wisdom and justice of the divine decree and endeavored to reconcile this disaffected being to the will of God. Christ was the Son of God; He had been one with Him before the angels were called into existence. He had ever stood at the right hand of the Father; His supremacy, so full of blessing to all who came under its benignant control, had not heretofore been questioned. The harmony of heaven had never been interrupted; wherefore should there now be discord? The loyal angels could see only terrible consequences from this dissension, and with earnest entreaty they counseled the disaffected ones to renounce their purpose and prove themselves loyal to God by fidelity to His government.

In great mercy, according to His divine character, God bore long with Lucifer. The spirit of discontent and disaffection had never before been known in heaven. It was a new element, strange, mysterious, unaccountable. Lucifer himself had not at first been acquainted with the real nature of his feelings; for a time he had feared to express the workings and imaginings of his mind; yet he did not dismiss them. He did not see whither he was drifting. But such efforts as infinite love and wisdom only could devise, were made to convince him of his error. His disaffection was proved to be without cause, and he was made to see what would be the result of persisting in revolt. Lucifer was convinced that he was in the wrong. He saw that "the LORD is righteous in all His ways, and holy in all His works" (Psalm 145:17); that the divine statutes are just, and that he ought to acknowledge them as such before all heaven. Had he done this, he might have saved himself and many angels. He had not at that time fully cast off his allegiance to God. Though he had left his position as covering cherub, yet if he had been willing to return to God, acknowledging the Creator's wisdom, and satisfied to fill the place appointed him in God's great plan, he would have been reinstated in his office. The time had come for a final decision; he must fully yield to the divine sovereignty or place himself in open rebellion. He nearly reached the decision to return, but pride forbade him. It was too great a sacrifice for one who had been so highly honored to confess that he had been in error, that his imaginings were false, and to yield to the authority which he had been working to prove unjust.

A compassionate Creator, in yearning pity for Lucifer and his followers, was seeking to draw them back from the abyss of ruin into which they were about to plunge. But His mercy was misinterpreted. Lucifer pointed to the long-suffering of God as an evidence of his own superiority, an indication that the King of the universe would yet accede to his terms. If the angels would stand firmly with him, he declared, they could yet gain all that they desired. He persistently defended his own course, and fully committed himself to the great controversy against his Maker. Thus it was that Lucifer, "the light bearer," the sharer of God's glory, the attendant of His throne, by transgression became Satan, "the adversary" of God and holy beings and the destroyer of those whom Heaven had committed to his guidance and guardianship.

Rejecting with disdain the arguments and entreaties of the loyal angels, he denounced them as deluded slaves. The preference shown to Christ he declared an act of injustice both to himself and to all the heavenly host, and announced that he would no longer submit to this invasion of his rights and theirs. He would never again acknowledge the supremacy of Christ. He had determined to claim the honor which should have been given him, and take command of all who would become his followers;

and he promised those would enter his ranks a new and better government, under which all would enjoy freedom. Great numbers of the angels signified their purpose to accept him as their leader. Flattered by the favor with which his advances were received, he hoped to win all the angels to his side, to become equal with God Himself, and to be obeyed by the entire host of heaven.

Still the loyal angels urged him and his sympathizers to submit to God; and they set before them the inevitable result should they refuse: He who had created them could overthrow their power and signally punish their rebellious daring. No angel could successfully oppose the law of God, which was as sacred as Himself. They warned all to close their ears against Lucifer's deceptive reasoning, and urged him and his followers to seek the presence of God without delay and confess the error of questioning His wisdom and authority.

Many were disposed to heed this counsel, to repent of their disaffection, and seek to be again received into favor with the Father and His Son. But Lucifer had another deception ready. The mighty revolter now declared that the angels who had united with him had gone too far to return; that he was acquainted with the divine law, and knew that God would not forgive. He declared that all who should submit to the authority of Heaven would be stripped of their honor, degraded from their position. For himself, he was determined never again to acknowledge the authority of Christ. The only course remaining for him and his followers, he said, was to assert their liberty, and gain by force the rights which had not been willingly accorded them.

So far as Satan himself was concerned, it was true that he had now gone too far to return. But not so with those who had been blinded by his deceptions. To them the counsel and entreaties of the loyal angels opened a door of hope; and had they heeded the warning, they might have broken away from the snare of Satan. But pride, love for their leader, and the desire for unrestricted freedom were permitted to bear sway, and the pleadings of divine love and mercy were finally rejected.

God permitted Satan to carry forward his work until the spirit of disaffection ripened into active revolt. It was necessary for his plans to be fully developed, that their true nature and tendency might be seen by all. Lucifer, as the anointed cherub, had been highly exalted; he was greatly loved by the heavenly beings, and his influence over them was strong. God's government included not only the inhabitants of heaven, but of all the worlds that He had created; and Lucifer had concluded that if he could carry the angels of heaven with him in rebellion, he could carry also all the worlds. He had artfully presented his side of the question, employing sophistry and fraud to secure his objects. His power to deceive was very great. By disguising himself in a cloak of falsehood, he had gained an advantage. All his acts were so clothed with mystery that it was difficult to disclose to the angels the true nature of his work. Until fully developed, it could not be made to appear the evil thing it was; his disaffection would not be seen to be rebellion. Even the loyal angels could not fully discern his character or see to what his work was leading.

Lucifer had at first so conducted his temptations that he himself stood uncommitted. The angels whom he could not bring fully to his side, he accused of indifference to the interests of heavenly beings. The very work which he himself was doing, he charged upon the loyal angels. It was his policy to perplex with subtle arguments concerning the purposes of God. Everything that was simple he shrouded in mystery, and by artful perversion cast doubt upon the plainest statements of Jehovah. And his high position, so closely connected with the divine government, gave greater force to his representations.

God could employ only such means as were consistent with truth and righteousness. Satan could use what God could not—flattery and deceit. He had sought to falsify the word of God and had misrepresented His plan of government, claiming that God was not just in imposing laws upon the angels; that in requiring submission and obedience from His creatures, He was seeking merely the exaltation of Himself. It was therefore necessary to demonstrate before the inhabitants of heaven, and of all the worlds, that God's government is just, His law perfect. Satan had made it appear that he himself was seeking to promote the good of the universe. The true character of the usurper and his real object must be understood by all. He must have time to manifest himself by his wicked works.

The discord which his own course had caused in heaven, Satan charged upon the government of God. All evil he declared to be the result of the divine administration. He claimed that it was his own object to improve upon the statutes of Jehovah. Therefore God permitted him to demonstrate the nature of his claims, to show the working out of his proposed changes in the divine law. His own work must condemn him. Satan had claimed from the first that he was not in rebellion. The whole universe must see the deceiver unmasked.

Even when he was cast out of heaven, Infinite Wisdom did not destroy Satan. Since only the service of love can be acceptable to God, the allegiance of His creatures must rest upon a conviction of His justice and benevolence. The inhabitants of heaven and of the worlds, being unprepared to comprehend the nature or consequences of sin, could not then have seen the justice of God in the destruction of Satan. Had he been immediately blotted out of existence, some would have served God from fear rather than from love. The influence of the deceiver would not have been fully destroyed, nor would be the spirit of rebellion have been utterly eradicated. For the good of the entire universe through ceaseless ages, he must more fully develop his principles, that his charges against the divine government might be seen in their true light by all created beings, and that the justice and mercy of God and the immutability of His law might be forever placed beyond all question.

Satan's rebellion was to be a lesson to the universe through all coming ages—a perpetual testimony to the nature of sin and its terrible results. The working out of Satan's rule, its effects upon both men and angels, would show what must be the fruit of setting aside the divine authority. It would testify that with the existence of God's government is bound up the well-being of all the creatures He has made. Thus the history of this terrible experiment of rebellion was to be a perpetual safeguard to all holy beings, to prevent them from being deceived as to the nature of transgression, to save them from committing sin, and suffering its penalty.

He that ruleth in the heavens is the one who sees the end from the beginning—the one before whom the mysteries of the past and the future are alike outspread, and who, beyond the woe and darkness and ruin that sin has wrought, beholds the accomplishment of His own purposes of love and blessing. Though "clouds and darkness are round about Him: righteousness and judgment [deliverance[2]] are the foundation of His throne." Psalm 97:2, R.V. And this the inhabitants of the universe, both loyal and disloyal, will one day understand. "His work is perfect: for all His ways are judgment [deliverance]: a God of truth and without iniquity, just and right is He." Deuteronomy 32:4.

---

2 See also Psalm 76:8, 9.

Chapter 1

Feast of Firstfruits: Christ, Our Representative— The Firstfruits Concept

Have you ever wondered why the Bible says that Jesus Christ is the only One who could have saved you?[1] Why could no one else have saved the human race? Why could an angel not do it? Why could we not save ourselves? After all, *we* are the ones who have sinned. We are responsible for our own choices. Have you ever wondered what it was that made *Jesus*, and no one else, qualified to do such a task?

Surprisingly, the answer is found in an obscure "dusty" old feast! Why a feast? Because the system of Hebrew worship tells us about the gospel and how the gospel works all through the ages. One of my favorite gospel authors makes the following statement, "So far as it was of divine institution, the entire system of Judaism was a compacted prophecy of the gospel."[2] If this is true, then this system of Judaism would be worth some serious study. So let's not waste any time. Let's get right into it.

In the Hebrew system, there were seven feast days, each of which has an antitypical fulfillment.[3] This fulfillment happens when the *type* (or model) meets the *antitype* (fruition and completion, that is, the "real thing"). You may have heard of Yom Kippur, the modern term for the biblical Day of Atonement. This feast is interesting, for some have written that we are living in the antitypical fulfillment of the Day of Atonement today, which we explore more fully in a later chapter.[4] The feast we are focusing on now is feast number three, the Feast of Firstfruits, which correlates to Christ's resurrection. This feast comes after the Passover, which reminds us of Christ's death, and the Feast of Unleavened Bread, which represents Christ's sinless life. But it happens before the Feast of Weeks, otherwise known as the Feast of Pentecost, which antitypical fulfillment gave the former rain of the Holy Spirit to the

---

1   See John 14:6: "I am the way, the truth, and the life: no man cometh unto the Father, but by me."
2   Ellen G. White, *The Desire of Ages*, p. 211.
3   The seven feasts are as follows: the Feast of the Passover, the Feast of Unleavened Bread, the Feast of Firstfruits, the Feast of Pentecost (or Weeks), the Feast of Trumpets, the Feast of the Day of Atonement, and the Feast of Tabernacles.
4   "We are in the great day of atonement, and the sacred work of Christ for the people of God that is going on at the present time in the heavenly sanctuary should be our constant study. We should teach our children what the typical Day of Atonement signified and that it was a special season of great humiliation and confession of sins before God. The antitypical day of atonement is to be of the same character. Everyone who teaches the truth by precept and example will give the trumpet a certain sound. You need ever to cultivate spirituality, because it is not natural for you to be heavenly-minded. The great work is before us of leading the people away from worldly customs and practices, up higher and higher, to spirituality, piety, and earnest work for God. It is your work to proclaim the message of the third angel, to sound the last note of warning to the world. May the Lord bless you with spiritual eyesight. I write this in love, seeing your danger. Please consider these things carefully and prayerfully" (Ellen G. White, *Testimonies for the Church*, vol. 5, p. 520).

apostles who founded the early Christian church. Because these feasts have an antitypical fulfillment, and because they all point to Christ, who is the antitypical fulfillment, it would be inconsistent with the prophetic purposes of these feasts and of Christ Himself to keep them literally today. But God encourages us to continually keep them in our hearts in heartfelt appreciation of what He has done, is doing, and what He is about to do.

The Feast of Firstfruits is important because it gives us an overview of who Christ is and His mission to save the human race. Therefore, this feast had to happen before the work of the Holy Spirit could begin in earnest. Because of this overview function, we will study the *representation* aspect of this feast first even though the feast is actually number three in the chronological order of the seven feasts. We will study the *harvest* aspect of the Feast of Firstfruits in a later chapter. What is true for the antitypical time of the former rain at the sowing time is also true for the antitypical time of the latter rain at the harvest. The work of the latter rain cannot happen in earnest without this understanding of Christ as our firstfruits. With all that said, let's look at this interesting feast—the Feast of Firstfruits.

In the history of the planet, there have been only two men who have ever represented the entire human race. The first man was Adam. The second is Jesus Christ. Throughout time there have been representatives of groups of people, but not of the whole human race. For example, politicians are elected for the specific purpose of representing various groups of people. A monarch represents a whole nation of people. A father represents his family. The concept is so widespread that every business and organization has agents who represent the whole or part of the company. Jesus and Adam are the only men who have ever represented the *entire* human race.

The third feast of the Hebrew economy is described in Leviticus 23:9–14 and points to the fact that Christ represents the human race:

> And the LORD spake unto Moses, saying, Speak unto the children of Israel, and say unto them, When ye be come into the land which I give unto you, and shall reap the harvest thereof, then ye shall bring a sheaf of the firstfruits of your harvest unto the priest: And he shall wave the sheaf before the LORD, to be accepted for you: on the morrow after the sabbath the priest shall wave it. And ye shall offer that day when ye wave the sheaf an he lamb without blemish of the first year for a burnt offering unto the LORD. And the meat offering thereof shall be two tenth deals of fine flour mingled with oil, an offering made by fire unto the LORD for a sweet savour: and the drink offering thereof shall be of wine, the fourth part of an hin. And ye shall eat neither bread, nor parched corn, nor green ears, until the selfsame day that ye have brought an offering unto your God: it shall be a statute for ever throughout your generations in all your dwellings.

So what is a "firstfruit"? Romans 11:16 tells us: "For if the firstfruit be holy, the lump is also holy: and if the root be holy, so are the branches." There are some people whose occupation is auditing.

Their job is to dig through the records of an organization to learn what the organization is doing. As an auditor, it is not possible, nor is it ordinarily necessary, to look at every transaction of an organization. Auditors use a procedure called "sampling." A sample is drawn from the whole population of transactions from which a conclusion can be drawn regarding the whole organization. Most often a conclusion can be drawn from the sample regarding a quantifiable margin of error. Regardless, the sample, if drawn from a true member of the population (This is the key!), can be said to "represent" the corporate whole.

In this feast, a sheaf of grain is drawn from the crop and waved before God, requesting His blessing on the crop itself and the use of it. Thus, the wave sheaf represents the harvest. Besides the presentation of the wave sheaf, a lamb was slaughtered and offered as a burnt sacrifice, representing the death of Christ and purification by fire.[5] Together these two actions carry the meaning of Christ's cleansing death being applied to the whole crop. Therefore, since Christ died for humankind and not for grain, the crop here represents something bigger than all the fields of grain in the world—it represents the whole human race. This is what Paul has in mind in his letters to the Romans and to the Ephesians.

As already stated, there have been only two men who have ever represented the entire human race. Paul's letter to the Romans describes them both: "It is true that through the sin of one man death began to rule, because of that one man. But how much greater is the result of what was done by the one man, Jesus Christ! All who receive God's abundant grace and the free gift of his righteousness will rule in life through Christ. So then, as the one sin condemned all men, in the same way the one righteous act sets all men free and gives them life" (Rom. 5:17, 18, Good News).

Adam, as the father of the human race, was our first representative. Unfortunately, as our representative, Adam sold the human race (and us with it) to Satan when he sinned. Jesus Christ completely reversed what Adam had done (and "much more"), thus saving the human race. This is what these verses are saying. In order to reverse what Adam did, Jesus had to re-qualify Himself to represent the human race and gain the victory as "us." This is how He won the whole human race back from Satan. The New English Bible clearly expresses the true meaning of Romans 5:18: "It follows, then, that as the issue of one misdeed was condemnation for all men, so the issue of one just act is acquittal and life for all men." And as a true representative of the human race, through the same power of God that is available to the rest of us, Christ could do this (John 5:19).

Regarding Christ's work as our representative, let's examine Ephesians 1:3-11:

> Blessed be the God and Father of our Lord Jesus Christ, who hath blessed us with all spiritual blessings in heavenly places in Christ: According as he hath chosen us in him before the foundation of the world, that we should be holy and without blame before him in love: Having predestinated us unto the adoption of children by Jesus Christ to himself, according to the good pleasure of his will, To the praise of the

---

5   The concepts of purification and "offering made by fire" will be presented in more detail in later chapters.

glory of his grace, wherein he hath made us accepted in the beloved. In whom we have redemption through his blood, the forgiveness of sins, according to the riches of his grace; Wherein he hath abounded toward us in all wisdom and prudence; Having made known unto us the mystery of his will, according to his good pleasure which he hath purposed in himself: That in the dispensation of the fulness of times he might gather together in one all things in Christ, both which are in heaven, and which are on earth; even in him: In whom also we have obtained an inheritance, being predestinated according to the purpose of him who worketh all things after the counsel of his own will:

Now let's think about this. Christ could do all this for us because He was the representative of the whole human race. If He came short in either criterion, He could not have saved us. But God is no respecter of persons, and He does not do anything halfway.[6] If you are a member of the human race, who did He die for? Of course, it would be for you—and everyone else who is a member of the human race. Christ died for you! He died for you even before you were born (Rev. 13:8). He died for you even before you committed (experientially) any sin. As the representative of the human race, Christ's perfect life, death, resurrection, and ascension were acts performed by Jesus "as" the human race, and therefore, it can be said that the corporate human race did all this "in Him." Because Christ is the representative of the human race, the whole human race is, therefore, in Him, even from before the foundation of the world. His death saved the human race from Satan. Since you are a member of the human race, as an individual, you are included as a beneficiary of this gift of salvation from sin and Satan (2 Tim. 1:9).

However, there is one caveat. Even though the whole human race has been given all things as a birthright possession in Christ our representative, as individuals we must make a decision regarding whether we want to *participate* in all this. At some point in our lives, God will present Himself to us, and we will have to decide for or against Him. God has given each of us the power to choose. Believe it or not, you and I can choose to discard this birthright from God and let the whole vast gift of righteousness and salvation go, just as Esau gave away his birthright to Jacob (Gen. 25:30–33). The Holy Spirit will work with all His power to keep you and me from making that decision, but God is a gentleman, and He will ultimately allow us to make our own choices in life.

Let us understand and appreciate the Gift He has given to us and the Price He paid for our salvation. By making what must be an active decision on our part to *reject* Christ as our representative, we effectively take ourselves "out" of Christ in our experience, at least temporarily.[7] If we choose Jesus as our representative (that is, we choose to *believe*[8]), we become His follower and are adopted into the

---

6   See Acts 10:34; Isaiah 55:11; and Luke 6:38.
7   This is not necessarily the same as the unpardonable sin.
8   I, personally, made this decision very early in life. By the time I was four years old, I was aware of this decision. I loved to go to church. I loved to talk about Jesus. If we missed church, which was only when someone was sick (and it only happened once), I was miserable in heart. At age eight I knew for sure what I wanted, and I ratified my decision. By age nine I knew I was going to be a minister; I just didn't know when. For some people this decision for Christ comes later

family of God.⁹ Then God, through the channel of our faith as a believer in Christ, can dispense to us the rich blessings of our inheritance (Eph. 1:11) held in trust for us. The decision for Christ *can* be repudiated later, which we must guard against.¹⁰ By our own choices of whether to participate "in Christ" (thus receiving the gift of His salvation into our experience), we can indeed, enter "into Christ" or depart "out of Christ" as our representative. Therefore, let it be your constant prayer that God will hold you, for He will hold you with a hand that will never let go. Only you can take yourself out of His hand.

This brings up an interesting question. What about those people who lived and died and sinned *before* Christ? Does He also represent *those* people? Let's take a closer look at a very interesting passage of Scripture that answers this question. Ephesians 1:3, 4 says, "Blessed be the God and Father of our Lord Jesus Christ, who hath blessed us with all spiritual blessings in heavenly places in Christ: According as he hath chosen us in him before the foundation of the world, that we should be holy and without blame before him in love."

So, *"before the foundation of the world,"* the godhead placed the whole human race in Christ. This is a vital concept to grasp. By doing this, He established the plan of salvation ahead of the time of need—a plan B, if you will, should man decide to sin. Therefore, everything Christ did, pertaining to the human race from "before the foundation of the world" and forward throughout all eternity, we did also "in Him," for He was the representative of the race even before we were created. After our parents sinned at the tree of knowledge of good and evil,¹¹ plan B was carried out, and humanity received a second chance. This second chance is called the "new covenant" and is based on this "in Christ" representative concept. Thus, those who lived and died and sinned before Christ are indeed included from "before the foundation of the world."¹²

After the creation of the human race but before sin entered, Jesus Christ represented the race as the Creator-owner of it. Adam also represented the race as the first created human being. When Adam sinned, death and condemnation befell humanity, and their nature changed, having at that moment

---

in life. For others, earlier. Some babies show their disposition clearly, and sometimes parents must immediately begin special work in earnest to win that child's heart. For more information, see Luke 1:39–44.

9   See John 1:12. Note: Adoption as a child of God is the very activity to which we were predestined in Ephesians 1:5. However, the choice is ours. God will not force us. For a discussion of predestination in Calvinism and Arminianism, see Appendix M titled "Christ, Our Representative."

10 See Luke 9:62; 1 Timothy 1:5–7, 19, 20; 4:1, 2, 10; and Galatians 1:6–8; 2:17, 18; 3:1–3.

11 The tree concept makes for an interesting metaphor and food for thought. Since humankind introduced eternal death and destruction to the human race at a tree, logically, death on a tree could possibly be associated with eternal death (Deut. 21:22, 23). If you carry forward the logic, death on a wooden cross could represent the kind of death that would eradicate all sin and ratify the gift of eternal life for all people. Christ, who did die on a wooden cross, did indeed gain the victory over all sin, death (including eternal death), and destruction for every human being.

12 Since "before the foundation of the world" (Eph. 1:4) we all were placed in Christ, we are in ignorant bliss, until, and even perhaps for awhile after, we are conceived. For some, this could conceivably happen later in life, even in old age. This ignorance begins to end when Jesus presents Himself to us, which could be at any stage in our lives. At that point, everything changes for us. We either begin to experience the blessings of the trust fund God holds for us "in Christ," or we go "out of Christ," which means we are on our own. If the latter happens, God continues to work to bring us back, but nothing is the same after our first encounter with God.

become fallen sinful human flesh.[13] After Adam and Eve sinned, because of the change in the nature of humanity, the execution of the plan of salvation had to involve a "new qualifying" of Christ to represent the race.[14] This qualification first had to prove that humanity was *not* qualified to fix the sin problem. Such deficiency is indicated by the replacing of the fig leaves in the garden with sheepskins (Gen. 3:21). Adam's attempt to fix the problem with the fig leaves represents the "old" covenant attempt by the human race to get "right" with God. The animal skins, requiring death and the shedding of blood, represents Christ, the "new" covenant Gift to humankind through the shedding of Jesus' blood on the cross.[15]

This process of proving humanity's incapability to qualify to represent the human race or to fix the sin problem, included the manifestation of the wickedness of the antediluvians, which resulted in the worldwide flood. This incapability was also manifested in the wickedness of the kings of Israel who, as kings, were *supposed* to represent God's people but ended up leading Israel into apostasy and captivity. The final result of Israel's wickedness culminated in the death of God on the cross, the destruction of Jerusalem in AD 66–70, and the scattering of the nation. Furthermore, the people failed to understand the significance of the temple ceremonies and feasts and how they pointed to Christ. We will look at the *how* of Christ's qualification as our representative in a minute, but first let's get an overview of the representative concept.[16]

The basic issue is this: Adam and Eve "blew it" in the Garden of Eden. They made the ultimate of "stupid mistakes." After Christ created the world, Adam had everything, including representative status of the human race. When Adam sinned, he allowed an enemy to conquer him, thus giving up his right to represent the human race. Satan, as conqueror, made the claim that he now represented the earth, as we see in the council meeting in Job 1, especially verses 6 and 7 (see also 2 Peter 2:19).

Since man (mankind, as represented by Adam) caused the problem, it was his responsibility to fix what he broke. However, now that man's nature had changed, he no longer had the ability to fix it because he could no longer live a perfect sinless life. He now had become fallen sinful human flesh, which, of itself, unaided by the power of God, is *incapable* of living a sinless life. A transaction needed to take

---

13   Adam, not Eve, represented the human race. You and I were created "in Adam" (in his loins, indicating subservience). Eve was created "from" Adam, not "in Adam," specifically, his side, indicating equality with Adam. However, because she was created from Adam, he also represented her.
14   As long as Adam had sinless human flesh, which was the condition in which he was placed when he was created, Christ could say He could represent what He created as it was when He created it. When the creation changed and became fallen sinful human flesh, which was something different than when it was created, Christ had to take on that new flesh in order to qualify to represent it, for His claim as Creator had lost some of its essence and significance.
15   We will study the two covenants later.
16   This process was coupled with the earthly priests and temple ceremonies (including this feast that we are now studying), which could never take away sins. The people had come to the place where they largely believed that they could represent themselves before God in bringing the sacrifices, believing that the sacrifices themselves saved them from their sins, which was a form of legalism. To point to Christ and His saving work were all these ceremonies were ever intended to do (see Heb. 9 and 10). On another note, this process also includes the final events of earth's history, which will culminate in the final scenes of the "Battle of Armageddon" when Satan and his forces will try to take the New Jerusalem and destroy God, as they proved when Christ died on the cross. By doing this, they think they can save themselves (see Rev. 16:16). Armageddon is interrupted by the earthquake and finished in Revelation 20.

place. In order to solve this problem, man needs something he does not have, that is, righteousness, and he has to give up something he does have, which is sin. Who will trade with him? Indeed, who would *want* to? An angel certainly could not fix it because humanity had not been created by an angel. That left Christ. As Creator, He carried the responsibility to fix what He made, a celestial "recall," so to speak. But how could He do it? What were His options?

God could simply have re-created humankind. However, by so doing He would have had to destroy Satan, as well, to prevent re-infestation. Had God done that, the universe would have served God out of fear rather than love, because of the feeling that would result—"If I don't 'measure up,' God will destroy me." This situation would never eradicate sin, for someone who is afraid is not made perfect. "There is no fear in love; but perfect love casteth out fear: because fear hath torment. He that feareth is not made perfect in love" (1 John 4:18).

Instead, God chose to make the transaction. This option requires the universe to see the end result of Satan's idea. When they fully see the results of sin, they will agree that God's ways truly are right and sin can never rise a second time, for even if it did, all would agree to the immediate removal of the culprit.

So God chose to make the exchange. This transaction is described in the Bible very shortly after Adam and Eve sinned. God was looking for the couple in the garden. For the first time, He did not find them in the usual manner because they were playing "hide and seek" with Him. Let's pick up the story in Geneses 3:7:

> And the eyes of them both were opened, and they knew that they were naked; and they sewed fig leaves together, and made themselves aprons. And they heard the voice of the Lord God walking in the garden in the cool of the day: and Adam and his wife hid themselves from the presence of the Lord God amongst the trees of the garden.
>
> And the Lord God called unto Adam, and said unto him, Where art thou? And he said, I heard thy voice in the garden, and I was afraid, because I was naked; and I hid myself. And he said, Who told thee that thou wast naked? Hast thou eaten of the tree, whereof I commanded thee that thou shouldest not eat?
>
> And the man said, The woman whom thou gavest to be with me, she gave me of the tree, and I did eat. And the Lord God said unto the woman, What is this that thou hast done? And the woman said, The serpent beguiled me, and I did eat. And the Lord God said unto the serpent, Because thou hast done this, thou art cursed above all cattle, and above every beast of the field; upon thy belly shalt thou go, and dust shalt thou eat all the days of thy life: And I will put enmity between thee and the woman, and between thy seed and her seed; it shall bruise [crush] thy head, and thou shalt bruise [crush] his heel.
>
> Unto the woman he said, I will greatly multiply thy sorrow and thy conception;

in sorrow thou shalt bring forth children; and thy desire shall be to thy husband, and he shall rule over thee. And unto Adam he said, Because thou hast hearkened unto the voice of thy wife, and hast eaten of the tree, of which I commanded thee, saying, Thou shalt not eat of it: cursed is the ground for thy sake; in sorrow shalt thou eat of it all the days of thy life; Thorns also and thistles shall it bring forth to thee; and thou shalt eat the herb of the field; In the sweat of thy face shalt thou eat bread, till thou return unto the ground; for out of it wast thou taken: for dust thou art, and unto dust shalt thou return.

And Adam called his wife's name Eve; because she was the mother of all living. Unto Adam also and to his wife did the LORD God make coats of skins, and clothed them. (Gen. 3:7–21)

When God told the serpent (Satan) that He was placing enmity between him and the woman (verse 15), He *made* the transaction through His all-powerful creative word (Gen. 1). Because God's word has inherently within it the power to create what it says, simply *saying* something sets it up as truth that is realized immediately, in trust, and experienced eventually, through believing.

When God makes a statement, His statement *creates* something so that when He spoke the Ten Commandments, they are actually ten promises! These are the things that you will actually do when you believe (cherish) God's promises to you. The ten promises are critical to understanding Exodus 20. God makes two statements in this passage in Genesis 3. First, by placing enmity between Satan and the woman, He reiterated that Christ remains the representative of the human race. Satan would not represent the human race, even as conqueror. The second statement, that the seed of the woman (Jesus Christ) would crush Satan's head,[17] compromised the spirit of conquest on the part of Satan. By making these dual statements, Christ gave humanity His own righteousness as a heritage and took humanity's sin away. Man simply needed to appreciate the gift—he simply needed to believe God's word (Gen. 15:6)—and that is still the issue today. If we refuse to believe, we call God a liar and thus spurn the gift. Consequently, while we are in unbelief, we will never realize the fulfillment of God's righteousness in our experience.

However, there is another problem. Since humanity's nature changed with the introduction of sin, Christ could no longer represent the human race as its Creator, for the human race had become something different than it was when Christ created it. Therefore, Christ, in order to represent the race, had to "re-qualify" as representative. Since He could not qualify as Creator, He had to qualify as a card-carrying member of the population. He had to become a man, taking humanity's fallen, sinful, flesh because that is the state of the human race that needed redemption.[18] By doing this, Christ effectively took our sins. By truly taking our fallen nature, He forged a heritage of a perfect life in fallen, sinful, human

---

17 See also Galatians 3:16, 29.
18 Man, as he was in sinless flesh, hardly needed any redemption for he was created perfect.

flesh—He won the battle with sin.

To summarize:

1. A *man* had to fix the problem because man caused it,
2. There had to be a *battle* to gain the victory over sin, regaining what was lost at the battle in Eden,
3. There had to be a *transaction*—an *exchange*—for humankind to do this, and
4. *Christ had to take our sins* and give us His righteousness.

As we contemplate Christ's gift of salvation, let's examine the five major concepts of soteriology, which is the study of salvation.[19] All of these concepts illustrate some truth about salvation, but only one is complete. In fact, it is so complete that it forms the structure upon which the whole plan of salvation hangs. Let's look briefly at these five concepts, four of which leave unanswered questions:

1. The "Moral Influence" concept
    a. *Theoretical Concept:* In this concept all the emphasis is on the cross, which is the revelation of God's love. our love is evoked as we witness this supreme revelation of God's love. The emphasis is on His death only, especially the gory and sensational aspects of it, coupled with humanity's response to that act of God.
    b. *Unanswered question:* There is no idea of any transaction taking place. Humanity needs what God has—His righteousness, His salvation. The idea that Christ changes or transforms and renews or redeems is not present.
    c. *Missing:* The transaction that transforms.
2. The "Satisfaction" concept
    a. *Theoretical Concept:* Our sin stained the honor of God, but God could forgive if He received a satisfaction that was sufficient to "satisfy" His wounded honor.
    b. *Unanswered question:* Our sin does stain the honor of God. Yet, the satisfaction has to come from the one who caused the problem (that is, from *humanity*) because the one who causes the problem is the one who is responsible to fix it. The problem here is that no mere human being is capable of providing that satisfaction. Neither could an angel do it, nor could one who is God only, as God is not man and thus cannot represent humankind. Remember, the angels did not cause Adam to fall; therefore, they have no responsibility to fix the problem. It was Adam's free choice, as it is today.[20]
    c. *Missing:* the representative *man* who satisfies.
3. The "Penal Substitution" concept

---

19 For more information, check out Harry Johnson's book *The Humanity of the Saviour*, which was published by Epworth Press in 1962, pages 205–221.
20 Lucifer did not cause the problem. He only made a suggestion. Adam, as the representative of the human race, made his own decision, so the problem and responsibility rests upon the human race. Lucifer *will* pay for his part played in the fall, but we must acknowledge that it was Adam and Eve's choice to disobey that led to the fall.

a. *Theoretical Concept:* Punishment is required by the law of God, and Christ bore this punishment in our stead. He did this by bearing our sins, which were laid upon Him.
   b. *Unanswered question:* How did He *get* our sins? In what *sense* can we say that Christ bore our sins or the sins of the whole world? After all, He was sinless, wasn't He? How could God punish a sinless being?
   c. *Missing:* How Christ got our sins.
4. The "Christ the Victor" concept
   a. *Theoretical Concept:* God, in Christ, fought the battle with sin and Satan, and through the cross gained the victory. Sin is defeated, punishment is canceled, and salvation is brought to a sinful human race.
   b. *Unanswered question:* In what manner did this combat take place?
   c. *Missing:* The location and manner of battle.

Please note: all of these concepts express some truth about salvation, and even, when used together, give a fairly good, though rough, "picture" of what God has done. But there is *one* concept that pulls it all together, so to speak, into one harmonious cohesive image.

5. The "Representative" concept[21]
   a. Christ, as perfect man and as our example and substitute, makes a response to God on our behalf as our representative. He did this by becoming one of us, taking our fallen sinful human flesh, including our sins, although He never committed any of His own. While in our flesh, He lived a sinless life, suffering temptation in all points as we (Heb. 4:15). Thus, as our representative, He reversed everything Adam did and He gave to the human race an heritage of righteousness, that is, victory over sin and Satan.
   b. Now let's pick apart the above statement and show how it answers all the questions:
      i. Christ, as perfect man and as our example and substitute, makes a response to God on our behalf as our representative, thus providing the *satisfaction* that answers the *second* concept. This also supplies the missing information of the representative man for the substitute required in the second concept.
      ii. He did this by becoming one of us, which is the prerequisite that qualifies Him to become a representative, *our* representative. He took our fallen, sinful, human flesh, thus bearing our sins in His body (1 Peter 2:24). This answers the *third* concept of how He got our sins—in His *flesh*, not His *life*.
      iii. Then, as our representative, through the sinless life He lived, He reversed everything Adam did, giving us the heritage of righteousness and life in exchange for the heritage of sin and death that we inherited from Adam, which is the missing transaction

---

21 See Appendix M titled "Christ, Our Representative: Treatise relating to Arminianism/Calvinism."

of the *first* concept.

    iv. As our representative, He lived a sinless life (thus conquering sin) while suffering temptation in all points as we, that is, in our fallen, sinful, human flesh. Thus He provided the missing location (His flesh) and manner of battle (through suffering and temptation) that addresses the *fourth* concept.

    v. Regarding the gift to the human race of the heritage of righteousness, which is the victory over sin and Satan, I want to emphasize the *heritage*. We receive it as an inheritance, *not* as wages (Rom. 5:18; 6:23; 8:16, 17; 1 Peter 1:3–5).[22] Christ is our agent (trustee) who holds our inheritance in a trust and dispenses the blessings of the inheritance as we need them.

c. With respect to the feast days, Christ's life, death, resurrection, and ascension (Eph. 1:3) were the fulfillment of his representative role to redeem the entire human race. What He did, He did as the human race; that is to say, the whole human race did it—in Him. What He did, He did for all humanity, whether people want to believe it or not. The first three of the seven feast days illustrate what Christ did for *all* people. The last three illustrate what Christ does only for those who *believe*. The fourth feast (Pentecost) is about the former rain of the Holy Spirit provided to all human beings, but received and appreciated by only a few. This feast acts as a transition between the two groups of feasts and represents each individual's decision. Regarding the latter rain, unless we are daily receiving the work of the *former* rain in the heart, we shall not recognize the manifestations of the Holy Spirit in the *latter* rain. It may be falling on hearts all around us, but we shall not discern or receive it.[23]

In order for a sample to qualify to represent the whole population (or corporate body), the sample must be a member of, and taken from, the corporate whole. This membership must be complete and must be official, that is, a "card carrying" membership is required. (In the case of political representation this is accomplished by the residency requirement.) Jesus is the current representative of the human race, a "sample" of one, if you will. So was Adam, when he was the representative of the race. Let's see how these two men qualified.

When Adam was created, God breathed into him, not just his one life, but the lives of the whole human race, including you and me! The original language of Genesis 2:7 ("And the LORD God formed man of the dust of the ground, and breathed into his nostrils the breath of life; and man became a living soul.") has the plural for "life"—"and [God] breathed into his nostrils the breath of *lives*." In the same corporate sense that God told Rebekah that "two nations" were in her womb (Gen. 25:23), God breathed into Adam the lives of the whole human race. And since we all

---

22   Peter discusses the extent of our inheritance in 1 Peter 1:6–9. Verse 9 tells us that the end, or fulfillment, of our faith is salvation that leads all the way (verse 4) to heaven and the new earth.

23   See Ellen G. White, *Testimonies to Ministers and Gospel Workers*, p. 507.

have descended from Adam, can anyone say he is not our father? Therefore, we are part and parcel with Adam, made out of the same "dough," so to speak—the same flesh and blood. Genetically, Adam was our representative.

But, as our representative, Adam sold us into sin and slavery. Therefore, a new representative had to be found for us and for him—one who could successfully represent the human race before the presence of a holy God.

Who would qualify for such a task? It could not come from within the human race, for we all had been sold "down the river," so to speak, and betrayed. None of the remaining race could qualify, for we are all sinners and could not stand before a holy God without a qualified representative mediator.[24] Someone had to take on human flesh—the same fallen, sinful flesh that the race had—and live a life in this human flesh. Also, the life lived in this same human flesh had to be a perfect life if this person was going to be able to represent the race in the presence of a holy God. Who would do it? Who *could* do it?

Well, the one who would qualify to do this also had to be one who was responsible to fix the problem. Blame, in this case, was not the issue—what mattered was, who was going to fix it. For such a person, there were two possibilities:

- First, since it was a *man* who brought sin and destruction to the human race, it needed to be a *man* who would be responsible to fix it. That man should have been Adam, except that Adam in his sin disqualified himself and the whole human race with him. He was unable to take that responsibility, even though he caused the problem.
- The second one who would carry responsibility was the one who created the "items" that became faulty. The One who created Adam and Eve would (and could) take upon Himself that responsibility to fix the problem (a celestial "recall," if you will). Who was that? Who was the active agent in creation? None other than Jesus Christ Himself, the second person of the Godhead (John 1:1–3; Eph. 3:9). Actually, Adam said it himself when he said in Genesis 3:12, "The woman whom *thou gavest* to be with me, she gave me of the tree, and I did eat." The gift of Eve to Adam (and also the creation of Adam himself) was an act of creation. The angels did not create anything; none of them could qualify—only Jesus Christ met the requirement. Although Christ was not to blame, even though Adam tried to push the blame on Him in this verse, God chose to fix it Himself.

Now we see a *dual* responsibility: Man, who sinned and brought this upon us, and God, who created the man who sinned. The solution required a man who creates—a God-man, so to speak. So, you see, the buck stopped at Jesus. It fell upon Him to fix the problem because He was the active agent in creation. However, He had to become a man in order to truly and completely represent the race and fulfill humanity's responsibility.

---

24 A mediator has a hard job because he or she has to represent both parties in a conflict. He or she has to qualify as (i.e., to be accepted by) both and bring the two opposing parties together. This, as 100 percent God and 100 percent man, Jesus did.

The answer to God's trial in the last days, in which He is charged with being a liar,[25] is who God is and what He can do in fallen, sinful human flesh through His all-powerful creative word. Jesus proved what God can do in fallen, sinful, human flesh when He relied on the word of the Father (John 5:19, 30). Let us now be His witnesses in His trial—a living demonstration of what God can do in *our* fallen, sinful human flesh, relying on His promise to hold us within His will.[26]

Both Satan and Jesus Christ claim to be your representative before the universe. It is your duty to make a decision. Who will you vote for?

Father, we believe; help our unbelief. Let it be as Thou hast said (Luke 1:38).

"And the word that was spoken to Jesus at the Jordan, 'this is My beloved Son, in whom I am well pleased,' embraces humanity. God spoke to Jesus as our representative. With all our sins and weaknesses, we are not cast aside as worthless. 'He hath made us accepted in the Beloved.' Ephesians. 1:6."[27]

"The most lowly and weak are bound by a chain of sympathy closely to His heart. He never forgets that He is our representative, that He bears our nature....

"But exalted 'to be a Prince and a Saviour, to give repentance to Israel, and remission of sins,' will Christ, our representative and head, close His heart, or withdraw His hand, or falsify His promise? No; never, never."[28]

---

25   See Genesis 2:16, 17 and 3:4 for the lies Satan told to Eve in regards to God's character.
26   See John 15:5; Jeremiah 31:31–33; Ezekiel 36:25–28; and Galatians 3:16, 29.
27   Ellen G. White, *The Desire of Ages*, p. 113.
28   Ellen G. White, *Testimonies to Ministers and Gospel Workers*, pp. 19, 20.

Chapter 2

Feast of the Passover: Christ, Our Salvation

Let's begin this chapter by examining Psalm 22:1–8, which describes the agony Christ felt while on the cross.

> My God, my God, why hast thou forsaken me? why art thou so far from helping me, and from the words of my roaring? O my God, I cry in the day time, but thou hearest not; and in the night season, and am not silent. But thou art holy, O thou that inhabitest the praises of Israel. Our fathers trusted in thee: they trusted, and thou didst deliver them. They cried unto thee, and were delivered: they trusted in thee, and were not confounded. But I am a worm, and no man; a reproach of men, and despised of the people. All they that see me laugh me to scorn: they shoot out the lip, they shake the head, saying, He trusted on the Lord that he would deliver him: let him deliver him, seeing he delighted in him.

Why did Jesus feel forsaken by the Father? Why did He allow Himself to get into such a vulnerable position?

The focus of this chapter is the Feast of the Passover, an important feast in the Hebrew system. For us to understand fully what this feast is all about, it helps to contemplate the mind of God a little bit. This psalm and some other scriptures will give us a knothole in the fence surrounding the mind of Jesus and provide a clue regarding what is going on. Psalm 22 and Psalm 69 describe Jesus Christ and what He felt while hanging on the cross.

Why did Christ feel forsaken by the Father on the cross? Part of the answer lies in 1 Peter 2:24: "Who his own self bare our *sins* in his own *body* on the tree, that we, being dead to *sins*, should live unto righteousness: by whose stripes ye were healed." Sin cannot exist in the presence of a holy God, for sin is destroyed in His presence (Deut. 4:24, 9:3; Heb. 12:29).[1] While on the cross, Jesus bore the sins of the whole world. Had the Father revealed His presence, Christ could not have borne our sins, for our sins He was bearing would have been destroyed and purged from the Father's presence.[2] For this reason the

---

[1] The context of the consuming fire of Hebrews 12 is the extraction of sin and the entering of holiness; the context of the consuming fire in Deuteronomy 4 is the extraction of idolatry, the placing of anything ahead of God.

[2] Had Christ *not* taken our fallen sinful human flesh, those same sins also would have been destroyed in His *own* presence. This is one reason why Jesus had to partake fully in humanity's flesh.

Father had to disguise His presence from the Son. Please note also that Christ bore our sins in His body, not in His life.[3] Jesus Himself could never be destroyed by the Father's presence because, though Jesus took fallen sinful human flesh, He never committed one wrong act or thought one wrong thought on His own. Instead, He dispatched temptation immediately through the power of the Holy Spirit—the same power that is available to each person (John 8:28)

However, there is more to it than that. If Christ is to represent the whole human race, what He did on the cross He would need to do *as* the human race.[4] And what He *did* on the cross would need to accomplish what this human race actually needed. We need salvation from sin and the penalty of it. "But we see Jesus, who was made a little lower than the angels for the suffering of death, crowned with glory and honour; that he by the grace of God should taste death for every man" (Heb. 2:9). Since the "wages of sin is death" (Rom. 6:23), Christ had to take the death that was ours. He bore our sins *as if* He had committed them Himself, for He was counted a transgressor, and because of that, His heart broke as He endured the terrible pain of our sin and the resulting separation from His Father. Notice what Psalm 69:1–4 says that Jesus did:

> Save me, O God; for the waters are come in unto my soul. I sink in deep mire, where there is no standing: I am come into deep waters, where the floods overflow me. I am weary of my crying: my throat is dried: mine eyes fail while I wait for my God. They that hate me without a cause are more than the hairs of mine head: they that would destroy me, being mine enemies wrongfully, are mighty: then I restored that which I took not away.

His job was to restore to the human race everything Adam had given away (Rom. 5). Because Adam brought sin, death, and separation from God (loss of intimacy) to the human race, Jesus' role was to also restore our standing of favor with God, which also logically results in the removal of the death penalty.

In Psalm 22:1 the Hebrew word *sh@agah* (sheh-aw-gaw'), translated "roaring," means "the roaring of a lion or the cry of a wretched person, wrung forth with grief." In *The Desire of Ages* Ellen White describes this more poignantly than I can:

> Upon Christ as our substitute and surety was laid the iniquity of us all. He was counted a transgressor, that He might redeem us from the condemnation of the law. The

---

3 One should not think of "sin" as some physical entity that can be transferred from one person to another. Christ bore our sins in His body by taking upon Him our fallen sinful human flesh (Heb. 2:14–16), which makes Hebrews 4:15 possible: "For we have not an high priest which cannot be touched with the feeling of our infirmities; but was in all points tempted like as we are, yet without sin." The guilt, the condemnation, the discouragement of the knowledge of sin and temptation were a fact in Christ's conscious experience, though He never actually committed any sin of His own. This enabled Him to "taste death for every man" (Heb. 2:9).

4 See chapter 1, "Feast of Firstfruits: Christ, Our Representative."

guilt of every descendant of Adam was pressing upon His heart. The wrath of God against sin, the terrible manifestation of His displeasure because of iniquity, filled the soul of His Son with consternation. All His life Christ had been publishing to a fallen world the good news of the Father's mercy and pardoning love. Salvation for the chief of sinners was His theme. But now with the terrible weight of guilt He bears, He cannot see the Father's reconciling face. The withdrawal of the divine countenance from the Saviour in this hour of supreme anguish pierced His heart with a sorrow that can never be fully understood by man. So great was this agony that His physical pain was hardly felt.

Satan with his fierce temptations *wrung* the heart of Jesus. The Saviour could not see through the portals of the tomb. Hope did not present to Him His coming forth from the grave a conqueror, or tell Him of the Father's acceptance of the sacrifice. He feared that sin was so offensive to God that Their separation was to be eternal. Christ felt the anguish which the sinner will feel when mercy shall no longer plead for the guilty race. It was the *sense of sin*, bringing the Father's wrath upon Him *as man's substitute*, that made the cup He drank so bitter, and *broke the heart* of the Son of God. (p. 753)

Hear Christ's cry: "My God, my God, why hast thou forsaken me? why art thou so far from helping me, and from the words of my roaring?" (Ps. 22:1). Now we begin to understand His pain, for He felt that His own existence was at stake. What Jesus felt was worse than death. The death that Christ took for us was not the physical death we all face before Christ returns, if we are not translated at His coming,[5] but that death the Bible calls the "second death." Let's look at Revelation 20 and break it up into sections:

The Binding of Satan and the Beginning of the Millennium (1000 Years)

"And I saw an angel come down from heaven, having the key of the bottomless pit and a great chain in his hand. And he laid hold on the dragon, that old serpent, which is the Devil, and Satan, and bound him a thousand years, and cast him into the bottomless pit, and shut him up, and set a seal upon him, that he should deceive the nations no more, till the thousand years should be fulfilled: and after that he must be loosed a little season" (verses 1–3).

During the Millennium

"And I saw thrones, and they sat upon them, and judgment was given unto them: and I saw the souls of them that were beheaded for the witness of Jesus, and for the word of God, and which had not worshipped the beast, neither his image, neither had received his mark upon their foreheads, or in their

---

5   See 1 Thessalonians 4:13–18 and 1 Corinthians 15:50–54.

hands; and they lived and reigned with Christ a thousand years.[6] But the rest of the dead lived not again until the thousand years were finished.[7] This is the first resurrection. Blessed and holy is he that hath part in the first resurrection: on such the second death hath no power, but they shall be priests of God and of Christ, and shall reign with him a thousand years" (verses 4–6).

The Release of Satan and the End of the Millennium

"And when the thousand years are expired, Satan shall be loosed out of his prison, and shall go out to deceive the nations which are in the four quarters of the earth, Gog, and Magog, to gather them together to battle: the number of whom is as the sand of the sea. And they went up on the breadth of the earth, and compassed the camp of the saints about, and the beloved city: and fire came down from God out of heaven, and devoured them. And the devil that deceived them was cast into the lake of fire and brimstone, where the beast and the false prophet are, and shall be tormented day and night for ever and ever" (verses 7–10).[8]

The Conclusion

"And I saw a great white throne, and him that sat on it, from whose face the earth and the heaven fled away; and there was found no place for them. And I saw the dead, small and great, stand before God; and the books were opened: and another book was opened, which is the book of life: and the dead were judged out of those things which were written in the books, according to their works. And the sea gave up the dead which were in it; and death and hell[9] delivered up the dead which were in them: and they were judged every man according to their works. And death and hell [the grave] were cast into the lake of fire. This is the second death. And whosoever was not found written in the book of life was cast into the lake of fire" (verses 11–15).

"And I saw a new heaven and a new earth: for the first heaven and the first earth were passed away; and there was no more sea" (Rev. 21:1).

Now let's look at Malachi 4:1 and Ezekiel 28:18, respectively, for additional insight into the lake of fire: "For, behold, the day cometh, that shall burn as an oven; and all the proud, yea, and all that do

---

6   If those who had been beheaded are living at *this* time, they must have been resurrected at the *beginning* of the 1000-year period.
7   This sentence about the "rest of the dead" is a parenthetical note and goes with verse 7.
8   The Greek word *aion* that is here translated "ever" has the root meaning "to breathe, blow, as to denote properly that which causes life, vital force" (cf. Thayer, *Greek-English Lexicon of the New Testament*, 1977). In other words, the devil shall be tormented day and night until his vital force is gone. This is supported by Malachi 4:1 and Ezekiel 28:18, both of which tell us that Satan is brought to ashes, to stubble, and burnt up. From this I conclude that the English "ever and ever" (or "forever") means (or should mean) forever as long as possible, an unknown amount of time. If I were to say, "This sore on my finger is lasting forever!", I am stating that the sore is taking too long to heal to satisfy me. This is not the same as "eternal," which is never ending. A fire that burns *forever* burns until it runs out of fuel, however long that may be. An *eternal* fire never runs out of fuel and never burns out. Torment that lasts *forever* lasts until the end of the life of the victim, however long that may be. Thankfully, God never allows anyone to suffer *eternal* torment.
9   "Hell" simply refers to the grave. The Greek word *hades* literally means "not to be seen"—"death and *the grave* delivered up the dead which were in them."

wickedly, shall be stubble: and the day that cometh shall burn them up, saith the LORD of hosts, that it shall leave them neither root nor branch"; "Thou [Satan] hast defiled thy sanctuaries by the multitude of thine iniquities, by the iniquity of thy traffick; therefore will I bring forth a fire from the midst of thee, it shall devour thee, and I will bring thee to ashes upon the earth in the sight of all them that behold thee."

I do not have enough time to do an exegesis of Revelation 20, but please follow along.

- The devil is bound on this earth for 1000 years after Christ comes to take His people to heaven (verse 2). He cannot deceive the nations any more (verse 3) because all those who chose to cling to sin died when they saw Christ's glory upon His return to claim His followers (see also Mal. 3 and 2 Thess. 2:8).
- During the 1000-year period, God's people are with Christ in heaven and reign with Him in judgment of the wicked (verse 4). God's people are referred to as the "first resurrection" because they were those who had lived and died before Jesus came and were resurrected at Jesus' second coming (verse 5). Notice that there is something called "the second death" that has no power over those resurrected in the "first resurrection" (verse 6). The second death has no power over God's people.
- After the 1000 years are over, Satan has his chance again (verse 7). The nations he deceives (verse 8) had been dead but now obviously have been resurrected (verse 13). These are they who "lived not again until the thousand years were finished" (verse 5). For the sake of discussion, we'll call this the "second resurrection," for this resurrection takes place 1000 years after the "first resurrection."
- It all finally ends with sin (and those who cling to sin) being burned up in the "lake of fire," which is called "the second death" (verses 14, 15). These are the ones who feel "the anguish which the sinner will feel when mercy shall no longer plead for the guilty race" (*The Desire of Ages*, p. 753). And *this* is what Christ felt on the cross.

This is why Christ said, as it is described in Psalm 69, "Save me, O God; for the waters are come in unto my soul. I sink in deep mire, where there is no standing: I am come into deep waters, where the floods overflow me. I am weary of my crying: my throat is dried: mine eyes fail while I wait for my God" (verses 1–3). What Jesus felt was the "second death." This is the anguish of permanent separation from the Father. This is the death that Jesus died for you and for me. The "first death," that physical death that takes us to the grave, is only temporary. The "second death" is permanent.

So why did Jesus have to go through all this? What was the purpose for His actions and the choice to put Himself in harms way? Genesis 3:15 gives us a clue. Talking to Satan, God says, "And I will put enmity between thee and the woman, and between thy seed and her seed; it shall bruise [Hebrew: crush] thy head, and thou shalt bruise [Hebrew: crush] his heel." By becoming human, Christ became the seed of the woman (Eve) and was subject to the law of heredity, taking upon Himself fallen, sinful, human flesh. He would crush Satan's head, but in the process, He would have His heel crushed—not a final death blow mind you, but still a crippling blow, agonizing to the core of His being. He felt the anguish that the sinner will feel when mercy shall no longer plead for the guilty race.[10] Christ did this to save humankind—Christ did this to save you and me. Christ completely undid all the sin and corruption that Adam brought upon the human race, and more (Rom. 5). And He did it through the promise of His word, which has inherent within it the power to create what it says (Gen. 1).

This promise is first given in Genesis 3:15. It is the same promise given to Abraham, although it is explained to Abraham in the most detail in Genesis 15 and 17.[11] This promise is also known as the "covenant" (Gal. 3:15–18).

> And when Abram was ninety years old and nine, the LORD appeared to Abram, and said unto him, I am the Almighty God; walk before me, and be thou perfect. And I will make my covenant between me and thee, and will multiply thee exceedingly. And Abram fell on his face: and God talked with him, saying, As for me, behold, my covenant is with thee, and thou shalt be a father of many nations. Neither shall thy name any more be called Abram, but thy name shall be Abraham; for a father of many nations have I made thee. And I will make thee exceeding fruitful, and I will make nations of thee, and kings shall come out of thee. And I will establish my covenant between me and thee and thy seed after thee in their generations for an everlasting covenant, to be a God unto thee, and to thy seed after thee. And I will give unto thee, and to thy seed after thee, the land wherein thou art a stranger, all the land of Canaan, for an everlasting possession; and I will be their God. And God said unto Abraham, Thou shalt keep my covenant therefore, thou, and thy seed after thee in their generations. (Gen. 17:1–9)

This covenant is also described by Jeremiah and is called the "new covenant": "Behold, the days come, saith the LORD, that I will make a new covenant with the house of Israel, and with the house of Judah: Not according to the covenant that I made with their fathers in the day that I took them by the hand to bring them out of the land of Egypt; which my covenant they brake, although I was an husband unto them, saith the LORD: But this shall be the covenant that I will make with the house of Israel; After those days, saith the LORD, I will put my law in their inward parts, and write it in their hearts; and will be their God, and they shall be my people" (Jer. 31:31–33).

Notice that God gave Abraham four things, which we all need to live happy and productive lives:

1. Deliverance – from sin and the second death: "Walk before me, and be thou perfect" (Gen. 17:1).
2. Family – a sense of belonging: "thou shalt be a father of many nations" (verse 4).

---

10 Satan's "head" is crushed in the lake of fire, sealing his fate for eternity. By the way, the lake of fire is prepared for the devil and his angels, not for humans (Matt. 25:41). However, because *sin* is the target of the lake of fire, those who cling to sin will burn with it, whether they be angelic or human.

11 This same promise is also given to Moses in Exodus 6:1–8. However, because it is given to Abraham in the most detail, it is often called the "Abrahamic" covenant, while the Genesis 3:15 promise, as given to Adam and Eve, is sometimes called the "everlasting" covenant, but they, with the "new" covenant, are all the same promise.

3. Intimacy – with God, as a good Friend: "the Lord *appeared* to Abram, and *said* unto him, I am the Almighty God" (verse 1).
4. Real estate – the new earth, as a place to call "home": "And I will give unto thee, and to thy seed after thee, the land wherein thou art a stranger, all the land of Canaan, for an everlasting possession; and I will be their God" (verse 8).

Since the earth we live on now is going to burn up and be made new (Rev. 21:1–8), such an "everlasting" possession would have to at least include real estate in the new earth. And since only righteousness can dwell in the new earth, this promise must also include the righteousness needed to live there, which it *does* in the "deliverance" portion of this promise.[12] And furthermore, Jeremiah tells us that God will write His law—His righteousness—in our *hearts*. This makes it so that keeping God's law of righteousness will be *as if* we are carrying out *our own* impulses, which will *not* be a burdensome chore (Matt. 11:28–30)

Now let's return to Genesis 17:7. This is where you, dear reader, have a special interest, because here is where you become a part of this story. "And I will establish my covenant between me and thee and thy seed after thee in their generations for an everlasting covenant, to be a God unto thee, and to thy seed after thee." Abraham's seed is Christ, as it says in Galatians 3:16, "Now to Abraham and his seed were the promises made. He saith not, And to seeds, as of many; but as of one, And to thy seed, which is Christ," and this seed includes all who are *in Christ*, as it says in Galatians 3:29, "And if ye be Christ's, then are ye Abraham's seed, and heirs according to the promise."

So, *you* are indeed an heir to this promise if you have not taken yourself out of Christ, for He is your representative. This promise is your heritage, which was sealed with God's oath at the sacrifice of Isaac: "And the angel of the Lord called unto Abraham out of heaven the second time, And said, By myself have I sworn, saith the Lord, for because thou hast done this thing, and hast not withheld thy son, thine only son: That in blessing I will bless thee, and in multiplying I will multiply thy seed as the stars of the heaven, and as the sand which is upon the sea shore; and thy seed shall possess the gate of his enemies; And in thy seed shall all the nations of the earth be blessed; because thou hast obeyed my voice" (Gen. 22:15–18).

And since, in a pledge, one swears by something greater than himself, God had no options for His oath. He had to swear by "Himself," that is, His own *existence*. He pledged His own existence on the completion of His promise to Abraham, and to us. And based on our study, we know that Jesus gave up the hope of His own existence while on the cross, since He felt the anguish the sinner will feel when mercy shall no longer plead for the guilty race—the anguish of permanent separation from the Father.

---

12   Any discussion of the new covenant, which is God's promise to all people, brings up the concept of the old covenant, which is our promise to God (Exod. 19:8), which we have no power to keep (Jer. 31:32). God does not expect us to promise to keep His law. He wants our hearts so that *He* can keep His *own* law in us (Jer. 31:31-33; Ezek. 36:26–28; Phil. 2:13). Israel's promise to God was broken soon after it was made by worshipping the golden calf, symbolized by the literal breaking (by Moses) of the stone tables written by God's own finger (Exod. 31:18–32:35; Jer. 31:32). The old covenant is called "old" because it was ratified first by the sacrifice of animals at Sinai (Exod. 24). The new covenant was ratified later by the sacrifice of Christ on the cross, as we are now studying.

That anguish is the permanent "second death" that is sealed by the "lake of fire" (Rev. 20:14). Thank God, Christ gained the victory over the second death and conquered it! We *never* have to be separated from Him.

In Exodus 6 God renews this promise to Moses: "Then the Lord said unto Moses, Now shalt thou see what I will do to Pharaoh: for with a strong hand shall he let them go, and with a strong hand shall he drive them out of his land. And God spake unto Moses, and said unto him, I am the Lord: And I appeared unto Abraham, unto Isaac, and unto Jacob, by the name of God Almighty, but by my name JEHOVAH was I not known to them. And I have also established my covenant with them, to give them the land of Canaan, the land of their pilgrimage, wherein they were strangers" (verses 1–4).

A few chapters later, in Exodus 12, God carries out His promise and delivers the "goods":

> "For I will pass through the land of Egypt this night, and will smite all the firstborn in the land of Egypt, both man and beast; and against all the gods of Egypt I will execute judgment: I am the Lord. And the blood shall be to you for a token upon the houses where ye are: and when I see the blood, I will pass over you, and the plague shall not be upon you to destroy you, when I smite the land of Egypt. And this day shall be unto you for a memorial; and ye shall keep it a feast to the Lord throughout your generations; ye shall keep it a feast by an ordinance for ever.… And the children of Israel went away, and did as the Lord had commanded Moses and Aaron, so did they. And it came to pass, that at midnight the Lord smote all the firstborn in the land of Egypt, from the firstborn of Pharaoh that sat on his throne unto the firstborn of the captive that was in the dungeon; and all the firstborn of cattle. And Pharaoh rose up in the night, he, and all his servants, and all the Egyptians; and there was a great cry in Egypt; for there was not a house where there was not one dead. And he called for Moses and Aaron by night, and said, Rise up, and get you forth from among my people, both ye and the children of Israel; and go, serve the Lord, as ye have said" (verses 12–31).

This was the first Passover, which was to be observed throughout Israel's generations.

If we turn now to the New Testament, we find that Christ fulfilled this oath by enduring the anguish of the second death: "For when God made promise to Abraham, because he could swear by no greater, he sware by himself [His own existence], Saying, Surely blessing I will bless thee, and multiplying I will multiply thee.[13] And so, after he had patiently endured, he obtained the promise. For men verily swear by the greater: and an oath for confirmation is to them an end of all strife. Wherein God, willing more abundantly to shew unto the heirs of promise the immutability of his counsel, confirmed it by an oath: That by two immutable things, in which it was impossible for God to lie, we might have

---

13   Read Genesis 17 for the context and Genesis 22:16, 17 for the oath.

a strong consolation, who have fled for refuge to lay hold upon the hope set before us: Which hope we have as an anchor of the soul, both sure and stedfast, and which entereth into that within the veil; Whither the forerunner is for us entered, even Jesus, made an high priest for ever after the order of Melchisedec" (Heb. 6:13–20).

The second death actually begins to take place in Matthew 27:46, "And about the ninth hour Jesus cried with a loud voice, saying, Eli, Eli, lama sabachthani? that is to say, My God, my God, why hast thou forsaken me?" Jesus is beginning to feel that anguish the sinner will feel when mercy no longer pleads for the guilty race—total separation from God. The oath Jesus took was that He would give up the hope of His own existence, taking the second death,[14] that He might seal His promise to us. Christ accomplished this while on the cross. After He suffered the anguish of the *second* death, He died the *first* death, from which He was resurrected three days later (Friday-death, Sabbath-rest, and Sunday-resurrection).[15]

Notice that Hebrews 6:20 calls Christ the forerunner, for Christ is our firstfruits, the head and representative of the human race.[16] What He did, we did (corporately) in Him. And as forerunner, He has gone before us to heavenly places, having taken us also (corporately) "in Him" (Eph. 2:6), to dispense our inheritance (individually) a little at a time as we need it most, culminating in this description in Revelation 20.

All of this discussion so far has been describing the Passover concept. Christ took our second death, which we deserve, that we might be "passed over" and not have to go through it.

Now let's look at the feast itself. The Scriptures describe the Feast of the Passover as follows:

> Speak ye unto all the congregation of Israel, saying, In the tenth day of this month they shall take to them every man a lamb, according to the house of their fathers, a lamb for an house: And if the household be too little for the lamb, let him and his neighbour next unto his house take it according to the number of the souls; every man according to his eating shall make your count for the lamb. Your lamb shall be without blemish, a male of the first year: ye shall take it out from the sheep, or from the goats: And ye shall keep it up until the fourteenth day of the same month: and the whole assembly of the congregation of Israel shall kill it in the evening. And they

---

14   Christ felt forsaken by the Father because the Father could not reveal His (sin eradicating) presence to the Savior. Christ had to bear the sins of the whole world and take our punishment. He accepted the penalty of the second death for us—that death from which there is no resurrection because the dying one has forsaken God. That death is eternal separation from God. It is because Jesus never committed any sin of His own that He was able to be resurrected, through His own power, as God (John 10:18).

15   This timeline is derived from the following: Mathew 27:45, 46, 50; John 19:31–33; Mathew 27:57–62; Mathew 28:1–6. Since the biblical reckoning of days begins at sunset the day before, Christ and His disciples could observe the Passover meal after sunset on Thursday night. Also in the biblical reckoning, the "first hour" of the day falls between what we today call 6:00 a.m. and 7:00 a.m., so that the "ninth hour" would begin at 3:00 p.m. Friday is called the day of preparation for the Sabbath.

16   See chapter 1, "Feast of Firstfruits: Christ, Our Representative."

shall take of the blood, and strike it on the two side posts and on the upper door post of the houses, wherein they shall eat it. And they shall eat the flesh in that night, roast with fire, and unleavened bread; and with bitter herbs they shall eat it. Eat not of it raw, nor sodden at all with water, but roast with fire; his head with his legs, and with the purtenance thereof. And ye shall let nothing of it remain until the morning; and that which remaineth of it until the morning ye shall burn with fire.

And thus shall ye eat it; with your loins girded, your shoes on your feet, and your staff in your hand; and ye shall eat it in haste: it is the Lord's passover. For I will pass through the land of Egypt this night, and will smite all the firstborn in the land of Egypt, both man and beast; and against all the gods of Egypt I will execute judgment: I am the Lord. And the blood shall be to you for a token upon the houses where ye are: and when I see the blood, I will pass over you, and the plague shall not be upon you to destroy you, when I smite the land of Egypt. And this day shall be unto you for a memorial; and ye shall keep it a feast to the Lord throughout your generations; ye shall keep it a feast by an ordinance for ever....

And ye shall take a bunch of hyssop, and dip it in the blood that is in the bason, and strike the lintel and the two side posts with the blood that is in the bason; and none of you shall go out at the door of his house until the morning. For the Lord will pass through to smite the Egyptians; and when he seeth the blood upon the lintel, and on the two side posts, the Lord will pass over the door, and will not suffer the destroyer to come in unto your houses to smite you. (Exod. 12:3–23)

Christ's death on the cross took place during the Hebrew Feast of the Passover on the very day and at the very hour (3:00 p.m.) of the evening sacrifice (Mark 15:33–37). Finally, Christ's hour that He spoke of came (John 2:4; 7:30; 8:20). The death of the sacrificial Passover lamb every year pointed forward to the death of Christ, the Lamb of God, and now His time had come and the sacrifice was made. Not only this, but the Passover lamb was set aside on the tenth day of the month; as its antitypical fulfillment, Christ drove out the moneychangers from the temple, after which the priests and rulers determined to kill Him at their earliest convenience, exactly four days before the Passover, which was another fulfillment of Bible prophecy.

The Passover is the kingpin feast in the Hebrew system. All the other feasts in the spiritual economy of this sacrificial system have this feast as their foundational support. Being the first of the seven feasts, the Passover is the opening statement made by God that, by itself, has all the elements needed to give us, corporately and individually, salvation from our sins as well as deliverance from the condemnation of God's broken law. Every subsequent feast has, as part of its ceremony, the sacrifice of animal(s), thus pointing back to the Passover as its basis.[17] Each subsequent feast adds details regarding the overview

---

17   The seven feasts and the mention of the sacrifice of animals are as follows: (1) Exodus 12:3; (2) Numbers 28:19; (3) Leviticus 23:12; (4) Leviticus 23:18; (5) Numbers 29:2; (6) Numbers 29:8; (7) Numbers 29:13.

of God's grand plan of salvation. They reveal to us the methods and plan of action on God's part in bringing an end to sin on this planet and eradicating sin for all eternity from the whole universe. They also reveal the unfolding of history, especially the final unfolding of events in earth's history and the ushering in of the new earth and a new era of government for the universe.

Furthermore, the Passover is the kingpin feast not only because it is the first one but because it represents the blood of Christ and His death on the cross, the completion of God's oath to save the human race. The Passover is the representative of the entire feast system, and Christ's death is the antitypical fulfillment of this feast. Therefore, while different aspects of Christ's ministry fulfill each feast individually (as the rest of this book will show), His death covers and fulfills the entire feast system corporately.

The *literal* Passover was at the exodus when the Hebrews were delivered from Egypt to go to the Promised Land. The *ceremonial* (or typical) Passover was observed every year and pointed forward to the antitypical fulfillment in Jesus Christ Himself. The *antitypical* Passover was fulfilled by Jesus Christ on the cross, where He sealed His promise of deliverance to the human race. In the final ceremonial Passover that Jesus observed with His disciples the evening before He died, He instituted the Communion service to replace the Passover observance.[18] He tied the Communion service to the Passover and the Promised Land by saying in Matthew 26:29, "But I say unto you, I will not drink henceforth of this fruit of the vine, until that day when I drink it new with you in my Father's kingdom."

In addition to participating in Communion, we can observe the Passover by constantly applying the blood of Christ to the doorposts of our *hearts* (which is a heartfelt appreciation for Jesus' sacrifice, that price of His eternal life, that secured our salvation) that the second death might harmlessly pass over us, too. Then the following text from Romans will remain true for us: "Nay, in all these things we are more than conquerors through him that loved us. For I am persuaded, that neither death [first death], nor life, nor angels, nor principalities, nor powers, nor things present, nor things to come, nor height, nor depth, nor any other creature, shall be able to separate us from the love of God, which is in Christ Jesus our Lord" (Rom. 8:37–39).

Amen. Let it be as Thou hast said.

---

18 Matthew 26:26–29; Mark 14:22–25; Luke 22:14–20. See Appendix L about keeping the literal feast day ceremonies today.

Chapter 3

Feast of Unleavened Bread: New Life

As we begin chapter 3, let's examine the Feast of Unleavened Bread in Leviticus 23:4–8 and Exodus 12:15–20.

> These are the feasts of the Lord, even holy convocations, which ye shall proclaim in their seasons. In the fourteenth day of the first month at even is the Lord's passover. And on the fifteenth day of the same month is the feast of unleavened bread unto the Lord: seven days ye must eat unleavened bread. In the first day ye shall have an holy convocation: ye shall do no servile work therein. But ye shall offer an offering made by fire unto the Lord seven days: in the seventh day is an holy convocation: ye shall do no servile work therein. (Lev. 23:4–8)

> Seven days shall ye eat unleavened bread; even the first day ye shall put away leaven out of your houses: for whosoever eateth leavened bread from the first day until the seventh day, that soul shall be cut off from Israel. And in the first day there shall be an holy convocation, and in the seventh day there shall be an holy convocation to you; no manner of work shall be done in them, save that which every man must eat, that only may be done of you. And ye shall observe the feast of unleavened bread; for in this selfsame day have I brought your armies out of the land of Egypt: therefore shall ye observe this day in your generations by an ordinance for ever. In the first month, on the fourteenth day of the month at even, ye shall eat unleavened bread, until the one and twentieth day of the month at even. Seven days shall there be no leaven found in your houses: for whosoever eateth that which is leavened, even that soul shall be cut off from the congregation of Israel, whether he be a stranger, or born in the land. Ye shall eat nothing leavened; in all your habitations shall ye eat unleavened bread. (Exod. 12:15–20)

Thus the Lord introduces the Feast of Unleavened Bread, a seven-day feast. Because it begins at sunset, say on a Friday, and would then end at sunset the following Friday, sometimes it is said to last, or include, eight days.¹ Sometimes the Feast of Unleavened Bread would be said to begin one day earlier (say Thursday at sunset) on Passover, because the Passover meal was also eaten with unleavened bread (thus adding another day to the count), as we see in Matthew 26:17. One could conceivably find a count of days for this feast ranging between seven and nine.

In order to learn what the leaven is all about, we will look to the New Testament and the words of Christ Himself in Matthew 16:5–12.

> And when his disciples were come to the other side, they had forgotten to take bread. Then Jesus said unto them, *Take heed and beware of the leaven of the Pharisees and of the Sadducees.* And they reasoned among themselves, saying, It is because we have taken no bread. Which when Jesus perceived, he said unto them, O ye of little faith, why reason ye among yourselves, because ye have brought no bread? Do ye not yet understand, neither remember the five loaves of the five thousand, and how many baskets ye took up? Neither the seven loaves of the four thousand, and how many baskets ye took up? How is it that ye do not understand that I spake it not to you concerning bread, that ye should beware of the leaven of the Pharisees and of the Sadducees? *Then understood they how that he bade them not beware of the leaven of bread, but of the doctrine of the Pharisees and of the Sadducees.*

Therefore, we see that the leaven refers to sin and false doctrine. Paul reinforces this in 1 Corinthians 5:6–8 as follows: "Your glorying is not good. Know ye not that a little leaven leaveneth the whole lump? Purge out therefore the old leaven, that ye may be a new lump, as ye are unleavened. For even Christ our passover is sacrificed for us: Therefore let us keep the feast, not with old leaven, neither with the leaven of malice and wickedness; but with the unleavened bread of sincerity and truth."

So you see that this feast is designed to point to a sinless situation as the reference in Exodus 12:17 indicates: "And ye shall observe the feast of unleavened bread; for in this selfsame day have I brought your armies out of the land of Egypt: therefore shall ye observe this day in your generations by an ordinance for ever."² Moreover, we know that time is a factor because this feast lasts a full seven days instead of just one, as the others we have studied so far. Therefore, the antitypical fulfillment will cover a period of time, even eternity, and not be a single event, such as the Passover or Pentecost.³ Note that Paul is revealing the antitypical fulfillment of the feasts of Passover ("Christ our passover") and Unleavened Bread ("keep the feast … with the unleavened bread of sincerity and truth") in 1 Corinthians 5:7, 8.

---

1   The "eight-day" count is according to normal waking hours: Day 1=First Thursday (for example) from sunset to retiring, Day 2=Friday all day (arising to retiring), Day 3=Saturday all day, Day 4=Sunday all day, Day 5=Monday all day, Day 6=Tuesday all day, Day 7=Wednesday all day, Day 8=Second Thursday arising to sunset.

2   In the Bible Egypt represents sin and bondage. Therefore, to be brought out of Egypt is to be brought out of bondage to sin. See also Exodus 20:1 and 2, which introduces the ten promises of deliverance from sin.

3   See the two chapters on the Feast of Firstfruits and the chapter on the Feast of the Passover.

Since these have been fulfilled antitypically in Christ's life and death, we do not need to literally observe these feasts today, but in our hearts.[4]

Numbers in the Bible are important, for there is meaning attached to them. These meanings add information that God is trying to convey and by that enhance our understanding of the feast days. Let us look into the concept of numbers in Bible symbolism. I will present just a few:

- The number 1 is used to express unity, singleness of purpose, and corporate oneness (John 17:11, 21–23; 1 Cor. 12:12–20; Eph. 4:4–6).
- The number 2 is used to express companionship. One example is that Jesus sent out His disciples in pairs (Luke 10). Another example is that the Old and New Testaments work together as a pair (Rev. 11:3, 4; Zech. 4:1–6).
- The number 3 is used to express perfection, especially as related to the heavenly trio that make up the Godhead (1 John 5:7, 8). We also find other Bible stories that refer to three, which indicates sufficiency or perfection, such as Jesus' death and resurrection on the third day (John 2:19, 20; see also Gen. 15:9 and Exod. 3:18; 8:27; 10:22; 23:14).
- The number 4 is used to express geography, especially when referring to the whole world, as in "the four corners [of the earth]" or "the four winds [of strife]" (Ezek. 37:9; Zech. 2:6; Rev. 7:1; 20:8).
- The number 7 is used to express completeness or fulfillment, as in "seven eyes," referring to complete wisdom and "seven days," referring to a complete amount of time, seven days being the basic structure of our calendar (Zech. 3:9; Rev. 5:6).
- The number 10 is used to express authority or law, as in the Ten Commandments, which we have already seen are God's ten spoken (and written) promises to us.[5]
- The number 12 is used to refer to God's government. For example, the nation of Israel has twelve tribes and the city of God has twelve gates, one for each tribe.[6] Jesus had twelve disciples/apostles to set up His church. These twelve were considered "official" and had to be replaced, such as when Matthias was elected to replace Judas (Acts 1:26).
- The number 1000 is used to express the raw power of God.[7]

Now it begins to get exciting. The discipline of mathematics (multiplication) can be applied to these numbers. For example, multiply 3 (perfection) with 4 (geography). The result is 12 (God's government). This is expressing perfection spread out everywhere—over the four corners of the earth—which is the realm of God's government. In addition, 10 to the power of 3, which is God's law (promises) x God's promises x God's promises, equals 1000 or God's raw power, which is inherent in His word. Do you see how this works?

---

4   See Appendix L.
5   See chapter 1, "Feast of Firstfruits: Christ, Our Representative."
6   The work of government is considered to take place at the "gate," which makes sense because that is where the traffic into and out of the city is controlled. Note that in the city are four sides facing each direction on the compass (indicating geography or territory) with each side having three gates (indicating perfection). The whole setup indicates perfect government in all directions.
7   See Joshua 23:10; Psalms 50:10; 90:4; 91:7; 105:8—all of which refer to the power of God using the number 1000.

Let's take another example. Revelation 7 and 14 discuss a group called the 144,000. This number is made up of 3 (perfection) x 4 (geography) x 12 (God's government)[8] x 1000 (God's raw power). Therefore, the people who make up this impressive group are fully controlled by God's perfect, all-encompassing, all-powerful government. Because they allow God to have full control, they present God's final warning to a dying world just before Jesus comes. The two-fold result of this supreme witness is God's vindication at His trial (Rev. 14:7) and the great multitude of Revelation 7:9–17 who stand before the throne of God.[9]

Now let's apply the number seven, which represents completion or completeness. The Feast of the Passover is just one day—a single event. Christ died only *once* for the human race. The Feast of Firstfruits is just one day—a presentation of the concept that Christ is the new head and representative of the human race because of the Passover.[10] The Feast of Unleavened Bread, however, is to last for seven days, representing a complete amount of time—all eternity.

When we take the lack of leaven, meaning without sin, and add to that the number seven, meaning all eternity, we get the following: *God's eternal life is a life without sin that never ends.*

The question we might ask now is, "So what? What makes this feast important?" In order to answer this question, let's look at Christ's life without sin and behold the Son of man. What is it going to take to satisfy God's standard of righteousness? "Be ye therefore perfect, even as your Father which is in heaven is perfect" (Matt. 5:48). Scripture will give us the answer, so let's look at Jesus' Sermon on the Mount. "And seeing the multitudes, he went up into a mountain: and when he was set, his disciples came unto him: And he opened his mouth, and taught them, saying, Blessed are the poor in spirit: for theirs is the kingdom of heaven" (Matt. 5:1–3).

Now take, for example, the following story Jesus told in Luke 18:9–14.

> And he spake this parable unto certain which trusted in themselves that they were righteous, and despised others: Two men went up into the temple to pray; the one a Pharisee, and the other a publican. The Pharisee stood and prayed thus with himself, God, I thank thee, that I am not as other men are, extortioners, unjust, adulterers, or even as this publican. I fast twice in the week, I give tithes of all that I possess. And the publican, standing afar off, would not lift up so much as his eyes unto heaven, but smote upon his breast, saying, God be merciful to me a sinner. I tell you, this man went down to his house justified rather than the other: for every one that exalteth himself shall be abased; and he that humbleth himself shall be exalted.

---

8   Note that God's government is squared—for emphasis (3 x 4 = 12 x 12 = 144, the square of 12).
9   The 144,000 are hereby "numbered," but "the great multitude" "no man could number" (Rev. 7:9). For a description of the awesome attributes of the 144,000, look at Revelation 14:1–5. A discussion of this passage will come in a later chapter.
10 By the way, some of the other feasts mention the firstfruits concept, so it is pervasively important. In all things, sealed by His death and punctuated by His resurrection that establishes His victory over death, Christ represents the human race before the universe. What makes the Feast of Firstfruits special is that this feast is devoted exclusively to the firstfruits concept, especially as it relates to the final harvest of the world.

Notice with whom the Pharisee was praying. It was not God, for God was not listening. He was talking to himself. The Pharisee was caught up in himself and his own "goodness." The publican,[11] on the other hand, knew he was rotten deep down to the core, and he plead with God for mercy. God can work with someone who feels that way. We are all rotten to the core because we all possess the same fallen sinful human flesh that we inherited from Adam. No one is any better than anyone else. We are all made out of the same stuff, and God is no respecter of persons. We need to realize that, given the same circumstances and opportunities, we are capable of doing the same things as the people we might otherwise look down on. We need to understand that, without the power of God to hold us, we would have done exactly what they did (except that perhaps we were not in the "right place at the right time"). Therefore, although we may not have actually robbed that bank, we should not be so quick to condemn.

"As we see souls out of Christ, we are to put ourselves in their place, and in their behalf feel repentance before God, resting not until we bring them to repentance. If we do everything we can for them, and yet they do not repent, the sin lies at their door; but we are still to feel sorrow of heart because of their condition, showing them how to repent, and trying to lead them step by step to Jesus Christ" (Ellen G. White, *Seventh-day Adventist Bible Commentary*, vol. 7, p. 960). We can all repent of (turn away from) the sins we see in others because we know that the sin we see in them is also in us. This is what it means to "feel repentance on behalf of others."

Now let's look at Jesus' story. With whom do you identify? Do you identify with the publican and say, "I am humble like he is"? If so, you are the Pharisee in your own self-righteous humility. If you identify with the Pharisee, you are the publican, because you realize that deep down inside, you are no better than anyone else is, yet you are willing to admit that you have a "holier than thou" attitude that comes forth in your behavior. This irony is a struggle we all have. It constantly tugs at you and me. We *want* to have, in our experience, the righteousness of Christ (what the Pharisee thinks he has), while at the same time we know that we are still sinners and in need of a Savior. Nevertheless, we do not want to believe that our sinfulness is as bad as all that we see on television or in the media. After all, we have never robbed a bank, have we? We just have these "little" things that do not amount to much. Maybe we occasionally slam a door in anger, which some people call "door swearing," or secretly eat the biggest piece of cake when no one is looking—but those things do not amount to much—or do they?

God wants us to reach a plane of performance higher than any of us can imagine! The statement "be ye therefore perfect, even as your Father which is in heaven is perfect" (Matt. 5:48) is a promise that God intends to carry out in us with our consent. God intends that we will have such complete deliverance and recovery from the power of the devil and be wholly separated from all sin that the result will fully destroy the work of Satan in our lives. In trying to get us to sin, the devil will be completely baffled and frustrated, for God's promise will turn us into a fortress impregnable to the assaults of Satan.[12]

Are we up to that? No, we are not. But God is! Let *Him* do it in *you*.

---

[11] Publicans were tax collectors under contract with the Roman government. Thus, they were considered traitors and cheaters notwithstanding the facts. Matthew was a publican.

[12] Ellen G. White, *The Desire of Ages*, p. 311.

So, with whom do you identify? The only way we can bless others is to realize that we are no better than anyone else. We need to be able to give to each other the benefit of whatever doubt we can dredge up. When we see people committing open or covert sins, we should realize that, in actuality, that could be us under different circumstances. Thus, although we cannot repent for others, we can *feel* repentance for sin we may never have committed because repentance is a turning away from sin. Thus, we can repent for *all* sin, not just sin we may have actually committed. This attitude can help others in their Christian journey, for we can be an example in bearing humility and in cherishing God's laws. The word for this concept is "corporate repentance."

As we travel the road of Christian experience, occasionally we will meet with disappointment and trials. Jesus said, "Blessed are they that mourn: for they shall be comforted" (Matt. 5:4). The most obvious reason for mourning is affliction or bereavement. Sometimes we want to blame God when we suffer affliction or when a loved one dies. Sometimes we ask, "How could a loving God do such a thing?" However, we are forgetting that it was not God who brought sin into the world. As a reminder, look at Genesis 3:1–6:

> Now the serpent was more subtil than any beast of the field which the LORD God had made. And he said unto the woman, Yea, hath God said, Ye shall not eat of every tree of the garden? And the woman said unto the serpent, We may eat of the fruit of the trees of the garden: But of the fruit of the tree which is in the midst of the garden, God hath said, Ye shall not eat of it, neither shall ye touch it, lest ye die. And the serpent said unto the woman, Ye shall not surely die: For God doth know that in the day ye eat thereof, then your eyes shall be opened, and ye shall be as gods, knowing good and evil. And when the woman saw that the tree was good for food, and that it was pleasant to the eyes, and a tree to be desired to make one wise, she took of the fruit thereof, and did eat, and gave also unto her husband with her; and he did eat.

Therefore, you see, this whole sin idea was Satan's to begin with. Moreover, please notice that the serpent said, "Ye shall not surely die." Ever since that day, people have been tempted to believe that everyone goes to heaven or to hell at the time they stop breathing. However, we must consult Scripture to determine the truth. Let's read Ecclesiastes 9:1–10:

> For all this I considered in my heart even to declare all this, that the righteous, and the wise, and their works, are in the hand of God: no man knoweth either love or hatred by all that is before them. All things come alike to all: there is one event to the righteous, and to the wicked; to the good and to the clean, and to the unclean; to him that sacrificeth, and to him that sacrificeth not: as is the good, so is the sinner; and he that sweareth, as he that feareth an oath. This is an evil among all things that are done under the sun, that there is one event unto all: yea, also the

> heart of the sons of men is full of evil, and madness is in their heart while they live, and after that they go to the dead. For to him that is joined to all the living there is hope: for a living dog is better than a dead lion. For the living know that they shall die: but the dead know not any thing, neither have they any more a reward; for the memory of them is forgotten.[13] Also their love, and their hatred, and their envy, is now perished; neither have they any more a portion for ever in any thing that is done under the sun. Go thy way, eat thy bread with joy, and drink thy wine with a merry heart; for God now accepteth thy works. Let thy garments be always white; and let thy head lack no ointment. Live joyfully with the wife whom thou lovest all the days of the life of thy *vanity* [breath, breathing[14]], which he hath given thee under the sun, all the days of thy vanity [breath]: for that is thy portion in this life, and in thy labour which thou takest under the sun. Whatsoever thy hand findeth to do, do it with thy might; for there is no work, nor device, nor knowledge, nor wisdom, in the grave, whither thou goest.

There you have it. Can anything be stated more plainly than that? *Satan* is the originator of sin, lies, and half-truths (which are really lies), not God. Moreover, since God knows everything, He knows what is best for us. When trials come and bereavement sets in, it is because God has something better for us. Furthermore, it is important for us to remember that God does not leave us comfortless. He sends us the divine Comforter (John 14:16, 17). When we mourn and are bereaved, God does not leave us alone in our grief. He who gave up His only Son knows how to comfort us, and He who became one of us knows how we feel. Let Him bless us during these times.

By the way, as we have already studied, those who go to the grave, though they are not aware of the passing of time, are resurrected, either in the first or second resurrection.[15] They just close their eyes and then wake up—like falling asleep and waking up in the morning (see John 11).

> But I would not have you to be ignorant, brethren, concerning them which are asleep, that ye sorrow not, even as others which have no hope. For if we believe that Jesus died and rose again, even so them also which sleep in Jesus will God bring with him. For this we say unto you by the word of the Lord, that we which are alive and remain unto the coming of the Lord shall not prevent [go before[16]] them which are asleep. For the Lord himself shall descend from heaven with a shout, with the voice of the archangel, and with the trump of God: and the dead in Christ shall rise first: Then we which are alive and remain shall be caught up together with them in the

---

13 They forget all they once remembered, as is explained in the sentence that follows.
14 The Hebrew word for vanity means breath, breathing, or a gentle breeze. The word is commonly used of anything transitory, evanescent, or frail, hence the idea of vanity.
15 See chapter 2, "Feast of the Passover: Christ, Our Salvation."
16 "Pre"=before, "vent"=go.

clouds, to meet the Lord in the air: and so shall we ever be with the Lord. Wherefore comfort one another with these words. (1 Thess. 4:13–18)

There is another form of mourning. Blessed are they also who weep with Jesus in sympathy with the world's sorrow and in sorrow for its sin. This comes out of the idea of corporate repentance, for if we feel repentance on behalf of others, we will have an accompanying feeling of sorrow. In addition, as we see things happening in our churches that are not right, we also feel a sense of sorrow, sighing and crying for the abominations that people do in the midst of the church. (In Ezekiel 9:4 the process begins with the ancient men in the sanctuary—the church leadership—and then goes throughout the whole church.)

When we see all this sin in our church, do we get angry? Frankly, I used to until I understood this concept of corporate repentance. Today, I just feel this deep sense of sorrow and pain—I hurt for the church when it strays from God's plan. But God will take care of His church.

The church, however, is not the only arena in which this plays out. What about our families? Our children? Our jobs? Our boss? Or … me?

How about it? Do you sorrow for your *own* sin? For what you are doing to your Savior, and to yourself?

Such mourning "shall be comforted." God reveals to us our guilt so that we may flee to Christ and let Him set us free from the experience of the bondage of sin and rejoice in the liberty of being sons and daughters of God. In true contrition, we may come to the foot of the cross and leave our burdens. The Lord has special grace for the mourner, and its power melts hearts and wins souls. His love opens a channel into the wounded and bruised soul and becomes a healing balsam to those who sorrow.

Typically, there are two ways we deal with the knowledge of our own sin. Either we shrug it off because, in our fallen sinful human flesh, it is hard for us to see our own sin or we wallow in self-pity as if there is no hope. Either response can be fatal if allowed to fester, because in either case we deny our true condition. God is not against us. He does not hate us. He is not trying to keep us out of heaven. In fact, our standing before God is one of *favor* until we *choose* to take ourselves out of His hands.

Ephesians 1:3–5 gives us this assurance: "Blessed be the God and Father of our Lord Jesus Christ, who hath blessed us with all spiritual blessings in heavenly places in Christ: According as he hath chosen us in him before the foundation of the world, that we should be holy and without blame before him in love: Having predestinated us unto the adoption of children by Jesus Christ to himself, according to the good pleasure of his will." Therefore, before God created this planet, He chose you and me to be holy and blameless before God in love and to one day be adopted into His family.[17]

Does this sound as if He hates us and is trying to keep us out of heaven? Does this sound as if He is waiting for us to straighten up before He will accept us? Does this sound as if we need to "accept"

---

17 He "chose" us by using His powerful word, which has within it the power to create (Gen. 1). He has created that holiness in each human being, even before we were born. If we believe (i.e., appreciate the gift and the price paid for that gift), we then begin to experience these things in our daily lives.

Him before He can accept us?[18] No! God has already accepted us. Even before we were born and had an opportunity to reject Him, God already accepted us. Think about it! God has *already* accepted *you*!

Can you shrug that off? Frankly, who would want to? However, does the knowledge of God's love for you and His acceptance of you cause you to feel about two inches tall? So often, we feel that we can never get it right so why try? Nevertheless, God has done it all, and He has given you everything He has: the gift of His Son Jesus and His righteousness, eternal life, and a royal heritage. It is yours to use or discard. You have a choice. Christ has given you all things, holding them in trust for when you need it most. Do you choose to believe? If you choose to believe, this righteousness of God will become yours in your experience—the actual good works of God. Is this news too good to believe?

Let's note what it says in Numbers 14:18: "The LORD is longsuffering, and of great mercy, forgiving iniquity and transgression, and by no means clearing the guilty, visiting the iniquity of the fathers upon the children unto the third and fourth generation."

The first part is obviously good news, because God does forgive us. Moreover, the reason He forgives us is because we are in His Son Jesus. We have been in Him since before the foundation of the world, before He created us. We are in Christ because Christ is our Creator,[19] and we are in Christ because He is the representative of the human race.[20] Now this is certainly good news!

However, the last part of the verse does not sound so good, does it? How can God forgive iniquity and transgression and still not clear the guilty? Isn't that what forgiveness is all about—clearing the guilty?

Yes and no. Yes, forgiveness is about clearing guilt, and no, forgiveness does not clear those who choose to remain guilty. This word forgive is actually made up of two words, "for" and "give." When God forgives, He actually "gives" "for." He *gives* us something in exchange *for* our iniquity and transgression. Therefore, when God forgives us, He takes away our sin and transgression and gives us, in exchange everything He has! He gives us His only Son with all of Christ's righteousness and good works forged out for us while He was living here on earth. In addition, through the process, He takes away the guilt. Rather than clearing the guilty, He takes away your guilt! This is the exchange. And it is yours by inheritance because you are in Christ.[21]

God beholds you as not guilty because you are in Christ, and the Father sees Christ, not you. Moreover, when you believe, the righteousness already given you begins to appear in your experience. When that happens, what happens to guilt? There is then nothing of which to be guilty! Remember, you have been in Christ since before the foundation of the world, and you are still in Christ today, unless … unless you take yourself out of His hands. You can do that, and *only* you can do that. Moreover, should you do that (let's hope you never do), you are no longer in Christ. Your protection is gone, and God sees you for who you are, a guilty sinner who is subject to the full condemnation of the law, and He cannot clear you.

---

18   See Appendix M titled "Christ, Our Representative: Treatise relating to Arminianism/Calvinism."
19   We *must* have been in Him before the foundation of the world, because when He created Adam, He breathed our lives into him. See chapter 1, "Feast of Firstfruits: Christ, Our Representative."
20   See chapter 1, "Feast of Firstfruits: Christ, Our Representative."
21   Ephesians 1:9–12; Galatians 3:16–18; Colossians 1:9–12.

So how can we take ourselves out of Christ? We do that through our own unbelief (see John 3:14–20; Rom. 14:10–12, which we discuss in more detail later). God's word has inherent within it the power to create what it says. Do you believe His word? Do you believe He has forgiven you and given you Christ's righteousness? If you do, God will begin to activate the righteousness He has already given you, and you will do the good works of God—not your works, mind you, but He does His good works in you, which is the *experience* of right doing.

Ezekiel 36:26–28 states, "A new heart also will *I* give you, and a new spirit will *I* put within you: and *I* will take away the stony heart out of your flesh, and *I* will give you an heart of flesh. And *I* will put my spirit within you, and *cause* you to walk in my statutes, and ye shall keep my judgments, and do them. And ye shall dwell in the land that I gave to your fathers; and ye shall be my people, and I will be your God."

Think about it! What reason do we have to feel sorry for ourselves when the Ruler of the universe has given us everything He has? Let's believe His promises and receive His gifts so that He can get on with adjusting our experience—our daily lives. He will do it. Will you let Him? Say "yes" to Him right now.

> God would not have us remain pressed down by dumb sorrow, with sore and breaking hearts. He would have us look up and behold His dear face of love. The blessed Saviour stands by many whose eyes are so blinded by tears that they do not discern Him. He longs to clasp our hands, to have us look to Him in simple faith, permitting Him to guide us. His heart is open to our griefs, our sorrows, and our trials. He has loved us with an everlasting love and with loving-kindness compassed us about. We may keep the heart stayed upon Him and meditate upon His loving-kindness all the day. He will lift the soul above the daily sorrow and perplexity, into a realm of peace.[22]

---

22 Ellen G. White, *Thoughts from the Mount of Blessing*, p. 12.

Chapter 4

Feast of Unleavened Bread: Under Control

You never knew there was so much wrapped up in this Feast of Unleavened Bread, did you? Well, we are not done. The Feast of Unleavened Bread has to do with our characters, which God develops in us as we move along our spiritual journey. In chapter 3 we explored the new life, new hope, comfort, and joy that has been given to all of us through the eternal life of Christ that He gave to us. Now let's continue to examine this eternal life that He has for us to enjoy, except in this chapter we will focus our thoughts on the joy we can receive in our experience when we say "yes" to God. Jesus' Sermon on the Mount is His message to us about our characters and tells us what God wants to do in each of us.

"Blessed are the meek: for they shall inherit the earth" (Matt. 5:5).

Paul expounded upon this thought in Romans 2:14–21, where he said, "Bless them which persecute you: bless, and curse not. Rejoice with them that do rejoice, and weep with them that weep. Be of the same mind one toward another. Mind not high things, but condescend to men of low estate. Be not wise in your own conceits. Recompense to no man evil for evil. Provide things honest in the sight of all men. If it be possible, as much as lieth in you, live peaceably with all men. Dearly beloved, avenge not yourselves, but rather give place unto wrath: for it is written, Vengeance is mine; I will repay, saith the Lord. Therefore if thine enemy hunger, feed him; if he thirst, give him drink: for in so doing thou shalt heap coals of fire on his head. Be not overcome of evil, but overcome evil with good."

"Far better would it be for us to suffer under false accusation than to inflict upon ourselves the torture of retaliation upon our enemies. The spirit of hatred and revenge originated with Satan, and can bring only evil to him who cherishes it. Lowliness of heart, that meekness which is the fruit of abiding in Christ, is the true secret of blessing. 'He will beautify the meek with salvation.' Psalm 149:4."[1]

Patience and gentleness when wronged are characteristics of those who dethrone self and allow God to be the supreme ruler of their soul. So I want to ask this question: Are you ready and willing to learn? If you are, then no suggestion—even if given in an accusatory spirit—will cause you to become defensive. No desire to elbow your way to the top will be allowed to control your actions. And you will say, as did John the Baptist, "He must *increase*, but I must *decrease*" (John 3:30). If you find yourself

---

1 Ellen G. White, *Thoughts from the Mount of Blessing*, p. 17.

becoming defensive when you feel you are under "attack" for something you said or did, then give your heart to God afresh that He might do *His* work in you.

"Blessed are they which do hunger and thirst after righteousness: for they shall be filled" (Matt. 5:6).

"Drop down, ye heavens, from above, and let the skies pour down righteousness: let the earth open, and let them bring forth salvation, and let righteousness spring up together; I the Lord have created it" (Isa. 45:8).

Coupled with, and opposite to, this idea of meekness is the sin of greed, the natural result of the selfishness of our fallen sinful human flesh. Jesus expounds upon this in Matthew 6:19–34:

> Lay not up for yourselves treasures upon earth, where moth and rust doth corrupt, and where thieves break through and steal: But lay up for yourselves treasures in heaven, where neither moth nor rust doth corrupt, and where thieves do not break through nor steal: For where your treasure is, there will your heart be also.
>
> The light of the body is the eye: if therefore thine eye be single, thy whole body shall be full of light. But if thine eye be evil, thy whole body shall be full of darkness. If therefore the light that is in thee be darkness, how great is that darkness!
>
> No man can serve two masters: for either he will hate the one, and love the other; or else he will hold to the one, and despise the other. Ye cannot serve God and mammon. Therefore I say unto you, Take no thought for your life, what ye shall eat, or what ye shall drink; nor yet for your body, what ye shall put on. Is not the life more than meat, and the body than raiment? Behold the fowls of the air: for they sow not, neither do they reap, nor gather into barns; yet your heavenly Father feedeth them. Are ye not much better than they? Which of you by taking thought can add one cubit unto his stature?
>
> And why take ye thought for raiment? Consider the lilies of the field, how they grow; they toil not, neither do they spin: And yet I say unto you, That even Solomon in all his glory was not arrayed like one of these. Wherefore, if God so clothe the grass of the field, which to day is, and to morrow is cast into the oven, shall he not much more clothe you, O ye of little faith? Therefore take no thought, saying, What shall we eat? or, What shall we drink? or, Wherewithal shall we be clothed? (For after all these things do the Gentiles seek:) for your heavenly Father knoweth that ye have need of all these things. But seek ye first the kingdom of God, and his righteousness; and all these things shall be added unto you. Take therefore no thought for the morrow: for the morrow shall take thought for the things of itself. Sufficient unto the day is the evil thereof.

What is your treasure? Obviously, the temporal things of this world do have value, much of which God has provided for our enjoyment—so do not hesitate to enjoy and appreciate these things.[2] However, what do you treasure in your heart? Everything we have on planet earth will burn someday. Can you say "goodbye" to all your earthly treasures today, even while you enjoy and appreciate them? We should constantly live in such a way that we can walk away from our temporal blessings without saying "goodbye." And the only way I know to do that is to say "goodbye" to everything right now, today, and every day, and live life in a constant state of thankfulness to God for what He has given us.

Before the foundation of the world, and again later, when Jesus was born in a barn 2,000 years ago (laying aside His divine prerogatives), God gave to us everything He has in His only Son, including righteousness and eternal life.

So, where is your treasure? Do you treasure mercy and goodness and truth?

"Blessed are the merciful: for they shall obtain mercy" (Matt. 5:7).

Let's look again at Moses' experience with God on Mount Sinai. This provides a picture of what God's character is and what He values: "And the Lord passed by before him, and proclaimed, The Lord, The Lord God, merciful and gracious, longsuffering, and abundant in goodness and truth, Keeping mercy for thousands, forgiving iniquity and transgression and sin, and that will by no means clear *the guilty*; visiting the iniquity of the fathers upon the children, and upon the children's children, unto the third and to the fourth *generation*" (Exod. 34:6, 7).

Note that *God* is merciful. However, as we have already seen, rather than confusing the issue by clearing the guilty, *Jesus takes away your guilt* by giving you *His righteousness*, which was forged out for you in the perfect life He lived in the same fallen sinful human flesh that you have.

"For God so loved the world, that he gave his only begotten Son,[3] that whosoever believeth in him should not perish, but have everlasting life. For God sent not his Son into the world to condemn the world; but that the world through him might be saved" (John 3:16, 17). Verse 17 is very plain. Jesus did not become a human being and take our flesh upon Him so that He could condemn us. Instead, He acquits us! But God is too honest to acquit a guilty person, so He must first remove our guilt. And He does that through the process of forgiveness that we have already discussed.

So, if *God* does not condemn us, who *does*? Verse 18 gives us the answer: "He that believeth on him is not condemned: but he that believeth not is condemned already, because he hath not believed in the name of the only begotten Son of God."

Those who *refuse to believe* the *word(s)* of God condemn themselves! Remember, God's word has inherent within it the power to create what it says. If we refuse to believe Him, we are in danger of sealing our own doom because we have cut off our only source of life and power. God has given us

---
2   We can enjoy all *good* things most when we remember that too much of any *good* thing is *still too much*.
3   This was done *before* the foundation of the world, as we have already seen.

everything we need to get to heaven. If we cut off the gift, whose fault is it if we are not there? Your fate is in your own hands. The choice is yours. What will you decide?

When you choose to believe, His righteousness begins to be displayed in your own experience. If you choose to throw this gift away through unbelief, your guilt remains. "And this is the condemnation, that light is come into the world, and men loved darkness rather than light, because their deeds were evil. For every one that doeth evil hateth the light, neither cometh to the light, lest his deeds should be reproved. But he that doeth truth cometh to the light, that his deeds may be made manifest, that they are wrought in God" (verse 19–21).

God does not *have* to condemn you, for you have done a good job of condemning yourself already by the choices you have made. Do not cherish any evil deeds.

Choose God now. He does not, nor will He ever, condemn you. Perish the thought, but if you were to choose to follow Satan and end up in the lake of fire, it will be by your own choice and you will admit that your disposition is fair in the end. Although the lake of fire was not made for unrighteous human beings,[4] it is a merciful act on God's part, because if He were to allow sinners to live in the earth made new (which, remember, is a land without sin), they would be miserable, for they would be living in eternal boring torture!

Choose God now. He comes to you right now in all of His mercy and all of His power on your behalf. Don't give Him the cold shoulder. The stakes are too high. "Whereby are given unto us exceeding great and precious promises: that by these ye might be *partakers of the divine nature*, having escaped the corruption that is in the world through lust" (2 Peter 1:4).

By allowing Christ to control your thoughts and your desires, you become a partaker of the divine nature, that is, you partake of the mind of God.[5] You can do this even though you live in fallen sinful human flesh, for Christ has already conquered that flesh in His own life. Let Him do it in you. He does not ask if we are worthy of His love, but He pours upon us the riches of His love, to *make* us worthy. What a God!

Job declared, "I delivered the poor that cried, and the fatherless, and him that had none to help him. The blessing of him that was ready to perish came upon me: and I caused the widow's heart to sing for joy. I put on righteousness, and it clothed me: my judgment was as a robe and a diadem. I was eyes to the blind, and feet was I to the lame. I was a father to the poor: and the cause which I knew not I searched out" (Job 29:12–16).

If we let Him, Jesus can use us to be His eyes and His feet for others in need. And the experience will be a joy to our hearts as well. "There are many to whom life is a painful struggle; they feel their deficiencies and are miserable and unbelieving; they think they have nothing for which to be grateful. Kind words, looks of sympathy, expressions of appreciation, would be to many a struggling and lonely one as the cup of cold water to a thirsty soul. A word of sympathy, an act of kindness, would lift burdens

---

4   "Then shall he say also unto them on the left hand, Depart from me, ye cursed, into everlasting fire, prepared for the devil and his angels" (Matt. 25:41).

5   "Let this mind be in you which was also in Christ Jesus" (Phil. 2:5).

that rest heavily upon weary shoulders. And every word or deed of unselfish kindness is an expression of the love of Christ for lost humanity."[6]

John reminded us that "we love, because he first loved us" (1 John 4:19, RSV).

"Blessed are the pure in heart: for they shall see God" (Matt. 5:8).

Let us also ponder the wisdom of the following texts: "He that loveth pureness of heart, for the grace of his lips the king shall be his friend" (Prov. 22:11); "But the wisdom that is from above is first pure, then peaceable, gentle, and easy to be intreated, full of mercy and good fruits, without partiality, and without hypocrisy" (James 3:17); "For now we see through a glass, darkly; but then face to face: now I know in part; but then shall I know even as also I am known" (1 Cor. 13:12).

Wouldn't you like to have God as your friend? He is easy to talk to and easy to be entreated. You can take your complaints to Him, and He will not think any less of you for doing so. He wants to be your friend. Remember, God *already* loves you. *There is nothing you can do to make Him love you more.* He longs to be your friend. Ask Him to give you pureness of heart—a longing to reflect His character. He will gladly honor that request: "A new heart also will I give you, and a new spirit will I put within you: and I will take away the stony heart out of your flesh, and I will give you an heart of flesh. And I will put my spirit within you, and cause you to walk in my statutes, and ye shall keep my judgments, and do them. And ye shall dwell in the land that I gave to your fathers; and ye shall be my people, and I will be your God. I will also save you from all your uncleannesses" (Ezek. 36:26–29).

The wisdom of God is pure, peaceable, gentle, easy to be entreated, full of mercy and good fruits, without partiality, and without hypocrisy. Wouldn't you like to have a friend like that? This is what you will see when you have God as your friend.

"Blessed are the peacemakers: for they shall be called the children of God" (Matt. 5:9).

"Peace I leave with you, my peace I give unto you: not as the world giveth, give I unto you. Let not your heart be troubled, neither let it be afraid" (John 14:27).

Please note that peace is a gift from God. It is *His* peace that He gives to us. We will not find peace by looking for it nor by trying to manufacture it. Neither do we find nor make peace by trying to placate people and caving in to the demands of sin. Therefore, I conclude that it is not the work of the peacemakers to "make people happy" as the world so often thinks. They are peacemakers because they tell people about the *gift* that God has given them. As peacemakers, they are content with what they have and with their situation, which is what Paul addressed when he spoke about being content in "whatsoever state I am" (Phil. 4:11). It is only possible to *have* peace if we appreciate what God has given us and the Price He paid for the gift. When we truly understand God's love for us, we

---

[6] Ellen G. White, *Thoughts from the Mount of Blessing*, p. 23.

will not discard the peace that He gives, the peace that reaches deep down inside you and evades the understanding of the world.

So what does it mean to have peace? Peace actually means to stop fighting and to be content with life despite the daily challenges that surround us. That may sound like an oversimplification, but in a practical matter, if you want to have peace with God, simply stop fighting Him and let him have His way with you. God will come to you from time to time and say, "There is something in your life that is hurting you. There is a fault or defect in your character that I need to take away. Will you let Me have it?"

Now we have a choice. We can either say "yes" or "no." We can yield to the work of the Holy Spirit in our lives or we can fight Him off and say, "No. I'd rather have this thing than You." If we say "yes," then God works in us "to will and to do" according to *His* "good pleasure" (Phil. 2:13). Notice that God does the "doing," but He also does the "willing." Even if you know you don't have the willpower to carry out what God wants, God will provide that, too. That is because there is power inherent in His word to create what He says. When He says there is something He wants us to do, He provides everything we need to accomplish the task—even the will to do it.

However, God is a Gentleman. If we say "no," He does not pressure us. If we rebuff Him, He will back off and come back again later to test us on the same point, only from a different angle—a different perspective, maybe. God has given us the power of choice. We can choose to say "no." However, I encourage you to always say "yes" to God.

"Therefore being justified by faith, we have peace with God through our Lord Jesus Christ" (Rom. 5:1).

Receive His peace, and you will know peace.

> **"Blessed are they which are persecuted for righteousness' sake: for theirs is the kingdom of heaven. Blessed are ye, when men shall revile you, and persecute you, and shall say all manner of evil against you falsely, for my sake. Rejoice, and be exceeding glad: for great is your reward in heaven: for so persecuted they the prophets which were before you"**
> **(Matt. 5:10-12).**

The antidote for slander is found in Proverbs 26:2: "As the bird by wandering, as the swallow by flying, so the curse causeless shall not come." This means that when someone talks behind your back about you, and maybe even tries to destroy your reputation, if your character is intact, those things that people say will not harm you permanently. They may light on you for a little while, but you will be vindicated later. When you are in God's hands, you are safe.

Your "reputation" is what *people* think about you. Your "character" is what *God* thinks about you. God knows whom you really are inside, and He knows what you do when no one else is around to see you. This is your character. Do not confuse what *people* think about you with your character, for people cannot control whom you really are inside. Only God can do that, and He *will* do that, but only with your permission.

When you desire to do God's will and allow Christ to have control of your life, Satan will hate it and will try to discourage you. Knowing this, when trials and persecutions come, we should rejoice that God is blessing us in this manner and honoring us in this way, for we are merely following in the footsteps of our Master. God sometimes allows situations to come to a *crisis* so that all can see His deliverance. The more marked the crisis, the more marked the deliverance. This is hard to remember during the close battles, but *do* remember that we are not fighting God, for He is on our side. In fact, there is no need for us to fight at all, for the battle is the Lord's. We are on the winning team. It is our job to make sure we stay on His team and are listening attentively to everything that He says.

There are many verses in the Old Testament where God reminded His people that *He* was the one fighting the battle:

- "And all this assembly shall know that the LORD saveth not with sword and spear: for the battle is the LORD's, and he will give you into our hands" (1 Sam. 17:47).
- "And he said, Hearken ye, all Judah, and ye inhabitants of Jerusalem, and thou king Jehoshaphat, Thus saith the LORD unto you, Be not afraid nor dismayed by reason of th**is** great multitude; for the battle is not yours, but God's" (2 Chron. 20:15).
- "Who is this King of glory? The LORD strong and mighty, the LORD mighty in battle" (Ps. 24:8).

> **"Ye are the salt of the earth: but if the salt have lost his savour, wherewith shall it be salted? it is thenceforth good for nothing, but to be cast out, and to be trodden under foot of men. Ye are the light of the world. A city that is set on an hill cannot be hid. Neither do men light a candle, and put it under a bushel, but on a candlestick; and it giveth light unto all that are in the house. Let your light so shine before men, that they may see your good works, and glorify your Father which is in heaven"**
> **(Matt. 5:13–16).**

Notice that verse 16 says to *let* your light shine, not "make" your light shine. How hard is that? Well, the hard part is to surrender your ego long enough to let God fight the battle of your witnessing. So often, we want to "sell" Jesus. However, Jesus is not a commodity that can be bought or sold. We don't need a punch line or any kind of "cleverness" or "design" to close the deal because the work of the conviction of the heart is the work of the Holy Spirit—the work of God, Himself.

Let's not take on God's work. Let Him do His work in you. Our witness is simply to tell what our experience with God has been and to allow God to display His work in us. Let the Holy Spirit do the convincing. He knows more than we do about the needs of those we work with. I have heard people say that it is time for them to put on their "Jesus hat" and go witness for Him. But, I ask, when do we ever take it off?

> **"Think not that I am come to destroy the law, or the prophets: I am not come to destroy, but to fulfil. For verily I say unto you, Till heaven and earth pass, one jot or one tittle shall in no wise pass from the law, till all be fulfilled. Whosoever therefore shall break one of these least commandments, and shall teach men so, he shall be called the least in the kingdom of heaven: but whosoever shall do and teach them, the same shall be called great in the kingdom of heaven. For I say unto you, That except your righteousness shall exceed the righteousness of the scribes and Pharisees, ye shall in no case enter into the kingdom of heaven"**
> **(Matt. 5:17-20).**

Look at Romans 10:4: "For Christ is the end of the law for righteousness to every one that believeth." Has this text ever bothered you? Is our Bible inconsistent? Jesus just told us that He did not come to destroy the law, but Paul tells us that Christ is the end of the law.

First, let me say that the Bible is consistent with itself. It does not say one thing in one place and the opposite someplace else. When interpreting what the Bible says, the main pillar rule is that although there were many human authors, there is only one *real* Author, and He is divine and does not make mistakes. All scripture is inspired by the Holy Spirit (2 Peter 1:16–21), and God never changes.

Therefore, when Paul tells us that Christ is the "end" of the law, logically, he cannot be saying that Jesus destroyed the law. That would mean that God is a liar, and that is not possible because God's word has inherent within it the power to create what it says (Gen. 1). It is impossible for God to lie; therefore, there must be a better interpretation of this text (Heb. 6:18; Titus 1:2).

Every journey has a beginning and an end, right? Every book has a beginning and an end, also. Can either be fulfilled without going all the way to the end? To say that Christ is the "end of the law" is simply to say that He completely fulfilled the law. He fulfilled the end purpose of the law.

Please notice that Matthew 5:17 goes beyond merely saying that Christ would *not destroy* the law, which is a passive statement, but it also says that He would *fulfill* the law, which is a positive action. The Bible is clear that Jesus fulfilled the law in the perfect life He lived for us, which is a precious heritage and is the lesson the Feast of Unleavened Bread teaches us.

> **"Ye have heard that it was said of them of old time, Thou shalt not kill; and whosoever shall kill shall be in danger of the judgment: But I say unto you, That whosoever is angry with his brother without a cause shall be in danger of the judgment: and whosoever shall say to his brother, Raca, shall be in danger of the council: but whosoever shall say, Thou fool, shall be in danger of hell fire. Therefore if thou bring thy gift to the altar, and there rememberest that thy brother hath ought against thee; Leave there thy gift before the altar, and go thy way; first be reconciled**

**to thy brother, and then come and offer thy gift"
(Matt. 5:21–24).**

God has already given us, as a heritage, everything He has, including His Son and all of His righteousness. Now He is encouraging you and me to receive these into our experience. If we have sinned against our brother or sister (neighbor, family member, coworker, church member, etc.) and have not made it right, and we know there is this issue with our brother, God does not want our gifts or offerings. To Him, such gifts are a self-righteous abomination.

It is God's goal to remove your sin and replace it with His righteousness, all in our daily experience. Therefore, when He comes to you and tells you that there is a sin or defect in your character that He wants to take away, cooperate with Him. He needs your permission to work in your life because He is a Gentleman and will not force Himself on you. The Lord has begun a good work in you. Let Him finish what He has started. If you refuse to cooperate with God (by saying "no" to Him), and then try to give Him offerings and gifts, well, how would that make *you* feel if someone tried to do something like that to you?

Now let's discuss how God works with anger. Many people have a mistaken idea about anger, and they think that one should *never* get angry. Anger is a legitimate emotion. According to the Bible, it is not a sin to be angry if you have good reason and you don't attack the person, just the idea that may be presented or expressed or the action that is being considered or carried out. Mathew 5:21 and 22 is talking about attacking the *person*, even wanting to kill him or her. Yet, even though it may never actually happen, Jesus says the thought itself is sin.

Read Ephesians 4:26, which says, "Be ye angry, and sin not: let not the sun go down upon your wrath." This means get over it. Let your anger inspire you to greater determination to do something positive to accomplish some good, but get over any animosity and attack the *idea*, not the *person*. Moreover, do not use your anger as an excuse to "get mad," which equals losing control. If you are in the right, there is no need to get defensive. Remember, God will be a calming influence. He will remove any desire for revenge if you let Him. And a "soft answer turneth away wrath" (Prov. 15:1).

**"Agree with thine adversary quickly, whiles thou art in the way with him;
lest at any time the adversary deliver thee to the judge, and the judge
deliver thee to the officer, and thou be cast into prison. Verily I say unto
thee, Thou shalt by no means come out thence, till thou
hast paid the uttermost farthing"
(Matt. 5:25, 26).**

Sometimes the fight is not worth the price. Let the Lord choose His own battles.

Just to give us an idea of the extent of the righteousness that the Lord has given to us in the perfect life that He lived in our flesh, Jesus has this to say:

> Ye have heard that it was said by them of old time, Thou shalt not commit adultery: But I say unto you, That whosoever looketh on a woman to lust after her hath

committed adultery with her already in his heart. And if thy right eye offend thee, pluck it out, and cast it from thee: for it is profitable for thee that one of thy members should perish, and not that thy whole body should be cast into hell. And if thy right hand offend thee, cut it off, and cast it from thee: for it is profitable for thee that one of thy members should perish, and not that thy whole body should be cast into hell. (Matt. 5:27–30)

Lest we get the impression that God would have us go around maiming ourselves, the eye and the hand are metaphors dealing with what we allow ourselves to *behold* (hence, the eye), and what we allow ourselves to *do* (thus, the hand).[7]

Sin is committed well before we carry out the act. There are five parts to committing sin: temptation, consideration, consent, plan, and action. Our five senses will perceive stimuli. Some of these stimuli will come in the form of temptation. The eye is probably the most used sense that receives stimuli, so Christ uses the eye to represent wisdom—the reception of stimuli.

When temptation comes in the form of stimuli, is that sin on our part? Remember, we are only responsible for what we can say "yes" or "no" to. We know temptation will come because we still live in a world full of sinful stimuli. This is the work of Satan connecting with our fallen sinful human flesh. The question at hand is, will we let him close the deal? Just be careful during the temptation stage that you do not place yourself purposely in the path of temptation, for us that would be the same as consent to such action. We can say "no" to that, too. We pray in the Lord's Prayer, "Lead us not into temptation." Let us not derail the Lord's own prayer. "For the grace of God that bringeth salvation hath appeared to all men, Teaching us that, denying ungodliness and worldly lusts, we should live soberly, righteously, and godly, in this present world" (Titus 2:11, 12).

When stimuli come in, we have to look at (*consider*) it long enough to sort through it to determine what it is. The sin comes when we *consent* to the idea. Just be careful during the consideration stage that the consideration itself does not begin to border on consent. Dismiss it with dispatch. Quick prayers work well here. The Lord provides instant power.

The *consent* to sin is the sin itself. Jesus has delivered us from the consent to sin, and we who believe can say with Joseph, "How then can I do this great wickedness, and sin against God?" (Gen. 39:9).

For example, we can consent to rob a bank, but if we lack the skills and equipment to carry out the task or the only thing that stops us is the fear of getting caught, have we really cherished God's law—His

---

7   The right hand for most people is the hand of power and action. Hence, in the Bible, the hand (especially the right hand) is the hand of action (Exod. 15:6; Deut. 33:2; Ps. 16:8, 11; 17:7; 18:35; 20:6; 21:8; 26:10; 44:3; 48:10; 60:5; 63:8; 73:23; Isa. 41:13; 45:1; 48:13). Other biblical metaphors are as follows: the eye is the seat of wisdom (what we see or perceive); the heart is the seat of the emotions; the head (or mind, soul) is the seat of the intellect; the forehead (frontal lobe) is the seat of decision-making; the reins (kidneys) are the seat of the motives (Ps. 7:9; 16:7; 26:2; Jer. 11:20; 17:10; 20:12; Rev. 2:23); the bowels are the seat of extreme (passionate) love or sympathy (especially regarding offspring or family; Gen. 43:30; 1 Kings 3:26; Ps. 22:14; Song of Sol. 5:4); the dress (especially the ornamentation) is the seat of righteousness (Isa. 61:10, 11); the spirit (that part of the mind that communicates with God) is the seat of the character; and the loins are the seat of posterity (Heb. 7:5–10).

gift of righteousness? Sin is committed in the mind; the flesh merely carries out (in *action*) the sin consented to, even if all we have done is to make plans.

"Let this mind be in you, which was also in Christ Jesus" (Phil. 2:5). Christ's mind never gave consent to sin even though He was bitterly tempted. Let His divine mind work in you. That is the partaking of the divine nature.

Here is a story about how Jesus, in a *legal* sense, as our representative, took upon Him the sin of humanity and gave to us an inheritance of righteousness, a conquering of sin.[8] The irony of this story is that Jesus kept the Feast of Unleavened Bread, not by *eating*, but by *fasting*. "Man shall not live by bread alone, but by every word that proceedeth out of the mouth of God" (Matt. 4:4).

> And Jesus being full of the Holy Ghost returned from Jordan, and was led by the Spirit into the wilderness, Being forty days tempted of the devil. And in those days he did eat nothing: and when they were ended, he afterward hungered. And the devil said unto him, If thou be the Son of God, command this stone that it be made bread. And Jesus answered him, saying, *It is written, That man shall not live by bread alone, but by every word of God.* And the devil, taking him up into an high mountain, shewed unto him all the kingdoms of the world in a moment of time. And the devil said unto him, All this power will I give thee, and the glory of them: for that is delivered unto me; and to whomsoever I will I give it. If thou therefore wilt worship me, all shall be thine. And Jesus answered and said unto him, *Get thee behind me, Satan: for it is written, Thou shalt worship the Lord thy God, and him only shalt thou serve.* And he brought him to Jerusalem, and set him on a pinnacle of the temple, and said unto him, If thou be the Son of God, cast thyself down from hence: For it is written, He shall give his angels charge over thee, to keep thee: And in their hands they shall bear thee up, lest at any time thou dash thy foot against a stone. And Jesus answering said unto him, *It is said, Thou shalt not tempt the Lord thy God.* And when the devil had ended all the temptation, he departed from him for a season. And Jesus returned in the power of the Spirit into Galilee: and there went out a fame of him through all the region round about. (Luke 4:1–14)

Moreover, from the pen of John, we read: "For all that is in the world, the lust of the flesh, and the lust of the eyes, and the pride of life, is not of the Father, but is of the world" (1 John 2:16).

---

8   "Holiness" is living a life without sinning. The holy angels do this. However, the holy angels do not have righteousness. Righteousness differs from holiness in that righteousness is meeting sin in your own flesh and conquering it, thus attaining the level of both holiness and righteousness. Christ took upon Himself the same fallen sinful human flesh that you and I have, and in that flesh conquered sin, thus giving us the heritage of righteousness. The "legality" of this transaction is that Christ did this as the representative and head of the human race. He effectively set up a "trust fund" of righteousness for you and me. What He did, He did *as* the entire human race in a corporate sense and because of that, we did it "in Him." When we hear this good news and believe the Bible (the creative word of Christ), and claim His promises, God can then begin to work this righteousness into our *experience*. See chapter 1, "Feast of Firstfruits: Christ, Our Representative."

I believe that when John wrote this, he had in mind Christ's forty-day sojourn in the wilderness as Luke described, for he lists in exact order the three temptations that Jesus endured. The first temptation was regarding food, or appetite, which is an example of the "lust of the flesh."[9] However, Jesus reminds us that if we cherish first the spiritual blessings of the kingdom of heaven He will provide all necessary temporal blessings (Matt. 6:33).

When the devil showed Jesus "all the kingdoms of the world in a moment of time" (the second temptation), Jesus told Satan to get out of the way. Through the "lust of the eyes," which is pleasure and power and otherwise known as greed, Satan tries to interpose himself between you and God so that we worship him. The problem is not with beauty, for there is nothing wrong with enjoying true satisfying beauty. Moreover, the proper use of power, as long as we acknowledge that all power comes from Jesus,[10] will promote the cause of Christ and assist others along the Christian way. The problem is a matter of worship. Satan will promise us the world[11] *if* we will worship him. We must decide whom we are going to worship. Choose Christ today!

The third temptation has to do with pride and presumption. So many times I have heard people say something to the effect of, "God told me to …" Please don't let me deceive you, God *does* tell us things from time to time. However, Satan will *also* try to tell us things. Therefore, we need to be careful to recognize the true work of the Holy Spirit in our lives—the true voice of God—and not assume that because we want to do something God is giving His stamp of approval.

So how can we know the will of God? The Bible is our foundational benchmark. The following quote is clear and straightforward and answers the question better than I can.

> There are three ways in which the Lord reveals His will to us, to guide us, and to fit us to guide others. How may we know His voice from that of a stranger? How shall we distinguish it from the voice of a false shepherd? [1] God reveals His will to us in His word, the Holy Scriptures. [2] His voice is also revealed in His providential workings; and it will be recognized if we do not separate our souls from Him by walking in our own ways, doing according to our own wills, and following the promptings of an unsanctified heart, until the senses have become so confused that eternal things are not discerned, and the voice of Satan is so disguised that it is accepted as the voice of God.
>
> [3] Another way in which God's voice is heard is through the appeals of His Holy Spirit, making impressions upon the heart, which will be wrought out in the

---

9   It could be food, sex, money, or anything that is a temporal blessing.
10 See Matthew 28:18–20. Notice what the "therefore" in verse 19 is referring to. When we talk about taking the gospel to the world, we like to emphasize the "go" and leave off the power. That is a recipe for disaster.
11 What right does Satan have to planet Earth that he thinks he can give it away as he chooses? Adam, as representative of the human race, did give it to him when he sinned, at the time that Satan conquered him; but Christ has won it back, partly by this exchange with Satan during the wilderness fast and also through the exchange in Genesis 3 in which He told Satan that he could never represent planet Earth because of the enmity He placed between human beings and Satan.

> character. If you are in doubt upon any subject you must first consult the Scriptures. If you have truly begun the life of faith you have given yourself to the Lord to be wholly His, and He has taken you to mold and fashion according to His purpose, that you may be a vessel unto honor. You should have an earnest desire to be pliable in His hands and to follow whithersoever He may lead you. You are then trusting Him to work out His designs, while at the same time you are co-operating with Him by working out your own salvation with fear and trembling. You, my brother, will find difficulty here because you have not yet learned by experience to know the voice of the Good Shepherd, and this places you in doubt and peril. You ought to be able to distinguish His voice.[12]

Abraham knew the voice of God. When God told him to sacrifice Isaac on Mount Moriah, Abraham recognized that it was God who was speaking to him, so there was no question or hesitation. He knew, also, that God's voice equals strength and power. Since God had promised that He would make of Abraham a great nation through Isaac, and no one else, not even his servant Eliezer or his firstborn Ishmael, Abraham reasoned that God would resurrect Isaac from the sacrificial ashes. Abraham was willing to allow God to have control; he was willing to be pliable in God's hands. He knew the voice of God and had faith in the word of his heavenly Father (Gen. 22; Heb. 11:8–12).

Do *we* believe the word of God? When we act according to our *own* will and follow the promptings of our *own* unsanctified hearts, it is pride and presumption at its "best." It is easy to receive strong impressions that are actually coming from Satan through our fallen sinful human flesh. If our hearts are unsanctified, if we do not set ourselves apart for God's use, if we do not allow God to have control, we will misunderstand and accept error for truth. *We need to know our Bibles*. We need a thorough understanding of the Scriptures so that we can know whether the impressions we receive and the events that happen in our lives are God's leading.

For this reason, we need to ask God to guide us when we study our Bibles. Without the guidance of God as we study, it is very easy to trip and fall. For example, in Luke 4:10, 11 Satan quoted Psalm 91:11, 12: "For he shall give his angels charge over thee, to keep thee in all thy ways. They shall bear thee up in *their* hands, lest thou dash thy foot against a stone." But he left out verses nine and ten, which say, "Because thou hast made the LORD, which is my refuge, even the most High, thy habitation; There shall no evil befall thee, neither shall any plague come nigh thy dwelling." Satan is very "good" at giving us half-truths.

Whenever we get a "strong impression" to do something, we need to first test it with the Bible to see whether it is consistent with God's written will. Now there may be situations that dictate a choice between two acceptable pathways or situations that Scripture does not clearly delineate. Under those conditions, we can allow God's providential workings (the events in our lives) to show us what the Lord's will is or what He will have us to do. Be patient and don't run ahead of God. Running ahead of

---

12 Ellen G. White, *Testimonies for the Church*, vol. 5, p. 512.

His timing is acting on a presumed understanding of His will, which means that in our pride we actually substitute our will for the will of God!

So once again, the question comes down to this, whom are we going to worship?

Jesus' response to Satan is interesting: "It is said, Thou shalt not tempt the Lord thy God" (Luke 4:12). He did not argue with His adversary about his misuse of Scripture. He acted as if Satan knew what he was doing, which he did. Rather than enter a pointless argument, He simply quoted Deuteronomy 6:16. Note that in every case, Jesus' response was from Scripture (Deut. 8:3; 6:13; 6:16). If you know your Bible, you have a powerful "weapon."

In Christ's forty-day fast, on behalf of the entire human race, Jesus gained the victory over appetite, greed, and presumption—all three major points of sin, representing all sin ever committed by any human being. Thus Jesus Christ, the Son of God, as the representative of the human race, in the same fallen sinful human flesh that you and I have, gained the victory over Satan with respect to "all that is in the world," as stated by the apostle John. By so doing, Christ won back all that Adam lost in Eden. Therefore, *in Christ*, God has already forged out and given you, as an inheritance, victory over the lust of the flesh, and the lust of the eyes, and the pride of life—appetite, greed, and pride.

Christ gained the victory and completely reversed what Adam did—and *more*[13]—by taking upon Himself "all that is in the world," all the sin that every inhabitant on this earth has had in them because of what our father Adam gave us corporately, plus all the sin that we, by our own volition, have committed by ourselves. Jesus gave of Himself for you and for me.

Receive the gift. Believe it. Cherish it. Once you do, you will begin to see it come alive in your experience. God has promised—and God cannot lie. Won't you receive it right now? Can the good news be better than we have thought—too good to believe? Then throw yourself upon the Rock and be broken. Tell Him, "I believe; help thou mine unbelief" (Mark 9:24, see also verse 23), and the Lord *will* make you whole.

---

13   See Romans 5:17–19. (The NEB says it quite clearly.)

Chapter 5

Feast of Unleavened Bread: Who God Is

We are continuing to discuss the Feast of Unleavened Bread. In this chapter we will focus on how the feast points to the life of Christ and His perfect character. Remember, no one could ever convict Jesus of committing sin. Please note this passage in John in which Jesus tells us who He is.

> Jesus went unto the mount of Olives. And early in the morning he came again into the temple, and all the people came unto him; and he sat down, and taught them. And the scribes and Pharisees brought unto him a woman taken in adultery; and when they had set her in the midst, They say unto him, Master, this woman was taken in adultery, in the very act. Now Moses in the law commanded us, that such should be stoned: but what sayest thou? This they said, tempting him, that they might have to accuse him. But Jesus stooped down, and with his finger wrote on the ground, as though he heard them not. So when they continued asking him, he lifted up himself, and said unto them, He that is without sin among you, let him first cast a stone at her. And again he stooped down, and wrote on the ground. And they which heard it, being convicted by their own conscience, went out one by one, beginning at the eldest, even unto the last: and Jesus was left alone, and the woman standing in the midst.
>
> When Jesus had lifted up himself, and saw none but the woman, he said unto her, Woman, where are those thine accusers? hath no man condemned thee? She said, No man, Lord. And Jesus said unto her, Neither do I condemn thee: go, and sin no more. Then spake Jesus again unto them, saying, I am the light of the world: he that followeth me shall not walk in darkness, but shall have the light of life. The Pharisees therefore said unto him, Thou bearest record of thyself; thy record is not true. Jesus answered and said unto them, Though I bear record of myself, yet my record is true: for I know whence I came, and whither I go; but ye cannot tell whence I come, and whither I go. Ye judge after the flesh; I judge no man. And yet if I judge, my judgment is true: for I am not alone, but I and the Father that sent me. (John 8:1–16)

Also, Jesus said in John 5:30, "I can of mine own self do nothing: as I hear, I judge: and my judgment is just [or true]; because I seek not mine own will, but the will of the Father which hath sent me."

I would like to make two points based on these passages. First, Jesus did not condemn the woman caught in adultery—*and neither will He condemn you*. Instead of condemning her, He judged her. Instead of words of condemnation, He spoke words of righteousness—into her. Moreover, instead of condemning *you*, He speaks righteousness into you.[1] Remember, God's word has inherent within it the power to create what it says. When He says, "You are perfect", or "Be ye therefore perfect, even as your Father which is in heaven is perfect" (Matt. 5:48), or "Go and sin no more" (as in our example), He *creates* that condition of righteousness *in you* as our divine Trustee to dispense to you what you need when you need it most.[2] This dispensation[3] then begins to take place upon the condition of belief when you believe the words of Christ. He has done, and continues to do, the same in you and in me that He did for the woman in John 8. *This* is how God judges us.

Second, this is who God is. So many people seem to think that God is a cruel, or at best, a heavy-handed taskmaster who is trying to keep us out of heaven. God is not like that. God is a kind and compassionate Friend who is trying to get us *into* heaven. He has already given each of us all the righteousness we need for entrance into heaven and the new earth. For each of us, He is waiting for us to say, "Thank you for saving my soul. Thank you for the infinite gift of your eternal life and your righteousness, purchased at an infinite price." This is what He is waiting for us to do. Let's not keep Him waiting any longer. He is anxious to begin to (or continue to) dispense His righteousness into *your* experience right now, and He longs to have you with Him in glory for eternity. You are free! For God does not condemn you. Make good use of the choice you have. The final closing of the conflict between good and evil will culminate in sorting out the issue of who God is. He is, *already*, the Savior of your soul.

Please notice that Jesus did not even condemn the Pharisees![4] They condemned themselves when they left the scene with the wind taken out of their sails. You see, Jesus merely did what the Holy Spirit does with you and me. He revealed to them their own sin (in their case by writing it down), thus causing them to be "convicted by their own conscience." Moreover, the part I like best is that He did not broadcast their sin to all present, but rather, He wrote it in the sand so that He could easily cover it over. This is the kind of God we follow.

If Jesus does not condemn anyone, what kind of judgment does Jesus pass? He says His judgment is true, which means He judges only truth. He tells us that this is because he would judge only in consultation with the Father. Yet, when you think about it, truth is the only kind of judgment He could possibly pass because His word has inherent within it the power to create what it says.[5] So that when He says, "Be ye therefore perfect," He creates in the subject the condition of perfection.

Moreover, Jesus has *already* passed this judgment. First He talks about casting out the devil through

---

1   Please see the previous discussion on who condemns.
2   Even though, for now, Christ our Trustee keeps it safe in Him.
3   A good study on dispensation is Ephesians 3.
4   There are passages in the Scriptures (e.g., Matthew 23) where Christ warned the Pharisees of the direction they were headed, calling them hypocrites, acknowledging the decisions they had already made so far; but even then, He did not condemn any individual. Jesus spoke the same righteousness to them as He has to everyone else.
5   Jesus cannot possibly be the minister of sin. He cannot create condemnation, even by speaking it. See Galatians 2:17.

His death on the cross: "Now is the judgment of this world: now shall the prince of this world be cast out. And I, if I be lifted up from the earth, will draw all men unto me" (John 12:31, 32). Additionally, included in this drawing to the foot of the cross is His judgment of eternal life for you and me. Paul writes about delivering us from the devil's power through the death of Christ: "Forasmuch then as the children are partakers of flesh and blood, he also himself likewise took part of the same; that through death he might destroy him that had the power of death, that is, the devil" (Heb. 2:14).

In John 3:14–21, Jesus also talks about His judgment on you and me using the metaphor of the snakebites in the wilderness (see Num. 21:4–9). His judgment on us is eternal life, which includes deliverance from sin: "And as Moses lifted up the serpent in the wilderness, even so must the Son of man be lifted up: That whosoever believeth in him should not perish, but have eternal life.[6] For God so loved the world, that he gave his only begotten Son, that whosoever believeth in him should not perish, but have everlasting life. For God sent not his Son into the world to condemn the world; but that the world through him might be saved" (John 3:14–17).[7]

All this happened 2,000 years ago. Therefore, someone might very well say, "If Satan was *destroyed* 2,000 years ago (see Heb. 2:14), why is he still around? This proves that the Bible cannot be true. We cannot rely on what it says." That is a legitimate question.

If this is your concern, I have good news! The Greek word that is translated "destroy" means "to paralyze," so the devil has been *paralyzed* by the death of Christ, and all power has been given to Christ by virtue of His death on the cross.[8] Therefore, the devil can still be around to tempt us even though he has been defeated. The only way Satan can have any power now is through *us* if we choose not to believe God. That is the only way. So do not let the devil have any power over you. Believe God's all-powerful Word.

> It is also written in your law, that the testimony of two men is true. I am one that bear witness of myself, and the Father that sent me beareth witness of me. Then said they unto him, Where is thy Father? Jesus answered, Ye neither know me, nor my Father: if ye had known me, ye should have known my Father also. These words spake Jesus in the treasury, as he taught in the temple: and no man laid hands on him; for his hour was not yet come. Then said Jesus again unto them, I go my way, and ye shall seek me, and shall die in your sins: whither I go, ye cannot come. Then said the Jews, Will he kill himself? because he saith, Whither I go, ye cannot come. And he said unto them, Ye are from beneath; I am from above: ye are of this world; I am not of

---

6 Please note that the eternal life that God refers to here is the *experience* of eternal life, actual righteousness and good works in the experience, because the experience is what happens to those who *believe*. God bestowed eternal life in *title* before the foundation of the world. Moreover, Jesus refers to the "good works" aspect of God's gift of experiential salvation in the next few verses. See John 3:18–21.

7 God *did* save the whole world on the cross by taking their penalty for sin, in *title*, for all humanity.

8 The devil will be destroyed in the lake of fire at the end of time (Matt. 25:41; Rev. 20:10). But until then, we are assured of Jesus' words: "All power is given unto me in heaven and in earth" (Matt. 28:18).

this world. I said therefore unto you, that ye shall die in your sins: for if ye believe not that I am he, ye shall die in your sins. Then said they unto him, Who art thou? And Jesus saith unto them, Even the same that I said unto you from the beginning. (John 8:17–25)

The question in verse 25—"Who art thou?"—is the question that must be settled before Jesus can come. *Who is God?* God has been on trial since before the foundation of the world, the question ultimately boiling down to, "Who is God? Is He who He says He is?" Moreover, the battlefield is the law, the Ten Commandments, because these ten promises make up the transcript of God's character, which is who He is. Please note that Jesus Himself brought up a legal issue regarding the admission of the testimony of the witnesses in verse 17. The plan of salvation is a legal matter, and the Bible is couched with legal language; hence Christ's reference to the law.

If God is on trial, then there must be some courtroom players. Who are they? What are they doing? Actually, they are all there. There is a defendant, a plaintiff, a judge, a jury, and witnesses. The Scriptures say this of the plaintiff:

> Thou hast been in Eden the garden of God; every precious stone was thy covering, the sardius, topaz, and the diamond, the beryl, the onyx, and the jasper, the sapphire, the emerald, and the carbuncle, and gold: the workmanship of thy tabrets and of thy pipes was prepared in thee in the day that thou wast created. Thou art the anointed cherub that covereth; and I have set thee so: thou wast upon the holy mountain of God; thou hast walked up and down in the midst of the stones of fire. Thou wast perfect in thy ways from the day that thou wast created, till iniquity was found in thee. By the multitude of thy merchandise they have filled the midst of thee with violence, and thou hast sinned … Thine heart was lifted up because of thy beauty, thou hast corrupted thy wisdom by reason of thy brightness … Thou hast defiled thy sanctuaries by the multitude of thine iniquities, by the iniquity of thy traffick; therefore will I bring forth a fire from the midst of thee, it shall devour thee, and I will bring thee to ashes upon the earth in the sight of all them that behold thee. All they that know thee among the people shall be astonished at thee: thou shalt be a terror, and never shalt thou be any more.[9] (Ezek. 28:13–19)

Notice that the plaintiff (Satan, Lucifer[10]) was perfect until iniquity, violence, sin, self-exaltation, corruption, and defilement was found in him. He had kept the law of God—for how long the Bible does

---

9 Oh well, so much for an eternal burning hell. By the way, in the Bible, "everlasting" and "forever" both mean "(ever) as long as it lasts"—that is, until it burns out, it cannot be quenched or put out. On the other hand, "eternal" means "never ending."
10 The king of Tyrus is a metaphor. He never was in heaven. This can only be describing Lucifer.

not say—however, at some point, he stopped keeping the law of God. The little seed of pride grew in his mind that he was pretty good. He was working elbow-to-elbow with God Himself, Jesus Christ, the archangel, and he got the heady idea that he could do as well as or better than God was doing.

Sadly that seed brought about his downfall: "How art thou fallen from heaven, O Lucifer, son of the morning! how art thou cut down to the ground, which didst weaken the nations! For thou hast said in thine heart, I will ascend into heaven, I will exalt my throne above the stars[11] of God: I will sit also upon the mount of the congregation, in the sides of the north:[12] I will ascend above the heights of the clouds; I will be like the most High. Yet thou shalt be brought down to hell, to the sides of the pit" (Isa. 14:12–15).

This idea of the covering cherub is an interesting one. Exodus gives us a conceptual aid: "And thou shalt make a mercy seat of pure gold: two cubits and a half shall be the length thereof, and a cubit and a half the breadth thereof. And thou shalt make two cherubims of gold, of beaten work shalt thou make them, in the two ends of the mercy seat. And make one cherub on the one end, and the other cherub on the other end: even of the mercy seat shall ye make the cherubims on the two ends thereof. And the cherubims shall stretch forth their wings on high, covering the mercy seat with their wings, and their faces shall look one to another; toward the mercy seat shall the faces of the cherubims be. And thou shalt put the mercy seat above upon the ark; and in the ark thou shalt put the testimony that I shall give thee. And there I will meet with thee, and I will commune with thee from above the mercy seat, from between the two cherubims which are upon the ark of the testimony, of all things which I will give thee in commandment unto the children of Israel" (Exod. 25:17–22).

The earthly sanctuary, which is the pattern of the true sanctuary in heaven,[13] illustrates two cherubs (angels, actually[14]) covering the mercy seat over the ark of God. Lucifer was one of them. We don't know for certain whom the other covering cherub is. Perhaps he is Gabriel, but we are not told. There has been some speculation that Michael the archangel might be that other covering cherub. However, it is not likely that Michael the archangel, who is Christ Himself,[15] would be that other cherub. "For the Lord himself shall descend from heaven with a shout, with the voice of the archangel, and with the

---

11   Stars represent angels or leaders (Rev. 1:20; 12:1, 4, 9).
12   This is speaking about the seat of God's throne (Ps. 48:1, 2). It is worthy of note that the entrance to the Hebrew temple faced east, and the table of shewbread with the twelve loaves in two stacks—one throne each for the Father and the Son—was on the north side of the first apartment.
13   See Exodus 25:8, 9 and Hebrews 8:1–5. The earthly sanctuary was a pattern of the true sanctuary in heaven. The earthly sanctuary describes and illustrates for us the actual workings of God for our salvation for the whole world and in our daily experience.
14   There is another order of angels called "seraph." Cherubs and seraphs are the only two orders of angels that we know of (Isa. 6:2, 6).
15   "Michael the archangel, when contending with the devil he disputed about the body of Moses, durst not bring against him a railing accusation, but said, The Lord rebuke thee" (Jude 1:9). Arch means "above and supporting," head, chief, or principal. Therefore, Michael, as the "archangel" is the "above and supporting" head of the angels. One does not actually have to *be* an angel to be the head of, have charge of, have responsibility for, or represent the angels and their work. Being the *creator* of the angels is sufficient for that responsibility. See chapter 1 for more discussion on the topic of representation and responsibility.

trump of God: and the dead in Christ shall rise first" (1 Thess. 4:16). However, in Exodus 25, where God establishes the mercy seat with the two cherubs, it is Christ ("Lord," Yahweh, Jehovah) who says He will communicate from *between* the two cherubs (see Exod. 25:1, 22.) Therefore, I conclude that Jesus Christ (Michael), who is not an angel, is not the other covering cherub.

From Ezekiel 28:15 we conclude that Satan had, at one time, been keeping the law of God. But he disobeyed at some point, which indicates that he *stopped* keeping the law of God. This also implies that Satan somehow concluded that the law of God was either unreasonable, impossible, or both. Satan made this decision while he was still in heaven and "wast upon the holy mountain of God," which implies that he had been given a ministry to the whole congregation of created beings of God. As one of the covering cherubs, this would be true.

However, Heaven was not thrilled with Lucifer's decision. The book of Revelation tells the story. "And there was war in heaven: Michael and his angels fought against the dragon; and the dragon fought and his angels, And prevailed not; neither was their place found any more in heaven. And the great dragon was cast out, that old serpent, called the Devil, and Satan, which deceiveth the whole world: he was cast out into the earth, and his angels were cast out with him. And I heard a loud voice saying in heaven, Now is come salvation, and strength, and the kingdom of our God, and the power of his Christ: for the accuser of our brethren is cast down, which accused them before our God day and night" (Rev. 12:7–10).

God has been on trial ever since all this happened. As the defendant, He needs witnesses, which is where you and I come in. We are His witnesses—good or bad, on God's side or on Satan's side. When the Bible talks about being God's witnesses, I believe that this scenario is the context. When God has His witnesses together, those who, through their lives, testify of who God is and what He can do in fallen sinful human flesh,[16] then the trial is over and the sentence can be carried out. Then Christ can come and receive His inheritance, which is you and me.

Satan has his witnesses too, for each person who refuses to believe what God says witnesses to the universe on Satan's behalf and adds credence to his claim that it is impossible to keep God's law. Yet, in the midst of his lies, there is truth. *Outside of God*, people cannot keep God's law. But with Christ in us, we can stand on His side and prove to the world that God's laws are just and good and not burdensome. So there you have it. The battle lines are drawn. Satan's charge is that *nobody* can keep God's law. Therefore, God only needs to prove that *somebody* can. Will you take God's side?

Let's continue our examination of John 8:

> I have many things to say and to judge of you: but he that sent me is true; and I speak to the world those things which I have heard of him. They understood not

---

16   That is, *their* flesh, the flesh of the witnesses—indwelling them through the power of the Holy Spirit—not just His flesh that *He* took. When Christ became a human being, taking upon Himself fallen sinful human flesh and living a perfect life in the same flesh you and I have, He demonstrated what He could do in the flesh that *He* took. Now the jury is waiting to see what He can do in the fallen sinful human flesh of people such as you and me. After all, *we* are the ones who need salvation.

that he spake to them of the Father. Then said Jesus unto them, When ye have lifted up the Son of man, then shall ye know that I am he, and that I do nothing of myself; but as my Father hath taught me, I speak these things. And he that sent me is with me: the Father hath not left me alone; for I do always those things that please him. (verses 26–29)

Jesus was ready to judge them, yet He was pleased to speak only what the Father wanted Him to say.[17] God will do the same for you (Ezek. 3:16–27, especially verses 26 and 27).

> As he spake these words, many believed on him. Then said Jesus to those Jews which believed on him, If ye continue in my word, then are ye my disciples indeed; And ye shall know the truth, and the truth shall make you free. They answered him, We be Abraham's seed, and were never in bondage to any man: how sayest thou, Ye shall be made free? Jesus answered them, Verily, verily, I say unto you, Whosoever committeth sin is the servant of sin. And the servant abideth not in the house for ever: but the Son abideth ever.[18] If the Son therefore shall make you free, ye shall be free indeed. I know that ye are Abraham's seed; but ye seek to kill me, because my word hath no place in you.
>
> I speak that which I have seen with my Father: and ye do that which ye have seen with your father. They answered and said unto him, Abraham is our father. Jesus saith unto them, If ye were Abraham's children, ye would do the works of Abraham. But now ye seek to kill me, a man that hath told you the truth, which I have heard of God: this did not Abraham. Ye do the deeds of your father. Then said they to him, We be not born of fornication; we have one Father, even God. Jesus said unto them, If God were your Father, ye would love me: for I proceeded forth and came from God;[19] neither came I of myself, but he sent me. (John 8:30–42)

Either Jesus is the Son of God or He is the biggest liar who ever lived! The final events of the world are all about who God is.

---

17 Please note that in verse 29 Jesus claimed for Himself infallibility and that no one challenged Him. None of us can say, "For I do *always* those things that please Him."

18 The principle that Jesus is expressing is this: The *servant* is not an heir, but the *son*, whether natural or adopted, *is* an heir. The servant *serves* for remuneration, the "goodies," so to speak. Then he goes home to his own activities. The heir *cares* about the estate. His primary concern is for the *father* and the father's *estate*. He suffers for the welfare of the estate. It is heart work with the heir. God does not want you to serve Him for the goodies, or to escape perceived bad consequences. He wants your whole heart. If you believe, you are an *heir, joint-heirs with Christ* (John 1:12; Rom. 8:17), not a servant. In these last days He is looking for a people who will vindicate His character and demonstrate what He can do in fallen sinful human flesh. He has faith that *you* will allow *Him* to do that in you! Moreover, anyone who chooses to be the servant of sin can only be a servant that way, never an heir. Such a person will not be able to abide in sin forever, for as the servant of sin, when sin is destroyed in the lake of fire, those who cling to sin will also be destroyed with their sin.

19 Jesus became incarnate and took human flesh.

> Why do ye not understand my speech? even because ye cannot hear my word. Ye are of your father the devil, and the lusts of your father ye will do. He was a murderer from the beginning, and abode not in the truth, because there is no truth in him. When he speaketh a lie, he speaketh of his own: for he is a liar, and the father of it. And because I tell you the truth, ye believe me not. Which of you convinceth me of sin? And if I say the truth, why do ye not believe me? (John 8:43–46)

No one could pin one sin on Jesus. This proves that Jesus is not a liar; He is who He says He is.

> He that is of God heareth God's words: ye therefore hear them not, because ye are not of God. Then answered the Jews, and said unto him, Say we not well that thou art a Samaritan, and hast a devil? Jesus answered, I have not a devil; but I honour my Father, and ye do dishonour me. And I seek not mine own glory: there is one that seeketh and judgeth. Verily, verily, I say unto you, If a man keep my saying, he shall never see death. (John 8:47–51)

Only God could say this (and the Jews recognized this in verse 53), for only the words of God have the power inherent within them to create what they say. Can any of us cause this statement to happen, "If a man keep my saying, he shall never see death" (verse 51)? Moreover, this cannot be referring to the first death, for Christians are still dying today. This must be referring to the second death. The Jews do not acknowledge this nuance, as is apparent from what follows:

> Then said the Jews unto him, Now we know that thou hast a devil. Abraham is dead, and the prophets; and thou sayest, If a man keep my saying, he shall never taste of death. Art thou greater than our father Abraham, which is dead? and the prophets are dead: whom makest thou thyself? Jesus answered, If I honour myself, my honour is nothing: it is my Father that honoureth me; of whom ye say, that he is your God:[20] Yet ye have not known him; but I know him: and if I should say, I know him not, I shall be a liar like unto you: but I know him, and keep his saying. Your father Abraham rejoiced to see my day: and he saw it, and was glad. Then said the Jews unto him, Thou art not yet fifty years old, and hast thou seen Abraham? Jesus said unto them, Verily, verily, I say unto you, Before Abraham was, I am. (John 8:52–58)

There you have it; the most powerful statement one could ever make in claiming to be God. Jesus claimed for Himself self-existence. By using the term "I am," Jesus claimed for Himself the state of having no beginning and no end. He is God. He was God in Israel's day. He was God before Abraham

---

20 In John 8:54, Jesus is referring back to His opening statement about witnesses (verses 17 and 18).

was born. He was God before Adam was created. He was God before the foundations of the world were laid. He was God before anything else existed.[21] He is God! Jesus could truthfully say, "I and my Father are one" (John 10:30). Jesus Christ is God today—and for all eternity—God and Man. Jesus Christ is *everything* to us, and yet the Pharisees refused to understand. Instead, "Then took they up stones to cast at him: but Jesus hid himself, and went out of the temple, going through the midst of them, and so passed by" (John 8:59).

Jesus, though God, was also man; and as man, He relied on the Father for everything, even the plan for His life. Jesus was to die on the cross. However, His time was not up. God has a plan for your life, too. The only one who can derail that plan is you. Let Him have your life, your thoughts, your desires, your plans, hopes, dreams, and aspirations today—and He will return them to you sanctified.

What does this mean to us? Read Matthew 5:48 for the answer: "Be ye therefore perfect, even as your Father which is in heaven is perfect."

No one could pin sin on Jesus Christ. He has already done the same for you, simply by speaking His righteousness to you, as you have just read.[22] He does not condemn you, but He lifts you up with His word. Will you let Him work His Word into your experience? This is what the Feast of Unleavened Bread is all about. Come to the table and feast!

Look at what Jeremiah and Ezekiel have to say to us regarding this subject.

> Behold, the days come, saith the LORD, that I will make a new covenant with the house of Israel, and with the house of Judah: Not according to the covenant that I made with their fathers in the day that I took them by the hand to bring them out of the land of Egypt; which my covenant they brake, although I was an husband unto them, saith the LORD: But this shall be the covenant that I will make with the house of Israel; After those days, saith the LORD, I will put my law in their inward parts, and write it in their hearts; and will be their God, and they shall be my people. (Jer. 31:31–33)

---

21 "And now, O Father, glorify thou me with thine own self with the glory which I had with thee before the world was" (John 17:5). This statement by Christ indicates that He knew He preexisted the creation of the world. Note John 1:1–3, 14, "In the beginning was the Word, and the Word was with God, and the Word was God. The same was in the beginning with God. All things were made by him; and without him was not any thing made that was made…. And the Word was made flesh, and dwelt among us, (and we beheld his glory, the glory as of the only begotten of the Father,) full of grace and truth." These statements indicate that Jesus Christ made all things. Therefore, He preexisted all things and created all things. Jesus Christ is the One speaking in Exodus 3:14: "And God said unto Moses, I AM THAT I AM: and he said, Thus shalt thou say unto the children of Israel, I AM hath sent me unto you." Micah 5:2 is also about Jesus Christ: "But thou, Bethlehem Ephratah, though thou be little among the thousands of Judah, yet out of thee shall he come forth unto me that is to be ruler in Israel; whose goings forth have been from of old, from everlasting." Jesus Christ *is* eternal life—in His person: "Jesus said unto her [Martha], I am the resurrection, and the life: he that believeth in me, though he were dead, yet shall he live: And whosoever liveth and believeth in me shall never die [the second death]" (John 11:25, 26).

22 We cannot claim infallibility for ourselves, but we can say that Christ has given to us His righteousness held in trust for us to be dispensed to our experience when we need it and will allow it to be used in us.

> A new heart also will I give you, and a new spirit will I put within you: and I will take away the stony heart out of your flesh, and I will give you an heart of flesh. And I will put my spirit within you, and cause you to walk in my statutes, and ye shall keep my judgments, and do them. (Ezek. 36:26, 27)

God will *cause* you to keep His law. Rather than to discard it or ignore it, God will write the law in your heart. If something is written in your heart, how difficult is it to perform that thing? Whatever is in your heart comes out naturally, right? It is as if you are carrying out your own impulses. In this case, God is the One who is performing His law in you under *His* impulses, but for all practical purposes, it is as if the impulses were your own.[23] It is being done that naturally. Let's continue reading from Ezekiel 36.

> And ye shall dwell in the land that I gave to your fathers; and ye shall be my people, and I will be your God. I will also save you from all your uncleannesses: and I will call for the corn, and will increase it, and lay no famine upon you. And I will multiply the fruit of the tree, and the increase of the field, that ye shall receive no more reproach of famine among the heathen. Then shall ye remember your own evil ways, and your doings that were not good, and shall lothe yourselves in your own sight for your iniquities and for your abominations. Not for your sakes do I this, saith the Lord God, be it known unto you: be ashamed and confounded for your own ways, O house of Israel. (Ezek. 36:28–32)

How shall we respond? Will you receive "the fruit of the tree, and the increase of the field, that ye shall receive no more reproach of famine among the heathen"?[24] Are you willing to allow God to bring you to the place where you *loathe* the sins you may now be committing or thinking right now?

O Lord God, grant us, *in our experience*, what You have already given us *in fact* and are holding *in trust* for us. Give us a delight for those things that are good and from You; cause us to abhor those things that are evil and from the devil; and grant us the proper balance of everything else. In Your all-powerful name, we ask it.

This is what the Feast of Unleavened Bread is all about. Come to the table—and feast!

> Now the God of peace, that brought again from the dead our Lord Jesus, that great shepherd of the sheep, through the blood of the everlasting covenant, Make you perfect in every good work to do his will, working in you that which is wellpleasing in his sight, through Jesus Christ; to whom be glory for ever and ever. Amen. (Heb. 13:20, 21)

---

23   Compare with *The Desire of Ages*, page 668.
24   See also John 15.

Chapter 6

Feast of Firstfruits: Christ, Our Harvest— The Fruit of Representation

The antitypical fulfillment of this feast is the resurrection of Jesus Christ from the dead. The Feast of Firstfruits was observed on the sixteenth day of the first month, two days after the Passover, which took place on the day of the week we call Friday. This feast represents the resurrection of Jesus on early Sunday morning.

We have already discovered that, in the history of this planet, there have been only two men who have ever represented the entire human race. The first man was Adam. The second is Jesus Christ. As our representative in heavenly places,[1] Jesus is our resurrection from the dead, and in reality, spiritually speaking, He pulls us into heaven with Him.

The third feast of the Hebrew economy is described in Leviticus 23:9–14:

> And the Lord spake unto Moses, saying, Speak unto the children of Israel, and say unto them, When ye be come into the land which I give unto you, and shall reap the harvest thereof, then ye shall bring a sheaf of the firstfruits of your harvest unto the priest: And he shall wave the sheaf before the Lord, to be accepted for you: on the morrow after the sabbath the priest shall wave it. And ye shall offer that day when ye wave the sheaf an he lamb without blemish of the first year for a burnt offering unto the Lord. And the meat offering thereof shall be two tenth deals of fine flour mingled with oil, an offering made by fire unto the Lord for a sweet savour: and the drink offering thereof shall be of wine, the fourth part of an hin. And ye shall eat neither bread, nor parched corn, nor green ears, until the selfsame day that ye have brought an offering unto your God: it shall be a statute for ever throughout your generations in all your dwellings.

Please note in verse ten that, for this feast, the firstfruit is the firstfruit of the *harvest*. The wave sheaf that was brought to the priest came from the harvest and represented the entire harvest of the giver. This wave sheaf is the *type*. It provided food for the priest as well as serving to remind the farmer

---

1 "Blessed be the God and Father of our Lord Jesus Christ, who hath blessed us with all spiritual blessings in heavenly places in Christ: According as he hath chosen us in him before the foundation of the world, that we should be holy and without blame before him in love" (Eph. 1:3, 4).

that God provided the harvest. The farmer dedicated to God the entirety of his harvest. What is good for the farmer is good for the rest of us, also.

As an example, let's discuss the matter of tithe. This dedication of the wave sheaf is what tithing does for us today (see Lev. 27:30–34). The 10 percent of our income that God asks of us represents *all* that He gives us and is a way of telling Him that all we *have* belongs to Him and, as such, is a means by which we can dedicate our temporal blessings back to Him. Another example is the Sabbath. The seventh day of the week represents the *entire* week of time and is a way of telling God that all we *are* belongs to Him and, as such, is a means by which we can dedicate our entire lives and spiritual blessings back to Him. (Because the Sabbath also memorializes His creative power, it also represents God's ability, by His all-powerful creative word, to re-create us[2] and to make us into the people He wants us to be through our willingness to let Him give to us the experience of His righteousness, when we choose to believe.)

There is another aspect of this feast that cannot go without mentioning. For the Israelites, this feast represented freewill offerings, which were in *addition* to the tithing program (Mal. 3:8–12). Therefore, it had more meaning than merely to provide for the earthly priesthood, to represent the temporal harvest, and to represent our acknowledgement of Him who owns us. In addition to the tithe, which, as already stated, is 10 percent of our net income, God asks us to give freewill thank offerings in heartfelt appreciation for what He has done for us and the price He has paid for our salvation. These are "freewill" offerings in that there is no definite amount that is specified, even though the offerings are indeed required. The poor widow who gave "all that she had" apparently did not know from where her next meal was going to come (Mark 12:44; see also Luke 21:4). This could have been in addition to her tithe, which surely had been returned at an earlier date, or it may have even been her tithe, having been saved for this purpose, and now her meager store of cash had run out. Either way, she gave out of a heartfelt appreciation, for she knew God would provide and would not let her down. So this feast also represents our thankfulness to God, a heartfelt appreciation for His love and His care for us.

This feast becomes even more important in our understanding when we combine these two representative concepts together into one Person. First, we know from chapter 1 that Jesus is the representative of the human race. Everything He did, *we* (i.e., the whole human race, corporately) did also *in Him*. Secondly, this feast represents the harvest, as we have just discussed.

By connecting this feast to Jesus Christ, we will be able to see that the antitypical fulfillment of this feast ultimately represents the harvest of the entire human race at the end of time, including, and especially, the two resurrections of the dead before the final fulfillment of earth's history. During the growing season, the immature good grain cannot easily be distinguished from the equally immature tares. They look so very much alike that they cannot be easily separated. At harvest time, the tares can be easily distinguished from the good grain and the separation can be accomplished readily. The good grain is harvested for use and the tares are sent to the burn pile.

Leviticus 23:11 says that the sheaf was to be waved on the day after the Sabbath. In today's calendar,

---

2   We are a new "act of creation," according to the original Greek in 2 Corinthians 5:17.

this would be Sunday. What could Christ do on Sunday (as the representative of the human race) that would attach Him firmly to the harvest of earth's history?

We know that the antitypical fulfillment of the Passover was the death of Christ on the cross—His freewill offering to us so that, individually, we don't have to die the second death. Christ's sacrifice happened on Friday afternoon. This is the *first* feast.

We know that the seven-day Feast of Unleavened Bread represents Christ's eternal and righteous life that He forged for us as our representative in the same fallen, sinful, human flesh that we have. He dispenses this righteous inheritance to us as we need it in our daily lives, from the "trust fund" that He has set up (as we remain believers in God).[3] The human race (corporately) lived that perfect life *in Christ*. This feast began on the Sabbath after the Passover. It is the *second* feast.

Something else happened that fateful weekend, early on Sunday morning. Look at what Paul tells us regarding another aspect of Christ as our representative:

> What shall we say then? Shall we continue in sin, that grace may abound? God forbid. How shall we, that are *dead to sin*, live any longer therein? Know ye not, that so many of us as were baptized into Jesus Christ were *baptized into his death*? Therefore we are buried *with him* by baptism into death: that like *as* Christ was raised up from the dead by the glory of the Father, even so we also *should walk* in newness of life. For if we have been *planted together* in the likeness of his death, we *shall* be also in the likeness of his resurrection: Knowing this, that our old man is crucified *with him*, that the body of sin might be destroyed [Greek: paralyzed], that henceforth we should not serve sin. *For he that is dead is freed from sin.* Now if we be dead *with* Christ, we *believe* that we *shall* also live with him: Knowing that Christ being raised from the dead dieth no more; death hath no more dominion over him. For in that he died, he died unto sin once: but in that he liveth, he liveth unto God. Likewise reckon ye also yourselves to be dead indeed unto sin, but alive unto God through Jesus Christ our Lord. Let not sin therefore reign in your mortal body, that ye should obey it in the lusts thereof. (Rom. 6:1–12)

According to verse three, when we are baptized, we acknowledge that Christ is our representative in death. Baptism is a very important individual acknowledgement and acceptance that Christ's death represents the death of the human race corporately, of which, individually, we are a part. When we are baptized, each baptismal candidate formally "elects" Jesus to represent him or her before the Father and the universe. When we "go under the water" and come forth again (Rom. 6:4, 5), we acknowledge publicly that we have chosen to receive His death and resurrection as our own personal spiritual experience

---

3   See Ephesians 1:3–14; 3:2–7 and Colossians 1:25–28. The word that is translated "dispensation" in the KJV means to manage, administer, dispense, especially as a steward (or trustee) of the property of others. Jesus Christ, as our representative, would be the trustee of our inheritance. Thus, He dispenses from our inheritance everything we need.

and that, as Jesus came forth from the grave alive, so we come forth from the watery "grave" alive in Him, for His second death is ours. This acknowledges that we have eternal life in Christ, for He took our eternal death as our representative (verse 4). By being baptized we are formally adopted into God's household as His child—His heir.

Because He represented us on the cross, our "old man" (our sinning mind) is crucified (that is, put to death) *in Him* with respect to sin (verse 6). It also means—as a result—that our "body of sin" (our fallen sinful human flesh) is paralyzed with respect to sin. The Greek word translated "destroyed" in the KJV is *katargeo,* which means to render idle or inoperative, hence to paralyze.[4] Fallen sinful human flesh is paralyzed with respect to sin by the power of the mind of Jesus Christ, that is, His all-powerful Word dwelling in us through the power of the Holy Spirit.[5]

As we receive (by believing) the *experience* of the crucifixion of our fallen sinful human mind that was forged out by Christ on the cross as our representative, that "hole" left by the death of our sinful mind is then filled (spiritually speaking) by the sinless mind of Christ, as verse 8 indicates. This change of mind is what happens when we live with Jesus (compare with Phil. 2:5). This is what "conversion" is: we receive this "change of mind"—and our baptism formally acknowledges all of this regarding the death and resurrection of Christ for us.

Our proper response to verse 11—"Likewise *reckon* ye also yourselves to be dead indeed unto sin, but alive unto God through Jesus Christ our Lord"—is simply to believe God's promise, His Word, to us. If we believe we have been freed from sin, we give permission for God to cause us to *act* that way (see verse 7). The sin that was removed from the human race corporately by the death, life, and resurrection of Christ is removed from each one of us individually in our daily experience when we choose to believe (verses 1, 2, and 12). Our proper response to Romans 6:11 is to say, "Amen. Thank you, God."

By the way, verses 9 and 10 indicate that Jesus needed to die one time only. His life, death, and resurrection represented the life, death, and resurrection for the entire human race corporately, which is what the first three feasts are all about. As individuals we are each members of the human race. As we daily die to self, Jesus does not need to die again for each of us, for His death represents and covers the entire human race (and there is only *one* of those). Individually, we experience that death when, having been confronted with the goodness of God, we choose to believe and thus allow God to control our minds. This is what it means to die to self.

Paul speaks elsewhere in the New Testament about the process of dying to self.

> I am crucified with Christ: nevertheless I live; yet not I, but Christ liveth in me: and the life which I now live in the flesh I live by the faith of the Son of God, who loved me, and gave himself for me. (Gal. 2:20)

---

4 It can also mean to cause to cease, to annul, to abolish. However, since our body is still *alive* after we come forth from the water of baptism, our fallen sinful human flesh does *not* cease and neither is it abolished.

5 It is interesting to note that though the NIV translates *katargeo* as "done away with," the margin in the NIV suggests "to be rendered powerless" as an alternative translation to replace the word "destroyed."

> For I delivered unto you first of all that which I also received, how that Christ died for our sins according to the scriptures; And that he was buried, and that he rose again the third day according to the scriptures:...
>
> Now if Christ be preached that he rose from the dead, how say some among you that there is no resurrection of the dead? But if there be no resurrection of the dead, then is Christ not risen: And if Christ be not risen, then is our preaching vain, and your faith is also vain. Yea, and we are found false witnesses of God; because we have testified of God that he raised up Christ: whom he raised not up, if so be that the dead rise not. For if the dead rise not, then is not Christ raised: And if Christ be not raised, your faith is vain; ye are yet in your sins. Then they also which are fallen asleep in Christ are perished.
>
> If in this life only we have hope in Christ, we are of all men most miserable. But now is Christ risen from the dead, and become the firstfruits of them that slept. For since by man [Adam] came death, by man [Christ] came also the resurrection of the dead. For as in Adam all die, even so in Christ shall all be made alive. But every man in his own order: Christ the *firstfruits* [three days after he died]; afterward they that are Christ's at his coming [the "first resurrection" at the second coming of Christ]. Then cometh the end [at the time of the "second resurrection" after the 1000 years], when he shall have delivered up the kingdom to God, even the Father; when he shall have put down all rule and all authority and power. For he must reign, till he hath put all enemies under his feet.
>
> The last enemy that shall be destroyed is death [in the lake of fire (see Rev. 20:14)]. For he [the Father] hath put all things under his [Christ's] feet. But when he [the Father] saith all things are put under him [Christ], it is manifest that he [the Father] is excepted, which did put all things under him. And when all things shall be subdued unto him [Christ], then shall the Son also himself be subject unto him [the Father] that put all things under him, that God [the Father] may be all in all. Else what shall they do which are baptized for the dead, if the dead rise not at all? why are they then baptized for the dead? And why stand we in jeopardy every hour? I protest by your rejoicing [boasting, glorying] which I have in Christ Jesus our Lord, I die daily. (1 Cor. 15:3, 4, 12–31)

Our baptism (representing our "walk" with Christ and acceptance of the fulfillment of the Feast of Firstfruits in our lives) is not, technically, the fulfillment of the Feast of Firstfruits. It is merely our proper response and reception of the gift that the feast represents. When combined with Christ having fulfilled this feast (antitypically) through His being resurrected on Sunday, His resurrection itself, made as the representative of the human race, has its own antitypical fulfillment—for the Feast of Firstfruits mainly represents the harvest, as Paul just discussed in the above text. Typically, this is the harvest of the farmer's crops. It also involves the full ripening and maturation of the grain, ready for use. Antitypically, that means God's people will be prepared to live in heaven and the new earth for all eternity, perfectly reflecting the character of God, *before* the harvest is accomplished.

For the antitypical fulfillment of Christ's resurrection as the harvest, let's look at Revelation 20. For an overview, I refer you back to the discussion on this passage that appears in chapter 2 on the Passover. This passage in Revelation 20 and 21 is one of my favorites because it describes the final events of earth's history and the rebuilding of the old earth (as we know it) into the new earth, a glorious and unmolested masterpiece of God's creation.

> And I saw an angel come down from heaven, having the key of the bottomless pit and a great chain in his hand. And he laid hold on the dragon, that old serpent, which is the Devil, and Satan, and bound him a thousand years, And cast him into the bottomless pit, and shut him up, and set a seal upon him, that he should deceive the nations no more, till the thousand years should be fulfilled: and after that he must be loosed a little season. And I saw thrones, and they sat upon them, and judgment was given unto them: and I saw the souls of them that were beheaded for the witness of Jesus, and for the word of God, and which had not worshipped the beast, neither his image, neither had received his mark upon their foreheads, or in their hands; and they lived and reigned with Christ a thousand years.… This is the *first* resurrection.
>
> Blessed and holy is he that hath part in the first resurrection: on such the second death hath no power, but they shall be priests of God and of Christ, and shall reign with him a thousand years. ["But the rest of the dead lived not again until the thousand years were finished,"[6] which marks the *second* resurrection. Note that the whole human race is now alive. This whole scenario is the harvest.] And when the thousand years are expired, Satan shall be loosed out of his prison, And shall go out to deceive the nations which are in the four quarters of the earth, Gog, and Magog, to gather them together to battle: the number of whom is as the sand of the sea.[7]
>
> And they went up on the breadth of the earth, and compassed the camp of the saints about, and the beloved city: and fire came down from God out of heaven, and devoured them. And the devil that deceived them was cast into the lake of fire and brimstone, where the beast and the false prophet are, and shall be tormented day and night for ever and ever. And I saw a great white throne, and him that sat on it, from whose face the earth and the heaven fled away; and there was found no place for them. And I saw the dead, small and great, stand before God; and the books

---

6   This is a quote from the first part of Revelation 20:5 (omitted above), which is a parenthetical note regarding the second resurrection. Contextually it belongs here.

7   This would be the completion of the battle of Armageddon that was paused for 1000 years. This is discussed in more detail in chapter 15 on the Feast of Tabernacles.

were opened: and another book was opened, which is the book of life: and the dead were judged out of those things which were written in the books, according to their works. And the sea gave up the dead which were in it; and death and hell delivered up the dead which were in them: and they were judged every man according to their works. And death and hell were cast into the lake of fire. This is the *second* death. And whosoever was not found written in the book of life was cast into the lake of fire. (Rev. 20:1–15)

The good news is that the lake of fire goes out. "For, behold, the day cometh, that shall burn as an oven; and all the proud, yea, and all that do wickedly, shall be stubble: and the day that cometh shall burn them up, saith the LORD of hosts, that it shall leave them neither root nor branch" (Mal. 4:1); "Thou Satan hast defiled thy sanctuaries by the multitude of thine iniquities, by the iniquity of thy traffick; therefore will I bring forth a fire from the midst of thee, it shall devour thee, and I will bring thee to ashes upon the earth in the sight of all them that behold thee" (Ezek. 28:18).

And now for the rest of the harvest scenario:

And I saw a new heaven and a new earth: for the first heaven and the first earth were passed away; and there was no more sea. And I John saw the holy city, new Jerusalem, coming down from God out of heaven, prepared as a bride adorned for her husband. And I heard a great voice out of heaven saying, Behold, the tabernacle of God is with men, and he will dwell with them, and they shall be his people, and God himself shall be with them, and be their God. And God shall wipe away all tears from their eyes; and there shall be no more death, neither sorrow, nor crying, neither shall there be any more pain: for the former things are passed away. And he that sat upon the throne said, Behold, I make all things new. And he said unto me, Write: for these words are true and faithful. And he said unto me, It is done. I am Alpha and Omega, the beginning and the end. I will give unto him that is athirst of the fountain of the water of life freely. He that overcometh shall inherit all things; and I will be his God, and he shall be my son. (Rev. 21:1–7)

This, dear friend, is the ultimate and final antitypical fulfillment of the Feast of the Firstfruits. I pray that you will choose to have a part in it.

These three feasts—the Passover, Unleavened Bread, and Firstfruits, all coming so close together—point to Jesus Christ and what He has done for you as part of the human race. To illustrate what this means for you today, there is a helpful and very interesting prophecy in Ezekiel 37:1–14:

The hand of the LORD was upon me, and carried me out in the spirit of the LORD, and set me down in the midst of the valley which was full of bones, And caused me to pass by them round about: and, behold, there were very many in the open valley; and, lo, they were very dry. And he said unto me, Son of man, can these bones live? And I answered, O Lord God, thou knowest. Again he said unto me, Prophesy upon these bones, and say unto them, O ye dry bones, hear the word of the Lord. Thus saith the Lord God unto these bones; Behold, I will cause breath to enter into you, and ye shall live: And I will lay sinews upon you, and will bring up flesh upon you, and cover you with skin, and put breath in you, and ye shall live; and ye shall know that I am the Lord. So I prophesied as I was commanded: and as I prophesied, there was a noise, and behold a shaking, and the bones came together, bone to his bone. And when I beheld, lo, the sinews and the flesh came up upon them, and the skin covered them above: but there was no breath in them.

Then said he unto me, Prophesy unto the wind, prophesy, son of man, and say to the wind, Thus saith the Lord God; Come from the four winds, O breath, and breathe upon these slain, that they may live. So I prophesied as he commanded me, and the breath came into them, and they lived, and stood up upon their feet, an exceeding great army.

Then he said unto me, Son of man, these bones are the whole house of Israel: behold, they say, Our bones are dried, and our hope is lost: we are cut off for our parts. Therefore prophesy and say unto them, Thus saith the Lord God; Behold, O my people, I will open your graves, and cause you to come up out of your graves, and bring you into the land of Israel. And ye shall know that I am the Lord, when I have opened your graves, O my people, and brought you up out of your graves, And shall put my spirit in you, and ye shall live, and I shall place you in your own land: then shall ye know that I the Lord have spoken it, and performed it, saith the Lord.

If you are willing, this prophecy is about you, for if you believe, you are adopted into God's house and become His own child—His heir. He can resurrect your dead heart and give you a heart of flesh and, thus, cause you to walk in His statutes in new life.[8] Indeed, He has already done this for you as your representative. I encourage you to say "yes" to God right now so that He might finish what He has started in you.

But I would not have you to be ignorant, brethren, concerning them which are asleep, that ye sorrow not, even as others which have no hope. For if we believe that Jesus died and rose again, even so them also which sleep in Jesus will God bring with him. For this we say unto you by the word of the Lord, that we which are alive and remain unto the coming of the Lord shall not prevent [go before] them which are

---

8   See Ezekiel 36, the whole chapter, but especially verses 26–28.

asleep. For the Lord himself shall descend from heaven with a shout, with the voice of the archangel, and with the trump of God: and the dead in Christ shall rise first: Then we which are alive and remain shall be caught up together with them in the clouds, to meet the Lord in the air: and so shall we ever be with the Lord. Wherefore comfort one another with these words. (1 Thess. 4:13–18)

Chapter 7

Feast of Weeks—Pentecost: A Transition

It is interesting to note that the seven feasts of the Jewish religious calendar target two different groups of people and are clustered together in a pattern. The first three of the seven feast days teach us what God did for the entire human race.

- Feast one, the Passover, represents Christ death on the cross, which was His gift to all human beings.
- Feast two, Unleavened Bread, represents Christ's perfect life lived in fallen sinful human flesh—a heritage for all people.
- Feast three, Firstfruits, teaches the concept that Christ represents, and is the Savior of, the entire human race before God and the universe from a legal perspective.

All three feasts illustrate what God has already done and/or is doing currently for *all* people, individually and corporately. The beginnings of all three feasts cluster within a three-day period in the first month of the Jewish religious calendar, and they are all completed within eight days.

Jumping forward a little bit, by contrast, feasts five, six, and seven represent what God does for all those who choose to *believe*. Some, but not all, of the human race will receive the full benefit of the ministry of Christ represented by these last three feasts. All in the human race will have to deal with the results of their own decisions. The beginnings of all three feasts cluster within a fifteen-day period in the seventh month of the Jewish religious calendar, and they are completed within three weeks.

Feast number four, however, is a transition between these two sets of feasts. This feast introduces the work of the Holy Spirit *on* the lives of *all people* and illustrates what He does *in* the lives of all who believe the good news of the first three feasts and are willing to allow God to work in them. Our reception of the Holy Spirit is the pivotal factor in this feast, which represents the point of human decision. This one-day feast takes place fifty days[1] after the Feast of Firstfruits, and thus we categorize it by itself.

These seven feasts resulted in three trips to Jerusalem each year. The first trip was in celebration of feasts one, two, and three. The second trip was in observance of feast four. And the last trip was in commemoration of feasts five, six, and seven. Sometimes these trips themselves are referred to as three "feasts" and numbered accordingly. For the sake of our discussion, we will refer to seven "feasts" and three "trips." This configuration forms an interesting comparison and corresponds exactly to the one above regarding the target groups—the human race corporate verses the human race as individuals

---

1   In Greek the word "Pentecost" means "the fiftieth," that is, the fiftieth day.

considering each individual (and each person's choices) separately.

God introduces feast number 4 as follows:

> And ye shall count unto you from the morrow after the sabbath, from the day that ye brought the sheaf of the wave offering; seven sabbaths shall be complete: Even unto the morrow after the seventh sabbath shall ye number fifty days; and ye shall offer a new meat offering unto the Lord. Ye shall bring out of your habitations two wave loaves of two tenth deals; they shall be of fine flour; they shall be baken with leaven; they are the firstfruits unto the Lord. And ye shall offer with the bread seven lambs without blemish of the first year, and one young bullock, and two rams: they shall be for a burnt offering unto the Lord, with their meat offering, and their drink offerings, even an offering made by fire, of sweet savour unto the Lord. Then ye shall sacrifice one kid of the goats for a sin offering, and two lambs of the first year for a sacrifice of peace offerings.
>
> And the priest shall wave them with the bread of the firstfruits for a wave offering before the Lord, with the two lambs: they shall be holy to the Lord for the priest. And ye shall proclaim on the selfsame day, that it may be an holy convocation unto you: ye shall do no servile work therein: it shall be a statute for ever in all your dwellings throughout your generations. And when ye reap the harvest of your land, thou shalt not make clean riddance of the corners of thy field when thou reapest, neither shalt thou gather any gleaning of thy harvest: thou shalt leave them unto the poor, and to the stranger: I am the Lord your God. (Lev. 23:15–22)

The antitypical fulfillment of this feast is described in Acts 2:1–4: "And when the day of Pentecost was fully come, they were all with one accord in one place. And suddenly there came a sound from heaven as of a rushing mighty wind, and it filled all the house where they were sitting. And there appeared unto them cloven tongues like as of fire, and it sat upon each of them. And they were all filled with the Holy Ghost, and began to speak with other tongues, as the Spirit gave them utterance."

Thus, the Lord introduced the Feast of Weeks, or Pentecost. Please note that the antitypical fulfillment of this feast happened on the exact day[2] of the Jewish feast of Pentecost—fifty days after the antitypical fulfillment of the Passover during which Christ died at the exact hour. The appearing of the cloven tongues of fire, representing the beginning of the office work of the Holy Spirit,[3] was the antitypical fulfillment of this feast. Therefore, the Feast of Weeks points to the work of the Holy Spirit in the "Christian" era.

---

2   This is the meaning of "fully come" in Acts 2:1.
3   The Holy Spirit, being an eternal being and the third Person of the Godhead, has been working all along, but His work took on an official capacity as the replacement for Christ's presence on earth when Christ ascended to begin His office work as High Priest in the heavenly sanctuary.

So, what does this mean for us today?

First, the Holy Spirit will take away your sin from your experience. How does this work in Scripture? Since the Holy Spirit descended as tongues of fire, we should consider this metaphor in Isaiah 33: "The sinners in Zion are afraid; fearfulness hath surprised the hypocrites. Who among us shall dwell with the devouring fire? who among us shall dwell with everlasting burnings? He that walketh righteously, and speaketh uprightly; he that despiseth the gain of oppressions, that shaketh his hands from holding of bribes, that stoppeth his ears from hearing of blood, and shutteth his eyes from seeing evil" (verses 14, 15). "For the LORD thy God is a consuming fire, even a jealous God" (Deut. 4:24).

Please notice that the passage in Isaiah first mentions the sinners and hypocrites[4] who dwell within the congregation of those who claim to be God's people. Then it tells us who can dwell in the devouring fire and everlasting burnings. The ones who can dwell in such a devouring fire are those who love God and allow Him to work out His righteousness in their lives. How can they dwell within the fire without being devoured? Because they walk righteously and speak uprightly and are not clinging to sin.[5]

From this, we can conclude that the "consuming fire" destroys sin. But what about those within the church who do *not* love God and do not allow Him to work out His righteousness in them? Matthew 13:30 comes to mind: "Let both grow together until the harvest: and in the time of harvest I will say to the reapers, Gather ye together first the tares, and bind them in bundles to burn them: but gather the wheat into my barn." If we allow God, He will consume the sin in us now. If not, He will wait until the lake of fire to consume our sin, at which time we will also be consumed if we have chosen to cling to sin.

Remember, God Himself is a "consuming fire" (Deut. 4:24). Therefore, the "consuming fire" represents the work of God Himself who, while we let Him, is removing the sin from our lives. It is quite fitting, therefore, that God would use tongues of fire to represent the work of the Holy Spirit, for "when he is come, he will reprove the world of sin" (John 16:8). What better way is there than fire to present the beginning of the special work of the Holy Spirit in removing the sins of the people in the Christian era and replacing the presence of Christ on earth?

> But now I go my way to him that sent me; and none of you asketh me, Whither goest thou? But because I have said these things unto you, sorrow hath filled your heart. Nevertheless I tell you the truth; It is expedient for you that I go away: for if I go not away, the Comforter will not come unto you; but if I depart, I will send him unto you. And when he is come, he will reprove the world of sin, and of righteousness,

---

[4] Hypocrites are people who profess beliefs and opinions they do not hold in order to conceal their real feelings or motives. Those who are allowing God to remove sin from their lives are not hypocrites.

[5] Please note what God says in Ezekiel 28:14, 15 about Satan before he fell: "Thou art the anointed cherub that covereth; and I have set thee so: thou wast upon the holy mountain of God; thou hast walked up and down in the midst of the stones of fire. Thou wast perfect in thy ways from the day that thou wast created, till iniquity was found in thee." Satan was able to walk in the consuming fire as long as he was perfect. How iniquity eventually could be found in him we do not know, but he must have consented to sin and, therefore, removed himself from the "stones of fire."

and of judgment: Of sin, because they believe not on me; Of righteousness, because I go to my Father, and ye see me no more; Of judgment, because the prince of this world is judged. I have yet many things to say unto you, but ye cannot bear them now. Howbeit when he, the Spirit of truth, is come, he will guide you into all truth: for he shall not speak of himself; but whatsoever he shall hear, that shall he speak: and he will shew you things to come. He shall glorify me: for he shall receive of mine, and shall shew it unto you. All things that the Father hath are mine: therefore said I, that he shall take of mine, and shall shew it unto you. A little while, and ye shall not see me: and again, a little while, and ye shall see me, because I go to the Father. (John 16:5–16)

In all the feasts except the Passover, an offering is made by fire, although Exodus 12 mentions roasting the Passover meal with fire (verse 8). Acts 2:3 mentions "tongues like as of fire," referring to the presence of the Holy Spirit at Pentecost. Examining other Bible texts that discuss fire, we find three scriptures that discuss gold tried in the, or with, or through fire (see Rev 3:18; 1 Peter 1:7, 8; and Zech. 13:9). We also find the phrase "devouring fire" used in the Bible in five places. This phrase refers to the presence of God. From this, we can conclude that all of the feasts carry this cleansing and deliverance-from-sin idea. The Feast of Weeks is the central feast in the Jewish calendar that has as its antitypical fulfillment the beginning work of the Holy Spirit in the Christian era, which will lead all the way to the end of time.

The Bible also talks about the lake of fire in five places (Rev. 19:20; 20:10, 14, 15; 21:8). One specific text, Matthew 25:41, tells us that the destructive "everlasting fire" was prepared for the *devil* and his *angels*, implying that God did not intend the lake of fire to be for humanity. However, the refining fire of God *is* for you, and it will remove your sin and purify your life *now* if you allow the Holy Spirit to finish His work in you. Do not cling to your sin and wait until it is too late, because the lake of fire completes the second death from which there is no recovery, for the results are everlasting. Please don't think of "the lake of fire" and "hell" as being the same thing. For example, "hell" simply refers to the grave (Greek Hades, literally, "not to be seen"), as we see in Revelation 20:13, 14: "Death and hell [the grave] delivered up the dead which were in them … and death and hell [the grave] were cast into the lake of fire."

Once the wicked are consumed, the lake of fire will go out, for there is no eternal torture. We know this to be true from Malachi 4:1: "For, behold, the day cometh, that shall burn as an oven; and all the proud, yea, and all that do wickedly, shall be *stubble*: and the day that cometh shall burn them up, saith the LORD of hosts, that it shall leave them neither root nor branch."

This feast is about choices. Which is it—life or death? The choice is yours. You cannot hide from making a decision.

The *second* meaning this feast has for us today is that we can know that the work of the Holy Spirit, while reproving the world of sin, will also lead us into correct doctrine. John 16:13 says, "Howbeit when he, the Spirit of truth, is come, he will guide you into all truth." Moses uses the metaphor of falling rain to describe "doctrine," or teaching, that is spoken by God, which, by the way, has inherent within it the power to create what it says. "Give ear, O ye heavens, and I will speak; and hear, O earth, the words of my mouth. My doctrine shall drop as the rain, my speech shall distil as the dew, as the small rain upon the tender herb, and as the showers upon the grass: Because I will publish the name of the LORD: ascribe ye greatness unto our God. He is the Rock, his work is perfect: for all his ways are judgment: a God of truth and without iniquity, just and right is he" (Deut. 32:1–4).

The metaphor of the falling rain becomes more important as time moves toward the culmination of earth's history and Satan puts forth superhuman effort to hide the truth. Pentecost was the time of the falling of the "former" rain of the Holy Spirit. The time of the culmination of earth's history is the time of the falling of the "latter" rain of the Holy spirit, which we will discuss later in this chapter.

The *third* meaning this has for us today is that the Holy Spirit is the divine Psychiatrist, a Comforter during this time of trial and the removal of sin. John 16:5–15 explains the work of the divine Comforter who is to "reprove [convince] the world of sin, and of righteousness, and of judgment [deliverance]" (verse 8). Judgment was passed and deliverance secured when Christ ascended the cross, which points to the first feast.[6] The work of the divine Comforter is to communicate this to us so that we can receive the comfort we need while God is purifying us. What is more comforting than the realization that our salvation and our place in heaven and the new earth is secure in God's hands, the title to our inheritance held in trust by the most trustworthy One in all the universe? This gives us confidence that we are secure in Christ and that we can go about each new day without looking over our shoulders wondering what will catch us next. If we have any questions, if we have any problems, we can go to the divine Psychiatrist for the comfort and guidance we need.

Fourthly, we can receive so much of the blessings of the Lord that our cup will overflow (Luke 6:38). This is in fulfillment of the Feast of Weeks prophecy in Leviticus 23:22 that says that the overflow will go to all around us for others to glean. Our job is to allow God to fill our cups—to say "yes" to Him when He speaks to our hearts through the Holy Spirit. It is His desire that our cups be full to overflowing. Notice in Hosea that God comes to us as the rain, so the metaphor of "pouring" and "overflowing" holds true: "Then shall we know, if we follow on to know the LORD: his going forth is prepared as the morning; and he shall come unto us as the rain, as the latter and former rain unto the earth" (Hosea 6:3).

By the way, Hosea 6 is very enlightening. Verse 2 talks about "raising us up" after three days, which is referring to Christ's resurrection as the representative of the entire human race—*we* were raised in Him (see chapter 1 of this book). However, notice in this text that there are two types of rain, the "latter" and the "former."

---

6   The work of the judge is to deliver as explained in Psalm 76:8, 9; Judges 2:16; and 1 Samuel 24:15. This Christ did on the cross by taking our penalty for sin. In John 12:31, 32 Jesus tells us that His death on the cross was the judgment of the world and His sacrifice brought about deliverance from sin and Satan. Therefore, the introduction of the Holy Spirit is to apply this deliverance in our daily lives, which is what happens when we believe. Satan is already a defeated foe. He has no power over us unless we allow him to have it (see Matt. 28:18).

In Joel 2 we read that the Lord will bring the rain and fill us with spiritual food by "pouring" out His Spirit upon us. From this, we can conclude that the work of the Holy Spirit is illustrated not only as a cleansing fire but also as a gently falling rain. And this rain God will pour out in the last days. Let us look at this passage of scripture.

> Fear not, O land; be glad and rejoice: for the Lord will do great things. Be not afraid, ye beasts of the field: for the pastures of the wilderness do spring, for the tree beareth her fruit, the fig tree and the vine do yield their strength. Be glad then, ye children of Zion, and rejoice in the Lord your God: for he hath given you the former rain moderately [literally, "in righteousness"], and he will cause to come down for you the rain, the former rain, and the latter rain in the first month [literally, "as at the first"]. And the floors shall be full of wheat, and the vats shall overflow with wine and oil. And I will restore to you the years that the locust hath eaten, the cankerworm, and the caterpillar, and the palmerworm, my great army which I sent among you. And ye shall eat in plenty, and be satisfied, and praise the name of the Lord your God, that hath dealt wondrously with you: and my people shall never be ashamed. And ye shall know that I am in the midst of Israel, and that I am the Lord your God, and none else: and my people shall never be ashamed. And it shall come to pass afterward [literally, "at the end"—see Acts 2:17, which is quoting Joel 2], that I will pour out my spirit upon all flesh; and your sons and your daughters shall prophesy, your old men shall dream dreams, your young men shall see visions: And also upon the servants and upon the handmaids in those days will I pour out my spirit. And I will shew wonders in the heavens and in the earth, blood, and fire, and pillars of smoke. The sun shall be turned into darkness, and the moon into blood, before the great and terrible day of the Lord come. (verses 21–31)

Revelation 18:1 says, "And after these things I saw another angel come down from heaven, having great power; and the earth was lightened with his glory." This statement begins chapter 18, which is a description of the latter rain and its work.

Joel mentions the two kinds of rain. From a temporal perspective, the "former" rain falls at the sowing time to germinate the seed.[7] The "latter rain" falls at the harvest time to mature and ripen the fruit. Without either of these former or latter rains, there is no harvest, no produce, no food for the table.

The metaphor of the rains applies to our *spiritual* food. The antitypical fulfillment of the Feast of Weeks, or Pentecost, is the *former* rain of the Holy Spirit, which germinates the seed of the Christian era "in righteousness" (Joel 2:23). This is true primarily for the corporate church down through the

---

7   In Israel sowing was done in the autumn.

years, but also for each person individually. When people hear the good news of what Christ has done for them, and choose to believe, they then receive the former rain to germinate the seed of the gospel in their hearts. Then at the end of time just before Jesus comes, they will receive the latter rain to mature them for the harvest—but only if they have first received the former rain and have germinated and grown during that time. This prerequisite is logical because there cannot be fruit without a vigorous plant.

The antitypical fulfillment of the latter rain comes during another feast called the Day of Atonement, which we will discuss later in this book. However, the Feast of Weeks *introduces* the latter rain because both the former and latter rains work together in the development of the church and the development of the individual. In the last days, God will employ the latter rain of the Holy Spirit to prepare God's people for the harvest of the earth—the second coming of Christ.

Many people, in looking for the latter rain, are expecting the tongues without the fire. The great manifestation of the former rain was the converting of 3,000 people in one day—an exciting event—and we look for such events in the manifestation of the latter rain. However, the true manifestation of both rains of the Holy Spirit is in the fire that purifies, not in the tongues that excite. The true rain of the Holy Spirit is a teaching—a doctrine that has as its effect the purification of God's people from sin. The work of the latter rain is to prepare the grain for the harvest—to accomplish a cleansing in the hearts of God's people in the last days so that Jesus can come.

We are in the last days! The dark day described in Joel 2:31 took place on May 19, 1780, when the sky became very dark and the sun took on a deep red hue. We do not need to keep looking to the future for these events to take place to signal the beginning of the last days. Now is the time of decision, for now is the time of the end. You can be part of the remnant—the last piece in the last days.[8] Please do not put it off. Choose Christ today.

As we close this chapter, ponder the following texts:
- "And it shall come to pass, that whosoever shall call on the name of the Lord shall be delivered: for in mount Zion and in Jerusalem shall be deliverance, as the Lord hath said, and in the remnant whom the Lord shall call" (Joel 2:32).
- "Ask ye of the Lord rain in the time of the latter rain; so the Lord shall make bright clouds, and give them showers of rain, to every one grass in the field" (Zech. 10:1).

---

8 The remnant is the last piece of the "bolt" of all of God's people.

Chapter 8

Feast of Trumpets: The History

"But if the watchman see the sword come, and blow not the trumpet, and the people be not warned; if the sword come, and take any person from among them, he is taken away in his iniquity; but his blood will I require at the watchman's hand" (Ezek. 33:6).

What happens when those who have been charged with watching for danger do not sound the alarm? What if they make some sort of a sound but it is not loud enough, or to the point, or, worse yet, it is the wrong signal? The watchmen are responsible to sound the trumpet with a certain sound to alert people to danger. If they fail in that mission, the enemy will succeed.

God introduces the Feast of Trumpets as follows, "And the Lord spake unto Moses, saying, Speak unto the children of Israel, saying, In the seventh month, in the first day of the month, shall ye have a sabbath, a memorial of blowing of trumpets,[1] an holy convocation. Ye shall do no servile work therein: but ye shall offer an offering made by fire unto the Lord" (Lev. 23:23–25).

This feast, which took place nine days before the colossal and important Feast of the Day of Atonement, served as an announcement and warning of the impending climactic event. The historic events of the Millerite movement of 1831 to 1844 aptly meet the criteria of announcing and warning the cataclysmic event of the antitypical cleansing of the sanctuary, which is leading to the end of the world. Therefore, the Millerite movement provided the antitypical fulfillment of the ancient Feast of Trumpets.

Ellen White has the following to say about William Miller and her conversion, an eyewitness report:

> In March, 1840, William Miller visited Portland, Maine, and gave his first course of lectures on the second coming of Christ. These lectures produced a great sensation, and the Christian church on Casco Street, occupied by Mr. Miller, was crowded day and night. No wild excitement attended these meetings, but a deep solemnity pervaded the minds of those who heard his discourses. Not only was there manifested

---

1 Literally, "a sabbath, a reminder signaled, a gathering holy," in other words, a memorial reminder signal. The original Hebrew text does not specifically mention trumpets. However, the trumpets aspect comes from Numbers 10:1–10, where it tells Israel to sound the clarion trumpets on the first day of every month. This month (month 7 in the religious calendar) is special because God adds a day of rest and a convocation on the first day to call attention to this month and to the feast that is to follow in nine days. Because this feast is the only feast that begins on the first day of any month, a day on which the trumpets would normally be blown, it is called the Feast of Trumpets. This feast is announcing a reminder.

a great interest in the city, but the country people flocked in day after day, bringing their lunch baskets, and remaining from morning until the close of the evening meeting.

In company with my friends I attended these meetings and listened to the startling announcement that Christ was coming in 1843, only a few short years in the future. Mr. Miller traced down the prophecies with an exactness that struck conviction to the hearts of his hearers. He dwelt upon the prophetic periods, and brought many proofs to strengthen his position. Then his solemn and powerful appeals and admonitions to those who were unprepared, held the crowds as if spellbound.

Special meetings were appointed where sinners might have an opportunity to seek their Saviour and prepare for the fearful events soon to take place. Terror and conviction spread through the entire city. Prayer meetings were established, and there was a general awakening among the various denominations, for they all felt more or less the influence that proceeded from the teaching of the near coming of Christ.[2]

The following quoted passages from the *Seventh-day Adventist Encyclopedia* give additional historical background on the Millerite movement.

MILLER, WILLIAM (1782–1849). American farmer and Baptist preacher who announced the imminent coming of Christ and founded the movement popularly known as Millerism, or the Millerite movement, characterized by a distinctive type of premillennialism and giving rise to a group of denominations classed as the Adventist bodies. Miller was born in Pittsfield, Massachusetts, and was reared in Low Hampton, in northern New York, almost on the Vermont line. As an ambitious frontier boy with an unquenchable desire for knowledge, he was largely self-educated. Upon his marriage to Lucy P. Smith in 1803, he moved to Poultney, Vermont. Through friendship with several prominent citizens who were deists, Miller abandoned his religious convictions and became an avowed skeptic.

In the War of 1812 Miller served as lieutenant and captain. At the close of the war he moved his family to Low Hampton, where he hoped to live quietly as a farmer through his remaining years. At various times he served his community as deputy sheriff and justice of the peace. But Miller was not at peace with himself, for he was at heart a deeply religious man. In 1816 he was converted. Concerning this he wrote in 1845:

---

2   Ellen G. White, *Testimonies for the Church*, vol. 1, p. 14.

> I saw that the Bible did bring to view just such a Savior as I needed; and I was perplexed to find how an uninspired book should develop principles so perfectly adapted to the wants of a fallen world. I was constrained to admit that the Scriptures must be a revelation from God; they became my delight, and in Jesus I found a friend (*Apology and Defence*, p. 5).

Challenged by his skeptical friends, he set out to study the Bible:

> I commenced with Genesis.… Whenever I found any thing obscure, my practice was to compare it with all collateral passages, and by the help of Cruden['s Concordance] I examined all the texts of Scripture.… Then by letting every word have its proper bearing on the subject of the text, if my view of it harmonized with every collateral passage in the Bible, it ceased to be a difficulty (*ibid.*, p. 6).

Miller concluded that Scripture "is its own interpreter," and that the words ought to be understood literally, that is, in their ordinary historical and grammatical sense, except in those instances where the writer used figurative language. In this Miller simply was following the path of conservative theologians. In his study of the prophecies he reached the conclusion that the writers pointed to his day as the last period of earth's history. Specifically, he put his first and greatest emphasis on the prophetic declaration, "Unto two thousand and three hundred days; then shall the sanctuary be cleansed" (Dan. 8:14), from which he reached his conclusion in 1818, at the close of two years' study of the Bible, that "in about twenty-five years [that is, about 1843] … all the affairs of our present state would be wound up" (*ibid.*, p. 12). Seeking to criticize his own conclusions and to examine all objections, he "was occupied for five years" (*ibid.*, p. 15) more in examining and re-examining the arguments for and against his beliefs.

Convinced of "the duty of presenting the evidence of the nearness of the advent to others" (*ibid.*), he tried to excuse himself on the ground that he was not a public speaker. He was "very diffident and feared to go before the world" (*ibid.*, p. 16). He wrote an extended statement of his beliefs to a minister friend named Andrus, in 1831, but he could not free his mind from that impelling sense of duty.

Finally in August, 1831, he covenanted with God that "if I should have an invitation to speak publicly in any place, I will go and tell them what I find in the Bible about the Lord's coming" (*ibid.*, p. 17). What he did not know was that even as he was making such apparently safe terms with the Lord, there was traveling down the highway a young man bearing an invitation for him to preach the following day. The tumult that this unexpected invitation produced in Miller's soul sent him to a nearby grove where he could pray. Into that grove went a farmer; out came a preacher. After dinner Miller left with the youth for nearby Dresden.

Invited to remain during the week, Miller found himself engaged in a revival. The preaching of the soon coming of Christ seemed naturally and inevitably to lead men to seek to make ready for that solemn event. Miller was soon to find himself in the position of having to turn down more requests than he filled simply because he could not be in more than one place at once, or because he had to spend some time on the farm.[3]

Miller and the Adventists. The "Millerites" actually called themselves Adventists, but were popularly known by the name of their leading exponent, William Miller, a New York farmer and a licensed Baptist preacher. Since the term "Adventist" is now often used in a broader sense or as a shortened form of Seventh-day Adventist, the more specific term "Millerite" is used here.

Miller first published his views on prophecy in 1832, but the year 1840 marks the launching of the movement on a wide basis. Miller's colleagues included ministers of various denominations, some of whom did not agree with his expectation that Christ would return in 1843/44 but were otherwise sympathetic with his views.

The principal doctrine on which the Millerite movement was considered to be based was not primarily the "definite time" of the Second Advent, but an interpretation of prophecy embodying (1) belief in "the Advent near" and (2) a distinctive view of the nature of the kingdom of God.

Part of an International Awakening. The Millerites regarded their movement as the continuation and culmination of an international awakening of interest in the Second Advent, and a proclamation of "the Advent near," that had developed almost simultaneously in many countries in the early 1800's. At that time the majority of Protestants were either indifferent to the Second Advent or were looking for it after a millennium of 1,000 (or 365,000) years of a spiritual reign, through the triumph of the church. It was against the latter view, called *post*millennialism, that nineteenth-century *pre*millennialists contended by their insistence that Christ would return before the millennium, and soon ... [Premillennialism is the belief that Christ will come *before* the 1000 years of Satan being confined to this planet.] Among them were Petri in Germany (before 1800), Gaussen in Switzerland, Irving and others in England, Wolff in Asia, and others elsewhere.

Similarities and Differences. The Millerites circulated the works of some of these writers and regarded these premillennialists as forerunners and colleagues. They

---

3   *Seventh-day Adventist Encyclopedia*, p. 889.

opened correspondence with some of the "friends of the advent near" in England, hoping that they could unite with them, but found their differing views on the second principal doctrine, the nature of the expected kingdom of God, an insuperable barrier.

A study of the writings on the prophecies in many countries shows that the Millerites were preceded by many expositors who held the same general historical interpretation of the outline prophecies of Daniel and the Revelation as they held, and even looked to 1843, 1844, or 1847 for the end of the 2300 days of Dan. 8:14 (the key prophecy on which Miller based his expectation of the Advent in or about 1843). Many expected, just as definitely and just as mistakenly as Miller, some momentous event or development of world history introducing, or leading to, the millennium, or the Second Advent.

What distinguished Miller's group from these other expositors was not the fact that the Millerites set dates, but the fact that they expected the Second Advent to bring the catastrophic end of the age, the cleansing of the world by fire, and the setting up of the eternal kingdom of the saints. Because the Adventists formed a large and vocal movement, their views were widely disseminated and discussed, and consequently their disappointment made headlines while the less spectacular predictions made by other expositors passed unnoticed or were forgotten. Furthermore, the Millerite movement, though interdenominational, eventually gave rise to several organized church bodies.[4]

The 2300 Days. The key prophetic period was that of the 2300 (Dan. 8:14) years (see Twenty-three Hundred Days),[5] ending with the cleansing of the sanctuary, which the Millerites believed to involve the final purification of the earth at the Second Advent. As noted earlier, Miller ended this period in or *about* 1843, but he never preached an exact date. Pressed to be more specific, he finally, by December, 1842, defined "1843," by which he meant the Jewish year, as probably "sometime between March 21st, 1843, and March 21st, 1844" (*The Signs of the Times*, 4:47, Jan. 25, 1843)—for he knew the Jewish religious year ran from spring to spring. (Other Millerite leaders, knowing that the Jewish calendar was lunar, began and ended the year with the new moon of April.)

When the "Jewish year 1843" passed (in the spring of 1844) without the return of the Lord, and the public expected the Millerites to "yield the whole question," Litch wrote:

---

4   Ibid., p. 892.
5   See Appendix E.

> The doctrine does not consist in merely tracing prophetic periods.... But the whole prophetic history of the world ... affords indubitable evidence of the fact, that we have approached a crisis. And no disappointment respecting a definite point of time can move them, or drive them from their position, relative to the speedy coming of the Lord ("The Rise and Progress of Adventism," *The Advent Shield*, 1:80, May, 1844).

Then he quoted the "Fundamental Principles" of the Millerites as published in their periodicals in 1843, adding this footnote:

> The above was written in the Jewish year 1843, which has now expired.... We can only wait ... continually looking for, and momentarily expecting, his appearing (*ibid.*).

The Shift From 1843 to 1844. It was not until the summer of 1844 that the majority of the Millerites began to pay serious heed to a few who had been insisting that the correct computation of the 2300 years and the 70 weeks would lead to an ending date in the autumn, on the day of the month the ancient sanctuary was cleansed, the tenth day of the seventh Jewish month, which they understood to fall in 1844 on Oct. 22.... On this day they believed that Christ would end His priestly ministry and emerge from the holy of holies, or heaven, to return to the earth to "bless His waiting people."

The Three Angels' Messages. The Millerites believed also that they were fulfilling the prophecy of the flying angel of Rev. 14:6, 7, the first of three ... , proclaiming, "The hour of his judgment is come," and many of them also gave the second angel's message, to come out of fallen Babylon (v. 8; cf. ch [Rev.] 18:4), advocating separation from hostile churches. They gave little or no attention to the message of the third angel (v. 9).[6]

The "Seventh-Month Movement" introduced the idea that these feast days we are studying had to do with present time even though, being a type and description of Christ's ministry, they were not observed in a literal sense because Christ has already fulfilled these feasts[7] in His life, death, resurrection, and ascension into heaven, where He is serving as the antitypical High Priest today:

SEVENTH-MONTH MOVEMENT. The climactic phase of the Millerite movement,

---

6 *Seventh-day Adventist Encyclopedia*, pp. 896, 897.
7 See Appendix L.

occurring during the summer and autumn of 1844, in which the proclamation of the "definite time" (Oct. 22) for the expected Second Advent, the tenth day of the seventh (Jewish) month, lent a heightened enthusiasm.

William Miller had not set a specific day for the Advent, but expected it at some time during the "Jewish year 1843," that is, the year 1843/1844 from spring to spring (see Millerite Movement, III, 5). This new definite date, which Miller did not preach and did not accept until shortly before it came, was calculated by several of his colleagues.

The year 1844, instead of 1843, was arrived at by Apollos Hale, Sylvester Bliss, and others, through the correction of a one-year error in computation from B.C. to A.D. dates. The month and day, worked out chiefly by Samuel Snow, were selected because (1) the expectation of the Advent was based chiefly on the calculation of the twenty-three hundred days (counted as years) according to the prophecy "Unto two thousand and three hundred days; then shall the sanctuary be cleansed" (Dan. 8:14); (2) the annual ritual cleansing of the ancient Hebrew sanctuary took place on the tenth day of the seventh month, called the Day of Atonement (see Lev. 16:16–19, 29–34); and (3) this Jewish calendar date was computed—not according to the current Jewish calendar, but according to an older form attributed to the Karaite Jews—as the equivalent of Oct. 22 in 1844.

This interpretation was developed, principally by Snow, out of Miller's suggestion (letter of May 3, 1843) that just as the ancient Hebrew spring festivals (Passover, Pentecost) were types of the death and resurrection of Christ, so the autumn festivals (Day of Atonement, Feast of Tabernacles) typified the Second Advent.

Miller had mentioned several events occurring on the tenth day of the seventh Jewish month (the Day of Atonement), such as the cleansing of the sanctuary, its furnishings, and its worshipers; the sounding of the jubilee trumpet signaling the release of all Israelites in bondage, a type of the final redemption; and the atonement made on that day, followed by the coming of the high priest out of the Holy of Holies, typical of Christ's priestly ministry ending at His second coming. Thus many looked to the autumn of 1843 "with much interest." Then, as Himes relates:

> Snow fully embraced the opinion that, according to the types, the advent of the Lord, when it does occur, must occur on the tenth day of the 7th month; but he was not positive as to the year. He afterwards saw that the prophetic periods do not actually expire until the present 1844; he then planted himself on the ground that about the 22nd of October—the tenth day of the seventh month of this present year—must witness the advent (*Advent Herald*, 8:93, Oct. 30, 1844).

The autumn expectation was based on the idea that the 70 weeks of years (beginning synchronously with the 2300 years)[8] began and ended in the seventh month; and on the application to Christ of the types of the ancient Mosaic festivals. The date was based on the following reasoning: Since Christ, our Passover, was crucified on the fourteenth of the first Jewish month, the day prescribed for the slaying of the Passover lamb, and because He rose again on the day of the wave sheaf (the sixteenth of the same month), it was logical to expect that Christ our great High Priest would fulfill the antitype of the Day of Atonement by coming from the Holy of Holies, or heaven, on the tenth day of the seventh month to bless His waiting people and to announce the beginning of the year of jubilee—the millennium.

It was in February, 1844, that both Hale and Snow published their revised reckoning, ending the 2300 years in 1844, and soon afterward Snow fixed on the tenth day of the seventh month, 1844. But acceptance was slow. Not until after midsummer, when Snow began to preach on the subject, notably at the camp meeting at Exeter, New Hampshire, in August, did the movement catch fire....

As the date approached, enthusiasm mounted, though not all the Millerites joined the seventh-month movement. One by one the Millerite leaders, who had been the last to take part in it, accepted the seventh-month message. William Miller and J. V. Himes, his lieutenant, came to the conclusion early in October that the movement must be the Lord's doing, and they too looked for the Advent on that October day....

Just as the great surge of enthusiasm over the October date separated the Millerites most completely from the world at large, so, after the Great Disappointment, when that day passed, it was the question of the significance of this seventh-month movement, the "true midnight cry," that drew the sharpest line of cleavage between the Millerites themselves. Had it been a colossal blunder, or had it been truly a fulfillment of prophecy—though not the fulfillment they had expected—and had God indeed been leading them in it, testing their devotion and their readiness to meet Christ?

In the aftermath ... the majority, including most of the leaders, came within a few months to the conclusion that it was "not a fulfillment of prophecy in any sense," that their prophetic chronology had been wrong, and that the fulfillments were yet in the future. Those who held that the movement had been led of God held that the timing was right and sought other explanations of their disappointment.

From the latter came the little groups that later became the SDA's [Seventh-day Adventists]. These refused to "deny their past experience," as most of the others seemed to them to have done. They sought another meaning in it and arrived at the

---

8   Read Daniel 8 and 9.

conclusion that the cleansing of the sanctuary was not the return of Christ but involved another phase of His priestly ministry before His return to this earth.⁹

God anticipated this great disappointment, so He warned us about it through the pen of John in the book of Revelation.

> And I saw another mighty angel come down from heaven, clothed with a cloud: and a rainbow was upon his head, and his face was as it were the sun, and his feet as pillars of fire [a description of Christ Himself (see Rev. 1:13–16)]:
>
> And he had in his hand a little book open [the book of Daniel, which had previously been closed, is now open to our understanding (see Dan. 12:4, 9–13)]: and he set his right foot upon the sea [populated area], and his left foot on the earth [unpopulated area—both the populated and unpopulated areas would combine to make up the whole world, as the metaphor of the earth and sea *themselves* would indicate],
>
> And cried with a loud voice, as when a lion roareth: and when he had cried, seven thunders uttered their voices.
>
> And when the seven thunders had uttered their voices, I was about to write: and I heard a voice from heaven saying unto me, Seal up those things which the seven thunders uttered, and write them not. [God's people will know what these thunders are as the events unfold.]
>
> And the angel which I saw stand upon the sea and upon the earth lifted up his hand to heaven, And sware by him that liveth for ever and ever, who created heaven, and the things that therein are, and the earth, and the things that therein are, and the sea, and the things which are therein, that there should be time no longer: [Note the reference to creation of the universe. This is Jehovah, the Creator, who creates by speaking—His voice having inherently within it the power to create what it says instantly (Gen. 1).¹⁰ Righteousness by faith, therefore, would be *believing* (faith) God's all-powerful inherently creative word and allowing Him to apply His promises (righteousness) to our lives. And so you can see that righteousness by faith is the underlying final issue in the last days of earth's history. The last line, "that there should be time no longer," indicates that time prophecy is ended. There is no time prophecy that ends after 1844.]
>
> But in the days of the voice of the seventh angel, when he shall begin to sound, the mystery of God should be finished [This is the completion of the work of God on

---

9   *Seventh-day Adventist Encyclopedia*, pp. 1337, 1338.
10 This has righteousness by faith implications. We must depend upon God's voice *only* to create righteousness in His people and not with our "help"—none of our *own* "righteousness" will do (Isa. 64:6). See chapter 11 of this book for more information about this idea.

the hearts of His people—"Christ in you, the hope of glory" (Col. 1:27). It denotes the completion of the work of Christ in the Most Holy Place of the heavenly sanctuary.], as he hath declared to his servants the prophets [Daniel, Isaiah, Joel, Malachi, etc.].

And the voice which I heard from heaven spake unto me again, and said, Go and take the little book [again, the book of Daniel] which is open in the hand of the angel which standeth upon the sea and upon the earth.

And I went unto the angel, and said unto him, Give me the little book. And he said unto me, Take it, and eat it up; and it shall make thy belly bitter, but it shall be in thy mouth sweet as honey.

And I took the little book out of the angel's hand, and ate it up; and it was in my mouth sweet as honey: and as soon as I had eaten it, my belly was bitter. [The message of Christ's coming in 1844 was sweet at first, but then it turned to bitter disappointment when He didn't come as expected. God knew this would happen, so He told us about it in the book of Revelation.]

And he said unto me, Thou must prophesy again before many peoples, and nations, and tongues, and kings. [In essence he is saying, "Don't quit now. You must tell the world about the work of Christ in the heavenly sanctuary—that He is removing the sins of His people so that He can return." This is the work that began in 1844. When the sins of God's people stop flowing into the sanctuary, Christ can complete His work as High Priest, for the "mystery of God should be finished" (Rev. 10:7) and the sanctuary will be cleansed at that time,[11] the work having been completed, thus preparing the way for Christ to come.]

Today we are living in the aftermath of the Great Disappointment:

Aftermath—Three-Way Split. After the great disappointment of Oct. 22, 1844, the Millerites—at least those who did not fall away in their disillusionment—split into three groups, differing according to their respective views of the cause of their error in expecting the return of Christ in 1844.

(1) The majority group, including, by April, 1845, Miller and most of the leaders. These held that they had been right in applying the 2300-day prophecy and the parable of the Bridegroom to the Second Advent; and that, therefore, since the Lord had not come they had been in error in the chronology; that there had been no fulfillment of prophecy in 1843–1844 and the "definite time" movement had been a mistake.

---

11 This is in fulfillment of Daniel 9:14. The next chapter explores this prophecy further.

(2) A minority group known as the "spiritualizers," or "spiritualists." These held that they had been right both in chronology and in the expected event: the Second Advent had actually occurred at the time specified, but as a spiritual coming, in His saints (the spiritualizers).... Many of these went into extreme splinter groups, and a number of them joined the Shakers.

(3) Another minority group, intermediate between the other two groups. Holding that the prophetic chronology had been correct, but that the error lay in the event expected, they rejected on the one hand the "spiritualist" view of an invisible Advent and a spiritual kingdom (they insisted that the Advent was personal, literal, and still future); on the other hand, they rejected the majority contention that the 2300 days had not ended and that the 1844 movement had been a complete mistake.

To this third group (as to the second) the majority party appeared to have abandoned the Adventist message by denying their past experience in the 1844 movement. The majority group, in turn, were inclined to condemn the third group, along with the second, for holding that the 2300 days had ended and that the "midnight cry" was valid.

Among this third group were the leaders of the future SDA's [Seventh-day Adventists], who arrived at the conclusion that the proper interpretation of the symbols indicated a different fulfillment—not the Second Advent by the final phase of Christ's ministry.[12]

Relation of SDA's [Seventh-day Adventists] to Millerism. The leaders of the small group that formed the nucleus of the organized SDA Church came out of the Millerite movement, and they regarded themselves as the true successors of the movement, as retaining and carrying on to completion the main principles of Millerite doctrine and correcting and clarifying the misunderstanding that had caused the disappointment and had resulted in the repudiation of the 1844 message by the leaders.

Retaining the distinctive principles of Millerite premillennialism, the SDA's modified certain points; for example, holding to the close of probation at the Second Advent but placing the renewal of the earth, and the establishment on it of the everlasting kingdom of the saints, at the end of the millennium. They accepted the minority view of conditional immortality. They explained the Disappointment by showing that the "cleansing of the sanctuary" represented not the end of the heavenly ministry of Christ, but a new phase of it.... Thus the doctrines of Millerism formed the background of many of the distinctive teachings of the SDA Church.

---

12 *Seventh-day Adventist Encyclopedia*, p. 897.

However, not all of these doctrines originated in Millerism …, and they were incorporated selectively into the structure of the SDA Church.[13]

Well, that is enough of the history for now. Later we will explore this subject further by digging into some prophecy in the book of Revelation, but for now, in the next chapter, we will study the prophecies found in Daniel 8 and 9 that caused all the commotion.

---

13   Ibid., p. 898.

Chapter 9

Feast of Trumpets: The Prophecy

So what was the big deal to William Miller and the others? What was the big idea that aroused so much excitement? It was none other than this idea of the Day of Atonement, the annual event of the cleansing of the earthly sanctuary. Since the earthly teaches us about the heavenly,[1] we should pay some attention to the prophetic meaning of this Jewish feast. God introduces the subject of the cosmic antitypical cleansing of the sanctuary in Daniel 8:

> In the third year of the reign of king Belshazzar a vision [Hebrew: *chazown*[2]] appeared unto me, even unto me Daniel, after that which appeared unto me at the first. And I saw in a vision [*chazown*]; and it came to pass, when I saw, that I was at Shushan in the palace, which is in the province of Elam; and I saw in a vision [*chazown*], and I was by the river of Ulai. Then I lifted up mine eyes, and saw, and, behold, there stood before the river a ram which had two horns: and the two horns were high; but one was higher than the other, and the higher came up last. I saw the ram pushing westward, and northward, and southward; so that no beasts might stand before him, neither was there any that could deliver out of his hand; but he did according to his will, and became great.
>
> And as I was considering, behold, an he goat came from the west on the face of the whole earth, and touched not the ground: and the goat had a notable horn between his eyes. And he came to the ram that had two horns, which I had seen standing before the river, and ran unto him in the fury of his power. And I saw him come close unto the ram, and he was moved with choler against him, and smote the ram, and brake his two horns: and there was no power in the ram to stand before him, but he cast him down to the ground, and stamped upon him: and there was none that could deliver the ram out of his hand. Therefore the he goat waxed very great: and when he was strong, the great horn was broken; and for it came up four notable ones toward the four winds of heaven.
>
> And out of one of them came forth a little horn, which waxed exceeding great,

---
1   See the preface to this book.
2   The Hebrew word translated "vision" here is the word *chazown*, which means to see, look, a sight (mental), *i.e.*, a dream, revelation, oracle—hence, "vision."

toward the south, and toward the east, and toward the pleasant land. And it waxed great, even to the host of heaven; and it cast down some of the host and of the stars to the ground, and stamped upon them. Yea, he magnified himself even to the prince of the host, and by him the daily sacrifice was taken away, and the place of the sanctuary was cast down. And an host was given him against the daily sacrifice by reason of transgression, and it cast down the truth to the ground; and it practised, and prospered.

Then I heard one saint speaking, and another saint said unto that certain saint which spake, How long shall be the vision [*chazown*] concerning the daily sacrifice, and the transgression of desolation, to give both the sanctuary and the host to be trodden under foot? *And he said unto me, Unto two thousand and three hundred days;*[3] *then shall the sanctuary be cleansed.* (Dan. 8:1–14)

This prophecy is at least partially interpreted in the same chapter. We pick up again in verse 19 and read through 27:

And he said, Behold, I will make thee know what shall be in the last end of the indignation: for at the time appointed the end shall be. The ram which thou sawest having two horns are the kings of Media and Persia. And the rough goat is the king of Grecia: and the great horn that is between his eyes is the first king. Now that being broken, whereas four stood up for it, four kingdoms shall stand up out of the nation, but not in his power. And in the latter time of their kingdom, when the transgressors are come to the full, a king of fierce countenance, and understanding dark sentences, shall stand up.

And his power shall be mighty, but not by his own power: and he shall destroy wonderfully, and shall prosper, and practise, and shall destroy the mighty and the holy people. And through his policy also he shall cause craft to prosper in his hand; and he shall magnify himself in his heart, and by peace shall destroy many: he shall also stand up against the Prince of princes; but he shall be broken without hand. And the vision [*mareh*[4]] of the evening and the morning [time portion] which was told is true: wherefore shut thou up the [entire] vision [*chazown*]; for it shall be for many days. And I Daniel fainted, and was sick certain days; afterward I rose up, and did

---

3   Literally, "evenings mornings."
4   The Hebrew word translated "vision" in this place is the word *mareh*, which means appearance, look, aspect, vision, sight, form, shape, view—hence, "vision." The meaning of this word is very similar to the word *chazown* (above), so much so that the meanings are virtually identical. However, there is a reason Daniel uses two different words for "vision" in chapters 8 and 9. When Daniel wants to refer to the *entire* vision of Daniel 8:1–14, he uses the word *chazown*. When he wants to refer to the *time aspect* of that prophecy (verse 14, "2300 evening-mornings"), he uses the word *mareh*. This relationship is established in Daniel 8:26, 27.

> the king's business; and I was astonished at the [time portion of the] vision [*mareh*[5]], but none understood it.

So we can see that the prophecy of the cleansing of the sanctuary involves world history. From this we know that the period of time covers at least Babylon, Medo-Persia, Greece, and the power that conquered Greece, which, from world history, we know is Rome. It tells us that this power (Rome) shall stand up against Christ and shall be broken by an unseen power. All this was written by Daniel during his lifetime and, in some cases, long before the predicted events happened. That should give us cause to think.

So how do we relate to the 2300 "evenings and mornings"? Can the number be literal? From Daniel's day, a literal reckoning would last a little more than six years and thus would probably end while Daniel was still alive. It, therefore, certainly would have ended before Greece and Alexander (the first king) came on the scene. So we know that the 2300 days has to be symbolic with reference to time. The next question is obvious. What, in that case, does a "day" represent in Bible prophecy?

We find a clue in Numbers 14:34: "After the number of the days in which ye searched the land, even forty days, *each day for a year*, shall ye bear your iniquities, even forty years, and ye shall know my breach of promise." (See also Ezekiel 4:6.)

If the "day-year" principal is correct, it should work out in the application of calculations in Bible prophecy, right? The answer is found in Daniel 9. I will insert comments as I quote the text.

> Yea, whiles I was speaking in prayer, even the man Gabriel, whom I had seen in the vision [*chazown*] at the beginning [the entire vision of Dan. 8:1–14], being caused to fly swiftly, touched me about the time of the evening oblation. And he informed me, and talked with me, and said, O Daniel, I am now come forth to give thee skill and understanding. At the beginning of thy supplications the commandment came forth, and I am come to shew thee; for thou art greatly beloved: therefore understand the matter, and consider the vision [*mareh*, that is, the *time portion* of the vision of chapter 8, as the rest of this explanation confirms].
>
> Seventy weeks [If we apply the day-year principal, this would be a total of 490 literal years.[6] From 457 BC (see below), this would take us (remember, there is no "year 0" between 1 BC and AD 1) to AD 34] are *determined* [literally meaning "cut off" (time wise, specifically from the 2300 days portion of the vision, *mareh*, of chapter 8)] upon thy people and upon thy holy city, to finish the transgression, and to make an end of sins, and to make reconciliation for iniquity, and to bring in everlasting righteousness, and to seal up the vision [*chazown*] and prophecy, and to anoint

---

5   Daniel's concern and confusion was regarding the *time aspect* of the prophecy, the "2300 evening-mornings."
6   Seven days times 70.

the most Holy. [Jesus did all of these things during His earthly life, between the years of 4 BC and AD 31.]

Know therefore and understand, that from the going forth of the commandment to restore and to build Jerusalem [This command was issued by the Persian King Artaxerxes I Longimanus in 457 BC.[7]] unto the Messiah the Prince shall be seven weeks [49 literal years—from 457 BC this would take us to 408 BC], and threescore and two weeks [69 weeks or 483 literal years—from 457 BC this would take us (remember, there is no "year 0" between 1 BC and AD 1) to AD 27]: the *street* shall be built again, and the *wall*, even in troublous times.[8] [The rebuilding of the *wall* was completed in 52 days, probably in 444 BC, soon after Nehemiah arrived for that purpose that same year. However, the meaning of the word translated "wall" is to sharpen (as in digging a new ditch), eager, diligent, sedulous; and the meaning of the word translated "street" is plaza (or forum), a place to conduct business, usually at the gate of the city where the government conducted business. Nehemiah 13:19 illustrates how the government would control activity at the gates of the cities.[9] Therefore, I conclude that Daniel 9:25 does not discuss the wall at all, but the setting up of a sharp and effective city government, of which the wall would be a part. The final touches to this activity are described in Nehemiah 13:23–31 when Nehemiah finished the cleansing of the priesthood. All this was accomplished within the 408 BC[10] deadline of Daniel 9:25 (after 7 weeks or 49 literal years from the decree to rebuild). And all of this was indeed accomplished during troublous times.[11]]

And after threescore and two weeks [62 weeks or 434 literal years to AD 27 (from 408 BC), again allowing for no "year 0."] shall Messiah be cut off [Again, cut off time wise: this is when Jesus began His ministry at age 30, having been born in 4 BC in the autumn.[12]], but *not for himself* [literally, no one with him[13]]: and the people

---

7   There were several such decrees, but the effective one was in 457 BC. This is the one that actually fulfills all the conditions. The others were only partial because they did not empower both civil and religious autonomy, or were merely for bolstering support.

8   Humphrey Prideaux makes the following statement about Daniel 9:25: "In the fifteenth year of Darius Nothus ended the first seven weeks of the seventy weeks of Daniel's prophecy. For then the restoration of the church and state of the Jews in Jerusalem and Judea was fully finished, in that last act of reformation, which is recorded in the thirteenth chapter of Nehemiah, from the twenty-third verse to the end of the chapter, *just forty-nine* years after it had been first begun by Ezra in the seventh year of Artaxerxes Longimanus" (*The Old and New Testament Connected in the History of the Jews*, vol. I, p. 322.; cf. Uriah Smith, *The Prophecies of Daniel and the Revelation*, p. 211).

9   "And it came to pass, that when the gates of Jerusalem began to be dark before the sabbath, I commanded that the gates should be shut, and charged that they should not be opened till after the sabbath: and some of my servants set I at the gates, that there should no burden be brought in on the sabbath day" (Neh. 13:19).

10 This occurred after 7 weeks, or 49 literal years, from the decree to rebuild.

11 See Ezra 4–7 and Nehemiah 1–6.

12 Yes, our calendars are off by four years.

13 "He is despised and rejected of men, a man of sorrows, and acquainted with grief: and we hid as it were our faces from him; he was despised, and we esteemed him not" (Isa. 53:3).

of the prince that shall come shall destroy the city and the sanctuary [Rome did this in AD 70]; and the end thereof shall be with a flood, and unto the end of the war desolations are determined.[14]

And he shall confirm the covenant[15] with many for one week [The final week, or 7 years, ending in AD 34 at the stoning of Stephen, thus beginning the wholesale persecution of the Christians by the Jews. Israel's time of probation ended at this point, ending the 490 years allotted to them (Dan. 9:24; Matt. 23:38).]: and in the *midst* [literally, "half"] of the week [3 1/2 years or AD 31 in the spring] he shall cause the sacrifice and the oblation to cease [Christ was the Passover lamb. His death ended the solemnity of the earthly sacrifices, for they all pointed to His supreme sacrifice.[16]], and *for* [literally, "upon"] the *overspreading* [literally, "extremity"] of abominations *he shall make it desolate* [literally, is "a desolator"], even until the *consummation* [literally, "complete end"], and that determined shall be poured upon the *desolate* [literally, "desolator."][17]

So it works! Applying the year-day principal to Daniel 9 explains it perfectly, so it must be right.[18] So—the obvious question—what about the 2300 days of Daniel 8:14?

Since the vision of Daniel 9 was "cut off" of the vision of Daniel 8, the earlier vision must begin at the same time. It would not make sense to cut it off at the *end* or at any time in the *middle*. From 457 BC, adding 2300 literal years, and recognizing there is no "year 0," we come to the year 1844!

---

14 The three "the's" and "shall be with" are added words. A literal translation of this sentence would read, "And its end shall be as a flood, and until an end of [all] war are determined desolations." After a four-year siege, Jerusalem was indeed destroyed in a rush. Also, as long as sin (and war) exist, there will be desolations.

15 This covenant is the covenant made to Adam and Eve (Gen. 3), Abraham (Gen. 12, 15, 17, and 22, the oath is in Gen. 22:16), Moses (Exod. 6), and to all in Christ (Heb. 6:13–18; Gal. 3:14–18, 29). Jeremiah calls it the "new" covenant in Jeremiah 31:31–33, and Ezekiel expresses the *results* of it in Ezekiel 36:26–28. Christ *confirmed* the covenant by carrying out the oath, pledging Himself and His own existence for the completion of His promise to humanity. He did this by giving up the hope of His own existence on the cross at Calvary. (See chapter 2 on the Passover.)

16 See Appendix L.

17 A literal Hebrew translation of Daniel 9:24–27 would be as follows: "Seventy weeks [490 literal years to AD 34] are cut off [from the 2300-day portion of the vision of chapter 8] as to your people and as to thy holy city, to finish the transgression, and to make an end of sins, and to atone for iniquity, and to bring in everlasting righteousness, and to seal up the [2300-day] vision and prophecy, and to anoint the most Holy. [Jesus did all of these things during His earthly life between the years of 4 BC and AD 31 (within the specified timeframe).] Then know and understand, from the issuing of the word to restore and to rebuild Jerusalem to Messiah the Prince shall be weeks seven, and weeks sixty and two Again it shall be built, with a sharp, effective, and diligent government forum, even in affliction of the times. And after the weeks sixty and two, shall be cut off Messiah [that is, set aside, at baptism], and no one will be with Him [for there will be few who understand]. And the city and the sanctuary shall be destroyed [in AD 70] by the people of a prince coming [Rome]. And its end shall be as a flood [rush], and until an end of [all] war are determined desolations. And He shall confirm the covenant with the many [all humankind] for one week. And at the half of that week He shall make cease sacrifice and offering [by dying on the cross: Christ was the One to whom the sacrifices were pointing (see Appendix L)], and upon the extremity of abominations is a desolator [Satan], even until the complete end. And that which was decreed shall be poured out upon the desolator."

18 For a timeline, see Appendix I.

Now there you have it. This is what excited William Miller and all those other Adventists all over the world. Christ was going to cleanse the sanctuary in 1844, on the literal Day of Atonement, October 22, reckoned as the ancient Hebrews would have reckoned it. As we studied in the previous chapter, those waiting for Christ's return were sorely disappointed when He didn't come. And yet, they had discovered an important Bible truth that unlocked another portion of Bible prophecy.

Chapter 10

Feast of Trumpets: The Event

As we begin this chapter and a discussion of the Feast of Trumpets, I want to examine Revelation 10:1–11.

> And I saw another mighty angel come down from heaven, clothed with a cloud: and a rainbow was upon his head, and his face was as it were the sun, and his feet as pillars of fire:[1] And he had in his hand a little book [Daniel] open:[2] and he set his right foot upon the sea, and his left foot on the earth,[3] And cried with a loud voice, as when a lion roareth: and when he had cried, seven thunders uttered their voices. And when the seven thunders had uttered their voices, I was about to write: and I heard a voice from heaven saying unto me, Seal up those things which the seven thunders uttered, and write them not.[4] And the angel which I saw stand upon the sea and upon the earth lifted up his hand to heaven, And sware by him that liveth for ever and ever, who created heaven, and the things that therein are, and the earth, and the things that therein are, and the sea, and the things which are therein, that there should be time no longer:[5]
>
> But in the days of the voice of the seventh angel, when he shall begin to sound, the mystery of God [the righteousness of God's people] should be finished,[6] as he hath declared to his servants the prophets. And the voice which I heard from heaven spake unto me again, and said, Go and take the little book which is open in the hand of the angel which standeth upon the sea and upon the earth. And I went unto the angel, and said unto him, Give me the little book. And he said unto me, Take it, and eat it up; and it shall make thy belly bitter, but it shall be in thy mouth sweet as

---

1 This is a description of Christ Himself.
2 The book of Daniel is unsealed and understood as prophesied in Daniel 12:9–13, for this is the "time of the end."
3 The metaphor of both feet on the earth and sea indicates His absolute control of the whole planet. The right side is the seat of action, and in Bible prophecy the seas indicate populated areas. Therefore, the position of His right foot on the sea indicates that Christ is acting upon the populated areas of the world.
4 Apparently, these things would be revealed at the proper time.
5 The final time prophecy in the Bible ends in 1844. There are no time prophecies that end after 1844. The time of the end of all sin is upon us today.
6 The mystery of God is "Christ in [us], the hope of glory" (Col. 1:25–28). The *finishing* of the mystery of God would, therefore, be the *sealing* in righteousness of God's people in the last days.

honey. And I took the little book out of the angel's hand, and ate it up; and it was in my mouth sweet as honey [something promising to be very pleasurable]: and as soon as I had eaten it, my belly was bitter [indicating a great disappointment].[7] And he said unto me, Thou must prophesy again[8] before many peoples, and nations, and tongues, and kings.

What is the sanctuary? Remember, Daniel 8:14 said that the "sanctuary" was to be "cleansed" in (or beginning in) 1844. It is obvious from history that the cleansing of the sanctuary was *not* the coming of Christ to set up His kingdom and usher in the millennium as was originally thought. Those who thought Christ would return in 1844 were greatly disappointed, but many did not lose faith. Instead, they continued their study of Scripture, which we will continue to do as well. So, what is the sanctuary, and how is it to be cleansed?

I have been able to identify three sanctuaries that are described in various scriptures. These three sanctuaries are as follows:

1. In heaven – "For he hath looked down from the height of his sanctuary; from heaven did the Lord behold the earth" (Ps. 102:19).
2. On earth – "And let them make me a sanctuary [on the earth (the type)]; that I may dwell among them. According to all that I shew thee, after the pattern of the tabernacle [in heaven (the antitype)], and the pattern of all the instruments thereof, even so shall ye make it" (Exod. 25:8, 9). "Who serve unto the *example* and *shadow* of heavenly things, as Moses was admonished of God when he was about to make the tabernacle: for, See, saith he, that thou make all things according to the pattern shewed to thee in the mount" (Heb. 8:5).
3. Our bodies – "But he spake of the temple of his body" (John 2:21). "What? know ye not that your body is the temple of the Holy Ghost which is in you, which ye have of God, and ye are not your own?" (1 Cor. 6:19).

Which of these were to be cleansed beginning in 1844? Well, the sanctuary on earth, the one that was made according to the pattern shown to Moses, does not function any more, for Christ Himself is the antitype of the Passover and all the feasts and services in the earthly sanctuary. We know this because at the moment of His death the veil in the temple was torn from top to bottom by an unseen hand,[9] exposing the Most Holy Place.

> And Jesus cried with a loud voice, and gave up the ghost. And the veil of the temple was rent in twain from the top to the bottom. And when the centurion, which stood

---

7   The prophecies of Daniel seemed very good at first, but the digestion process took God's people through bitter disappointment until the message was fully digested and understood.
8   The message to His church is, "Don't give up. You still have a great work to do. However, the message is something different than what you originally thought it would be."
9   It had to have been done by an angel because a human being would have needed a ladder to reach the top of the veil if he wanted to start the tear there.

over against him, saw that he so cried out, and gave up the ghost, he said, Truly this man was the Son of God. (Mark 15:37–39)

Jesus, when he had cried again with a loud voice, yielded up the ghost. And, behold, the veil of the temple was rent in twain from the top to the bottom; and the earth did quake, and the rocks rent; And the graves were opened; and many bodies of the saints which slept arose, And came out of the graves after his resurrection, and went into the holy city, and appeared unto many. (Matt. 27:50–53)

And it was about the sixth hour, and there was a darkness over all the earth until the ninth hour.[10] And the sun was darkened, and the veil of the temple was rent in the midst.[11] And when Jesus had cried with a loud voice, he said, *Father, into thy hands I commend my spirit:* and having said thus, he gave up the ghost. Now when the centurion saw what was done, he glorified God, saying, Certainly this was a righteous man. (Luke 23:44–47)

When Jesus died, offering Himself as the sacrificial Lamb, all the services surrounding the work of the earthly sanctuary and feast days officially came to an abrupt halt. Any services that may have been performed after that were bereft of meaning, for the object they pointed to had already taken place

Now let's take a closer look at portions of the above texts. Did you notice the part about the resurrection of the saints and the darkness? These events speak to the magnitude of Jesus' death. At the moment that Jesus took His last breath, there was an earthquake that freed some who had died for Christ. These bodies lay exposed on the ground for the rest of Friday and all day Sabbath until they were resurrected with Christ on Sunday morning, at which point they entered the city and appeared before the people. What a witness!

In addition to that, at noon, which some believe was the time Jesus was put on the cross, until 3:00 p.m. when He died, there was darkness in the land around the area of Jerusalem—a sort of supernatural "solar eclipse" if you will. God wanted to call attention to the events of the cross because Christ's sacrifice is our salvation. In like manner, the Feast of Trumpets was to announce the nearness of the

---

10 The people in Bible times reckoned time from dawn, dividing the light part of the day into twelve equal parts. From our reckoning (on the average), dawn would correspond to approximately six o'clock in the morning. For practical discussion, the "sixth hour" would be approximately noon our time, and the "ninth hour" would be approximately 3:00 p.m. our time, which, by the way, was precisely the time (*i.e.,* the ninth hour) of the evening sacrifice at the temple. Christ died at the exact time of the evening sacrifice! God is very precise in His timing of things.

11 This would be in the *middle* of the sanctuary—the veil between the holy and the Most Holy apartments. There was another veil at the front end of the holy place (the first apartment) at the entrance. In my opinion, the word "midst" refers to the middle of the temple, that is, the second veil—the one between the two apartments and at the entrance to the Most Holy Place. It can't refer to the place on the veil that the tear started because of Matthew 27:51 and Mark 15:38 that plainly indicate the veil was torn from top to bottom. Additionally, it is unlikely that it is referring to the veil being torn in the midst of the *veil* (itself) because these same two texts specifically use the phrase "into two" and not "midst." I believe that if Luke had wanted to say "into two," he would have used the same specific phrase that Mathew and Mark used.

work of the Day of Atonement, which was the meeting of God with His people to remove their sin in preparation for the final feast.

Each of the three descriptions in Matthew, Mark, and Luke mentions a tearing of a veil in the temple. This would be the veil that separates the first apartment of the sanctuary from the second apartment—the holy place from the Most Holy Place. The holy place ministry involved the daily ministry of sacrifices brought by sinners to acknowledge God's forgiveness and removal of sin(s) committed during the course of everyday life. The one who had committed a sin would bring a lamb or other offering to be slain before a priest by the hand of the individual, thus acknowledging what our sin does to God. The priest would then take the blood of the animal, or a part of the offering, and sprinkle it in the first apartment on the altar of incense to remit the sin committed and metaphorically transfer the sin into the sanctuary. This rite of service took place daily all year long until the annual cleansing of the sanctuary by the high priest. The cleansing of all the sins that had accumulated in the holy place throughout the year was done on the Feast of the Day of Atonement.

No one was ever to enter the second apartment of the sanctuary except the high priest, and then only once a year on the Day of Atonement. To do so by anyone else or even by the high priest himself on any other day resulted in the death of the trespasser.[12] Obviously, the Most Holy Place was very sacred to God. No one was even to *look* inside of it lest they die. So when the veil between the two apartments was torn, it exposed the sacred chamber to all eyes, yet no one died, thus signifying that the services were no longer sacred, for the meaning had departed. And to happen just as the priest was offering the daily evening sacrifice gave the rending of the veil even more significance, because this was an official service and it was being attended by a large number of eyewitnesses. All would know that the sacredness had departed at that precise moment. (For an expanded discussion of this subject, see Appendix L.)

So, as you can see from this study, the second option, the earthly sanctuary in the temple, cannot possibly be the one being cleansed beginning in 1844, because the services therein ended at the time of Christ's death. This leaves two more options: the sanctuary in heaven and the sanctuary of our hearts. Could either of these be the sanctuary Daniel wrote about?

---

12 For a description of the events surrounding the Day of Atonement, read Leviticus 16. The terms "tabernacle of the congregation" and "tent of meeting" both refer to the sanctuary. The "live goat" is a symbol of Satan and his angels who will be held prisoner on a desolate earth during the 1000 years with no one to deceive (see 2 Peter 2:4; Rev. 20).

Chapter 11

Feast of the Day of Atonement: The Coverage

Let's look at the Day of Atonement itself and see whether that will give us a clue about which sanctuary is being cleansed. Remember, the antitypical Feast of the Day of Atonement was to begin on October 22, 1844, the date being calculated by applying the prophecies of Daniel 8 and 9 with the ancient Jewish calculation of when the earthly Day of Atonement *would* have been held had it been calculated for the year 1844. As we have already seen, the earthly sanctuary in the temple cannot possibly be the one being cleansed beginning in 1844, because the services therein had ended at the time of the death of Christ in AD 31. This leaves two more options as to what sanctuary is to be cleansed: the sanctuary in heaven or the sanctuary in our hearts.

The sanctuary in heaven still exists. In fact, it will never go away. As we know from chapter 10, the heavenly sanctuary is the antitypical sanctuary of which the earthly sanctuary was only a type. The earthly sanctuary was cleansed at the end of the annual cycle because of sin in Israel; therefore, we conclude that the heavenly sanctuary also must be cleansed at some point in time because of sin in the universe. Since the cleansing of the heavenly sanctuary is the antitypical fulfillment of the *real* Day of Atonement, the prophecies of Daniel would indicate that we are living in the time of that feast *now*, which means that we are living in the time of the end of the cycle of sin! This is a sobering thought.

If we are living in the time of the cleansing of the *heavenly* sanctuary, how should that affect *us*? Does this have any bearing on us today? What does it matter to us which sanctuary is being cleansed? In what manner does one cleanse such a thing as a sanctuary? Should we be doing something?

Let's try to answer some of these questions. Have you ever tried to dry a sink? No? Most of the time we just let the water drain out and let the sink dry by itself, right? Usually, we prefer to let it air-dry, not really caring whether or how fast it might dry. However, (please bear with me for the sake of discussion, assuming a dry sink is somehow important), how fast would the sink dry if we let the faucet run? It would never dry, would it? As long as water was running into the sink, the sink could never dry out, no matter how many times you tried to wipe it with a dry cloth. If you want to dry a sink, the first thing you have to do is to stop the flow of water.

The same thing is true for the sanctuary (and this *is* important). As long as the sins of the people keep flowing into the sanctuary, the sanctuary can never be cleansed. At some point, the sins of God's people have to stop flowing into the sanctuary so that Christ can complete His work as High Priest and the sanctuary can finally be cleansed. The idea of a "holy convocation" is that God's people all come together for the purpose of meeting with God to receive instructions or other blessings at His hand. It is a time for Him to communicate with His people in a special way or to accomplish a special work—in them, on them, to them, and/or for them. The Day of Atonement is just such a holy convocation. The Day of Atonement is the time when God meets with His people in a special way to fully, completely, and finally cleanse the hearts of His people so that the sins can stop flowing into the sanctuary to be removed in the daily ministry—this daily ministry being the method Christ has used for thousands of years, before 1844. So not only is the sanctuary in *heaven* to be cleansed, but also, individually, the sanctuary of the *hearts of God's people* have to be cleansed *first*.

So as to be clear, this "meeting" is not a physical gathering of God's people in a stadium or any such place. It is a meeting of God with His people in their hearts. See Revelation 7 and 14 for a description of God's people in the last days just before He comes, and notice the idea of worshipping God as creator. As creator, God has inherent in His voice the power to create what it says, and that includes the creation of righteousness in the hearts of His people.

Jesus Christ is the antitypical high priest. After His death and resurrection, when He ascended, He went to heaven to begin the high priestly ministry in the heavenly sanctuary—the daily service. Examine the following verses that speak of the calling of Jesus as high priest:

- "The LORD hath sworn, and will not repent, Thou art a priest for ever after the order of Melchizedek" (Ps. 110:4).
- "As he saith also in another place, Thou art a priest for ever after the order of Melchisedec" (Heb. 5:6).
- "Called of God an high priest after the order of Melchisedec" (Heb. 5:10).
- "Whither the forerunner is for us entered ["within the veil" of the heavenly sanctuary, verse 19], even Jesus, made an high priest for ever after the order of Melchisedec" (Heb. 6:20).
- "If therefore perfection were by the *Levitical* priesthood, (for under it the people received the law,) what further need was there that *another* priest should rise after the order of *Melchisedec*, and *not* be called after the order of *Aaron*?" (Heb. 7:11).
- "For he testifieth, Thou art a priest for ever after the order of Melchisedec" (Heb. 7:17).
- "(For those priests were made without an oath; but this with an oath by him that said unto him, The Lord sware and will not repent, Thou art a priest for ever after the order of Melchisedec:)" (Heb. 7:21).

Melchisedec was the ruler of a place called Salem in Abraham's day and was also a priest of God *before* the "official" earthly Levitical (Aaron) priesthood was set up in Moses' day (see Heb. 7:11, above). Little is known about Melchisedec other than what is said about him in Genesis 14. Salem is mentioned in Psalm 76 as being the place in Israel of the dwelling of God and the place of God's tabernacle. From this, it would appear as if Melchisedec represents a type of Christ. Since Christ was ordained and trained[1] by *God* and never an *earthly* priest, a priest after the order of Melchisedec would be someone ordained and/or trained by *God* and *not* by the "official" order of earthly ordination. God will use such

---

1   Jesus was trained at home, not in the "official" schools (Luke 2:40; John 7:15).

people in the last days. Some of them will make up at least part of the 144,000.[2]

Since the priesthood of Melchisedec was *not* after the *earthly* order of Aaron, it must be referring to the *heavenly* priesthood of Christ. And a priesthood "after the *order* of Melchisedec" would refer to, and be synonymous with, a *heavenly* priesthood, organized after the order of *Christ*, of which Jesus Christ is the High Priest. Let's look at Hebrews 8:1–13:

> Now of the things which we have spoken this is the sum: We have such an high priest, who is set on the right hand of the throne of the Majesty in the heavens; A minister of the sanctuary [literally, "holy things"], and of the *true* tabernacle, which the *Lord* pitched, and *not man*. For every high priest is ordained to offer gifts and sacrifices: wherefore it is of necessity that this man [Christ] have somewhat also to offer. For if he were on *earth*, he should *not* be a priest, seeing that there are [already] priests that offer gifts according to the law: Who serve unto the *example* and *shadow* of heavenly things, as Moses was admonished of God when he was about to make the tabernacle: for, See, saith he, that thou make all things according to the pattern shewed to thee in the mount [From Exod. 25:40].
>
> But now hath he obtained a more excellent ministry, by how much also he is the mediator of a better covenant, which was established upon better promises [God's *own* promise, not man's]. For if that first covenant [the "old" (human) promise] had been faultless, then should no place have been sought for the second [the "new" (godly) covenant promise]. For finding *fault* with *them* [the *people* kept breaking the old covenant], he saith, Behold, the days come, saith the Lord, when I will make a *new* covenant with the house of Israel and with the house of Judah: Not according to the covenant that I made with their fathers in the day when I took them by the hand to lead them out of the land of Egypt [the "old" (human) covenant; Exod. 19:8]; because they continued *not* in my covenant, and I regarded them not, saith the Lord.
>
> For this is the [*new* (godly)] covenant that I will make with the house of Israel after those days, saith the Lord; *I will put* my laws into their *mind*, and write them in their *hearts*:[3] and I will be to them a God, and they shall be to me a people: And they shall not teach every man his neighbour, and every man his brother, saying, Know the Lord: for all shall know me, from the least to the greatest [because they will see

---

[2] The heavenly order of priesthood does not take anything away from the earthly order of priesthood. God uses both orders. For an example of the work of those from the heavenly order of priests, see *The Great Controversy*, page 606, "As the time comes for [the third angel's message of Revelation 14] to be given with greatest power, the Lord will work through humble instruments, leading the minds of those who consecrate themselves to His service. The laborers will be qualified rather by the unction of His Spirit than by the training of literary institutions. Men of faith and prayer will be constrained to go forth with holy zeal, declaring the words which God gives them."

[3] When the law is written in the heart, doing God's will becomes as natural as a heartbeat, as if carrying out our own impulses, even though those impulses come from God. Compare with Genesis 3:15: "I will *put* enmity between thee [Satan] and the woman."

God's work manifest in His people]. For I will be merciful to their unrighteousness, and their sins and their iniquities will I remember no more.[4] In that he saith, A *new* covenant, he hath made the first *old*. Now that which decayeth and waxeth old is ready to vanish away. [The *old* (human) covenant promise has been condemned to the trash heap.]

As you can see, the book of Hebrews has much to say about the subject of Christ's heavenly high priestly ministry. Chapter nine is even more descriptive. Let's take a look:

> Then verily the first [old] covenant had also ordinances of divine service, and a worldly [earthly] sanctuary [literally, "holy place"].[5] For there was a tabernacle made; the *first* [this would be a room, sometimes called "apartment" or "tabernacle"], wherein was the candlestick, and the table, and the shewbread; which is called the sanctuary [literally, "holy" also called the "holy place"; the terms "holy of holies," "most," or "holiest" are not used here]. And after the second veil[6] [was the *second* room], the tabernacle which is called the Holiest of all [literally, "holy of holies," also called the "Most Holy Place" or just "Most Holy"]; Which had the golden censer, and the ark of the covenant overlaid round about with gold, wherein was the golden pot that had manna, and Aaron's rod that budded, and the tables of the covenant; And over it the cherubims of glory shadowing the mercyseat; of which we cannot now speak particularly.[7]
>
> Now when these things were thus ordained, the priests went always [daily] into the first tabernacle, accomplishing the service of God. But into the second went the high priest alone once every year, not without blood, which he offered for himself, and for the errors of the people: The Holy Ghost [God Himself] this signifying, that

---

4   The author has been quoting from Jeremiah 31:31–34.
5   This is referring to the "old" covenant promise of the people to do God's will (Exod. 19:8), which caused God to *set up* the earthly priestly sanctuary system of sacrifices. These sacrifices were to constantly remind the people that it would *not* be through *their* promise to do God's will, but through the sacrificial blood of Christ that God's promise of righteousness (the "new" covenant) would be completed in us. (Not through Abraham's *own* work of begetting Ishmael, but through *God's* work of *causing* Abraham and Sarah to have the promised Isaac—the cutting off of the work of the flesh.) The constant influx of their sins into the sanctuary should have been an adequate illustration of the mutability of the people's promise of Exodus 19:8 (the setting up of the *old* covenant)—underscoring the impossibility of human beings to keep their promise of doing God's will, the flesh being weak (Rom. 8:3). See Exodus 24 for the description of the service in which the people *confirm* their promise to God and when He ratifies it with animal sacrifices, thus establishing the earthly sacrificial services—all pointing to Christ's antitypical death wherein He Himself ratified the "new" covenant. By the way, the new covenant is called "new" even though it was in existence since before the world was created (see Eph. 1) because it was ratified (by Christ's sacrifice on the cross) *after* the ratification of the "old" covenant (by animal sacrifices) in Exodus 24.
6   The first apartment had a veil at its entrance also.
7   The author appears to be trying to avoid going off onto a tangent, this information not being pertinent to his point. The articles of furniture in these two rooms are described in Exodus 25. There is a discussion of the covering cherubs earlier in this book.

the way into [literally, purpose of, manner of, way of thinking of] the holiest of all [literally, "holies"—the *heavenly* sanctuary[8]] was not yet made manifest [perceived or understood], while as the first [earthly] tabernacle was yet standing [literally, functioning]:[9] Which was a *figure* [symbol] for the time then present, in which were offered both gifts and sacrifices, that could *not* make him that did the service perfect, as pertaining to the conscience; Which stood only in meats and drinks, and divers washings, and carnal ordinances, imposed on them until the time of reformation.

But Christ being come an high priest of good things to come, by a [through the] *greater and more perfect* tabernacle, *not* made with hands, that is to say, *not* of this [earthly] building [therefore, heavenly]; Neither by [through] the blood of goats and calves, but by [through] his *own* blood he entered in [past tense—it happened upon His ascension] once[10] [for all] into the [heavenly] holy place [literally, "holies"—sanctuary (in actuality, the first apartment)[11]], having obtained [again, past tense—it was confirmed on the cross] eternal redemption for us. [We have been given salvation.][12] For if the blood of bulls and of goats, and the ashes of an heifer sprinkling the unclean, sanctifieth to the purifying of the flesh: How much more shall the blood of Christ, who through the eternal Spirit offered himself without spot to God, purge your conscience from dead works to serve the living God?

And for this cause he is the mediator of the *new* testament [covenant], that by means of death, for the redemption of the *transgressions that were under the first testament* ["old" covenant—the people kept breaking their promise], they which are called might receive the promise of eternal inheritance.

For where a testament is, there must also of necessity be the death of the testator. For a testament is of force after men are dead: otherwise it is of no strength at all while the testator liveth. Whereupon neither the first testament [old covenant] was dedicated without blood. For when Moses had spoken every precept to all the people according to the law, he took the blood of calves and of goats, with water, and scarlet

---

8 If Paul had meant to refer to the second apartment here, I believe he would have used the term "holy of holies," as he did in verse 3. The term in the English, "holiest of all," is not implied in the Greek, giving me the impression that the King James translators understood this to refer to the sanctuary in heaven, which is logical from the context.

9 A literal translation of Hebrews 9:8 would read as follows: "The Holy Ghost [God Himself] this signifying, that the purpose of the heavenly sanctuary was not yet perceived, while the earthly sanctuary was still functioning."

10 The Greek word can mean once, at once, all at once, or once for all. The context would suggest the latter.

11 I believe from the context that Paul is referring to the first apartment because he doesn't mention the second apartment (after verse 3) until verses 25 and 26, and that is in the context of the end of the world, holding consistency with the earthly symbol of the high priest entering the Most Holy Place only at the end of the year. The only exception to this annual restriction is at the time the temple was inaugurated, as discussed in a later paragraph, in Hebrews 9:18-23. For a brief discussion of the temple inauguration and its timing in type and antitype, see Appendix J.

12 A literal translation of Hebrews 9:12 would read as follows: "Neither through the blood of goats and calves, but through his own blood, Jesus Christ entered once for all into the heavenly sanctuary [first apartment], having obtained [on the cross] eternal redemption for us."

wool, and hyssop, and sprinkled both the book, and all the people, Saying, This is the blood of the testament which God hath enjoined unto you. Moreover he sprinkled with blood both the tabernacle, and all the vessels of the ministry. [Exod. 24] And almost all things are by the law purged with blood; and without shedding of blood is no remission.

It was therefore necessary that the *patterns* of things in the heavens should be purified with these; but the *heavenly* things *themselves* with *better* sacrifices than these. For Christ is not entered into the holy places made with hands [literally, "holies"—the earthly sanctuary], which are the *figures* of the *true*; but into *heaven itself*, now to appear in the presence of God for us: Nor yet that he should offer himself often, as the high priest entereth into the [most[13]] holy place [literally, "holies"—sanctuary] *every year* with blood of others; [Christ enters the Most Holy Place of the heavenly sanctuary only once (at the end of the world).] For then [because] must he *often* have suffered [metaphorically, He does not die on the cross every time someone commits a sin] since the foundation of the world: but now *once in the end of the world* hath he appeared [*will He appear*] to put away sin by [through] the sacrifice [on the cross] of himself.[14] [He appears in the heavenly Most Holy Place at the time of the end of the world (1844) to put away sin forever by claiming His one-time sacrifice on the cross, which was once and for all time.] And as it is appointed unto men once to die, but after this the judgment: So Christ was *once* offered [on the cross] to bear the sins of many; and unto them that look for him shall he appear the second time [Christ will come to get His people] without sin [having completed the cleansing of the heavenly sanctuary, including the hearts of His people] *unto salvation* [at the "end of the world," ushering in the millennium of wilderness[15] and the new earth after that].

So Jesus Christ is the antitypical High Priest; and we are living in the time of the gathering of God's people for the *work* of the heavenly High Priest. He is cleansing the heavenly sanctuary and beginning the next step in eradicating sin from the universe.

The Day of Atonement is introduced by God in Leviticus 23:26–32 as follows:

And the Lord spake unto Moses, saying, Also on the tenth day of this seventh month there shall be a day of atonement: it shall be an holy convocation unto you; and ye shall afflict your souls, and offer an offering made by fire unto the Lord. And ye shall

---

13 We know from the context that Paul is referring to the Most Holy Place.
14 A literal translation of Hebrews 9:26 would read as follows: "Because must he often have suffered from the foundation of the world. But now once at the completion of the ages for [the] putting away of sin through the sacrifice of him [on the cross] who will appear."
15 The "scapegoat" was part of the earthly Day of Atonement service. See Leviticus 16:5, 7–10 where the scapegoat, representing Satan, was led into the wilderness to die.

do no work in that same day: for it is a day of atonement, to make an atonement for you before the Lord your God. For whatsoever soul it be that shall not be afflicted in that same day, he shall be cut off from among his people. And whatsoever soul it be that doeth any work in that same day, the same soul will I destroy from among his people. Ye shall do no manner of work: it shall be a statute for ever throughout your generations in all your dwellings. It shall be unto you a sabbath of rest, and ye shall afflict your souls: in the ninth day of the month at even, from even unto even, shall ye celebrate [literally, "rest" on] your sabbath.

The details of the events of this day are given in Leviticus 16, which was mentioned previously in this book. It is a good study, which we can save for another time. What we want to cover now are the big ideas, the main points, so we will concentrate on chapter 23. There are four main ideas in the Day of Atonement, as follows:

- Holy convocation (verse 27)
- Afflict your souls (verse 27)
- Offering made by fire (verse 27)
- You shall do no work (verse 28)

Because the Day of Atonement comes near the end of earth's history as we know it, one would expect to see some cataclysmic events surrounding such an end-time scenario, for major changes never come without opposition. One should also expect to see changes in the way God's people have been behaving over the years because the Day of Atonement is a time for "repenting and confessing sins." God is doing such a work in these last days as has never been called for before. He is preparing a people for the coming cataclysmic events leading up to and beyond the second coming of Christ. Therefore, these four main ideas God introduces in the Day of Atonement come to us as four major reforms He makes in His people in the last days.

We will devote this chapter to the idea of the holy convocation. Similarly, each of the other three reforms will have an entire chapter devoted to them as well. Each of these reforms is very important, because without all four of them taking place in God's people, Jesus cannot come. God is fundamentally and particularly a God of order, and He will not come while His people are in disarray.

The Bible describes a holy convocation in Exodus 19: "And the Lord said unto Moses, Lo, I come unto thee in a thick cloud, that the people may hear when I speak with thee, and believe thee for ever. And Moses told the words of the people unto the Lord. And the Lord said unto Moses, Go unto the people, and sanctify them to day and to morrow, and let them wash their clothes, And be ready against the third day: for the third day the Lord will come down in the sight of all the people upon mount Sinai" (verses 9–11).

When God met with His people for an important meeting, He had them wash their clothes. Thus, you can see that clothing is important to God, and not just clothing, but all of our apparel because, in addition to washing their clothing, He had them remove their jewelry, as is described in the convocation after the golden calf incident: "And when the people heard these evil tidings, they mourned: and no man did put on him his ornaments. For the LORD had said unto Moses, Say unto the children of Israel, Ye are a stiffnecked people: I will come up into the midst of thee in a moment, and consume thee: therefore now put off thy ornaments from thee, that I may know what to do unto thee. And the children of Israel stripped themselves of their ornaments by the mount Horeb [Sinai]. And Moses took the tabernacle, and pitched it without the camp, afar off from the camp, and called it the Tabernacle of the congregation. And it came to pass, that every one which sought the LORD went out unto the tabernacle of the congregation, which was without the camp" (Exod. 33:4–7).

In Bible prophecy jewelry and fine clothing are a symbol of righteousness, either a person's *own* righteousness (put on by the person) or *God's* righteousness (put on by God). The operative word here is "who." The whole issue depends on *who* the acting agent is. If we try to dress ourselves, it is none other than self-righteousness and sin.[16] If we allow God to dress us, it can only result in righteous good works being done in and through God's willing servant,[17] through the power of the Holy Spirit.

An example of God putting righteousness on a man is found in Isaiah 61: "I will greatly rejoice in the LORD, my soul shall be joyful in my God; for *he* hath clothed me with the garments of salvation, *he* hath covered me with the robe of righteousness, as a bridegroom *decketh himself* with ornaments [literally, wears opulent priestly[18] garments], and as a bride *adorneth herself* with her jewels [literally, to make to pass over in an aggressive manner, as in what we might call today a "make over"; again, there is this idea of opulence]. For as the earth bringeth forth her bud, and as the garden causeth the things that are sown in it to spring forth; so the *Lord GOD* will *cause* righteousness and praise to spring forth before all the nations" (verses 10, 11).[19]

Another example is found in Ezekiel 36: "A new heart also will *I* give you, and a new spirit will *I* put within you: and *I* will take away the stony heart out of your flesh, and *I* will give you an heart of flesh. And *I* will put my spirit within you, and *cause* you to walk in my statutes, and ye shall keep my judgments, and do them. And ye shall dwell in the land that I gave to your fathers; and ye shall be my people, and I will be your God" (verses 26–28).

An example of a person putting on his or her *own* righteousness (with God providing the remedy)

---

16   "But we are all as an unclean thing, and all our righteousnesses are as filthy rags; and we all do fade as a leaf; and our iniquities, like the wind, have taken us away" (Isa. 64:6).

17   "Then answered Jesus and said unto them, Verily, verily, I say unto you, The Son can do nothing of himself, but what he seeth the Father do: for what things soever he doeth, these also doeth the Son likewise" (John 5:19). "I can of mine own self do nothing: as I hear, I judge: and my judgment is just; because I seek not mine own will, but the will of the Father which hath sent me" (verse 30). Even Jesus did not rely on Himself!

18   The words "himself" and "herself" are added words. They are not in the original. The idea the author is trying to convey here is a state of being, that is, opulent and priestly, not the *act* of putting it on. The author is indicating that God spares nothing for the good of His people (see also Luke 6:38). This is confirmed by the earlier statements that *God* has clothed me; *God* has covered me; and the later statement that *God* will *cause* righteousness to spring forth.

19   A literal translation of Isaiah 61:10, 11 would read as follows: "I will greatly rejoice in the LORD, my soul shall be joyful in my God; for he hath clothed me with the garments of salvation; he hath covered me with the robe of righteousness; as a bridegroom wears opulent priestly garments and as a bride receives her complete makeover. For as the earth bringeth forth her bud, and as the garden causeth the things that are sown in it to spring forth; so the Lord GOD will cause righteousness and praise to spring forth before all the nations."

is found in Revelation 3: "Because thou sayest, I am rich, and increased with goods, and have need of nothing; and knowest not that thou art wretched, and miserable, and poor, and blind, and naked: I counsel thee to buy of me gold tried in the fire, that thou mayest be rich; and white raiment, that thou mayest be clothed, and that the shame of thy nakedness do not appear; and anoint thine eyes with eyesalve, that thou mayest see" (verses 17, 18).

We tend to think that we are OK and that there is nothing *very* wrong with us, maybe just a few small things we need to "work on," but God wants us to see ourselves in our true condition. And He wants us to exchange our own self-righteousness for His true righteousness, allowing *Him* to put *His* own apparel upon us. Zechariah gives us a very good understanding of what happens to our own righteousness when we let God "dress us."

> And he shewed me Joshua the high priest standing before the angel of the Lord, and Satan standing at his right hand to resist him. And the Lord said unto Satan, The Lord rebuke thee, O Satan; even the Lord that hath chosen Jerusalem rebuke thee: is not this a brand plucked out of the fire? Now Joshua was clothed with filthy garments, and stood before the angel. And he answered and spake unto those that stood before him, saying, Take away the filthy garments from him. And unto him he said, Behold, I have caused thine iniquity to pass from thee, and *I* will clothe thee with change of raiment. And I said, Let them set a fair mitre upon his head. So they set a fair mitre upon his head, and clothed him with garments. (Zech. 3:1–5).

Notice that Zechariah is talking about the high priest, someone who on the surface looks about as righteous as it is possible to look on the outside, but God says he is wearing filthy garments. And before the robe of righteousness can be put on him, the old filthy garments, which represent Joshua's sins, must first be removed. God's robe of righteousness is not a cover-up of sins.

Today we are living in the antitypical Day of Atonement, the day when God, in judgment (i.e., deliverance), is removing the sins of His people before He comes to take them home to heaven. God wants His last-day people to look the part. He wants to set His people apart as a spectacle, so that when they sound the warning of the coming cataclysmic events people will listen.

> The Lord standeth up to plead, and standeth to judge the people [at the time of the end—the time of the antitypical Day of Atonement]. The Lord will enter into judgment with the ancients [the leadership] of his people, and the princes thereof: for ye have eaten up the vineyard; the spoil of the poor is in your houses. What mean ye that ye beat my people to pieces, and grind the faces of the poor? saith the Lord God of hosts. Moreover the Lord saith, Because the daughters of Zion are haughty, and walk with stretched forth necks and wanton eyes, walking and mincing as they go, and making a tinkling with their feet: Therefore the Lord will smite with

a scab the crown of the head of the daughters of Zion, and the LORD will discover their secret parts. In that day the LORD will take away the bravery of their tinkling ornaments about their feet, and their cauls [a covering like a net for the head, worn by women], and their round tires like the moon [hoops—tires back *then* were made of wood or metal], The chains, and the bracelets, and the mufflers, The bonnets, and the ornaments of the legs, and the headbands, and the tablets [a flattish piece of jewelry], and the earrings, The rings, and nose jewels, The changeable suits of apparel [literally, festal, for special occasions, such as changing into an evening gown], and the mantles [cape or loose fitting over-garment], and the wimples [a garment worn around the neck and chin, and which usually covers the hair], and the crisping pins [for curling and intermingling ringlets of hair], The glasses, and the fine linen, and the hoods, and the vails.

And it shall come to pass, that instead of sweet smell there shall be stink; and instead of a girdle a rent; and instead of well set hair baldness; and instead of a stomacher [an ornamental covering for the chest worn by either men or women] a girding of sackcloth; and burning instead of beauty. Thy men shall fall by the sword, and thy mighty in the war. And her gates shall lament and mourn; and she being desolate shall sit upon the ground. And in that day [the time of judgment and the end of the world] seven women [*all* of the churches[20]] shall take hold of one man [Christ], saying, We will eat our *own* bread, and wear our *own* apparel: only let us be *called* by thy name [Christian], to take away our reproach. (Isa. 3:13–4:1)[21]

Let's look at what God has to say in Numbers 15:38–41: "Speak unto the children of Israel, and bid them that they make them fringes in the borders of their garments throughout their generations, and that they put upon the fringe of the borders a ribband of blue: and it shall be unto you for a fringe, that ye may look upon it, and remember all the commandments of the LORD, and do them; and that ye seek not after your own heart and your own eyes, after which ye use to go a whoring: that ye may remember, and do all my commandments, and be holy unto your God. I am the LORD your God, which brought you out of the land of Egypt, to be your God: I am the LORD your God."

Here God shows us that He wants to use the way people dress to distinguish *His* special group of people from the rest of the world. God does not ask His people to place blue borders on their garments today, but instead, to dress simply and modestly, which is different from the way the world dresses. Their dress is to remind them that they are God's commandment-keeping people and that He will bring them through the time of trouble in a miraculous manner and, just as miraculously, keep them from

---

20 In Bible prophecy the number seven indicates completeness (Matt. 18:21, 22) and a woman represents a church (Jer. 6:2; Isa. 54).

21 This is a description of what we are doing when we live by the old covenant, trying of ourselves to keep God's law. The result is sin and self-righteous attitudes.

the bondage of sin to serve Him as a holy people.

The judgment ultimately means deliverance to God's people. And yet there are some who do not choose to be a distinct, separate people, who choose not to be recognized as God's followers who keep the law of the Ten Commandments and who God is delivering from sin. God's people are known to be His followers as soon as they are seen, for God, through the simple means of dress, distinguishes them as His. Did you notice what the women in the last days are saying? "We will eat our *own* bread [we will eat what *we* want to eat], and wear our *own* apparel [we will wear what *we* want to wear]: only let us be called by thy name [Christians], to take away our reproach" (Isa. 4:1). Later on in Isaiah, he reminds us that "we are *all* as an unclean thing, and all *our* righteousnesses are as filthy rags; and we all do fade as a leaf; and our iniquities, like the wind, have taken us away" (Isa. 64:6).

Let us have our filthy rags taken away and allow God to put His righteousness on us, both in *deed* and in *symbol*, whereby, through symbol, we acknowledge that it is God who is doing this and not us.

One might wonder how God wants His people to dress. As a historical commentator, Ellen G. White has had much to say about dress, since the subject of dress was a major issue during her lifetime. In the early 1800s, the ladies' dresses were very long, and they dragged in the water, dirt, and filth, thus spreading disease. Then the pendulum swung the other way, and the dresses became too short, even sometimes resembling the dress of men. Here are a few excerpts of what Ellen White had to say about the matter:

> I was shown that God would have us take a course consistent and explainable. Let the sisters adopt the American costume [see below] and they would destroy their own influence and that of their husbands. They would become a byword and a derision. Our Saviour says: 'Ye are the light of the world.' 'Let your light so shine before men, that they may see your good works, and glorify your Father which is in heaven.' There is a great work for us to do in the world, and God would not have us take a course to lessen or destroy our influence with the world. (Ellen G. White, *Testimonies for the Church*, vol. 1, p. 458)

> In wide contrast with this modest dress is the so-called American costume [for more details, see Appendix H], resembling very nearly the dress worn by men. It consists of a vest, pants, and a dress resembling a coat and reaching about halfway from the hip to the knee. This dress I have opposed, from what has been shown me as in harmony with the word of God; while the other I have recommended as modest, comfortable, convenient, and healthful. (Ellen G. White, *Testimonies for the Church*, vol. 1, p. 465)

> I saw that God's order has been reversed, and His special directions disregarded, by those who adopt the American costume. I was referred to Deuteronomy 22:5: "The

> woman shall not wear that which pertaineth unto a man, neither shall a man put on a woman's garment: for all that do so are abomination unto the Lord thy God." God would not have His people adopt the so-called reform dress [the American costume]. It is immodest apparel, wholly unfitted for the modest, humble followers of Christ.
>
> There is an increasing tendency to have women in their dress and appearance as near like the other sex as possible, and to fashion their dress very much like that of men, but God pronounces it abomination. 'In like manner also, that women adorn themselves in modest apparel, with shamefacedness and sobriety.' 1 Timothy 2:9. (Ellen G. White, *Testimonies for the Church*, vol. 1, p. 457)

God has a Day of Atonement message to give to the world today. He wants to have a special meeting with His people to communicate His special blessings for them and for the whole world. If we are to have an influence with the world in giving the final, last-day message, God wants His people to speak consistently—in mouth, pen, deed, and in appearance.

The Day of Atonement is a holy convocation, a most solemn meeting between God and His people in the last days of earth's history. The sanctuary that is now being cleansed is not only the heavenly sanctuary but also the sanctuary of our hearts.

Chapter 12

Feast of the Day of Atonement: The Affliction

I want to begin this chapter by reading Isaiah 58:3: "Wherefore have we fasted, say they, and thou seest not? wherefore have we afflicted our soul, and thou takest no knowledge? Behold, in the day of your fast ye find pleasure, and exact all your labours." As we move through this chapter, you will see the importance of paying attention to God's creative word, in full submission to what you hear.

Do you remember what the women in Isaiah 4 said? "And in that day seven women shall take hold of one man, saying, We will eat our own bread, and wear our own apparel: only let us be called by thy name, to take away our reproach" (Isa. 4:1).

The "one man" is Christ. "That day" is the time of the end—the time of judgment and deliverance. The "seven women" represent all churches (Jer. 6:2; Isa. 54:1–17; Matt. 18:21, 22). The churches want to do what *they* want to do, yet they want to be given a cloak of legitimacy by being called Christians. They want to be associated with Christ, yet they desire to do their own thing rather than follow His will. And Isaiah tells us that this happens in two areas: dress and diet.

If you love somebody you want to do those things that give them pleasure, right? And if the person you love happens to be God, wouldn't you want to worship Him the way He wants to be worshipped—to do those things that will honor the One who has done so much for you? God is particular. He cares about how He is worshipped. He is also a jealous God, One who is jealous for your welfare and cares about what happens to you, especially when it comes to judgment and deliverance.

Isaiah 4:1 is referring to the last days in earth's history. We know this because of what we read in Isaiah 3:13: "The LORD standeth up to *plead*, and standeth to *judge* [deliver] the people."

There were various times of judgment in the Old Testament, which also pointed to the future. The old saying is still true, "If we do not learn from history, we are bound to repeat it." What time is there in earth's history that is more applicable to judgment than today? Old Testament prophecies that refer to judgment are pointing right at us and giving us instruction for today, the antitypical time of the cleansing of the heavenly sanctuary—the time of judgment and deliverance. Moreover, Jesus will *stand up* to accomplish this. The time is critical; the events are important.[1]

We have already discussed dress, but what does diet have to do with the judgment? Is this subject

---

1   "And at that time shall Michael stand up, the great prince which standeth for the children of thy people: and there shall be a time of trouble, such as never was since there was a nation even to that same time: and at that time thy people shall be delivered, every one that shall be found written in the book" (Dan. 12:1).

really mentioned in the Day of Atonement context in Leviticus 23? Remember, Leviticus 23 mentions four main ideas involving the Day of Atonement:

- Holy convocation (verse 27)
- Afflict your souls (verse 27)
- Offering made by fire (verse 27)
- You shall do no work (verse 28)

We will devote this chapter to the affliction of our souls.

The idea of afflicting our souls is that of searching our hearts—a humble acknowledgement that God is all-powerful and that we are as weak as grass (Isa. 40). We, therefore, have no strength to stand unless God holds us up. Without Him we are destined to shrivel, die, and blow away in the wind. Afflicting our souls also includes an understanding that, if we let Him, God will work in us to change our hearts that we might truly reflect His divine character. David said, "Search me, O God, and know my heart: try me, and know my thoughts: And see if there be any wicked way in me, and lead me in the way everlasting" (Ps. 139:23, 24). In these last days of judgment and deliverance, this is the constant prayer of God's people who are looking for His soon return. This *is* the Day of Atonement work of the cleansing of sin in the hearts of God's people. God is coming to you and to me and saying, "There is something in your life that is a fault or a defect that is preventing you from reaching your highest potential in Me. Will you let Me have it?"

What is your answer? Tell Him now that you would rather have Him than the things of this world that you are holding onto. How you answer this question will demonstrate who or what you worship, for to put anything ahead of God and His will is idol worship.

This is the work of atonement and cleansing. Yet God never asks us to do anything except what He gives us power to do. We know that His word alone has the power inherent within it to create what it says. But God never does anything halfway. He pours out His blessings in a cup that overflows. Luke 6:38 says, "Give, and it shall be given unto you; good measure, pressed down, and shaken together, and running over, shall men give into your bosom. For with the same measure that ye mete withal it shall be measured to you again." So let's give everything we have, and everything we are, to God and see what He will do with it. (By the way, it's all His anyway. All He asks us to do is to acknowledge that fact.)

So what "extra" did God give us? He wants to communicate with us while He cleanses us. He has a special work for His people to do in the last days. In order to accomplish this work, He needs us to have a clear mind by watching what we eat. Have you ever tried to concentrate after a big Thanksgiving dinner? For our brain to do its best work, it is best not to eat a big meal first. After a big meal, the blood that previously might have been allocated to the brain is sent to the stomach to work on the huge task at hand of digesting all that food.

Therefore, in these last days, when God is removing the sins of the people, thus cleansing the heavenly sanctuary, He needs us to avoid large quantities of food or rich food that will clog our body and brain, thus spoiling our health. He wants us to eat lightly because He has a special message to send to and through His people.

In the antitypical Day of Atonement, when so much is at stake, we must afflict ourselves, meaning to bestow labor or exercise oneself; to afflict, depress, oppress; to *be* afflicted, depressed, oppressed; to submit oneself to any one; or to fast.

If we look back to the children of Israel as an example, for 40 years before entering the Promised Land, God gave them manna to eat, thereby, lightening their diet (see Exod. 16; Num. 11). And because of the light diet, God was able to communicate His mysteries to them. Ancient Israel searched their hearts, repented, and fasted.[2] Now that we are at the threshold of entering the promised land of the New Jerusalem, God wants to lighten our diet by following the principles of Daniel and his three friends.

> In the third year of the reign of Jehoiakim king of Judah came Nebuchadnezzar king of Babylon unto Jerusalem, and besieged it. And the Lord gave Jehoiakim king of Judah into his hand, with part of the vessels of the house of God: which he carried into the land of Shinar to the house of his god; and he brought the vessels into the treasure house of his god. And the king spake unto Ashpenaz the master of his eunuchs, that he should bring certain of the children of Israel, and of the king's seed, and of the princes; Children in whom was no blemish, but well favoured, and skilful in all wisdom, and cunning in knowledge, and understanding science, and such as had ability in them to stand in the king's palace, and whom they might teach the learning and the tongue of the Chaldeans. And the king appointed them a daily provision of the king's meat, and of the wine which he drank: so nourishing them three years, that at the end thereof they might stand before the king....
>
> But Daniel purposed in his heart that he would not defile himself with the portion of the king's meat, nor with the wine which he drank: therefore he requested of the prince of the eunuchs that he might not defile himself. Now God had brought Daniel into favour and tender love with the prince of the eunuchs. And the prince of the eunuchs said unto Daniel, I fear my lord the king, who hath appointed your meat and your drink: for why should he see your faces worse liking than the children which are of your sort? then shall ye make me endanger my head to the king.
>
> Then said Daniel to Melzar, whom the prince of the eunuchs had set over Daniel, Hananiah, Mishael, and Azariah, Prove thy servants, I beseech thee, ten days; and let them give us pulse[3] to eat, and water to drink. Then let our countenances be looked upon before thee, and the countenance of the children that eat of the portion of the king's meat: and as thou seest, deal with thy servants. So he consented to them in this matter, and proved them ten days.

---

2   We must do no less. Well, almost no less. Had God expected His people to perform a literal fast until He came, the movement of 1844 would have died out within about six weeks! In Moses' day, the people fasted for one day. Today, God has instituted the best thing for the long haul—a light diet.

3   The word in the original language means vegetables (as sown) and/or herbs.

> And at the end of ten days their countenances appeared fairer and fatter in flesh than all the children which did eat the portion of the king's meat. Thus Melzar took away the portion of their meat, and the wine that they should drink; and gave them pulse. As for these four children, God gave them knowledge and skill in all learning and wisdom: and Daniel had understanding in all visions and dreams.
>
> Now at the end of the days that the king had said he should bring them in, then the prince of the eunuchs brought them in before Nebuchadnezzar. And the king communed with them; and among them all was found none like Daniel, Hananiah, Mishael, and Azariah: therefore stood they before the king. And in all matters of wisdom and understanding, that the king enquired of them, he found them ten times better than all the magicians and astrologers that were in all his realm. And Daniel continued even unto the first year of King Cyrus. (Dan. 1:1–21)

This diet makes sense because it is the diet that God gave to Adam and Eve in the Garden of Eden. "And God said, Behold, I have given you every herb bearing seed [grain], which is upon the face of all the earth, and every tree, in the which is the fruit of a tree yielding seed [fruit and nuts (legumes)]; to you it shall be for meat [food]. And to every beast of the earth, and to every fowl of the air, and to every thing that creepeth upon the earth, wherein there is life, I have given every green herb [vegetables (stems, leaves, and roots)] for meat: and it was so" (Gen. 1:29, 30). "And the LORD God commanded the man, saying, Of every tree of the garden thou mayest freely eat: But of the tree of the knowledge of good and evil, thou shalt not eat of it" (Gen. 2:16, 17).

So, fruit, grain, and nuts (i.e., legumes) were given to human beings for food, and to the animals God also gave vegetables. Only one otherwise "edible" plant was forbidden, that being the tree of the knowledge of good and evil. It should be noted here that humanity's first disagreement with God, resulting in the first sin, was over diet.

After Adam and Eve sinned, they, too, were given vegetables to eat: "And unto Adam he said, Because thou hast hearkened unto the voice of thy wife, and hast eaten of the tree, of which I commanded thee, saying, Thou shalt not eat of it: cursed is the ground for thy sake; in sorrow shalt thou eat of it all the days of thy life; Thorns also and thistles shall it bring forth to thee; and thou shalt eat the herb of the field [same as the "green herb" above]; In the sweat of thy face shalt thou eat bread, till thou return unto the ground; for out of it wast thou taken: for dust thou art, and unto dust shalt thou return" (Gen. 3:17–19).

Only after the flood (when all the vegetation was destroyed except what was kept safe in the ark) was flesh food allowed. We know God made provision for this food shortage because He permitted seven of the "clean" (edible) animals to enter the ark, and only two of the unclean (Gen. 7:2). Certainly this was intended only for a limited time in order to meet the emergency food shortage, because the life of each man and woman was shortened with every animal they killed for food.

And God blessed Noah and his sons, and said unto them, Be fruitful, and multiply, and replenish the earth. And the fear of you and the dread of you shall be upon every beast of the earth, and upon every fowl of the air, upon all that moveth upon the earth, and upon all the fishes of the sea; into your hand are they delivered. Every moving thing that liveth shall be meat for you; even as the green herb have I given you all things. But flesh with the life thereof, which is the blood thereof, shall ye not eat. And surely your blood of your lives will I require; at the hand of every beast will I require it, and at the hand of man; at the hand of every man's brother will I require the life of man. (Gen. 9:1–5)

And man's life *was* shortened—from over 900 years (Gen. 5) to approximately 70 (Ps. 90:10).

We may not see a tenfold increase in intelligence by today's IQ charts, but if we were to follow the same diet as Daniel and his friends we would see a notable difference in our health. It has been documented that lacto-ovo[4] vegetarians average about 61 percent reduction in coronary heart disease deaths and total vegetarians about 86 percent reduction in the same from that of the normal population.[5]

These numbers do not indicate a total elimination of disease, but they do indicate a significant reduction of occurrences. As good as that is, a mere elimination of disease is not the point of what God is looking for. What God wants are people He can "talk to" and who will respond instantly to His promptings, for He has a special message to bring to the world just before He comes and He seeks a group of people who will allow God to gain for them victory over all sin and who will deliver the message.[6] This is what God wants to accomplish in His people in the last days.[7]

Diet is not the only aspect of this "fast" idea. There are eight principles to the reform in health that God wants to do in His people. These eight principles are as follows:

1. **Nutrition** – Eat your vegetables, plus fruit, nuts, and grains. Select a good variety, and eat as much fresh and raw as possible. A target of at least 50 percent of the total diet should be fresh[8] or raw.[9]
2. **Exercise** – Walking is a great form of exercise, is simple and inexpensive. Take a 30-minute

---

[4] Lacto refers to milk and ovo refers to eggs. Lacto-ovo vegetarians refer to those vegetarians who consume eggs and milk from non-human sources. Total vegetarians do not eat any poultry or dairy products.

[5] Neil Nedley, M.D., *Proof Positive: How to Reliably Combat Disease and Achieve Optimal Health through Nutrition and Lifestyle*, p. 84.

[6] Victory does not come through diet, by the way, but through the blood of Christ; don't think changing your lifestyle will save you. Good health will make life easier, but only Christ Himself saves anyone (see 1 Peter 1:19; Rev. 7:14; 12:11).

[7] See Revelation 14 in which the people are described in the first five verses and the message is described starting with verse six. The understanding of this passage is a subject for another venue, but you should be able to see that both the people and the message are special.

[8] A good definition of "fresh" would be as close to the garden as possible in terms of time, with the only processing being washing, peeling, and cutting.

[9] A good definition of "raw" would be not heated above 104–120 degrees. Any temperature above or within this range begins to break down the enzymes needed for digestion and other functions of the body. Other processes could include drying (at temperatures below 104 degrees) or fresh freezing that would still maintain the quality of raw.

walk per day at least four days each week.

3. **Water** – Drink plenty of pure, fresh water from the best possible source. For most people about 64 ounces per day is adequate. Distilled is good, although distilled water should be supplemented with trace mineral tablets.
4. **Sunshine** – It is important to get out of doors in the sunshine while properly protected, *without* chemical sunscreens.[10] But remember to not overdo it—one can get enough sun while merely walking.
5. **Temperance** – Actually, abstemiousness[11]—"too much of any *good* thing is still too much," and "any amount of any *bad* thing is always too much."
6. **Air** – Pure, fresh air is vital to our health. Outside activities and country living in the great outdoors is a blessing. Again, walking will help you to get plenty of fresh air.
7. **Rest** – For many people, two hours of sleep *before* midnight is worth more than four hours of sleep *after* midnight.[12] From this I have concluded that it's best to be in bed with the lights out by 10:00 p.m.
8. **Trust** – When we trust in divine power, depend on God's providence, and yield to His will for our lives, we find happiness and peace, which is what this book seeks to promote.

God wants His people in the last days to be constantly looking for ways to improve their health along these eight principles, doing the best they can, given the circumstances in which God has placed them. Some people live in places where fresh fruits and vegetables are often difficult or impossible to obtain. Some people live in a situation where their food is pre-prepared, such as if you are in college. If you can't change your location, simply do the best you can with what the Lord has provided.

However, some of us have more control of our circumstances. If this is true for you, and healthful living that follows these eight principles has not been your habit in the past, there is good news! These eight principles spell out *"New Start."* Ask God now to give you a new start. He will do it. It is never too late to start.

For more information on healthful living, please see Appendix G. Remember, it is God's desire that "above all things that thou mayest prosper and be in health, even as thy soul prospereth" (3 John 1:2).

---

10   If you are a total vegetarian, which is recommended. A wide-brimmed hat and/or well-placed bandanas make a good natural sunscreen, should sunscreen be needed for special health situations. Long sleeves also provide a good natural sunscreen and can actually be cooler while blocking the sun from heating your skin. However, you don't want to cover up so much as to miss the sun altogether.

11   Temperance is being moderate and careful in all things. Abstemious also involves completely leaving off certain things, a step further.

12   "I know from the testimonies given me from time to time for brain workers, that sleep is worth far more before than after midnight. Two hours' good sleep before twelve o'clock is worth more than four hours after twelve o'clock" (Ellen G. White, *Manuscript Releases*, vol. 7, p. 224).

Chapter 13

Feast of the Day of Atonement: Offering by Fire

As we begin this chapter on the third reform God wants to make in His people during the Feast of the Day of Atonement, I want to examine a few passages of Scripture that talk about fire.

> That the trial of your *faith*, being much more precious than of gold that perisheth, though it be tried with *fire*, might be found unto praise and honour and glory at the appearing of Jesus Christ. (1 Peter 1:7)

> Behold, I will send my messenger, and he shall *prepare the way before me*: and the Lord, whom ye seek, shall suddenly come to his temple, even the messenger of the covenant, whom ye delight in: behold, he shall come, saith the Lord of hosts. But who may *abide*[1] the day of his coming? and who shall stand when he appeareth? for he is like a refiner's *fire*, and like fullers' soap: And he shall sit as a *refiner and purifier* of silver: and he shall purify the sons of Levi, and purge them as gold and silver, that they may offer unto the Lord an *offering* in righteousness. Then shall the offering of Judah and Jerusalem be pleasant unto the Lord, as in the days of old, and as in former years. And I will *come near to you to judgment*; and I will be a swift witness against the sorcerers, and against the adulterers, and against false swearers, and against those that oppress the hireling in his wages, the widow, and the fatherless, and that turn aside the stranger from his right, and fear not me, saith the Lord of hosts. For I am the Lord, I change not; therefore ye sons of Jacob are not consumed. (Mal. 3:1–6)

> Also on the tenth day of this seventh month there shall be a *day of atonement*: it shall be an holy convocation unto you; and ye shall afflict your souls, and offer an *offering* made by *fire* unto the Lord. (Lev. 23:27)

Malachi is describing the Day of Atonement when he is talking about the offering made by fire. However, in addition to understanding what he has to say about this offering itself, let's not lose sight

---

1 That is, not resist it (see John 15:1–9).

of what God has to say in all this discussion about who the *messenger* is because the messenger flavors the subject matter. Much of who this messenger is has to do with the timing of the message, so let's look and see what the Bible has to say:

> For, behold, the day cometh, that shall burn as an oven; and *all the proud, yea, and all that do wickedly, shall be stubble: and the day that cometh shall burn them up*, saith the Lord of hosts, that it shall leave them neither root nor branch. But unto you that fear my name shall the Sun of righteousness arise with healing in his wings; and ye shall go forth, and grow up as calves of the stall. And ye shall tread down the wicked; for they shall be ashes under the soles of your feet in the day that I shall do this, saith the Lord of hosts. Remember ye the law of Moses my servant, which I commanded unto him in Horeb [Sinai] for all Israel,[2] with the statutes and judgments.[3] Behold, I will send you *Elijah the prophet* before the coming of the *great and dreadful day of the Lord*: And he shall turn the heart of the fathers to the children, and the heart of the children to their fathers, lest I come and smite the earth with a curse. (Mal. 4:1–6)

The messenger preparing the way before the Lord (Mal. 3:1) brings the message of Elijah.[4] The "great and dreadful day of the Lord" (Mal. 4:5) has to be the time of His second coming and the end of the world, beginning with the time of preparation just *before* His second coming all the way through the lake of fire and the destruction of the wicked. This is because of what it says happens to the wicked. Therefore, this would be today's time period, for these things are yet to happen.

Our God is a consuming fire. The very presence of God consumes sin as if it were dry tinder. That is why God cannot appear to us in all His glory (Exod. 33:18–23). That is why the wicked are destroyed by the brightness of His coming (2 Thess. 2:8). It is one of the reasons Jesus came to us as a human being. It is why, also, that while dying on the cross, Jesus could not see the Father's reconciling face or even perceive His presence at the cross. Christ had taken our sin upon Him. If He had perceived the Father's presence while bearing our sins, those sins He was bearing would have been consumed by the Father's presence, freeing Christ of His responsibility. Jesus had to deal with our sin and had to take our penalty, our second death.[5]

God's presence not only consumes sin, but it consumes everything attached to it. If we refuse to let go of our sin, we will be consumed with it, ultimately, in the lake of fire at the end of the thousand years. Instead, if we let go of our sin *now* and let God have it *now*, God will consume the sin *from* us. This is why He is described as a *refining* fire (Mal. 3:2), for He refines us, purifies us, and prepares us to stand

---

2 This references the Ten Commandment moral law given on Mount Sinai.
3 These would be the ceremonial, health, and civil laws of Israel given in the first five books of the Bible.
4 You can read about this message in 1 Kings, chapters 16–18.
5 The essence of the second death is the anguish sinners will feel when they realize they are about to be banished for all eternity from the presence of God, who is the source of all life.

before God without a mediator when Christ finally leaves His cleansing work in the Most Holy Place of the heavenly sanctuary to come and receive His own. Let Him have your sin today. By doing so you can live in the fire of God today.

During that time of preparation just before the second coming of Christ, God's people will come to understand their ancestral history; hence, the turning "the heart of the fathers to the children, and the heart of the children to their fathers" (Mal. 4:6). They will appreciate and respond to (*i.e.*, repent of) their history, lest they repeat it.

There are a number of texts in the Old Testament that address the issue of iniquity throughout generations.

> Thou shalt not bow down thyself unto them, nor serve them:[6] for I the LORD thy God am a jealous God, visiting the iniquity of the *fathers* upon the children unto the third and fourth generation of them that hate me. (Deut. 5:9)

> Wilt thou judge them, son of man, wilt thou judge [deliver][7] them? cause them to know the abominations of their fathers. (Ezek. 20:4)

> Moreover the word of the LORD came unto me, saying, Now, thou son of man, wilt thou judge, wilt thou judge the bloody city? yea, thou shalt shew her all her abominations. (Ezek. 22:1, 2)

> If they shall *confess their iniquity, and the iniquity of their fathers*, with their trespass which they trespassed against me, and that also they have walked contrary unto me; And that I also have walked contrary unto them, and have brought them into the land of their enemies; if then their uncircumcised hearts be humbled, and they then accept of the punishment [Hebrew: allow me to make you acceptable] of their iniquity [refining fire]: Then will I remember my covenant with Jacob, and also my covenant with Isaac, and also my covenant with Abraham will I remember; and I will remember the land. The land also shall be left of them, and shall enjoy her sabbaths, while she lieth desolate without them: and they shall accept of the punishment [Hebrew: allow me to make you acceptable] of their iniquity [again, refining fire]: because, even because they despised my judgments [deliverance], and because their soul abhorred my statutes. And yet for all that, when they be in the land of their enemies, I will not cast them away, neither will I abhor them, to destroy them utterly, and to break my *covenant with them*:[8] for I am the LORD their

---

6   This is speaking about idolatry in any form, either physical or mental.
7   The work of the judge is to deliver as explained in Psalm 76:8, 9; Judges 2:16; and 1 Samuel 24:15.
8   Note the continued importance God places on His covenant promise to us, that *He* will give us the righteousness He wants us to have. "Enjoying the Sabbath" is just such a rest from our *own* efforts and our *own* "trying" to keep God's law

> God. But I will for their sakes remember the *covenant of their ancestors*, whom I brought forth out of the land of Egypt in the sight of the heathen, that I might be their God: I am the Lord. (Lev. 26:40–45)

Bringing His people "out of the land of Egypt in the sight of the heathen" is what God wants to do for His people in these last days—getting ready to bring them out of this world to heaven to prepare for the establishment of the "new earth" (Rev. 21). This "offering made by fire" is very much about repentance from historical (as well as current) sin, both their own and ancestral.

There is a popular opinion that one has to commit sin experientially before one can repent of it. We may be tempted to think, "If *I* did not do it, why do *I* have to repent of it?" To "repent" (verb) means:
1. To turn from sin and to dedicate oneself to the amendment of one's life [physical]
2. To feel regret or contrition; to change one's mind [mental][9]

So even though *I* did not physically rob that bank, yet because I have the same fallen sinful human flesh that Adam had after he sinned, that sin is in me, and it is only by the power of God that I can turn away from that or any other sin. The same can be said for anyone. Therefore, it is possible (and necessary) that we turn away from all sin ever committed on the face of the planet, for those are the sins that put God on the cross—my sins, your sins, and those of everyone, for Christ took on all sin and died and took the penalty of sin for all humanity. So when we hear in the news about sins committed, we may not need to repent for the murderer's specific crime itself, but we can *feel* repentance on his behalf for we know that his sin is in us, too, because we are all children of Adam. We can feel regret and contrition on behalf of the sins of others and resolve to allow God to have control of our lives so that we may avoid that same action. Also, since we know that the same sin dwells in us, we cannot look down on or condemn anyone who commits sin(s) because we know that we are capable of doing the same thing(s). This is what "visiting the iniquity of the fathers upon the children unto the third and fourth generation" is all about (Deut. 5:9). But our repentance goes beyond the third and fourth generation all the way to Adam, which is called "corporate repentance."

While we are on this subject, let's talk about the "sins of the fathers." Is it possible that in the last days some might conclude that "good enough for my father (ancestral traditions)" does *not necessarily* mean good enough for me? Is it possible that the "old time religion" that may have been good enough for our ancestors in *their* time may need some revising for the last days before Jesus comes? It is worthy of our thought.

There are four common attributes used in the Bible that identify the message of the last days of earth's history:
1. It is called "Elijah" the prophet. This is a prophetic message of repentance. It is a refining work that takes us all the way into righteousness, which is doing what is right. This issue is about

---

(legalism).

[9] *Webster's Seventh New Collegiate Dictionary* (G. & G. Merriam Co., 1967), p. 727.

who God is and what He can do (1 Kings 18:36–38).
2. It is a message to prepare the way for God the King. A favorite phrase is "the kingdom of heaven is at hand" for God is about to reveal who He is and/or He is about to take the throne.
3. It is a voice crying in the wilderness because relatively few are listening, for it is an unpopular message.
4. The message would point to the "covenant" that is God's promise to *give* us the righteousness and repentance we need.

However, Jesus has something interesting to tell us about Elijah in His day. Note that this is called a "great" time and does not talk about it being "dreadful," since Christ's first coming was as a docile teacher, not as a dreadful conqueror:

> And it came to pass, when Jesus had made an end of commanding his twelve disciples, he departed thence to teach and to preach in their cities. Now when John had heard in the prison the works of Christ, he sent two of his disciples, And said unto him, Art thou he that should come, or do we look for another?[10] Jesus answered and said unto them, Go and shew John again those things which ye do hear and see: The blind receive their sight, and the lame walk, the lepers are cleansed, and the deaf hear, the dead are raised up, and the poor have the gospel preached to them. And blessed is he, whosoever shall not be offended in me. And as they departed, Jesus began to say unto the multitudes concerning John, What went ye out into the wilderness to see? A reed shaken with the wind? But what went ye out for to see? A man clothed in soft raiment? behold, they that wear soft clothing are in kings' houses. But what went ye out for to see? A prophet? yea, I say unto you, and more than a prophet. For this is he, of whom it is written, Behold, *I send my messenger before thy face, which shall prepare thy way before thee*. Verily I say unto you, Among them that are born of women there hath not risen a greater than John the Baptist: notwithstanding he that is least in the kingdom of heaven is greater than he [talking about John's humility]. And from the days of John the Baptist until now the kingdom of heaven suffered violence, and the violent take it by force. For all the prophets and the law prophesied until John. And if ye will receive it, *this is Elias,*[11] *which was for to come*. He that hath ears to hear, let him hear. (Matt. 11:1–15)

So John the Baptist gave the Elijah message in Christ's day 2,000 years ago. Elijah did not need to come, for John gave the message. Yet we can see from Malachi that there will be another time, a later

---

10 John was actually looking for the "dreadful" attribute even back then, for the popular opinion of the day was that the Messiah would come as a conqueror and take the temporal throne away from Rome. To John, Jesus seemed to be dragging His feet, but His "time was not yet."
11 "Elias" is the Greek form of the Hebrew name "Elijah."

dreadful time, in which the Elijah message will be given. Again, Elijah doesn't need to come this third time either, for the message will be given by others. In Elijah's day, it was Elijah. In Christ's day, it was John the Baptist. The precedent is established. Therefore, we should expect that in the climax of earth's history God will raise another messenger. We will see who that is a little later.

Matthew also tells us of the nature of this message:

> In those days came John the Baptist, preaching in the wilderness of Judaea, And saying, *Repent ye: for the kingdom of heaven is at hand.* For this is he that was spoken of by the prophet Esaias, saying, *The voice of one crying in the wilderness, Prepare ye the way of the* Lord, *make his paths straight.*[12] And the same John had his raiment of camel's hair, and a leathern girdle about his loins; and his meat was locusts and wild honey. Then went out to him Jerusalem, and all Judaea, and all the region round about Jordan, And were baptized of him in Jordan, *confessing their sins.* (Matt. 3:1–6)

Please note that Matthew tells us that the message John was giving was the message found in the book of Isaiah, chapter 40. Notice also that John ate and dressed simply (see chapters 11 and 12 of this book). The word that is translated "locusts" refers to the locust tree, a hard-wooded leguminous tree. A very popular fruit from the locust family of trees is "carob," which grows in the Mediterranean area, is naturally sweet, and is eaten in place of chocolate by many people.[13]

Isaiah 40 is a very interesting chapter, but we'll just look at verses 1 through 8:

> Comfort ye, comfort ye my people, saith your God. Speak ye comfortably to Jerusalem, and cry unto her, that her warfare is accomplished, that her iniquity is pardoned: for she hath received of the Lord's hand *double* for all her sins. The *voice of him that crieth in the wilderness, Prepare ye the way of the* Lord, *make straight in the desert a highway for our God.* Every valley shall be exalted, and every mountain and hill shall be made low: and the crooked shall be made straight, and the rough places plain: And the *glory* of the Lord shall be *revealed*, and all flesh shall see it together: for the *mouth* of the Lord hath spoken it. The voice said, Cry. And he said, What shall I cry? All flesh is grass, and all the goodliness thereof is as the flower of the field: The grass withereth, the flower fadeth: because the spirit of the Lord bloweth upon it: surely the people is grass. The grass withereth, the flower fadeth: but the *word* of our God shall stand for ever.

---

12 Jesus is quoting from Isaiah 40:3. "Esaias" is the Greek form of the Hebrew name "Isaiah."
13 From Wikipedia, the free encyclopedia, "Locust tree can mean: [1] Any of a number of tree species in the genera Gleditsia or Robinia, including: Honey locust ... a leguminous tree with pods having a sweet, edible pulp [or] Black locust ... a leguminous tree with toxic pods but useful for making honey; [2] Or less commonly, 'African locust bean tree' (Parkia biglobosa), which is also known as néré; [3] Also not commonly, the carob tree, Ceratonia siliqua, whose pods are called locust beans."

The Elijah message that John was giving is found in Isaiah.[14] It is, first of all, a message of comfort. This is because the war is over and a pardon has been issued. So often we read about what God wants to do in us, and we try as hard as we can to do it ourselves, but we fail every time. God says, "Stop fighting! Let *Me* accomplish My righteousness in you." Second Corinthians 5:19 says, "To wit, that God was in Christ, reconciling the [whole] world [including you] unto himself, not *imputing* their trespasses unto them; and hath committed unto us the word of reconciliation." In other words, God does not hold anything against you. And John 6:28 and 29 says: "Then said they unto him, What shall we do, that we might work the works of God? Jesus answered and said unto them, *This is the work of God, that ye believe on him whom he hath sent.*" So believe Him and relax! Your warfare is accomplished by, and in, Christ. This is the promise of God's covenant, for He will write His law in your heart (see Jer. 31:31–33). If you will relax and let Him do His work, He will use you to spread the word of His reconciliation in you as a "sermon in shoes" by your words and/or deeds. Jesus' gift is there for the receiving: "Come unto me, all ye that labour and are heavy laden, and I will give you rest. Take my yoke upon you, and learn of me; for I am meek and lowly in heart: and ye shall find rest unto your souls. For my yoke is easy, and my burden is light" (Matt. 11:28–30).

Another aspect of the "warfare" that is accomplished is that God's people do not have to point out, or fight against, the "Baal worship" of false doctrine. When the truth is presented in its proper light, all false ideas will become plain in contrast to the truth. Those who choose to listen to God will see the difference plainly and respond accordingly. However, there will come a time when modern day "Elijahs" will have to plainly point to specific issues, for not everyone will choose to listen to God. And God never allows people to die without a warning.

In Isaiah 40:2 it says that "she hath received of the LORD's hand double for all her sins." That doesn't sound very comforting, does it? But there it is. We have received (already, past tense) *double* for our sins. Well, at least, if it is in the past tense, the bad news is out, and we have reached the bottom already. Hopefully, we can only go up from here. But isn't that the truth when God has control of your life?

Now let's look more closely at what God has given to us for our sins. We know that we deserve punishment for our sins—we deserve to die the second, eternal, death, as we read in Scripture.[15] But,

---

14 Matthew 3:3 and Isaiah 40:3 confirm the identity of the message because the message is a voice crying in the wilderness that prepares the way for a coming King.

15 Matthew 10:28 says, "And fear not them which kill the body, but are not able to kill the soul: but rather fear him which is able to destroy both soul [mind, including the spirit] and body in hell [the second, eternal, death in the lake of fire]." Revelation 21:8 reads, "But the fearful, and unbelieving, and the abominable, and murderers, and whoremongers, and sorcerers, and idolaters, and all liars, shall have their part in the lake which burneth with fire and brimstone: which is the second death." And Malachi 4:1 says, "For, behold, the day cometh, that shall burn as an oven; and all the proud, yea, and all that do wickedly, shall be stubble; and the day that cometh shall burn them up, saith the LORD of hosts, that it shall leave them neither root nor branch." Without branches, there is no plant. Without roots, there is no growth. Both the mind (with the spirit) and the body are destroyed, never to rise again. Now read Romans 1:18–20: "For the wrath of God is revealed from heaven against all ungodliness and unrighteousness of men, who hold [suppress] the truth in righteousness; Because that which may be known of God is manifest in them; for God hath shewed it unto them. For the invisible things of him from the creation of the world are clearly seen, being understood by the things that are made, even his eternal power and Godhead; so that they are without excuse."

contrary to popular belief, God is not in the business of punishment, He is the business of *salvation* and *reclamation from sin*. See what God says in Ezekiel 33:11: "Say unto them, As I live, saith the Lord God, I have no pleasure in the death of the wicked; but that the wicked turn from his way and live: turn ye, turn ye from your evil ways; for *why will ye die*, O house of Israel?" And John 3:17 reminds us that "God sent not his Son into the world to condemn the world; but that the world through him might be saved."

The very first statement Isaiah makes, even the very first word, is that this is a message of *comfort*. Therefore, I have concluded that what Israel receives is not double jeopardy, but a double blessing! And these blessings are indeed for our sin, the purpose of which is to remove our sins, not to punish us for our sins.

What, specifically, could this double blessing be? Verses 5 and 8 tell us: "And the *glory* of the Lord shall be revealed, and all flesh shall see it together: for the mouth of the Lord hath *spoken* it.... The grass withereth, the flower fadeth: but the *word* of our God shall stand for ever." The double blessing is 1) righteousness (glory[16]) and 2) power to accomplish this goodness in our various experiences, for God's word has inherent within it the power to create what it says.[17] God creates righteousness in us simply by speaking it, and when we choose to believe God's word, His righteousness becomes real in our various daily experiences—the actual good works of God—and He speaks righteousness to us through His covenant promise.[18]

Verses 3 and 4 of Isaiah 40 simply identify the message itself by mentioning two of the four attributes of the message. "The voice of him that crieth in the wilderness, Prepare ye the way of the Lord, make straight in the desert a highway for our God. Every valley shall be exalted, and every mountain and hill shall be made low: and the crooked shall be made straight, and the rough places plain." Besides the fact that Jesus flat out tells us this, the Elijah message is also identified in Isaiah. God wants to make sure we understand.

As the voice is "crying in the wilderness," it would appear that the message is unpopular—and so it is. The ratio of priests on top of Mount Carmel was a staggering 450 for Baal versus 1 for Jehovah.[19] The message will be uncomfortable to those who cling to sin, worldliness, and/or self-righteousness.

The unflattering part of the message is given to us in verses 6 through 8: "All flesh is *grass*." We don't want to think of ourselves as being grass, "which to day is, and to morrow is cast into the oven" (Matt. 6:30), do we? But Jesus admitted that about Himself when He said, "I can of mine own self do nothing" (John 5:30). He relied upon the Father for obedience the same as we do, for He took upon Himself our fallen sinful human flesh. But the good news here is that "the word of our God shall stand for ever" (Isa. 40:8); that is, His all-powerful *creative* word. God's word holds us and sustains us in righteousness. And that is the joyous message for the last days.

---

16 See Exodus 33:18, 19 where, in the answer to Moses' request to see God's *glory*, God shows him the *goodness* of His character.
17 See Genesis 1 regarding the instantaneous creative power in God's word.
18 The two covenants are discussed in chapter 1 of this book.
19 This ratio would seem to indicate that the Elijah message would give plenty of room for the proponents of false doctrine to make their point, as the activities on Mount Carmel that monumental day would indicate. The priests of Baal had all day to implore their god to act—so, too, it will be in the modern showdown to come.

Looking back at Malachi 3:1 we read that the messenger brings the message of Elijah, which is a message of comfort, for it is the message of God's promise to write His laws on the hearts of His believers. Verses 2 and 3 tell us that this is a message of cleansing ("fullers' soap"), refinement ("refiner's fire"), purging ("purge them as gold and silver"), and purification ("refiner and purifier of silver" to "purify the sons of Levi [the clergy]"). An offering such as this would definitely be "pleasant unto the Lord" (verse 4). God would then come "near to [us] to judgment" (verse 5). That is, He will come near to us in deliverance[20] because He will deliver us from our sin(s), in our experience, and from those who would oppress His people, for He is a jealous God and a consuming and refining fire in favor of His people who receive joyfully all that God has for them.[21] This conclusion is given in Malachi 3:6: "For I am the Lord, I change not; therefore ye sons of Jacob are not consumed."

So far, we have identified the message and a little of what it is about, but we have not answered the other two questions of who this messenger is and the specific time of when the message begins to be given. We also haven't addressed the statement in Malachi 3:1 that reads "and the Lord, whom ye seek, shall suddenly come to his temple." Where is the Lord going? And why does He do it in such a sudden fashion? What temple is He entering so suddenly?

As we have already discussed, the earthly sanctuary cannot possibly be the one being cleansed beginning in 1844 because the services therein had already ended at the time of Christ's death. This leaves two more options. They are the sanctuary in heaven and the sanctuary of our hearts. Could either of these be the temple of Malachi 3:1?

The sanctuary in heaven still exists. In fact, it will never go away. This sanctuary in heaven, then, *must* be the sanctuary that is being cleansed. And so it is true—but is that all?

The rest of the answer is that the Lord is cleansing the hearts of His people *before* He can finish cleansing the heavenly sanctuary. All this began in 1844, which is when the heavenly High Priest suddenly (*i.e.*, unexpectedly) entered the Most Holy Place of the heavenly temple when everyone was expecting Him to come to the earth to establish His earthly kingdom. This fulfills exactly the prophecy of Malachi 3:1: "And the Lord, whom ye seek, shall suddenly come to his temple." So we have answered the question of when—1844.

Now let's turn our attention to addressing who the messenger is for these last days before Jesus comes. Revelation 14 tells us who is preparing the way and the message they bring. I will comment as

---

20   The work of the judge is to deliver as explained in Psalm 76:8, 9; Judges 2:16; and 1 Samuel 24:15. Christ did this on the cross by taking our penalty for sin. In John 12:31, 32 Jesus tells us that His death on the cross already passed judgment deliverance. Therefore, we can almost always interchange these two words, for they go together. Even in the refusal of the gift, God delivers the wicked from their misery in the lake of fire. From A. T. Jones, *The Consecrated Way to Christian Perfection*, we read: "The finishing of the mystery of God is the ending of the work of the gospel. And the ending of the work of the gospel is, *first, the taking away of all vestige of sin* and the bringing in of everlasting righteousness—Christ fully formed—within each believer, God alone manifest in the flesh of each believer in Jesus, and, *secondly*, on the other hand, the work of the gospel being finished means only the destruction of all who then shall not have received the gospel (2 Thessalonians. 1:7–10), for it is not the way of the Lord to continue men in life when the only possible use they will make of life is to heap up more misery for themselves" (p. 117, emphasis original).

21   See Exodus 20:5; Exodus 34:14; Deuteronomy 4:24.

I quote the text:

> And I looked, and, lo, a Lamb [Christ is the Lamb of God, the sacrifice for the whole world] stood on the mount Sion [Mount Zion is figurative for the place where God's people dwell and can be found], and with him an hundred forty and four thousand [This number can be literal but is at least figurative. They allow God to have full control of their thoughts and decisions (12 x 12 x 1000 = 144,000)[22] and note that they stand *on* Mount Zion with Him, so they are separate from the rest of Zion.], having his *Father's name* [God's character[23]] written in their foreheads. [The frontal lobe is the seat of human decision making (the mind) and is found in that part of the brain just behind the forehead. The 144,000 allow God to control their decisions, the essence of the new covenant, which writes God's promises and His law on our minds.[24]]
>
> And I heard a voice from heaven, as the voice of many waters, and as the *voice of a great thunder* [a description of the voice of God]: and I heard the voice of harpers harping with their harps:
>
> And they sung as it were a *new song*[25] [a special experience] before the throne, and before the four beasts, and the elders: and no man could learn that song but the hundred and forty and four thousand, which were redeemed from the earth.
>
> These are they which were not defiled with women[26] [not associated with false churches or false doctrine]; for they are virgins [they have a pure faith and belief system]. These are they which follow the Lamb whithersoever he goeth. These were redeemed from among men, being the *firstfruits*[27] [Having the character of God written in their minds, they *represent* the human race redeemed.] unto God and to the Lamb.
>
> And in their mouth was found *no guile* [not even deceitfulness, nor cunningness, nor craftiness, nor duplicity; that is, straightforward and transparent]: for they are *without fault before the throne of God.*[28] (Rev. 14:1–5)

---

22 See the chapter on the Feast of unleavened Bread for a discussion on the meanings of numbers in Bible prophecy.
23 See Exodus 33:13–19; 34:4–7.
24 This is the new covenant promise of God (see Jer. 31:31–33; Ezek. 36:26–28).
25 The new song is the song of Moses and the Lamb (Rev. 15:3). We will sing about Christ, the sacrifice for the world, the promise of God, deliverance from sin, the gift of repentance, and the law and the character of God. The 144,000 are the leaders in ministering these attributes to the world.
26 A woman in Bible prophecy refers to a church (see Jer. 6:2; Isa. 54, especially verse 6).
27 See chapter 1 on the Feast of Firstfruits.
28 God's covenant promise to Abraham included being able to walk before God and be perfect (Gen. 17:1). This perfection is even that of the Father (Matt. 5:48). The 144,000 have received this in their experience because they *believe* (John 6:29).

What comes next is the message they bring:

> And I saw another angel fly in the midst of heaven, having the everlasting gospel [good news] to preach unto them that dwell on the earth, and to every nation, and kindred, and tongue, and people,
>
> Saying with a loud voice, Fear God, and give glory to him; for the *hour of his judgment is come* [God is the defendant on trial.]: and worship him that made heaven, and earth, and the sea, and the fountains of waters. [This identifies God as Creator. That is who He is. His trial, which has been going on ever since Satan sinned in heaven, is to settle for all eternity the question of who God is and what He can do in fallen sinful human flesh. Just as He created all things by the words of His mouth, so by the words of His mouth He re-creates us into a new act of creation (2 Cor. 5:17; yes, the Greek supports this rendering). Christ, as the firstfruits of the human race, has done all this and will do this in the experience of those who believe—a message of true righteousness by faith as opposed to righteousness by human acts (works). The 144,000 lead out in the reception of this gift and are at the forefront of delivering the Elijah message of repentance. They now, with and in Christ, are the firstfruits of the human race. This is the Day of Atonement—the time when humanity becomes "at-one" with God, preparing the way before Him.]
>
> And there followed another angel, saying, Babylon[29] is fallen, is fallen, that great city,[30] because she made all nations drink of the wine of the wrath of her fornication [false doctrine (particularly a false concept of righteousness by faith) and spiritual adultery—a union is made that never should happen].
>
> And the third angel followed them, saying with a loud voice, If any man worship the *beast and his image* [We will discuss the beast and his image in the next chapter.], and receive his *mark* [sign of authority] in his *forehead* [the seat of decisions], or in his *hand* [the seat of action (You don't have to actually *believe* it, just *doing* it is sufficient.)],
>
> The same shall drink of the wine of the wrath of God, which is poured out without mixture into the cup of his indignation; and he shall be tormented with fire and brimstone [the "lake of fire," the second, and eternal, death (Rev. 20:14, 15)] in the presence of the holy angels, and in the presence of the Lamb:
>
> And the smoke [Smoke is the *result* of the fire, not the fire itself.] of their torment ascendeth up for ever and ever [The result of the lake of fire is the second,

---

29 We'll discuss how to know who Babylon is in a later chapter.
30 Note the metaphor. Ancient Babylon fell when King Belshazzar took the sacredness of God (in the form of the golden vessels set aside for use only in God's temple) and treated that sacredness as common, committing blasphemy through praising the "gods" of gold, silver, brass, iron, wood, and stone (Dan. 5:4). Please note: we can do the same things. When we take the sacred things of God and treat them as common, we are in danger of identifying with modern "Babylon." More on this in the next chapter.

eternal death. Forever is only forever as long as it lasts, in this case, for all eternity, that is, *eternal* death. The fire itself will go out,[31] but the *results* will last for all eternity. There is no recovery from the second death.]: and they have *no rest day nor night* [because they refuse to rest from their own works of trying to save themselves (a result of a false concept of righteousness by faith], who worship the beast and his image [until the lake of fire finally puts them out of their misery], and whosoever receiveth the *mark* [sign of authority] of *his name* [his character]. (Rev. 14:6–11)

You don't want to receive the sign of authority of the beast power of Babylon by believing him or, even if you *don't believe* him, by doing his will through fear, because that will place you in sympathy with him. So how does one avoid following the beast? Look at the next verse! Revelation 14:12 says, "Here is the patience of the saints: here are they that *keep the commandments of God*, and the *faith of Jesus.*"

The "faith *of* Jesus" is Christ's faith. God, and God alone, through His all-powerful creative Word saves us through His promise to do so—*without* our "help." The Elijah message given by the 144,000 is nothing more and nothing less than the message of true righteousness by faith. It is a message of repentance and a turning away from the world because of a heartfelt reception of God's gift of Christ's character lived by Him in us. This righteous character becomes real in our experience, causing us to do the actual good works of God. This is what true righteousness by faith is. This, *righteousness by faith* in its true understanding, is the issue in the last days before Jesus comes, during this Day of Atonement. If you want to avoid the mark of the beast, then believe in Jesus Christ, claim His promise to you, which allows *God* to keep His laws and statutes in *you*—through *His* faith—and thus, receive God's own seal and protection (see Acts 16:31).

The message promoted by the beast power of Babylon and his image is that you can save *yourself* by *doing* what the ecclesiastical and civil leaders tell you to do, which is self-righteousness by works and filthy rags according to God (Isa. 64:6). The message promoted by God is that:

1. He has *already* (past tense) given you salvation from sin and its penalty;
2. He delivers you *now* from the power of sin in your *experience (today)* when you believe His *promise* to you (the new covenant); and
3. As you *continue* to believe, He *will* (in the future) deliver you from the presence of sin by taking you to heaven and establishing you in the earth made new.[32]

God has given you all things in Christ, and He did this before the foundation of the world. All you have to do is believe it, and His righteousness will become yours in your experience. If you reject

---

31 "For, behold, the day cometh, that shall burn as an oven; and all the *proud, yea, and all that do wickedly, shall be stubble: and the day that cometh shall burn them up*, saith the LORD of hosts, that it shall leave them neither root nor branch" (Mal. 4:1).

32 The penalty, the power, and the presence of sin represent the three basic tenses of the word deliverance and are sometimes called "the three P's."

it, you will receive the mark of the beast power of Babylon, the mark of self-righteousness and human works.

Ultimately, this final conflict settles into two major opposing conceptual ideas.

1. In one corner is righteousness by faith (salvation by God's word *only*, His promise to all humankind) as indicated for all to see by receiving God's seal;
2. And in the other corner is legalism, which is doing things for the purpose of saving *yourself*. Legalism is generally manifested by trying to do "good works," either to try to get God to change His mind about you because you think God is against you[33] or to obey human laws that go against the law of God. Either of these excuses for self-preservation is borne of unbelief and is a refusal to take God at His all-powerful word. This is indicated for all to see by receiving the beast's mark.[34]

This group of people—the 144,000—is a special group. Revelation 7 tells us more about them:

> And after these things I saw four angels standing on the four corners of the earth, holding the four winds [of strife] of the earth, that *the wind should not blow* on the earth, nor on the sea, nor on any tree. [The final time of trouble is being held back. (More on this later.)]
>
> And I saw another angel ascending from the *east* [It is said that Christ will return to earth from the east (Matt. 24:27); hence, the temple of God faces east.], having the *seal of the living God* [more on the seal later]: and he cried with a loud voice to the four angels, to whom it was given to hurt the earth and the sea,
>
> Saying, Hurt not the earth, neither the sea, nor the trees, till we have *sealed* [This is God's preserving seal of quality—a settling into truth so that they cannot be moved.] the servants of our God in their *foreheads* [the seat of decisions—each individual makes his/her own choice].
>
> And I heard the number of them which were sealed: and there were sealed an hundred and forty and four thousand of *all the tribes of the children of Israel*.[35] (Rev. 7:1–4)

In verses 5–8 all twelve tribes are listed, 12,000 from each, indicating that the 144,000 represents the whole government and priesthood of God's people, because they listen attentively to, and believe, the all-powerful, creative word of God. (See Exodus 19:5, 6, which records God's introduction of His

---

33 God has already given you eternal life, and you will experience it unless you refuse to believe (see 1 John 5:13). You really don't want Him to change His mind, do you? (Caution: do not confuse eternal life with immortality. Eternal life is now. Eternal life carries with it all the blessings and righteousness of God. Immortality comes later when Jesus comes to take His people home. Until God's people have received immortality, it is always possible for them to repudiate eternal life and throw it away.)
34 The seal and the mark are covered in the next chapter.
35 This is referring to spiritual Israel—"Israel" means "overcomer."

new covenant promise to Israel.[36])

> After this [after the sealing of the 144,000, and at the time of judgment[37]] I beheld, and, lo, a *great multitude*, which no man could number [This "great multitude" is a different group from the 144,000, since the great multitude is not associated with a number.], of all nations, and kindreds, and people, and tongues, stood *before the throne* [inside the New Jerusalem], and before *the Lamb* [Christ, the Great Sacrifice for the race], clothed with *white robes* [the righteousness of Christ (see verse 14)], and *palms* in their hands [The waving of palm branches took place during a time of celebration. The people of Israel waved palm branches during the triumphal entry of Christ into Jerusalem for His "earthly" coronation as King of the Jews.[38] The great multitude in *this* scene are preparing for the "official" coronation of Christ as King of His soon-to-be re-united universal kingdom. The palm branches represent their joint-triumph with Christ, as they are joint-heirs with Him (Rom. 8:17).];
>
> And cried with a loud voice, saying, Salvation to our God which sitteth upon the throne, and unto the *Lamb* [again, Christ, the Sacrifice for the human race].
>
> And all the angels stood round about the throne, and about the elders and the four beasts, and fell before the throne on their faces, and worshipped God,
>
> Saying, Amen: Blessing, and glory, and wisdom, and thanksgiving, and honour, and power, and might, be unto our God for ever and ever. Amen. (Rev. 7:9-12)

The description of the great multitude in verses 9–12 is a parenthetical note reminding us that there are others who are saved besides the 144,000. *All* of God's righteous people wear white robes, for

---

36 Bear in mind as you read this passage that the word "obey" in the original language means "to listen attentively" and the word "keep" in the original means "to watch, guard, or cherish." If we listen attentively, we will cherish with a heartfelt appreciation His promise to cause us to do His will, and we place ourselves in a position to receive His gift of righteousness in our experience.

37 The setting is the judgment of the wicked. It occurs on earth after the 1000 years in heaven, after the second resurrection when the New Jerusalem descends, and just before the lake of fire cleanses the old earth while the new earth is being re-created. There are a great number of people who stand with the 144,000 inside the New Jerusalem to witness the "official" coronation of Christ as King. In fact, with a few notable exceptions beyond the scope of this book, the whole human race is present. This is the only time that everyone is present all in one place at the same time. There are actually four times of "coronation" of Christ for His work that I have been able to identify, not all of which actually involve placing a crown on His head. They are as follows: 1) His coronation with the crown of thorns on the cross (His "actual" coronation), 2) His triumphal entry into Jerusalem (as the earthly King of Israel), 3) the casting of the crowns at His feet in heaven by His saints at the beginning of the 1000 years, and 4) at the close of the 1000 years when the wicked are resurrected. The last coronation is considered the "official" act, establishing Him finally and irrevocably as King of the universe.

38 A donkey ride was a customary event for the coronation ceremonies for a new king, and the people knew it—hence the palm branches (see Matt. 21). Although Christ's "actual" coronation was the cross, and His crown was a crown of thorns, indicating that Jesus took upon Himself the curse, the sins, of all humanity (see Gen. 3:17, 18), in Matthew 21 Christ established His authority over the temple of God. Regarding this event, the priests and rulers challenged Him, for they also knew the meaning of the donkey ride.

the white robes are symbolic of Christ's' righteousness. This great multitude includes those of God's people throughout the ages who died in Christ and are resurrected at His coming. The 144,000 experience the "time of trouble, such as never was since there was a nation" (Dan. 12:1) and are translated from the earth without seeing death. In Rev. 7:13, the description goes back to the 144,000:

> And one of the elders answered, saying unto me, What are these which are arrayed in white robes? and whence came they?
>
> And I said unto him, Sir, thou knowest. And he said to me, These are they which came out of great tribulation [We shall discuss the great tribulation in a later chapter.], and have *washed their robes, and made them white in the blood of the Lamb* [the righteousness of Christ has been dispensed into the experiences of God's people].
>
> Therefore are they before the throne of God, and serve him day and night in his temple: and he that sitteth on the throne shall dwell among them [because they came through the great tribulation].
>
> They shall hunger no more, neither thirst any more; neither shall the sun light on them, nor any heat. For the Lamb which is in the midst of the throne shall feed them, and shall lead them unto living fountains of waters: and God shall wipe away all tears from their eyes. (Rev. 7:13–17)

As we learned in chapter 6, the date for the beginning of the cleansing of the sanctuary was October 22, 1844. This is the precise date that Christ entered the Most Holy Place ministry in the heavenly sanctuary and began the special work of cleansing the hearts of God's people so He could stop the flow of sins into the sanctuary and come to receive His people. Because people were expecting Jesus to return to the earth on October 22, 1844, His entrance into the Most Holy place of the heavenly sanctuary was unexpected and, therefore, sudden (Mal. 3:1). Malachi 3 is a prophecy of the Feast of the Day of Atonement, and it tells us what this feast is all about and what is happening. God's people should allow God to brace them spiritually, intellectually, emotionally, and physically[39] for the work God is doing and will be doing in them as He uses them to "prepare the way before" Him (Mal. 3:1). He will have a people who will be a "sermon in shoes." They will *live* the Elijah message, for, in addition to the life Christ lives in them, they will have a global Mount Carmel experience in which Satan will try to duplicate God's response by calling fire down from heaven (1 Kings 18; Rev. 13:13). Fasten your seat belts, for we are in for quite a ride. It is a time of decision for the world.

From Alonzo T. Jones, *The Consecrated Way to Christian Perfection*, we read:

> The service in the earthly sanctuary shows also that in order for the sanctuary to be cleansed and the course of the gospel service there to be finished, it must first be

---

[39] Health and dress reform.

finished *in the people* who have a part in the service. That is to say: In the sanctuary itself, transgression could not be finished, an end of sins and reconciliation for iniquity could not be made, and everlasting righteousness could not be brought in, until all this had been accomplished *in each person* who had a part in the service of the sanctuary. The sanctuary itself could not be cleansed until each of the worshipers had been cleansed. The sanctuary itself could not be cleansed so long as, *by the confessions of the people and the intercessions of the priests*, there was pouring into the sanctuary a stream of iniquities, transgression, and sins. The cleansing of the sanctuary, *as to the sanctuary itself*, was the taking out of and away from the sanctuary all the transgressions of the people which, by the service of the priests, had been taken into the sanctuary during the service of the year. And this stream must be stopped at its fountain in the hearts and lives of the worshipers, before the sanctuary itself could possibly be cleansed.

Therefore the very first work in the cleansing of the sanctuary was the cleansing of the people. That which was preliminary and essential to the cleansing of the sanctuary itself, to the finishing of the transgression and bringing in everlasting righteousness, there, was the finishing of transgression, and the making an end of sins, and making reconciliation for iniquity, and bringing in everlasting righteousness *in the heart and life of each one of the people* themselves. When the stream that flowed into the sanctuary was thus stopped at its source, then, and then alone, could the sanctuary itself be cleansed from the sins and transgression which, *from the people, by the intercession of the priests*, had flowed into the sanctuary.

And all that "was a figure for the time then present"—a "figure of the true." Therefore by this we are plainly taught that the service of our great High Priest in the cleansing of the true sanctuary must be preceded by the cleansing of each one of the believers, the cleansing of each one who has a part in that service of the true High Priest in the true sanctuary. It is plain that transgression must be finished, an end of sins and reconciliation for all iniquity must be made, and everlasting righteousness must be brought in, in the heart's experience of every believer in Jesus, before the cleansing of the true sanctuary can be accomplished.

And this is the very object of the true priesthood in the true sanctuary. The sacrifices, the priesthood, and the ministry in the sanctuary which was but a figure for the time then present, could not really take away sin, could not make the comers thereunto perfect. Whereas the sacrifice, the priesthood, and the ministry of Christ in the true sanctuary does take away sins forever, does make the comers thereunto *perfect, does perfect "forever* them that are sanctified." (pp. 117–119, emphasis original)

So the message that "prepares the way before me" (Mal. 3:1) must at a minimum include the cleansing and purification of the hearts of God's people.

Prior to 1844, God's ministry to the people, besides the normal round of daily ministry pertaining to everyday life, was to prepare them for their eventual (and inevitable) death. The ministry since 1844, besides the normal round of daily ministry pertaining to everyday life and, also, to prepare them for their eventual (but *no longer* inevitable) death, is a ministry to prepare the world for Christ's second coming. When He comes, He will put away sin forever and set up His temporal kingdom on earth. Therefore, the ministry since 1844 has been one of preparing a people to be translated without seeing death. This reform in the gospel message and corporate repentance on the part of God's people must be completed before Christ can come, for this would answer the charge of the plaintiff in God's trial—"it is impossible to keep God's law."

For many centuries there was no imminent need to emphasize the coming of Christ and His eternal kingdom, nor the corporate[40] purification from sin. Therefore, some of the gospel message had been allowed to take a back seat and had become stagnated from disuse. In the nineteenth century it was a new thought and new concept to many.

Ellen White wrote, "Great truths that have lain unheeded and unseen since the day of Pentecost, are to shine from God's word in their native purity."[41]

To re-introduce old doctrines dating back to the writings of Paul and the time of Pentecost, God raised up two men for this purpose. Their names were Alonzo Trévier Jones and Ellet Joseph Waggoner. Listen to what a contemporary has to say about these men:

> The Lord in His great mercy sent a most precious message to His people through Elders Waggoner and Jones. This message was to bring more prominently before the world the uplifted Saviour, the sacrifice for the sins of the whole world. It presented justification through faith in the Surety; it invited the people to receive the righteousness of Christ, which is made manifest in obedience to all the commandments of God. Many had lost sight of Jesus. They needed to have their eyes directed to His divine person, His merits, and His changeless love for the human family. All power is given into His hands, that He may dispense rich gifts unto men, imparting the priceless gift of His own righteousness to the helpless human agent. This is the message that God commanded to be given to the world. It is the third angel's message, which is to be proclaimed with a loud voice, and attended with the outpouring of His Spirit in a large measure.[42]

---

40 Individually there was always emphasis on purification from sin, but since 1844 God has sought to purify His people as a group, to make up His 144,000.
41 *Fundamentals of Christian Education* (Nashville, TN: Southern Publishing Association, 1923, p. 473).
42 Ellen G. White, *Testimonies to Ministers and Gospel Workers*, pp. 91, 92.

> This is the very work which the Lord designs that the message He has given His servants shall perform in the heart and mind of every human agent.... God gave to His messengers just what the people needed. Those who received the message were greatly blessed, for they saw the bright rays of the Sun of Righteousness, and life and hope sprang up in their hearts. They were beholding Christ.... The Lord would have these grand themes studied in our churches.[43]

I have heard it said that "no matter what you do there is always somebody who doesn't like it" and these new thoughts of this message did not come without their share of opposition. Those in leadership positions opposed it because it threatened the status quo. Jesus states the condition of the situation as follows:

> And as Moses lifted up the serpent in the wilderness, even so must the Son of man be lifted up: That whosoever believeth in him should not perish, but have eternal life. For God so loved the world, that he gave his only begotten Son, that whosoever believeth in him should not perish, but have everlasting life. For God sent not his Son into the world to condemn the world; but that the world through him might be saved. He that believeth on him is not condemned: but he that believeth not is condemned already, because he hath not believed in the name of the only begotten Son of God. And this is the condemnation, that light is come into the world, and men loved darkness rather than light, because their deeds were evil. For every one that doeth evil hateth the light, neither cometh to the light, lest his deeds should be reproved. But he that doeth truth cometh to the light, that his deeds may be made manifest, that they are wrought in God. (John 3:14–21)

It is the purpose of this book to bring truth to light. When God comes to a person and presents him with truth, it is to bring righteousness to that person and cleanse him from sin. There is something in his life that is hurting him, and God wants to change it or remove it altogether.

As we have already mentioned, God is the ultimate Gentleman. He will not *force* obedience. If a person does not want to change, God backs off and maybe tries again later, perhaps from another perspective. Should this person continue to reject the work of God in his life, he places himself under his own condemnation through the choices he makes. I pray that *you* will not hesitate to allow God to make these changes in and for you. Unfortunately, there are some who did not allow God this privilege:

> An unwillingness to yield up preconceived opinions, and to accept this truth, lay at the foundation of a large share of the opposition manifested at Minneapolis[44] against

---

43   Ibid., pp. 95, 96.
44   Minneapolis was the site of the General Conference session in 1888.

the Lord's message through Brethren [E.J.] Waggoner and [A.T.] Jones. By exciting that opposition Satan succeeded in shutting away from our people, in a great measure, the special power of the Holy Spirit that God longed to impart to them. The enemy prevented them from obtaining that efficiency which might have been theirs in carrying the truth to the world, as the apostles proclaimed it after the day of Pentecost [reference to the *former* rain of the Holy Spirit, specifically, the efficiency of it]. The light that is to lighten the whole earth with its glory [a reference to the *latter* rain of the Holy Spirit (Rev. 18)] was resisted, and by the action of our own brethren has been in a great degree kept away from the world.[45]

That was the situation in 1888. There are some today who will tell you that the message has been accepted and we are now over that hump and are moving forward. However, the greatest argument against all this is the fact that we are still here on this earth. The efficiency to carry the gospel truth to the whole world is not yet manifest, even with all our modern technology. At the time of Pentecost, under the full manifestation of the *former* rain, the gospel went forth with speed. During the last days before Christ comes, the gospel, under the full manifestation of the *latter* rain, will go forth with *lightning* speed (Ezek. 1:8, 14).[46] But, sadly, it has been more than 120 years since 1888—the gospel is stagnated—and Christ has yet to come.

It is my prayer that soon the condition of things will change and that God will have His day in court. This means that His witnesses will be ready to testify on His behalf through their lives, that is, through their actions, their lifestyle, and their words. They can do this because they have allowed Him to have full control of their thoughts and have not hesitated to allow Him to make the necessary changes in their lives.

"Only those who, in their attitude before God, are filling the position of those who are repenting and confessing their sins in the great anti-typical day of atonement, will be recognized and marked as worthy of God's protection. The names of those who are steadfastly looking and waiting and watching for the appearing of their Saviour—more earnestly and wishfully than they who wait for the morning—will be numbered with those who are sealed."[47]

How is it with you, dear reader? Will you allow God to make the necessary changes in *your* life? Remember how we started this chapter:

Behold, I will send my *messenger*, and he shall *prepare the way before me*: and the Lord, whom ye seek, shall suddenly come to his temple, even the *messenger of the covenant*, whom ye delight in: behold, he shall come, saith the Lord of hosts.

---

45 Ellen G. White, *Selected Messages*, book 1, pp. 234, 235.
46 Ellen G. White, *Testimonies for the Church*, vol. 5, p. 754.
47 Ellen G. White, *Testimonies to Ministers and Gospel Workers*, p. 445.

> But who may *abide* the day of his coming? [i.e., not resist it[48]] and who shall stand when he appeareth? for he is like a refiner's *fire*, and like *fullers' soap*:
>
> And he shall sit as a *refiner and purifier* of silver: and he shall *purify the sons of Levi*, and *purge them as gold and silver*, that they may offer unto the Lord an *offering in righteousness*.
>
> Then shall the offering of Judah and Jerusalem be pleasant unto the Lord, as in the *days of old*, and as *in former years*.
>
> And I will *come near to you to judgment*; and I will be a swift witness against the sorcerers, and against the adulterers, and against false swearers, and against those that oppress the hireling in his wages, the widow, and the fatherless, and that turn aside the stranger from his right, and fear not me, saith the Lord of hosts.
>
> For I am the Lord, I change not; therefore ye sons of Jacob are not consumed.

This explains why the gospel of today is a message of refinement, purification, repentance, and reform.

This also explains why, in these last days, for those participating in preparing the way before the King that there is a reform in health (including diet) and also in dress.

In the next chapter, we will discuss the fourth reform, a reform in "rest." The final issue in the history of the world is what true righteousness by faith really is—and it is all wrapped up in the idea of "rest."

---

48   See John 15:1–9.

Chapter 14

Feast of the Day of Atonement: A Call to Rest

Hebrews 4:8–11 introduces the topic of Sabbath rest, which we will be discussing in this chapter. "For if Jesus [Joshua][1] had given them rest, then would he not afterward have spoken of another day. There remaineth therefore a rest [Sabbath observance] to the people of God. For he that is entered into his rest, he also hath ceased from his own works, as God did from his. Let us labour therefore to enter into that rest, lest any man fall after the same example of unbelief."

Prior to 1844, God's ministry to the people, besides the normal round of daily ministry pertaining to everyday life (corresponding to the *first* apartment ministry in the heavenly sanctuary), was to prepare them for their eventual, and inevitable, death. The ministry since 1844, besides the normal round of daily ministry pertaining to everyday life, is a ministry to prepare the world for the second coming of Christ, at which time He will banish sin forever and set up His temporal kingdom on earth. All this relates to the *second* apartment ministry in the heavenly sanctuary. This reform in the gospel message and corporate repentance purification on the part of God's people must be completed before Christ can come, for this will answer the charge of the plaintiff in God's trial that "it is impossible to keep God's law." This also explains why, in these last days, there are reforms in health and dress for those participating in preparing the way before the King. In this chapter, we will discuss the fourth reform, a reform in "rest." The final issue in the history of the world is what true righteousness by faith really is—a *resting* in the work of God.

> And the Lord[2] spake unto Moses, saying, Also on the tenth day of this seventh month there shall be a day of atonement: it shall be an *holy convocation* unto you [washing clothes and dress reform]; and ye shall *afflict your souls* [fasting and health reform], and offer an *offering made by fire* [gospel reform and corporate repentance, a heart purification] unto the Lord. And ye shall do *no work* in that same day: for it is a day of atonement, to make an atonement for you before the Lord your God. For whatsoever soul it be that shall not be *afflicted* in that same day, he shall be *cut*

---

[1] "Jesus" is the Greek form of "Yeshua" or "Joshua."
[2] This is the Hebrew word for Jehovah (displayed in the KJV in small caps). The root meaning of the word is "to be" or "to exist" as in Exodus 3:14: "I Am That I Am," as if to say, "I ever shall be the same that I am today." Christ uses this thought to refer to Himself as the self-existent one in John 8:58: "Before Abraham was, I am." It is the name given to the second person of the Godhead—Jesus Christ. (See Appendix K.)

off from among his people. [If you refuse health reform, you will not participate in preparing the way before the King.] And whatsoever soul it be that doeth any *work* in that same day, the same soul will I *destroy* from among his people. [If you refuse this reform in *rest*—well, the stakes are higher.³] Ye shall do *no manner of work*: it shall be a statute for ever throughout your generations in all your dwellings. It shall be unto you a *sabbath of rest*, and ye shall afflict your souls: in the ninth day of the month at even, from even [sunset] unto even, shall ye celebrate [observe] your sabbath. (Lev. 23:26–32)

There are four verses relating to rest, representing 57 percent of the total number of verses pertaining to the Day of Atonement. That should tell us of the importance God places on this concept of rest. Note the difference in the language between "cut off" (verse 29) and "destroy" (verse 30, more on this later).

Related to this concept of Sabbath, which means rest, is the concept of the sealing of the 144,000. Let's revisit the 144,000 for a moment:

And after these things I saw four angels standing on the four corners of the earth, holding the four winds of the earth, that the wind should not blow on the earth, nor on the sea, nor on any tree. And I saw another angel ascending from the east, having the *seal* of the living God: and he cried with a loud voice to the four angels, to whom it was given to hurt the earth and the sea, Saying, Hurt not the earth, neither the sea, nor the trees, till we have sealed the servants of our God in their foreheads. And I heard the number of them which were sealed: and there were sealed an hundred and forty and four thousand of all the tribes of the children of Israel. (Rev. 7:1–4)

What is a seal? This must be important because the four angels holding the four winds that hurt the earth, the sea, and the trees are waiting for this sealing process to be completed. In Bible prophecy the sea represents a populated area, the earth represents an unpopulated area, the trees represent leadership, and the grass represents the average person.⁴ These four winds that hurt the earth and the sea (in both heavily populated and sparsely populated areas) represent the four winds of strife, the strife that comes upon the world in the last days. These four winds represent the final time of trouble, which

---

3   Exodus 31:14, 15, says, "Ye shall keep the sabbath therefore; for it is holy unto you: every one that defileth it shall surely be put to *death* [In Israel's day this would have represented both the first and the second deaths. In today's environment, this would represent at least the second death.]: for whosoever doeth any work therein, that soul shall be *cut off* from among his people. [Neither will you participate in preparing the way before the King.] Six days may work be done; but in the seventh is the sabbath of rest, holy to the Lord: whosoever doeth any work in the sabbath day, he shall surely be put to death." Exodus 35:2 reiterates the Sabbath rest: "Six days shall work be done, but on the seventh day there shall be to you an holy day, a sabbath of rest to the Lord: whosoever doeth work therein shall be put to death."

4   See Revelation 13:11; 17:1; Isaiah 10:22; 17:12, 13; 40:7; Micah 5:7; Hosea 1:10; and Psalm 1.

is the great tribulation. This time of trouble will not come until after God's people have been sealed, so this sealing must be important. Such a sealing has Passover implications (regarding the time of trouble and the seven last plagues[5]) when the Israelites sealed their doorposts with the blood of the lamb (representing Christ) and were protected from the angel of death.[6] Note that God's people are sealed in their *foreheads*, representing the frontal lobe—the seat of decision making. It's a matter of what one chooses to believe.

A seal, among other things, is a symbol or mark of office. Such a seal has three basic parts:
1. The name of the official
2. The title
3. The jurisdiction of authority

For example:
1. Abraham Lincoln, President, United States of America
2. John Smith, Notary Public, State of Florida

Well, God has a seal too:
1. Jehovah, Creator, Everything in the Universe

This seal is found in the fourth commandment in Exodus 20—the heart of the Ten Commandments:

> Remember the sabbath day, to keep it holy. Six days shalt thou labour, and do all thy work: But the seventh day is the sabbath of the LORD [Jehovah] thy God: in it thou shalt not do any work, thou, nor thy son, nor thy daughter, thy manservant, nor thy maidservant, nor thy cattle, nor thy stranger that is within thy gates: For in six days *the LORD* [1-Jehovah, His name] *made* [2-Creator, His title] *heaven and earth, the sea, and all that in them is* [3-The whole universe, His jurisdiction], and rested the seventh day: wherefore the LORD blessed the sabbath day, and hallowed it. (Exod. 20:8–11)

Verse 11 verifies the seal of God: "The LORD [Name: Jehovah] made [Title: Creator] heaven and earth, the sea, and all that in them is [His jurisdiction of authority: all things]." *This is His seal. This is who He is.*

The Sabbath and what it represents is actually the focus of Satan's charge against God. He claims that God's law is unfair because it is impossible to keep. Since the law of God is really the transcript of His character (the written description of who He is), the Sabbath focuses on the very essence of God in His trial against Satan. And when God's people are sealed, this is what they receive in their foreheads. By their own decision and choice, for they are not forced to do anything they don't believe, they receive His mark, His flag or standard, of who He is—the Sabbath. The work of God's people in the last days

---

5 See Revelation 16. The subject of the seven last plagues is beyond the scope of this book, so we will not attempt a detailed comprehensive presentation of them right now.

6 Exodus 11 and 12.

is to take the "witness stand" and testify of who He is and what He can do in fallen sinful human flesh, including our own. The Sabbath is a day of rest because we rest in the work of *God*, as Genesis shows us, forsaking our *own* works, our *own* attempts to keep God's law:

> And God saw every thing that he had made, and, behold, it was very good. And the evening and the morning were the sixth day. Thus the heavens and the earth were finished, and all the host of them. And on the seventh day God ended his work which he had made; and he *rested on the seventh day* from all his work which he had made. And God *blessed* the seventh day, and *sanctified* it:[7] because that in it he had rested from all his work which God created and made. (Gen. 1:31–2:3)

Thus God finished His act of creation. Similarly, when God works on *us*, it is another "act of creation" (see 2 Cor. 5:17; Gal. 6:15—the Greek rendering for "new creature" is "act of creation"). Note the language in the following texts that indicates that God's Sabbath seal is used as a sign.[8] The two words are synonyms. God's Sabbath seal is the sign of who God is and who God's people are. Furthermore, the seal is a sign that God's people belong to Him and are set apart for holy use.

> Nevertheless the foundation of God standeth sure, having this *seal* [sign], The Lord knoweth them that are his. And, let every one that nameth the name of Christ depart from iniquity. (2 Tim. 2:19)

> Moreover also I gave them my sabbaths, to be a *sign* [seal] between me and them, that they might know that I am the Lord that sanctify them. (Ezek. 20:12)

> And hallow my sabbaths; and they shall be a *sign* between me and you, that ye may know that I am the Lord your God. (Ezek. 20:20)

> Speak thou also unto the children of Israel, saying, Verily my sabbaths ye shall keep: for it is a *sign* between me and you throughout your generations; that ye may know that I am the Lord that doth sanctify you. (Exod. 31:13)

> It is a *sign* between me and the children of Israel for ever: for in six days the Lord made heaven and earth, and on the seventh day he rested, and was refreshed. (Exod. 31:17)

---

7   To "sanctify" means to be set apart for holy use.
8   "And he received the *sign* of circumcision, a *seal* of the righteousness of the faith which he had yet being uncircumcised: that he might be the father of all them that believe, though they be not circumcised; that righteousness might be imputed unto them also" (Rom. 4:11).

Notice that this is a loyalty issue. It is a sign of God's authority over the individual and over all humanity. God's right to rule is placed in the fourth commandment, and this seal will be placed in the foreheads of those who know God.

This is what the Day of Atonement, the holy convocation, is all about. Remember, God is on trial! He is answering Satan's charges against Him through His people.

> Bring forth the blind people that have eyes, and the deaf that have ears.[9] Let all the nations be gathered together, and let the people be assembled: who among them can declare this, and shew us former things? let them bring forth their witnesses, that they may be justified: or let them hear, and say, It is truth. Ye are my witnesses, saith the LORD, and my servant whom I have chosen: that ye may know and believe me, and understand that I am he: before me there was no God formed, neither shall there be after me. I, even I, am the LORD; and beside me there is no saviour. I have declared, and have saved, and I have shewed, when there was no strange god among you: therefore ye are my witnesses, saith the LORD, that I am God. [Notice that the issue in God's trial is who God is.] Yea, before the day was I am he; and there is none that can deliver out of my hand: I will work, and who shall *let* [Hebrew: change, bring back, reverse] it? Thus saith the LORD, your redeemer, the Holy One of Israel; For your sake I have sent to Babylon, and have brought down all their nobles, and the Chaldeans, whose cry is in the ships. I am the LORD, your Holy One, the creator of Israel, your King. (Isa. 43:8–15)

> And I saw another angel fly in the midst of heaven, having the everlasting gospel to preach unto them that dwell on the earth, and to every nation, and kindred, and tongue, and people, Saying with a loud voice, Fear *God* [1-Jehovah, His name], and give glory to him; for the hour of *his judgment* [God's trial] is come: and worship him that *made* [2-Creator, His title] *heaven, and earth, and the sea, and the fountains of waters* [3-The whole universe, His jurisdiction]. (Rev. 14:6, 7)

This is who He is—His *seal* in the book of Revelation indicates that Jehovah is the Creator of the universe, and everything is under his authority.

God's trial in the last days is all about who He is and what He can do in fallen, sinful human flesh. And the 144,000 are His witnesses! God introduces them just *before* the announcement of God's trial (see Rev. 14:1–5).

On the other side of the coin, God's seal has an antithesis—the mark of the beast. This mark is ultimately for those who throw off the rule of God in their lives.

---

9 Selective sight and selective hearing—they hear and see very well, but they choose not to.

> And there followed another angel, saying, Babylon is fallen, is fallen, that great city, because she made all nations drink of the wine of the wrath of her fornication [This stands for false doctrine and spiritual adultery, the latter representing a union that never should happen. Babylon is considered the northern king because the king of Babylon was the king who attacked Israel from the north. This "king" being from the north would have additional significance because God's throne is considered to dwell in the "north."[10] In other words, this king will claim to sit on the seat of God.[11]]
>
> And the third angel followed them, saying with a loud voice, If any man worship the *beast and his image*, and receive his *mark* [sign of authority] in his *forehead* [the seat of decisions], or in his *hand* [the seat of action; you don't have to actually *believe* it, just *doing* it would be sufficient], The same shall drink of the wine of the wrath of God, which is poured out without mixture into the cup of his indignation; and he shall be *tormented with fire and brimstone* [the "lake of fire" (Rev. 20:14, 15), which completes the second, and eternal, death] in the presence of the holy angels, and in the presence of the Lamb. (Rev. 14:8–10)

See Revelation 13 for a description of the two political, ecclesiastical, and/or ideological powers (beasts), which shows that the second beast power sets up an image to the first beast power. An image is something set up that looks (and/or acts) like the original, a visible (and/or tangible) representation. In this case political authority will be used to enforce worship of a false god in the form of the first beast—effectively the union of church and state, a type of fornication, for this union should never take place. To receive or worship the image of the beast is to allow state political authority to dictate who or what you worship.

> And the *smoke*[12] [results, that being the second death] of their *torment* [failed attempts to save themselves—no rest, but "endless" works] ascendeth up *for ever and ever* [Forever is only for as long as it lasts, which in this case is for all eternity, that is, *eternal* death. The fire itself will go out,[13] but the *results* will last for all eternity. There

---

10   "For thou [Lucifer] hast said in thine heart, I will ascend into heaven, I will exalt my throne above the stars of God: I will sit also upon the mount of the congregation, in the sides of the *north*" (Isa. 14:13). "Beautiful for situation, the joy of the whole earth, is mount Zion, on the sides of the *north*, the city of the great King" (Ps. 48:2).

11   By contrast, the southern king to Israel would be Egypt, which boasted an atheistic viewpoint, as evident by the king of Egypt asking, "Who is the LORD?" (Exod. 5:2). These "kings" are not literal places today (Babylon no longer exists, and Egypt is primarily Muslim), but they represent two opposing *ideologies*. One claims to sit on God's throne, and the other claims that God does not exist and need not be reckoned with. Neither of the northern or southern "kings" is correct in their ideologies, and both have a disdain for God and His people. Please note that in Daniel 11 there is a description of a battle between the "king of the south" and the "king of the north." *These* "kings" are a separate subject altogether and are for another time and another book.

12   Smoke is the result of the fire, not the fire itself.

13   "For, behold, the day cometh, that shall burn as an oven; and all the proud, yea, and all that do wickedly, shall be stubble: and the day that cometh shall burn them up, saith the LORD of hosts, that it shall leave them neither root nor branch" (Mal. 4:1).

is no recovery from the second death.]: and they have *no rest day nor night* [because they refuse to rest from their own works of trying to save themselves (until the lake of fire finally puts them out of their misery)[14]], who worship the beast and his image, and whosoever receiveth the *mark of his name* [the sign of the authority and character, respectively, of the northern king]. Here is the patience of the saints: here are they that keep [cherish] the commandments of God [all ten of them], and [cherish] the faith of Jesus. (Rev. 14:11, 12)

The "faith *of* Jesus" is Christ's faith. God, and God alone, through His all-powerful creative Word *only*, saves us. He does not save us with our "help." The Elijah message given by the 144,000 is nothing more or less than the message of true righteousness by faith, a heartfelt repentance. This is the issue in the last days before Jesus comes. This is the antitypical fulfillment of the Day of Atonement.

So, true righteousness by faith, a heartfelt repentance, is the *foundational issue* in the last days before Jesus comes.

Now you know the antitypical fulfillment of the Day of Atonement. All four parts of this day point to one thing—God's people will be at *one* with Him, and God *Himself* will make that happen with their permission. Will you give Him permission to make that happen in you?

The seal of God (i.e., God's holy Sabbath) represents righteousness by the faith of Jesus through His all-powerful inherently creative word spoken to all people and received into the experience of those who appreciate the gift and the price paid for it. Assuming this is true, it is only logical that the mark of the beast must, therefore, represent a false "sabbath" of some sort, which would actually be humanity's substitute for God's word, an attempt to save oneself apart from God's plan, which is a form of legalism.

In one corner we have God's Sabbath seal, representing His creative power—His word that has inherent within it the power to create what it says—creating all things, including righteousness (actual acts of good works) in the believer of the true God (a true and mature understanding of Him), a sign of Jehovah's authority. And in the other corner, we have the mark of the beast, which represents a false "sabbath" idea based on a person's attempt to save oneself through performing acts of self-righteousness, either through fear of punishment or hope of reward, a sign of the beast power's authority. The mark of the beast will be enforced by civil authority—the "image to the beast"—the union of church and state.

If this is true, then we have a face-off of epic proportions, for it is the final showdown before the end of the world and Christ's second coming, which will usher in the millennium and establish His eternal kingdom. This showdown will answer the questions of who God is and "what He can do in fallen sinful human flesh." We must pay attention if we want to be on the right side. The seriousness of this issue raises two equally serious questions. First, how can we know the difference between the

---

14 This torment of endless attempts at self-righteousness and self-salvation can only result in misery. God, in His mercy, does not even allow sinners to be tormented unmercifully for eternity, but allows the lake of fire to relieve them of their own self-inflicted torture.

two sides and which side we are on, and second, when and in what manner does this marking/sealing take place?

Let's answer the second question first. When and in what manner does this marking/sealing take place? With the Sabbath issue clearly set before us and the consequences clearly understood,[15] whoever shall trample upon God's law in order to obey a human enactment receives the mark of the beast,[16] for they have chosen to give their allegiance to a power of another instead of God. On the other side of the coin, especially while facing civil penalties for doing so, whoever chooses God's Sabbath sign of His authority receives the seal of God. At the point a person chooses to follow truth or error, God or Satan, and cannot possibly change one's mind, he or she is sealed, or "marked."

While we know that those who have died are sealed in their decision, those of us who are still alive do not know when, nor whether, our sealing has taken place because only God knows the heart well enough to know whether we have "settled" in our mind where we stand. We don't even know our *own* hearts that well (Jer. 17:9).[17] So, although we can know the circumstances under which this decision is made in individual hearts (even in our own), God will not allow us to know the fact and finality of our own sealing, for we really do not need to know, do we? Think about it. If we make the right decision against the pressure of civil enforcement and know we are sealed so that we could not be moved from the truth, we might become complacent and lax in our prayer life, thus losing our saltiness. It is an oxymoron, for we would be in danger of forfeiting the sealing, meaning we never were really "sealed" in the first place. It is better that we do not know. It eliminates confusion.

The first question, how can we know the *true* Sabbath from a *false* "sabbath," is of significantly greater importance, although just as serious, for we can know the answer for ourselves, and it affects our eternal destiny. Actually, it is not as hard as it might appear. To detect a counterfeit one must be intimately connected with the truth and know it inside and out. There are many ways to make a counterfeit, for the possibilities of minor imperfections are endless. But if we know the true specimen well, all counterfeits will be clearly spotted. If we know the true Sabbath of God, we will be able to identify all counterfeit false "sabbaths."

With this in mind, let's look again at the Sabbath commandment. God has made it easy to tell His Sabbath, for He selected a specific day of the week. What *day* is the Sabbath? The Bible tells us the day in the fourth commandment: "*Remember the sabbath day, to keep it holy. Six days shalt thou labour, and do all thy work:* But the *seventh day* is the sabbath of the LORD thy God: *in it thou shalt not do any work,* thou, nor thy son, nor thy daughter, thy manservant, nor thy maidservant, nor thy cattle, nor thy

---

15 Such consequences can be as simple as civil penalties enforced by the government promoting a false "sabbath" (Rev. 13:7) versus eternal penalties for purposely setting aside any part of God's Ten Commandments. This is where fear of punishment and hope of reward steps in.

16 Note: a person can keep *both* "sabbaths" without trampling upon God's law. It is never a sin to worship God on any (or every) day of the week. It is only when one knowingly is breaking God's true Sabbath and at the same time is keeping a human enactment, enforcing the false "sabbath" that the mark of the beast is applied. The next chapter will discuss the situation when a human law specifically forbids worship on God's true Sabbath.

17 It can help somewhat, however, to ask ourselves these questions while looking into a mirror. It will cause us to think.

stranger that is within thy gates: For in six days the Lord made heaven and earth, the sea, and all that in them is, and rested the seventh day: wherefore the Lord blessed the sabbath day, and hallowed it" (Exod. 20:8–11).

So the seventh day of the week is the Sabbath. We know it has to do with the weekly cycle because the other six days are clearly implicated. So what day is the seventh day of the week? If you look at most calendars, the seventh day would be Saturday. Is Saturday God's Sabbath? If Saturday is the Sabbath, then any of the other six days of the week would *not* be God's Sabbath. That's easy, isn't it?

Or is it? Hasn't the calendar been changed? Maybe the weekly cycle has changed. Maybe we missed a day sometime over the centuries. Why would it matter, anyway? After all, what is in a day? Isn't one set of 24 hours just like every other?

If you don't think it matters, think about this. Isn't one baby just like another? I mean, they all have one head, two arms, two legs, two ears, two eyes, one nose, a mouth, ten fingers, ten toes, and they all cry. What if the nurses at the hospital confused your child with another one and brought you a different baby since they all look alike with the same blankets and hospital caps? They're all the same, aren't they? I'm sure you are saying, "Of course not! Each child is different and special to their parents."

How about celebrations and events? What if your husband or wife forgot your anniversary or another special day? How would your child feel if you forgot to attend their piano recital, but instead showed up at the concert hall two days later?

Let's return to the question of the Sabbath. Does it matter to God what day of the week we worship on or how we keep the day? If we are particular about people and special events, don't you think the King of the universe has an opinion about the rest day He hallowed at the end of Creation? Let's spend a few minutes looking at the Sabbath from God's perspective. How does God feel about this? There is a passage in the book of Jeremiah that sheds some light on the way the Lord feels about the Sabbath.

"Thus said the Lord unto me; Go and stand in the gate of the children of the people, whereby the kings of Judah come in, and by the which they go out, and in all the gates of Jerusalem; And say unto them, Hear ye the word of the Lord, ye kings of Judah, and all Judah, and all the inhabitants of Jerusalem, that enter in by these gates: Thus saith the Lord; Take heed to yourselves, and bear no burden on the sabbath day, nor bring it in by the gates of Jerusalem; Neither carry forth a burden out of your houses on the sabbath day, neither do ye any work, but hallow ye the sabbath day, as I commanded your fathers" (Jer. 17:19–22).

Now let's examine Isaiah 58:13, 14: "If thou turn away thy foot from the sabbath [stop treading on it], from doing *thy* pleasure [activities[18]] on my holy day; and call the sabbath a delight, the holy of the Lord, honourable; and shalt honour him, not doing thine *own* ways, nor finding thine *own* pleasure [activities], nor speaking thine *own* words: Then shalt thou *delight thyself in the Lord;* and I will *cause* thee to ride upon the high places of the earth, and feed thee with the heritage of Jacob thy father: *for the mouth of the Lord hath spoken it.*"

---

18 In the original, the word means pursuit or ardour (as in affair or matter), hence activities. For God's people the Sabbath is very pleasurable.

Please notice the language in verse 13. God calls it *His* holy day. It is *His* day. It belongs to *Him*. And in verse 14, note the power of His *word*.

What does Jesus think about this? Let's turn to Mark 2:27, 28: "And he said unto them, The sabbath was made for man, and not man for the sabbath: Therefore the Son of man is Lord also of the sabbath." And Matthew 12:8 says the same thing: "For the Son of man is Lord even of the sabbath day."

So Jesus says that He is Lord of this day. This means that He is in charge of this day. It is *His* day. It belongs to *Him*—it is the "Lord's day."

And He set the example; He observed it Himself. "And he came to Nazareth, where he had been brought up: and, as his *custom* was, he went into the synagogue on the sabbath day, and stood up for to read" (Luke 4:16).

We have already established that the Lord's day has to be the seventh day of the week, but if you turn to Genesis 1, you will find something very interesting regarding how God measures time.

> And God called the light Day, and the darkness he called Night. And the evening and the morning were the first day. (Gen. 1:5)
>
> And God called the firmament Heaven. And the evening and the morning were the second day. (verse 8)
>
> And the evening and the morning were the third day. (verse 13)
>
> And the evening and the morning were the fourth day. (verse 19)
>
> And the evening and the morning were the fifth day. (verse 23)
>
> And God saw every thing that he had made, and, behold, it was very good. And the evening and the morning were the sixth day. (verse 31)

Do you see a pattern? How does God render His days? The answer is clear from Creation that the day begins with the evening first and then the morning. This corresponds with sunset and dawn. The sunset comes in the evening and the dawn comes in the morning. Each day on our calendar, according to the reckoning of the Lord, begins and ends at sunset.

It is only by custom that today we reckon a day from midnight to midnight. For business purposes, it is a matter of convenience. And that's OK for business. But let's think about God's Sabbath for a minute. If God wants us to *remember* this day, which He says He does in the fourth commandment, then doesn't it make sense to begin the day at a time when we are awake to enjoy the entrance of it, and also end it at a time when we can easily mark the conclusion of it? Sunset gives us a clear distinction of time so that we can appreciate the beginning and ending of Sabbath. If Sabbath were to be from midnight to midnight, it would enter and depart at a time when most of us are unconscious. We would not even be aware that anything special was happening, and the day itself would be fuzzy for we would effectively begin the Sabbath when we would wake up in the morning and end it when we would go to sleep at night. We would miss its specialness.

Leviticus 23:32 also documents the beginning and ending of Sabbath: "From even unto even, shall ye celebrate [observe] your sabbath."

The gorgeous sunset punctuates the Sabbath. What better way could there possibly be to usher in God's special day than by a beautiful sunset! God knew what He was doing when He completed His work of creating the world and made a day of rest. "Thus the heavens and the earth were finished, and all the host of them. And on the *seventh day* God ended his work which he had made; and he *rested* on the seventh day from all his work which he had made. And God *blessed* the seventh day, and *sanctified* it [set it apart for holy use]: because that in it he had rested from all his work which God created and made" (Gen. 2:1–3).

The seventh day of the week is Saturday. And most calendars show it that way. Most calendars show that the week begins with Sunday and ends with Saturday, the seventh day. Of course, there are a few calendars that begin the week with Monday and end with Sunday. I have a pocket calendar that has one page for each week, and once again, for convenience of business, Monday is the first day of the week, but on all of the displays of a whole *month*, the week begins with Sunday, and Saturday is the seventh day.

There have been changes in the calendar over the years. The biggest change was made in 1582 when ten days were dropped from the calendar. October 1582 had only 21 days in it (the day after October 4 was October 15). This was done to correct a calculation error that had accumulated over a long time.[19] But even though this change was made, the weekly cycle of days was not touched. In fact, the seven-day cycle as we know it today has *never* changed. France tried a ten-day cycle for awhile, but it failed miserably and didn't last long.

So don't let any calendar throw you. Even if lawmakers were to pass a law that said all calendars had to make Tuesday the last day of the week, such action would not change the Sabbath to Tuesday, for no human can change a law established by God.

The seventh day of the week is Saturday in English, but in many countries and languages, the name of the seventh day actually means Sabbath. For example, in Spanish the name for the day is *Sabbado*, which means "the Sabbath." In Greek Friday is *Paraskeue'* (pronounced Par-ask-yoo-*ay'*) and Saturday is *Sab'baton* (*Sab'*-bat-on), which is translated "the day of preparation" and "the Sabbath," respectively.[20]

---

19 A year is not 365 days. It is approximately 365.2425 days. One must account for that extra time—24 days must be added over each 100-year period. If prior to 1582 a leap year was observed *every* four years without a break (25 instead of 24), it would take 1000 years to build up those ten extra days. Additionally, every fourth century, the year 2000 being the last one, the leap year *is* observed, thus partially accounting for the leftover .0025 of a day. Because of the slow and continuous change in the orientation of the earth's rotational axis and changes in the equinoxes themselves, other modifications are made to the calendar from time to time.

20 "And that day was the *preparation*, and the *sabbath* drew on" (Luke 23:54). "The Jews therefore, because it was the *preparation*, that the bodies should not remain upon the cross on the *sabbath* day, (for that sabbath day was an high day,) besought Pilate that their legs might be broken, and that they might be taken away" (John 19:31). These passages use the same Greek words that are still being used today.

Remember, the sixth day was used as a day of preparation for the Sabbath, and for forty years God used food, in the form of manna (that white substance that fell from the sky six days a week), to introduce this concept to the Jewish people after being freed from Egyptian captivity. When the manna fell, they were to take an extra portion on the sixth day because on the Sabbath there would not be any, for God was giving them a day of rest (Exod. 16).

God appears to be very particular as to how He wants us to keep the Sabbath. He does not want it to degenerate into just another day; He wants it to remain special to us.

So how does He want us to remember it? Let's take another look at Isaiah 58:13, 14:

> If thou turn away thy foot from the sabbath, from doing *thy* pleasure [business, activities] on my holy day; and call the sabbath a delight, the holy of the LORD, honourable; and shalt honour him, not doing thine *own* ways, nor finding thine *own* pleasure [activities], nor speaking thine *own* words: *Then* shalt thou *delight thyself in the LORD;* and I will *cause* thee to ride upon the high places of the earth, and feed thee with the heritage of Jacob thy father: *for the mouth of the LORD hath spoken it."*

Let's look at this passage phrase by phrase.

"Turn away thy foot from the sabbath."

In other words, stop treading on it. Cease stepping on it. Desist from stomping on it. Stop kicking dirt on it. Please treat the Sabbath with the respect it deserves.

Refrain "from doing thy pleasure on my holy day."

If you take this at face value, you could easily get the wrong idea and this can appear to you as very bad news! God does not intend to take away our *fun* on the Sabbath. Indeed, it is a very pleasurable day.

The Hebrew word for "pleasure" is *chephets* (*khay'*-fets), which *can* mean pleasure, but in this use of the word, it means pursuit, ardour, affair, or matter. In other words, God says, "I'd like you to refrain from pursuing your *own* affairs and I would like you to put off your *own* matters (secular business and secular play) for 24 hours so we can meet together for a close, personal, and special quiet time together (sacred business and sacred enjoyment). I would like to give you quality time one day each week on a special day that I have already set aside for this purpose. This will be a special time that I can communicate my righteousness to you." Not bad, when you think about it.

"Nor finding thine own pleasure."

Again, this is the same Hebrew word and a reference to our *own* affairs. God has mentioned this twice, thus underscoring its importance.

"Nor speaking thine own words."

Once again God says it, only this time it is a reference to what we *say*. It may be that we do not *do* a certain thing on Sabbath, but God says He does not want us even to *talk* about it, either. The Sabbath is to be a day wholly set aside for our special sacred time together with Him and with each other.

Also, consider this: the best way to avoid *talking* about something is to avoid *thinking* about it. Let God place your mind on sacred subjects. We might also note here what God says in Nehemiah 10:31 regarding buying and selling on Sabbath: "And if the people of the land bring ware or any victuals on the sabbath day to sell, that we would not buy it of them on the sabbath."

"Call the sabbath a delight, the holy of the Lord, honourable."

This is not a day to be sad and morose. It is a day of joy, not in the sense of a *celebration* but in the sense of quiet rest and peaceful joy. (We will *celebrate* when Jesus comes as described in this book in the section on the Feast of Tabernacles.) It is also a day of good works and acts of mercy and kindness. Not that these are not done during the regular work week, but the Sabbath is a day especially set aside for this.

For insight into appropriate Sabbath activities, let's turn to Matthew 12.

> Or have ye not read in the law, how that on the sabbath days the priests in the temple profane the sabbath, and are blameless? [This is in reference to preachers. They work on the Sabbath and earn a living, but that's what they are supposed to do.] But I say unto you, That in this place is one greater than the temple. [Jesus is speaking of Himself.] But if ye had known what this meaneth, I will have mercy, and not sacrifice, ye would not have condemned the guiltless. For the Son of man is Lord even of the sabbath day. [There is that statement again, this time in context.]
>
> And when he was departed thence, he went into their synagogue: And, behold, there was a man which had his hand withered. And they asked him, saying, Is it lawful to heal on the sabbath days? that they might accuse him. And he said unto them, What man shall there be among you, that shall have one sheep, and if it fall into a pit on the sabbath day, will he not lay hold on it, and lift it out? How much then is a man better than a sheep? Wherefore it is lawful to do well on the sabbath days. Then saith he to the man, Stretch forth thine hand. And he stretched it forth; and it was restored whole, like as the other. (Matt. 12:5–13)

"For I desired mercy, and not sacrifice; and the knowledge of God more than burnt offerings" (Hosea 6:6). God has no pleasure in meaningless rites. The sacrifices were not for the purpose of trying to make God *approve* of us (as if we could get God to change His mind[21]), but to point to the removal

---
21 When you consider that God has already given us all things, including salvation, who would *want* God to change His mind?

of sin when Jesus died on the cross. As Jesus demonstrated in healing the man with the withered hand on Sabbath, it is lawful to do acts of mercy on the Lord's day. That's what the Sabbath is for. It is good to help our neighbor (even animals) in an emergency. It is good to pull the ox out of the ditch, even on the Sabbath. We just need to be sure we don't *push* the ox into the ditch so he needs to be pulled out. That's a whole different matter.

When you do these things that Isaiah 58:13, 14 tells us about, you will "delight thyself in the Lord," and *God* will "*cause* thee to ride upon the high places of the earth," and He will "feed thee with the heritage of Jacob thy father: for the mouth of the Lord hath *spoken* it."

And, remember, inherent in God's spoken word is the power to create what it says. The only way we can fail is through our own unbelief. Therefore, you can claim His promise and hold Him to the completion of it.

Will you believe today? The choice is yours. God will not force your hand.

There was a time some years ago, after I became a pastor and the Sabbath became a regular work day for me, when I began to see the Sabbath as drudgery—a continual round of work added to my other duties. I talked to God about it, and I asked Him to give me a delight for the Sabbath, claiming His promise. The response was immediate and lasting. Now I look forward to the day as never before. If you are struggling with this idea of Sabbath observance, or maybe you too feel that it is drudgery, take your problem to God and He will give you the delight He has promised.

"Thus saith the Lord; Take heed to yourselves, and bear no burden on the sabbath day, nor bring it in by the gates of Jerusalem; Neither carry forth a burden out of your houses on the sabbath day, neither do ye any work, but hallow ye the sabbath day, as I commanded your fathers" (Jer. 17:21, 22). God does not want us to carry a burden on the Sabbath day,[22] which is what drove the Jewish leaders to enact laws to require the people to honor God's Sabbath. Although they were *trying* to do what was right, the Pharisees became so legalistic about the way they kept the Sabbath that they could not even carry a handkerchief on it. If you wanted to carry a handkerchief with you, you had to pin it to your garment, so then it could be considered part of your clothing, and thus not be a burden. In fact, there were thousands of rules like this. That's not what the Sabbath is all about, friends. This is not about legalism—trying to save ourselves. God has already given us salvation. Although the Jewish people *wanted* to do what was right, although they *wanted* to honor God, they still missed the mark and fell short because of all their *trying*. They tried too *hard*; they tried in their own strength, which is weakness. If they had *believed* God and simply said thank you with their hearts, God would have caused them to ride on the high places of the earth.

God wants us to *unload* our burdens, not add more. God wants us to pause and rest. And the whole reason God wants us to put our personal agendas aside on Sabbath is so that we can understand that God wants us to unload our burden of sin—and along with it our burden of trying to keep God's law. The Ten Commandments are all about *God* delivering from bondage, the bondage of sin, as symbolized

---

22 Either temporal or spiritual, let God have all your worries before the Sabbath begins.

by the miraculous physical escape from Egypt. The Sabbath is God's *memorial* to all of that.[23]

One of my favorite authors put it this way:

> It is clear that mere bodily recuperation is not the object of the Sabbath day, and that merely refraining from bodily toil does not at all constitute the sum of Sabbath-keeping. Yet entire cessation from our *own* work, of whatever kind it may be, is enjoined on the seventh day. This, not alone for the purpose of giving us time to contemplate the works of God without interruption, but to impress a much needed lesson of trust in God. As we cease all our labor by which we earn our living, we are reminded of the fact that God supplies us not only with spiritual blessings, but also with all temporal necessities [food, clothing, shelter]. We thereby acknowledge that although, in obedience to His command, we labor for our daily bread, we are as dependent upon Him as though we did nothing. [In other words, even though we *work* for what we get, it is still *God* who *provides* for us—*as if* we actually had done nothing at all for it. For it is a gift.]
>
> A proper understanding of the Sabbath and its object, therefore, would forever set at *rest* the inquiry that often arises in the minds of persons who are convinced that they ought to obey God in the matter of Sabbath observance. The question is, "If I should keep the seventh day, how could I make a living? I shall doubtless lose my position, and since comparatively few people keep that day, and it is the principal business day of the week, I shall not be able to find employment. What can I do?" I say such a question will never be *asked* by one who knows the nature and object of the Sabbath. He will know that the Sabbath *itself* points out the answer. The very *idea* of Sabbath observance is *that* of perfect trust in God, whose power brought the universe from nothing, and upholds it, and whose love for His creatures is equal to His power to do them good.
>
> It will also solve the question, or rather prevent its arising, as to whether a man should in an extremity labor on the Sabbath in harvest, when that seems to be the only hope of securing the crop. [In other words, a storm is coming and it looks as if I will lose my crop. Should I harvest it on the Sabbath?] He will know that the God who alone can make the corn grow, is fully able to protect it, or to make ample provision for him in *another* way if it should be destroyed. But all will understand that perfect Sabbath-keeping is consistent with bestowing all needful care upon the afflicted; for the Sabbath itself reminds us that God is "gracious and full of compassion."...
>
> During the six days [of creation week] God had been speaking the words that

---

23 "The works of the Lord are great, sought out of all them that have pleasure therein. *His* work is honourable and glorious: and his righteousness endureth for ever. He hath made his wonderful works to be remembered [literally: a memorial]: the Lord is gracious and full of compassion" (Ps. 111:2-4).

brought the earth to its perfect condition. Then He rested. He ceased speaking, and His word, which liveth and abideth forever, continued to uphold that which was created. *So* God rested upon His word. He could rest from the work of creation in perfect confidence that His word would uphold the universe. So when we keep the Sabbath of the Lord, we simply take the rest that comes from settling down upon the promises of God.

Thus it is that "we which have believed do enter into rest." And he that hath *entered into rest*, he also hath *ceased* from his *own* works, as God did from *His*. Before men fully accept the simple word of the Lord, *everything* is from *self*. The works of the flesh are only sin; and even though men *profess* to serve God, and have *earnest desires* to do right, their *own* works to that end are dismal failures. "All our righteousnesses are as filthy rags." *Isaiah* 64:6. But when we realize the power of the *word* of God, and know that it is able to build up those who trust it, then we *cease* our *own* works, and allow *God* to work in us, both to *will* and to *do* of *His* good pleasure. *Then* all our works are *wrought in Him*, and they are *right*. *This is indeed rest*. The rest that comes when we *realize* that salvation does *not* come from *ourselves*, but from the *word* which *made* the heavens and the earth, and which also upholds them, is the rest which the Sabbath brings to us when it is kept as the Lord designs.[24]

What more can I say? The Sabbath means rest from legalism.

So what kinds of activities can we do on the Sabbath? Consider the following: religious meetings such as church worship services and evangelism, vespers programs, Bible studies, visitation (hospitals, nursing homes, those who are housebound or who may be discouraged), medical services that relieve pain and suffering, watching religious programming on television, listening to sacred music, reading sacred material, playing games that have a Sabbath theme, enjoying nature by going for a walk through the woods, etc. As an example, for those who have passes, going to the zoo would be a good nature walk.

What kinds of things would we not want to do on the Sabbath? Think about these: regular business that we do for a living, regular housework, gardening and lawn work, washing dishes (if possible), listening to secular music, watching secular television, reading secular material, or engaging in athletics or other secular games, etc.

Guard carefully the edges of the Sabbath. Be careful about what is the last thing you do in the hour or two before sunset. For example, don't choose a secular activity that will likely be interrupted by the setting of the sun, thus causing you to think about it during the Sabbath, anticipating finishing it once the sun sets. I call this "slamming into the Sabbath." Many people close their businesses at noon on Fridays in order to avoid this situation.

I like to think of the Sabbath as starting 15 to 30 minutes before the actual start of the Sabbath. This helps me to prepare my mind for resting on God's special day. Now, as the Sabbath is closing, I like to

---

24 E. J Waggoner, *Gospel in Creation*, pp. 66–69.

wait until it is obviously dark outside before beginning any secular activity. However, on a rainy day, you can get a false dark signal.

Ellen White wrote the following entry in her diary, dated Friday, February 21, 1896:

> This day is preparation day. We would come up to the Sabbath with our work closed up in proper shape and not dragging into the Sabbath. We must commence in the morning to look after every piece of clothing if we have neglected to do this through the week, that our garments may be neat and orderly and comely to appear in the place where God's people assemble to worship Him.... Entering upon new business should be avoided, if possible, but endeavor to close up the things already started that are half accomplished. Prepare everything connected with the household matters so that there shall be freedom from worries, and the mind be prepared to rest and to meditate upon heavenly things.
>
> There needs to be much more close investigation of the week past. Review it and see if, as a branch of the living Vine, you have drawn nourishment from the parent Vine to bear much fruit to the glory of God. If there has been feverish excitement, if hasty words have been spoken, if passion has been revealed, these have surely been the working on Satan's side of the question. Clear the heart by confession. Sincerely make everything right before the Sabbath. Examine your own selves, whether ye be in the faith....
>
> The humble dependence upon God, the faith that takes Him at His word and trusts Him at all times and under all circumstances, is the wearing of the yoke of Christ.

These ideas are only a beginning. Let the *Lord* speak to your own heart regarding what He has for you on the Sabbath day. We cannot fathom what the Lord has in store for His people, but if we desire His will for our lives, we know that His Word has inherent within it the power to create what it says.

In Hebrews 4:1–11 Paul differentiates between temporal and spiritual rest. He tells us that we receive God's spiritual (true) rest through believing His promise, which is true Sabbath observance. He illustrates how those in Israel in Joshua's day, through unbelief, did not accept the rest that God promises (and the seventh-day Sabbath memorializes) and, therefore, died in the wilderness, never reaching the Promised Land. He then implores us to work to find God's true rest in our lives today—rest in God's promise to give us His righteousness and rest from trying to save ourselves:

> Let us therefore fear, lest, a promise being left us of entering into his *rest*,[25] any of you should seem to come short of it.

---

25 The Greek word *katapausis* means temporal rest. All the references to "rest" in this passage, *except one*, uses this Greek word. Although it means a temporal rest, Paul is using it to refer to rest in God's strength. The change of words employed in verse nine emphasizes the true meaning of Sabbath observance.

> For unto *us* was the gospel preached, as well as unto *them* [Heb. 3:7–11, unbelieving Israel in the wilderness during Moses' day]: but the word preached did not profit them, not being mixed with *faith* in them that heard it.
>
> For we which have *believed* do enter into rest, as he said, As I have sworn in my wrath, if they shall [never] enter into my rest[26] [It is our choice whether we will believe.]: although the works were finished [creation was finished, including the Sabbath, and the power of God's word to give the righteousness the Sabbath memorializes] from the foundation of the world.
>
> For he spake in a certain place of the seventh day on this wise, And God did rest the seventh day from all his works. And in this place again, *If* they *shall* enter into my rest. Seeing therefore it remaineth that *some* must enter therein, and they to whom it was first preached entered *not* in because of *unbelief*:
>
> Again, he limiteth a certain day, saying in David, To day, after so long a time; as it is said, To day if ye will hear his voice, harden not your hearts [Ps. 95:7, 8]. For if Jesus [Joshua,[27] again, in the wilderness] had given them rest, then would he not afterward have spoken of another day.
>
> There remaineth therefore a rest [Greek: *sabbatismos*, Sabbath observance] to the people of God. For he that is entered into his rest, he also hath ceased from his *own* works [legalism, trying to save oneself or trying to convince God to change His mind and save you], as God did from his.
>
> Let us *labour* therefore to enter into that rest [Work hard to find God's rest. Stop trying to save yourself. This will take a constant heartfelt surrender to God's power and a repudiation of your own.], lest any man fall after the same example of unbelief.

Let's look at Mathew 11, which once again brings up the Elijah message: "And it came to pass, when Jesus had made an end of commanding his twelve disciples, he departed thence to teach and to preach in their cities. Now when John had heard in the prison the works of Christ, he sent two of his disciples, And said unto him, Art thou he that should come, or do we look for another? Jesus answered and said unto them, Go and shew John again those things which ye do hear and see: The blind receive their sight, and the lame walk, the lepers are cleansed, and the deaf hear, the dead are raised up, and the poor have the gospel preached to them. And blessed is he, whosoever shall not be offended in me."

---

26 This is a quote from Psalm 95:11, which, along with verse 10, says, "Forty years long was I grieved with this generation, and said, It is a people that do err in their heart, and they have not known my ways: Unto whom I sware in my *wrath* that [The Hebrew word translated "that" is an emphasized "if," as in "Lo! If!"] they should not [never; the Hebrew is an absolute negation "never"] enter into my rest." God *really wants* His people to enter into *His* rest, doesn't He? He would swear in His wrath *if* His people should *never* enter His true rest from trying to save themselves or trying to impress God to save them—something He has already done. Thankfully, they will enter His true rest in the last days before Jesus comes.

27 "Jesus" is the Greek form of "Yeshua" or "Joshua."

The Elijah message is one of power. When we cherish the Sabbath and pay attention to God's promise, His power is poured out in our lives. For an example of this, I have one final story, which Dr. Lucile C. Lacy, a professor in the music department at Oakwood University, Huntsville, Alabama, shared with me about her life experience.

> When I was a teenager, a high-school teacher told me that I would never be successful in my life, and that I'd be a detriment to society. I was devastated.
>
> After completing a master's degree in music teacher education from George Peabody College for Teachers [Nashville, Tennessee], I taught college for several years. Then I prayed, 'Lord, if it is your will for me to pursue the doctoral degree, prepare the way.' Unexpectedly, I was awarded a United Negro College Fund Teaching Grant for $10,000, renewable annually. This to me seemed a notable honor for one who had been told by a professional educator that I had no future.
>
> I wanted to get my doctoral degree from Ohio State University. From a pool of 400 applicants, I was one of the ten accepted into the program. Soon I met Professor 'X' who told me that, as a Seventh-day Adventist, I had no chance of succeeding at OSU if I missed the Friday night and Saturday sessions. I left his office determined to complete the program *and* keep the Sabbath.
>
> One Friday afternoon, Professor 'X' gave the class an almost impossible 'take home' final examination. It was due on Monday and would require exhaustive research in the library all weekend.
>
> Two hours before sunset on Friday, I closed up all my studies and prepared for the Sabbath. Saturday evening I learned my classmates had spent all Friday evening and all day Saturday in the library and were far from finished. By Sunday evening, after ten hours of research, I had answered three of the exam's ten questions. I stopped and communed with God for one hour. Then, one hour before the library closed, I was impressed to walk down the stacks. Praying silently, with tears running down my cheeks, I felt nothing but despair…
>
> …when suddenly, in front of me, a book dropped from the shelf and fell open to a page of information I needed. I quickly picked up the book and continued to walk down the aisle when *another* book fell from the shelf. Books began falling from high and low, faster and faster. Each book was opened to an exact answer. I grabbed a cart and moved quickly down the aisle picking up books. The library assistants heard the sounds of the books falling from the shelves and asked if I knew who was throwing the books? I just smiled through my tears, rejoiced in the Lord, and kept on picking up those books.
>
> I was the only student in the class who completed the entire exam. Professor 'X' was shocked.

"O that my ways may be steadfast in keeping Thy statutes" Psalm 119:5, RSV[28]

And Matthew 28:18 says, "And Jesus came and spake unto them, saying, All *power* is given unto me in heaven and in earth." This power will be revealed in His people in the last days just before Jesus comes. *This* is the Elijah message, and the *Sabbath* is the memorial thereof.

If anyone comes to you and says that you *cannot* worship on God's holy day, the seventh day Sabbath, RUN!

---

[28] This story originally appeared in an e-mail. It is printed with permission.

Chapter 15

Feast of Tabernacles

So far, we have studied six feasts:
- Feast 1 is the **Passover,** representing Christ's sacrificial death for the human race.
- Feast 2 is **Unleavened Bread,** representing Christ's perfect life as our heritage
- Feast 3 is **Firstfruits,** representing the resurrection of Christ as the representative of the human race, who, in that capacity, took us corporately and individually (in title) to the harvest of the earth, that is, heaven and the new earth to be created.
- Feast 4 is **Pentecost,** representing the early rain of the Holy Spirit.
- Feast 5 is **Trumpets,** representing the announcement of the convocation of the Day of Atonement, which was soon to take place.
- Feast 6 is the **Day of Atonement,** representing preparation for the second coming of Christ, a "meeting of the minds" of God and humankind.

Antitypically, with the exception of the harvest of the earth, the first five have been fulfilled already. We are living in feast number six, and feast number seven is soon to happen.

God introduces the seventh and final, **Feast of Tabernacles,** in Leviticus 23:33–44 as follows:

> And the Lord spake unto Moses, saying, Speak unto the children of Israel, saying, The fifteenth day of this seventh month shall be the feast of tabernacles for seven days unto the Lord. On the first day shall be an holy convocation: ye shall do no servile work therein. Seven days ye shall offer an offering made by fire unto the Lord: on the eighth day shall be an holy convocation unto you; and ye shall offer an offering made by fire unto the Lord: it is a solemn assembly; and ye shall do no servile work therein....[1]
>
> Also in the fifteenth day of the seventh month, when ye have gathered in the fruit of the land, ye shall keep a feast unto the Lord seven days: on the first day shall be a sabbath, and on the eighth day shall be a sabbath.
>
> And ye shall take you on the first day the *boughs* of goodly trees, branches of palm trees, and the boughs of thick trees, and willows of the brook; and ye shall *rejoice* before the Lord your God seven days. And ye shall keep it a feast unto the Lord seven days in the year. It shall be a statute for ever in your generations: ye shall celebrate it in the seventh month. Ye shall dwell in *booths* seven days; all that are

---

[1] Verses 37 and 38 are a parenthetical note. We will look at them later.

Israelites born shall dwell in booths: That your generations may know that I made the children of Israel to dwell in booths, *when I brought them out of the land of Egypt*: I am the LORD your God.

And Moses declared unto the children of Israel the feasts of the LORD.

Here is a description from one of my favorite Bible authors:

> The Feast of Tabernacles was the closing gathering of the year. It was God's design that at this time the people should reflect on His goodness and mercy. The whole land had been under His guidance, receiving His blessing. Day and night His watchcare had continued. The sun and rain had caused the earth to produce her fruits. From the valleys and plains of Palestine the harvest had been gathered. The olive berries had been picked, and the precious oil stored in bottles. The palm had yielded her store. The purple clusters of the vine had been trodden in the wine press.
>
> The feast continued for seven days, and for its celebration the inhabitants of Palestine, with many from other lands, left their homes, and came to Jerusalem. From far and near the people came, bringing in their hands a token of rejoicing. Old and young, rich and poor, all brought some gift as a tribute of thanksgiving to Him who had crowned the year with His goodness, and made His paths drop fatness. Everything that could please the eye, and give expression to the universal joy, was brought from the woods; the city bore the appearance of a beautiful forest.
>
> This feast was not only the harvest thanksgiving, but the memorial of God's protecting care over Israel in the wilderness. In commemoration of their tent life, the Israelites during the feast dwelt in booths or tabernacles of green boughs. These were erected in the streets, in the courts of the temple, or on the housetops. The hills and valleys surrounding Jerusalem were also dotted with these leafy dwellings, and seemed to be alive with people.
>
> With sacred song and thanksgiving the worshipers celebrated this occasion. A little before the feast was the Day of Atonement, when, after confession of their sins, the people were declared to be at peace with Heaven. Thus the way was prepared for the rejoicing of the feast. "O give thanks unto the LORD; for He is good: for His mercy endureth forever" (Psalm 106:1) rose triumphantly, while all kinds of music, mingled with shouts of hosanna, accompanied the united singing. The temple was the center of the universal joy. Here was the pomp of the sacrificial ceremonies. Here, ranged on either side of the white marble steps of the sacred building, the choir of Levites led the service of song. The multitude of worshipers, waving their branches of palm and myrtle, took up the strain, and echoed the chorus; and again the melody was caught up by voices near and afar off, till the

encircling hills were vocal with praise.

At night the temple and its court blazed with artificial light. The music, the waving of palm branches, the glad hosannas, the great concourse of people, over whom the light streamed from the hanging lamps, the array of the priests, and the majesty of the ceremonies, combined to make a scene that deeply impressed the beholders. But the most impressive ceremony of the feast, one that called forth greatest rejoicing, was one commemorating an event in the wilderness sojourn.

At the first dawn of day, the priests sounded a long, shrill blast upon their silver trumpets, and the answering trumpets, and the glad shouts of the people from their booths, echoing over hill and valley, welcomed the festal day. Then the priest dipped from the flowing waters of the Kedron a flagon of water, and, lifting it on high, while the trumpets were sounding, he ascended the broad steps of the temple, keeping time with the music with slow and measured tread, chanting meanwhile, "Our feet shall stand within thy gates, O Jerusalem." Psalm 122:2.

He bore the flagon to the altar, which occupied a central position in the court of the priests. Here were two silver basins, with a priest standing at each one. The flagon of water was poured into one, and a flagon of wine into the other; and the contents of both flowed into a pipe which communicated with the Kedron, and was conducted to the Dead Sea. This display of the consecrated water represented the fountain that at the command of God had gushed from the rock to quench the thirst of the children of Israel. Then the jubilant strains rang forth, "The Lord Jehovah is my strength and my song;" "therefore with joy shall ye draw water out of the wells of salvation." Isaiah 12:2, 3.[2]

The Feast of the Day of Atonement was a solemn affair. It was (and still is, because we are still in it) a time for confessing sin and allowing God to remove sin from our hearts. However, the Feast of Tabernacles was quite opposite, for God said the Israelites were to celebrate and rejoice. Yet, the antitypical Feast of Tabernacles is in the future, for we are currently still in the Feast of the Day of Atonement. Notice that dress ("holy convocation"), gospel ("offering made by fire"), and the Sabbath ("no work") are still implicated during the Feast of Tabernacles. Only health ("afflicting the soul") is not, perhaps because God's people are under special care during this time.[3] Daniel wrote this thought

---

2   Ellen G. White, *The Desire of Ages*, pp. 447–449.

3   "The Lord has shown me repeatedly that it is contrary to the Bible to make any provision for our temporal wants in the time of trouble. I saw that if the saints had food laid up by them or in the field in the time of trouble, when sword, famine, and pestilence are in the land, it would be taken from them by violent hands and strangers would reap their fields. Then will be the time for us to trust wholly in God, and He will sustain us. I saw that our bread and water will be sure at that time, and that we shall not lack or suffer hunger; for God is able to spread a table for us in the wilderness. If necessary He would send ravens to feed us, as He did to feed Elijah, or rain manna from heaven, as He did for the Israelites" (Ellen G. White, *Early Writings*, p. 56)

about the time of trouble.

> And at that time shall Michael stand up, the great prince which standeth for the children of thy people: and there shall be a *time of trouble, such as never was since there was a nation even to that same time*: and at that time thy people shall be delivered, every one that shall be found written in the book. And many of them that sleep in the dust of the earth shall awake, some to everlasting life, and some to shame and everlasting contempt. And they that be wise shall shine as the brightness of the firmament; and they that turn many to righteousness as the stars for ever and ever. But thou, O Daniel, shut up the words, and seal the book, even to the time of the end: many shall run to and fro, and knowledge shall be increased. (Dan. 12:1–4)

Both Leviticus, previously read, and this passage in Daniel are describing the same event, even though on the surface the two statements may appear to be opposites. Leviticus says we will rejoice, and Daniel describes a "time of trouble such as never was." How can this be both a time of trouble and a time of rejoicing?

Well, it depends on which side of the fence you choose to be on in that day. Today we are living in the antitypical Day of Atonement. Today we are allowing God to remove our sins so that we can stand before God without a mediator so that Christ can leave the heavenly sanctuary to come get His people. For those who allow Christ to do this, God's protection will hover over His people while the time of trouble bursts upon the world. Cataclysmic natural phenomena, oppressive government legislation, and opposition from degenerate humanity will inconvenience them during this time, yes, even persecute them; yet, although His people may suffer, God will protect them from the plagues that will come upon the earth.[4] For this reason, and because God is about to put an end to all sin and come and receive His inheritance—us—God's people rejoice.

If you choose to believe, God will number you among His people who will receive His protection. Those who choose *not* to believe place themselves among the transgressors who will receive the mark of the beast, experience the plagues, and finally end up in the lake of fire where God will mercifully allow them to receive the second death. They may talk about being Christians. They may *say* they believe God's word, even to the point of approaching His throne (north) and looking for His second coming (east). But they steadfastly continue in their own way and will not submit to God's word in their lives. They will be persecuting God's people who are carrying God's truth while claiming to look for His truth.[5] This whole scenario is the "battle of Armageddon," of which the gathering for the climax is

---

4 The persecution comes largely *because* of this protection, for the world will notice that a certain group is being protected somehow, but they will interpret that to mean that God's people are *causing* the problems that are coming upon the world. Hence, they will be persecuted. Such persecution will tend to weed out unbelievers who may be trying to attach themselves to God's people solely for the purpose of avoiding the plagues. This protection is not without precedent, however, for God protected His people from the plagues of Egypt in Moses' day (Exod. 8:22, 23), including the tenth plague that is linked to the Passover as described in Exodus 12.

5 Amos 8:11, 12 says, "Behold, the days come, saith the Lord God, that I will send a famine in the land, not a famine of

mentioned in Revelation 16:16 just before the last of the seven last plagues.

This battle between good and evil that we call "the battle of Armageddon" began with Lucifer's sin in heaven and has been increasing with intensity as each year passes. The battle climaxes during the seventh plague, is interrupted by the second coming of Christ, resumes after the 1000 years that Satan is bound in the wilderness, and culminates with the lake of fire and the destruction of Satan, his angels, the impenitent, and the earth as we know it. Then the earth will be made new and the righteous will live in bliss for eternity. The second death of impenitent human beings is merciful because it removes the transgressor from the misery and boredom of trying to live for all eternity in a place where there is nothing to do, for there will be no sin there.[6]

> The finishing of the mystery of God is the ending of the work of the gospel. And the ending of the work of the gospel is, *first, the taking away of all vestige of sin* and the bringing in of everlasting righteousness—Christ [in character] fully formed—within each believer, God alone manifest in the flesh of each believer in Jesus, and, *secondly*, on the other hand, the work of the gospel being finished means only the destruction of all who then shall not have received the gospel (2 Thessalonians 1:7–10), for it is not the way of the Lord to continue men in life when the only possible use they will make of life is to heap up more misery for themselves.[7]

The booths made out of branches and leaves mentioned in Leviticus represent God's people living in the wilderness during the time of trouble described by Daniel. Notice that Leviticus 23:43 refers to the time when God brought Israel out of the land of Egypt. They lived in the wilderness during that time of transition. It was indeed a time of trouble, for God allowed them to be backed into a corner where there was no way out. On one side they had the Red Sea. On the other side they had a mountain. Moreover, coming toward them on the attack from the third side was the army of Egypt. They were trapped! However, God provided a miraculous way of escape—*through the sea on dry ground!*

God's people will indeed need to flee to the wilderness in the last days just before Jesus comes. Listen to what Revelation 13:15–17 says: "And he had power to give life unto the image of the beast, that the image of the beast should both speak, and cause that as many as would not worship the image of the beast should be killed. And he causeth all, both small and great, rich and poor, free and bond, to receive a mark in their right hand, or in their foreheads: And that no man might buy or sell, save he that had the mark, or the name of the beast, or the number of his name."

We already know that the mark of the beast is a false Sabbath. We know also that God's true Sabbath is the seventh day of the week, that is, Friday sunset until Saturday sunset. The beast, therefore,

---

bread, nor a thirst for water, but of hearing the words of the Lord: And they shall wander from sea to sea, and from the north even to the east, they shall run to and fro to seek the word of the Lord, and shall not find it."
6   As we have already studied, the lake of fire will not last eternally, but will eventually go out, which in itself is merciful.
7   A. T. Jones, *The Consecrated Way to Christian Perfection*, p. 117, emphasis original.

is anyone who will try to influence *by force* the observance of any day other than God's true Sabbath day. As to who that is, it will become painfully plain at that time. In the meantime, one only needs to be paying attention to see who might be agitating any day other than God's true Sabbath. The law against buying or selling that accompanies the attempt to force observance of a false Sabbath, coupled with a threat to destroy (even with a death decree) those who observe the true Sabbath of God,[8] drives God's people into the wilderness where God will provide for them Himself. Some may quite literally be dwelling in "booths" during that time.[9] This flight parallels the flight of the Christians from Jerusalem just before the destruction of that city in AD 66–70, as Jesus warned in Mathew 24, Mark 13, and Luke 21.

The antitypical fulfillment of the Feast of Tabernacles is still in the future. Just as the Feast of Tabernacles in the *earthly* sanctuary began after the Day of Atonement was completed, so today, the antitypical Feast of Tabernacles will begin after Jesus Christ, our heavenly High Priest, completes His "Day of Atonement" work in the Most Holy Place of the heavenly sanctuary. God can do this because the sins of His people will have stopped flowing into the sanctuary, and Christ can finish the cleansing of the sanctuary, thus securing the fulfillment of Daniel 8:14, the completion of the antitypical fulfillment of the Feast of the Day of Atonement.

Christ will then be ready to leave the sanctuary.[10] Revelation describes His departure as follows:

> And when he had opened the seventh seal, there was silence in heaven [This is because no one is there, all have left for earth—even all the angels!] about the space of half an hour.[11] And I saw the seven angels which stood before God; and to them were given seven trumpets. And another angel came and stood at the altar, having a golden censer; and there was given unto him much incense, that he should offer it with the prayers of all saints upon the golden altar which was before the throne. And the smoke of the incense, which came with the prayers of the saints, ascended up before God out of the angel's hand. And the angel took the censer, and filled it with fire of the altar, and cast it into the earth: and there were voices, and thunderings, and lightnings, and an earthquake. (Rev. 8:1–5)

---

8   The ultimate method of Satan's persuasion is to threaten destruction (the first death), for this is the most he can do to anyone. It always has been and always will be so. Throughout the time of earth's history, many people have been put to death defending the cause of God, but at *this* time in earth's history, after the close of probation, the devil will be completely thwarted in his attempts to put God's people to death.

9   Temporary housing, even caves, etc.

10 When Christ's work is completed in the sanctuary, He stands up (Dan. 12:1), makes the announcement of the close of probation (Rev. 22:11, 12), which, by the way, human beings do not hear, and the seven last plagues begin to fall (Rev. 16), which Daniel 12:1 calls the "time of trouble, such as never was." Christ actually *leaves* the sanctuary during the seventh and final plague as described by the seventh seal of Revelation 8:1–5. That happens after the hail described in Revelation 16:21. (The description of the seventh plague is begun in Revelation 16:17–21, continued in Revelation 8:1–5; 19:6–18; 11:19; 6:14–17, and completed in Revelation 20:1–6. The book of Revelation has many flashbacks and historical sketches; it is not a continuous story line.)

11 In prophetic time, applying the year-day principle, this represents about 15 literal days.

The censer represents the work of the priestly office, in this case the work of the High Priest in the heavenly sanctuary. His work as priest is now finished, so He does not need the censer any longer and He casts it to the earth. As the golden censer "cascades" to earth, Christ's attention now shifts from the sanctuary to events on earth. When He casts down the golden censer, He picks up the "golden scepter," a reference to the work of a King. This is when He doffs His priestly garments and dons His kingly robes. It is now time for Christ to come and rescue His people.

The following verses speak of God's scepter and His title of King of the universe.

- "The sceptre shall not depart from Judah, nor a lawgiver from between his feet, until Shiloh come; and unto him shall the gathering of the people be" (Gen. 49:10).
- "I shall see him, but not now: I shall behold him, but not nigh: there shall come a Star out of Jacob, and a Sceptre shall rise out of Israel, and shall smite the corners of Moab, and destroy all the children of Sheth" (Num. 24:17).
- "But unto the Son he saith, Thy throne, O God, is for ever and ever: a sceptre of righteousness is the sceptre of thy kingdom" (Heb. 1:8).

In spite of events heating up, it is worth noting that in that day, people will be engaged in normal activities of daily living. Jesus describes it thusly:

> But as the days of Noe [Noah] were, so shall also the coming of the Son of man be.
>
> For as in the days that were before the flood they were *eating and drinking, marrying and giving in marriage* [normal activities of daily living], until the day that Noe entered into the ark,
>
> And knew not until the flood came, and took them all away; so shall also the coming of the Son of man be. [They were caught by surprise.]
>
> Then shall two be in the field; the one shall be taken, and the other left. [The work in the field signifies preparing the harvest. This represents those who are preparing for translation without seeing death while sounding the warning of the soon coming of Christ, which is a good thing to do. Yet even this good work is no guarantee of salvation. Some will be lost because their motives are wrong—they are working for their own salvation, having thrown away their birthright possession.]
>
> Two women shall be grinding at the mill; the one shall be taken, and the other left. [The phrase "women shall be" is not in the original Greek. Therefore, this statement is for both men and women. Grinding at the mill signifies preparing flour for bread. This represents those who are teaching the word of God, especially the message of the cross, which again, is a good thing to do.[12] Yet, even this good work is no guarantee

---

12   "For the bread of God is he which cometh down from heaven, and giveth life unto the world" (John 6:33). "And Jesus said unto them, I am the bread of life: he that cometh to me shall never hunger; and he that believeth on me shall never thirst" (verse 35). "I am the living bread which came down from heaven: if any man eat of this bread, he shall live for ever: and the bread that I will give is my flesh, which I will give for the life of the world" (verse 51). "And when he had given thanks, he brake it [the bread], and said, Take, eat: this is my body, which is broken for you: this do in remembrance of me" (1 Cor. 11:24).

of salvation. Some will be lost, having thrown away their birthright possession. Christ gave us salvation even before we were able to respond with any good works.]

Watch [pay attention] therefore: for ye know not what hour your Lord doth come. [One can be thoroughly involved in the work of God—even to the point of neglecting our own communication with Him so that we ourselves are found on the wrong side of the fence. Preparing for the second coming—frankly, health reform, dress reform, even teaching the word of God and the Sabbath can become legalistic when done out of fear of loss or hope of reward. Actually, we do not have to worry about these things if we are paying attention to the promptings of the Holy Spirit, because He will guide us to do right, if we are willing.]

But know this, that if the goodman of the house had known in what watch the thief would come, he would have watched, and would not have suffered his house to be broken up.

Therefore be ye also ready [constantly paying attention to the promptings of the Holy Spirit]: for in such an hour as ye think not the Son of man cometh.

Who then is a faithful and wise servant [those who profess to be God's people], whom his lord hath made ruler over his household, to give them meat in due season [faithfully feeding the flock with timely words of truth and encouragement]?

Blessed is that servant, whom his lord when he cometh shall find so doing.

Verily I say unto you, That he shall make him ruler over all his goods.

But and if that evil servant shall say in his heart, My lord delayeth his coming [not paying attention to the promptings of the Holy Spirit];

And shall begin to smite his fellowservants [gossip and backbiting], and to eat and drink with the drunken [giving up on health reform];[13]

The lord of that servant shall come in a day when he looketh not for him, and in an hour that he is not aware of,

And shall cut him asunder, and appoint him his portion with the hypocrites: there shall be weeping and gnashing of teeth [In the case of health reform, this would be manifest in poor health, disease, pain, and the first death—the same health problems as those of the world. In the case of gossip and backbiting, this would be manifest in the second death]. (Matt. 24:37–51)

The following verses provide us additional insight on the events of the last days. This is a dual prophecy, which means it applies both to those in Christ's day 2,000 years ago and, in addition, to those at the

---

13 "And in that day seven women shall take hold of one man, saying, We will eat our *own* bread, and wear our *own* apparel: only let us be called by thy name [Christian], to take away our reproach" (Isa. 4:1). See also chapter 12 in this book, "Feast of the Day of Atonement: The Affliction."

end of time—a parallel application, the destruction of Jerusalem itself being a prophecy of the last days:[14]

> O Jerusalem, Jerusalem, thou that killest the prophets, and stonest them which are sent unto thee, how often would I have gathered thy children together, even as a hen gathereth her chickens under her wings, and ye would not! Behold, your house is left unto you desolate. For I say unto you, Ye shall not see me henceforth, till ye shall say, Blessed is he that cometh in the name of the Lord. (Matt. 23:37–39)

> And Jesus went out, and departed from the temple: and his disciples came to him for to shew him the buildings of the temple. And Jesus said unto them, See ye not all these things? verily I say unto you, There shall not be left here one stone upon another, that shall not be thrown down. [This refers to the destruction of Jerusalem in AD 70.] And as he sat upon the mount of Olives, the disciples came unto him privately, saying, Tell us, when shall these things be? and what shall be the sign of thy coming, and of the end of the world?
>
> And Jesus answered and said unto them, Take heed that no man deceive you. For many shall come in my name, saying, I am Christ; and shall deceive many. [Some may even say, "I have the truth. Follow me."[15] Jesus elaborates on this in verses 23–28.] And ye shall hear of wars and rumours of wars: see that ye be not troubled: for all these things must come to pass, but the end is not yet. For nation shall rise against nation, and kingdom against kingdom: and there shall be famines, and pestilences, and earthquakes, in divers places. [Do I need to tell you that wars, earthquakes,[16] famines, and pestilences are increasing today and have been for some time? If you need to, you may check the historical records.] All these are the beginning of sorrows.
>
> Then shall they deliver you up to be afflicted, and shall kill you [Some may experience the first death.]: and ye shall be hated of all nations for my name's sake. [In Luke 21:18 Jesus adds, "But there shall not an hair of your head perish." He is saying that even though they may inflict the first death, they cannot cause you to suffer the second death (Matt. 10:28).]
>
> And then shall many be offended, and shall betray one another, and shall hate one another. And many false prophets shall rise, and shall deceive many. And because iniquity shall abound, the love of many shall wax cold. But he that shall endure unto the end, the same shall be saved.

---

14 Luke 21 is on the same subject as Mathew 24.
15 Anyone who asks you to follow them is standing in the place of God. A true follower of God will point to the Bible and to Christ and say, "Follow Him."
16 Earthquakes that happen under water are called tsunamis.

> And this gospel of the kingdom shall be preached in all the world for a witness unto all nations; and then shall the end come. When ye therefore shall see the abomination of desolation, spoken of by Daniel the prophet, stand in the holy place, (whoso readeth, let him understand:) [This can also be in reference to Luke 21:20: "And when ye shall see Jerusalem compassed with armies, then know that the desolation thereof is nigh."] (Matt. 24:1–15)

Before we move on to the rest of Matthew 24, I want to spend a few minutes addressing the destruction of Jerusalem. Several furlongs[17] of space around Jerusalem were considered "sacred ground." In AD 66, during the typical Feast of Tabernacles, the Roman army began the attack on Jerusalem. It ended four years later in AD 70. It was a good time to attack because virtually the whole population of Israel was in the city. The Roman soldiers approached the city, placed their standards (flags) in the sacred area, and then unexpectedly left for almost six months.[18] This gave the Christians time to flee the city, assuming they had left immediately while the feast was in session, which they did.[19] The placing of a false standard (or flag) on holy ground, thus claiming it as its own,[20] is the "transgression of desolation" mentioned in Daniel 8:13. This event represents the union of organized religion and civil government, in this case by the Roman armed forces (representing civil government) with their false standards[21] (as opposed to God's true standard, all ten of His commandments) claiming sacred territory (a reference to religious activity).

Today we call this the union of church and state. This union officially attacks God's own true standard (or law) represented by the "sacred ground." For us, during the time of trouble to come, the placing of a false standard will happen again in a spiritual sense regarding the sacred ground of the Sabbath when civil government, with the cooperation and instigation of organized religion, will try to restrict worship on God's true Sabbath. This is the abomination or transgression of desolation. Then it is time to flee. God's people will not have time to pack, but God will protect their flight. Interestingly, in each case, the Feast of Tabernacles is the time to flee. In Christ's day, 2,000 years ago, their flight did indeed take place during the typical Feast of Tabernacles. Today, during the time of trouble to come, the flight of God's people will actually take place during the antitypical Feast of Tabernacles. Logically, this anti-Sabbath law and resultant flight will mark the end of the antitypical Day of Atonement and begin the antitypical Feast of Tabernacles.

Now let's resume our examination of Matthew 24, picking up at verse 16:

---

17 A furlong is one-eighth of a mile.
18 Ellen G. White, *The Great Controversy*, pp. 26-31. The battle resumed during the Feast of the Passover.
19 The people who would ordinarily have inhabited the countryside were at the feast so that flight of the Christians, who were under persecution by the Jews, who ordinarily inhabited the now vacant countryside, was easier. When the time comes for *you* to flee, do not wait.
20 A couple of well-documented modern-day examples of a country placing a flag as a symbol of dominion took place when the United States placed their flag at Iwo Jima in 1945 during World War II and on the moon in 1969.
21 Standards represent authority. A flag placed in the ground represents the authority of the one placing the flag. A standard also is that which one in authority establishes as a rule or model for the measure of quantity, extent, value, or quality—a criterion or test. The Ten Commandments are such a standard.

Then let them which be in Judaea flee into the mountains: [Luke 21:21 gives us a little more detail: "Then let them which are in Judaea flee to the mountains; and let them which are in the midst of it depart out; and let not them that are in the countries enter thereinto." The "booths" of the antitypical Feast of Tabernacles represent this very activity to happen in the future. In the typical flight of ancient Israel, many Christians fled to the city of Pella among rugged hills and sharp valleys of the nearby land of Perea. Pella had been destroyed and left a wilderness several years before, but it still had a good water supply.]

Let him which is on the housetop not come down to take any thing out of his house: Neither let him which is in the field return back to take his clothes. [There will be no time to pack] And woe unto them that are with child, and to them that give suck in those days![22] But pray ye that your flight be not in the winter, neither on the sabbath day: [God will protect His people and also His day.]

For then shall be great tribulation, such as was not since the beginning of the world to this time, no, nor ever shall be. And except those days should be shortened, there should no flesh be saved: but for the elect's sake those days shall be shortened. [The time of trouble will not last a long time.]

Then if any man shall say unto you, Lo, here is Christ, or there; believe it not. For there shall arise false Christs, and false prophets, and shall shew great signs and wonders; insomuch that, if it were possible, they shall deceive the very elect. Behold, I have told you before. [See verse 5.] Wherefore if they shall say unto you, Behold, he is in the desert; go not forth: behold, he is in the secret chambers; believe it not. [Stay away from false prophets and false teachers and study for yourselves.]

For as the lightning cometh out of the east, and shineth even unto the west; so shall also the coming of the Son of man be. [All people will see Him at the same time. This implies that Christ will not touch the ground when He comes, for all will see Him. If someone claiming to be Christ is standing on the ground, run!]

For wheresoever the carcase is [the false prophet or teacher], there will the eagles be gathered together. [False prophets and teachers and those who follow them will all be destroyed with the sin to which they cling. Luke 21:24 expounds upon this verse: "And they shall fall by the edge of the sword, and shall be led away captive into all nations: and Jerusalem shall be trodden down of the Gentiles, until the times of

---

22 Ellen White gives us the following insight into the death of those we love before the time of trouble. "It is not always safe to ask for unconditional healing…. He [God] knows whether or not those for whom petitions are offered would be able to endure the trial and test that would come upon them if they lived. He knows the end from the beginning. Many will be laid away to sleep before the fiery ordeal of the time of trouble shall come upon our world" (*Counsels on Health*, p. 375). "The Lord has often instructed me that many little ones are to be laid away before the time of trouble. We shall see our children again. We shall meet them and know them in the heavenly courts" (*Selected Messages*, book 2, p. 259).

the Gentiles be fulfilled." [The Jewish people certainly fell by the sword and are still scattered all over the world today. And today Jerusalem is in the control of Gentiles. When the New Jerusalem comes down out of the sky, that will mark the fulfilling of the time of the Gentiles (see Revelation 21:2, 27).]

Immediately after the tribulation of those days shall the sun be darkened, and the moon shall not give her light, and the stars shall fall from heaven, and the powers of the heavens shall be shaken: [Typically, these signs have already been fulfilled.[23] Antitypically, these signs are still in the future and come during the seven last plagues.]

And then shall appear the sign of the Son of man in heaven:[24] and then shall all the tribes of the earth mourn, and they shall see the Son of man coming in the clouds of heaven [again, not touching the ground] with power and great glory.

And he shall send his angels with a great sound of a trumpet, and they shall gather together his elect from the four winds, from one end of heaven to the other. [He is still not touching the ground. He sends the angels to get His people.]

Now learn a parable of the fig tree; When his branch is yet tender, and putteth

---

23 See also Luke 21:25: "There shall be signs in the sun, and in the moon, and in the stars." Now read Luke 21:32: "This generation shall not pass away, till all be fulfilled." This is an example of the dual prophecy idea because this was fulfilled almost immediately on the mount of transfiguration (see *Desire of Ages,* p. 422). But we have *also* understood this to refer to the generation that *first* recognized these signs as signs of the soon coming of Jesus, that is, the first Adventist generation (see *Desire of Ages,* p. 632). And we can apply it to the second coming of Christ (see *The SDA Bible Commentary,* p. 1110).

Then came the Lisbon earthquake. It has been said that the Lisbon earthquake of 1755 not only shook Europe physically, but it shook the *thinking* of the people in *that* generation in a manner similar to the way nuclear fission has shaken *our* thinking today. It opened a new order of things and a new pattern of thought. It was a separation point in human history. That earthquake was the fulfillment of the opening of the *sixth seal* of Revelation 6; followed by the dark day of May 19, 1780, followed by the moon appearing as blood. People who studied their Bibles recognized this as *precisely* the fulfillment of the prophecy of Luke 21. Then came the falling stars of 1833, more fulfillment of prophecy. Jesus said that the generation that saw *all* those signs, not necessarily those who lived in 1755 and saw only the first or second signs, but those who also *recognized* them as *the fulfillment* of the promise of Jesus' soon coming, "this generation shall not pass until *all* be fulfilled." In 1888 the beginning of the latter rain started. From 1833 to 1888 is 55 years, well within the lifetime of a human being. (This information was adapted from a sermon by Robert J. Wieland; used with permission.)

24 The showdown on Mount Carmel, as documented in 1 Kings 18:36–44, was a prophecy of the "time of trouble" when God proves Himself before His accusers. We find in this passage a clue of what the "sign of the Son of man" will look like. "And it came to pass at the time of the offering of the evening sacrifice, that Elijah the prophet came near, and said, Lord God of Abraham, Isaac, and of Israel, let it be known this day that thou art God in Israel, and that I am thy servant, and that I have done all these things at thy word. Hear me, O Lord, hear me, that this people may know that thou art the Lord God, and that thou hast turned their heart back again. Then the fire of the Lord fell, and consumed the burnt sacrifice, and the wood, and the stones, and the dust, and licked up the water that was in the trench. And when all the people saw it, they fell on their faces: and they said, The Lord, he is the God; the Lord, he is the God. And Elijah said unto them, Take the prophets of Baal; let not one of them escape. And they took them: and Elijah brought them down to the brook Kishon, and slew them there. And Elijah said unto Ahab, Get thee up, eat and drink; for there is a sound of abundance of rain. So Ahab went up to eat and to drink. And Elijah went up to the top of Carmel; and he cast himself down upon the earth, and put his face between his knees, And said to his servant, Go up now, look toward the sea. And he went up, and looked, and said, There is nothing. And he said, Go again seven times. And it came to pass at the seventh time, that he said, Behold, there ariseth *a little cloud out of the sea, like a man's hand*. And he said, Go up, say unto Ahab, Prepare thy chariot, and get thee down that the rain stop thee not."

forth leaves, ye know that summer is nigh: So likewise ye, when ye shall see all these things, know that it is near, even at the doors. Verily I say unto you, This generation shall not pass, till all these things be fulfilled. [See verse 29.] Heaven and earth shall pass away, but my words shall not pass away. But of that day and hour knoweth no man, no, not the angels of heaven, but my Father only. [Not even Jesus knows ahead of time the day of His coming.]

The "time of the Gentiles," as mentioned in Luke 21:24, is true in a corporate sense.[25] This era began when corporate Israel finally and officially rejected Jesus Christ as the Messiah at Christ's crucifixion in the midst of the week in Daniel 9:27 and culminated with the stoning of Stephen at the end of that week, at the end of the "Jewish era" prophecy of Daniel 9. Thus began the era of "spiritual Israel" that includes Christian Jews and Christian Gentiles (see Rom. 9–11, especially 11:25–27), hence the "time of the Gentiles." The time of the Gentiles ends with the coming of the Messiah and the establishment of His eternal kingdom and culminates with the descent of the New Jerusalem in Revelation 21.

There is an interesting passage in the Bible regarding this idea of watching and being ready. Matthew 25 tells us about it:

> Then shall the kingdom of heaven be likened unto ten virgins, which took their lamps, and went forth to meet the bridegroom. And five of them were wise, and five were foolish. They that were foolish took their lamps, and took no oil with them: But the wise took oil in their vessels with their lamps. While the bridegroom tarried, they all slumbered and slept. And at midnight there was a cry made, Behold, the bridegroom cometh; go ye out to meet him. Then all those virgins arose, and trimmed their lamps. And the foolish said unto the wise, Give us of your oil; for our lamps are gone out. But the wise answered, saying, Not so; lest there be not enough for us and you: but go ye rather to them that sell, and buy for yourselves. And while they went to buy, the bridegroom came; and they that were ready went in with him to the marriage: and the door was shut. Afterward came also the other virgins, saying, Lord, Lord, open to us. But he answered and said, Verily I say unto you, I know you not. Watch therefore, for ye know neither the day nor the hour wherein the Son of man cometh.

Ordinarily, in Bible prophecy, a woman represents a church.[26] However, in this case, all ten women represent the professed people of God living during the last days. They are the guests at the wedding. They are waiting for the word that it is time to enter the sanctuary to witness the wedding "ceremony."

---

25 Individually, ancestral Jewish people experience salvation today by becoming Christians.
26 See Jeremiah 6:2 and Isaiah 54, especially verses 5, 6, and 17.

In the meantime, they are living during the antitypical Day of Atonement. Are they doing the heart searching required on that day? Some are. Others are not.

The bridegroom is Christ. The ten women are not the "bride." The "bride" is the church, the corporate body of God's people through all time who will inhabit the New Jerusalem.[27] In addition, the "ceremony" itself is the second coming of Christ and the resurrection of the saints—the gathering of His people from all time; in other words, the Feast of Tabernacles. The "consummation" of the wedding takes place during the 1000 years of time Christ spends with His church and culminates with the New Jerusalem descending in "all her glory"—glory provided by Christ Himself. The oil represents the work of the Holy Spirit.[28] The oil in the lamps represents the former rain work of the Holy Spirit; whereas the oil in the vessels (an emergency supply carried separately) represents the latter rain work of the Holy Spirit.[29]

In this parable God's professed people have "accepted" Christ, some only in a superficial way, perhaps, but they have taken a stand for Christ, have been baptized, and have joined the church. This is the work of the former rain of the Holy Spirit. No one will be able to receive the latter rain without first receiving this former rain. However, even though they have received the former rain of the Holy Spirit, they are yet deficient in the extra oil for the last days. They need the extra oil of the work of the latter rain of the Holy Spirit, the time of refreshing, to refresh their lamps when their lamps go out because of the wait. As this is being written, it has been more than 150 years since the work of the cleansing of the sanctuary began in 1844, which signaled the beginning of the wedding and the beginning of the work of the Bridegroom in this story, and it has been more than 120 years since God brought the beginning of the latter rain, the extra oil. It is easy to see how the lamps could go out.[30] Nevertheless, if they receive the work of the latter rain that began in 1888, God's people will be ready when the Bridegroom comes to take them home.

> "The law was our schoolmaster to bring us unto Christ, that we might be justified by faith" (Galatians 3:24). In this scripture, the Holy Spirit through the apostle is speaking especially of the moral law. The law reveals sin to us, and causes us to feel

---

27   See Revelation 19:5–9; 21:2, 9, 10, and onward.
28   See Zechariah 4:1–6.
29   For a discussion of the former and latter rains of the Holy Spirit, see chapter 7, "The Feast of Weeks."
30   "Many do not realize what they must be in order to live in the sight of the Lord without a high priest in the sanctuary through the time of trouble. Those who receive the seal of the living God and are protected in the time of trouble must reflect the image of Jesus fully. Their robes must be spotless, their characters must be purified from sin by the blood of sprinkling. Through the grace of God and their own diligent effort [that is, *decisive surrender*; Ellen G, White talks more about what she means by "diligent effort" (which is humanity's part in overcoming evil) in *Christ's Object Lessons*, pp. 61 (yield) and 331 (submit)], they must be conquerors in the battle with evil. While the investigative judgment is going forward in heaven, while the sins of penitent believers are being removed from the sanctuary, there is to be a special work of purification, of putting away of sin, among God's people upon earth. I saw that many were neglecting the preparation so needful and were looking to the time of "refreshing" and the "latter rain" to fit them to stand in the day of the Lord and to live in His sight. Oh, how many I saw in the time of trouble without a shelter! [No "booths!"] They had neglected the needful preparation; therefore they could not receive the refreshing that all must have to fit them to live in the sight of a holy God" (Ellen G. White, *Maranatha*, p. 254).

our need of Christ and to flee unto Him for pardon and peace by exercising [the gift of] repentance toward God and faith toward our Lord Jesus Christ [already provided].

    An unwillingness to yield up preconceived opinions, and to accept this truth, lay at the foundation of a large share of the opposition manifested at Minneapolis against the Lord's message through Brethren [E. J.] Waggoner and [A. T.] Jones. By exciting that opposition Satan succeeded in shutting away from our people, in a great measure, the special power of the Holy Spirit that God longed to impart to them. The enemy prevented them from obtaining that *efficiency* which might have been theirs in carrying the truth to the world, as the apostles proclaimed it after the day of Pentecost. [This is a reference to the former rain, specifically, the *efficiency* of it.] The light that is to lighten the whole earth with its glory [the latter rain (Rev. 18:1)] was resisted, and by the action of our own brethren has been in a great degree kept away from the world.[31]

As Matthew 25:2 tells us, five virgins were wise and five were foolish. The wise virgins, realizing that the coming of the Bridegroom could possibly be delayed, prepared a vessel of extra oil. In today's scenario, the antitypical fulfillment of this idea would be to receive at least the *beginning* of the latter rain, which you can see came to us first during a meeting held in Minneapolis, Minnesota, in 1888.

    The people were not expecting the latter rain to begin to fall in such a gentle manner. We tend to think that the latter rain is merely a special and mighty manifestation of God's power in His people. However, the Bible indicates the manner in which we should expect to encounter the latter rain. It comes as a teaching:

> Give ear, O ye heavens, and I will *speak*; and hear, O earth, the *words of my mouth*. [Get ready! God is about to create.]
>
>   My doctrine [the teachings and words of God's mouth] shall drop as the rain, my speech [again, the teaching and words of God's mouth] shall distil as the dew, as the *small rain* upon the tender herb, and as the *showers* upon the grass: [Note: the latter rain begins gently, almost imperceptibly such as the distillation of dew, and crescendos to a climax and a great shower.]
>
>   Because I will publish the name [character[32]] of the Lord: ascribe ye greatness unto our God. He is the Rock, his work is perfect: for all his ways are judgment [deliverance]: a God of truth and without iniquity, just and right [righteous] is he. (Deut. 32:1–4)

---

31   Ellen G. White, *Selected Messages*, book 1, pp. 234, 235.
32   God's people "publish" His character in their lives through teaching, lifestyle, and example as God lives His life in them.

God's "rain" is doctrine. It is His teaching—the word from His mouth that has inherent within it the power to create what it says. It is full of deliverance from sin and from all the enemies of God. When He speaks, He creates righteousness, and when we listen attentively and believe, that righteousness then enters into our daily experience. This is what happened at Pentecost when the tongues of fire lighted on the disciples—it was the manifestation of the *former* rain. The same is true today when we receive the work of the messengers of God that came in 1888 and incorporate the belief system thus presented. The work of 1888 was just the beginning of the latter rain. The full manifestation of the power of it will come during the time of the Feast of Tabernacles through those who have received the beginning of it during the Feast of the Day of Atonement. Thus, the antitypical fulfillment of the five wise women will be realized, for God's people (corporately[33]) will be fitted for the final events before Jesus comes and will safely be brought through the time of trouble, as indicated by Daniel in Daniel 12:1. During all this, God will use them to give a clear final warning, for God does not do anything important without warning the world. "Surely the Lord God will do nothing, but he revealeth his secret unto his servants the prophets" (Amos 3:7).

All of this applies to the church corporately as well as to each of us individually, as does our next text that follows. The Laodicean church is the final entry in the history of God's corporate church. The word means "a people judged."

> And unto the angel of the church of the Laodiceans write; These things saith the Amen [Christ Himself], the faithful and true witness [making a statement, sounding a warning], the beginning [originator, head] of the creation of God [Christ is depicted as the creator of all things. Remember, His *word* has inherent within it the power to create what it says. What follows is His warning.];
>
> I know thy works, that thou art neither cold nor hot [lukewarm—wanting to *look* good, but not wanting to *be* good or allow God to have control]: I would thou wert cold or hot. [Get off the fence and take one side or the other. God can more easily work with someone openly against Him than one who is self-reliant and self-righteous.]
>
> So then because thou art lukewarm,[34] and neither cold nor hot, I will [Greek:

---

33   Individually, the experiences of His people will vary, but God will always keep them from sin as long as they choose to remain His.

34   Who likes to drink lukewarm water? Water is good, and good for you, at room temperature, but lukewarm water is just *above* room temperature. It can be unappetizing because it is neither cold nor hot. People who are "lukewarm" *spiritually* have a knowledge of truth in their minds but they have not allowed God to transform their hearts. Thus, they have an intellectual understanding without the emotional response. Their lives look good on the surface but lack depth and spiritual discernment or spiritual understanding ("eyesalve"). Therefore, they capitulate when trials come, when it is time to stand for Christ, because their faith (that "gold tried in the fire") is dead. Their self-righteousness is filthy rags, and God considers them to be spiritually naked, lacking the "white raiment." God can work with people who are "hot," that is, they are both intellectually knowledgeable and emotionally involved. God can also work with people who are "cold," because they are unavoidably ignorant about God. Thus, their emotions cannot be *expected* to favor Him, yet they are still open-minded. Acts 17:30 expresses the idea very well: "And the times of this ignorance God winked at; but now commandeth all men

mello—am *about* to] spue [*emeo*—to vomit] thee out of my mouth. [I feel sick to my stomach, even nauseous, because you are lukewarm.],[35]

Because thou sayest, I am rich, and increased with goods [I possess all truth], and have need of nothing [I don't need to learn any more]; and knowest not that thou art wretched, and miserable, and poor, and blind, and naked [in understanding the gospel]:

I counsel thee to buy [purchase or trade in your old, preconceived ideas] of me gold tried in the fire, that thou mayest be rich [in faith and *agape*[36]]; and white raiment [the righteousness of Christ[37]], that thou mayest be clothed, and that the shame of thy nakedness do not appear; and anoint thine eyes with eyesalve, that thou mayest see [spiritual discernment and understanding].

As many as I love [*pheleo*—God likes each of us warmly and tenderly], I rebuke and chasten: be zealous therefore, and repent. [Go ahead and make the "purchase." Give up your own ways and preconceived ideas and let Me give you My righteousness.]

Behold, I stand at the door, and knock [In the Greek, it means He keeps on knocking.[38]]: if any man hear my voice [pay attention and receive His all-powerful creative word], and open the door [say "yes" and believe], I will come in to him, and will sup with him, and he with me. [Christ dwells in our hearts through faith—a living connection directly with Heaven—when we believe.]

To him that overcometh [through the death of Christ (Rev. 7:14; 12:1)] will I grant to sit with me in my throne [God intends to make the human race rulers in the universe—"Lords" and "Ladies," "Princes" and "Princesses"—royalty in the courts of heaven—joint heirs with Christ (Rom. 8:17).], even as I also overcame [We die *with* Christ, sharing His death and allowing His death to become ours, spiritually speaking (Rom. 6:1–6).], and am set down with my Father in his throne. [We choose to remain in Christ, who rules in heaven.]

He that hath an ear, let him hear what the Spirit saith unto the churches [Jesus said this, as if to say, "This is important. Pay attention."]. (Rev. 3:14–22)

---

every where to repent." Others who are spiritually cold are those who may be angry with Him (usually out of ignorance), for they are at least willing to admit their emotions on the one hand, or, on the other hand, are not pretentious, for they do not pretend to know Him or love Him. God cannot work with those who are "lukewarm," even though they are *called* Christians, for, although they *claim* to follow Him, they are not willing to *listen* to Him, which results in them missing the creative power of His word in their lives. They think they know it all, as Revelation 3:17 indicates. Thus, they refuse God's grace for themselves, and they block the way for others to come to know Christ and His power in *their* lives.

35 Note: Christ does not actually throw up His church. He just feels nauseous.
36 See 1 Peter 1:7, 8.
37 See Isaiah 61:10. White indicates purity; whereas, dirty garments indicate self-righteousness.
38 In Song of Solomon 5:2 (Septuagint) we find the bride brushing off the Bridegroom, which matches the Laodicean attitude.

The reason God created the human race was to replace the evil angels that fell with Lucifer, which was about one third of the total population of angels.[39] Lucifer had wanted to "horn in" on the Godhead to rule as God (Isa. 14:14). Having created man and woman in the image of God, yet just below the angels,[40] God intended to raise them to a little above the angels had they passed the test in the garden. However, it is not too late. Because God's people will be humble enough to allow Him to have complete control of their lives, He will cause them to rise from being a little lower than the angels to being a little higher than the angels, placing His people in rulership positions. The disciples argued among themselves about who was going to be the greatest in the kingdom of heaven, but God says that those who are the *least* (in their own minds) will be the *greatest* (in God's mind).[41]

The attack on the Sabbath is actually an attack on righteousness by faith because God's Sabbath is a memorial of creation: "For in six days the LORD made heaven and earth, the sea, and all that in them is, and rested the seventh day: wherefore the LORD blessed the sabbath day, and hallowed it" (Exod. 20:11). The Sabbath, therefore, represents God's all-powerful creative word that has the power inherent within it to create what He says. Through the power of His voice, He creates righteousness in His people. He speaks it, and thus they are *made* righteous—and when they listen attentively and believe, they begin to *act out* that righteousness—in actual good works in their experience.[42]

This is righteousness by faith. The issue is all about who God is and what He is capable of doing in fallen sinful human flesh! This includes the fallen sinful human flesh that He took when He became a baby and also the fallen sinful human flesh that you and I have. (See chapters 11 and 12 on the Feast of the Day of Atonement.)

> And it shall come to pass, that every one that is left [those who believe and kept watch with God's people] of all the nations which came against Jerusalem [Historically, these are enemies (unbelievers) of God and His people, yet there are some within their ranks who will choose to believe.] shall even go up from year to year to worship the King, the LORD of hosts, and to keep the feast of tabernacles. [These are people who were formerly unbelievers, enemies of God and His people. They receive the

---

39 See Revelation 12:4. "Star(s)" in Bible prophecy refer to a leadership, messenger(s), or angel(s). Revelation 1:20; 12:1, 4, 9. "God made the world to enlarge heaven. He desires a larger family of created intelligences.… Human beings were a new and distinct order. They were made 'in the image of God,' and it was the Creator's design that they should populate the earth" (*The SDA Bible Commentary*, vol. 1, p. 1081). "God created man for His own glory, that after test and trial the human family might become one with the heavenly family. It was God's purpose to re-populate heaven with the human family, if they would show themselves obedient to His every word" (Ibid., p. 1082). "Heaven will triumph, for the vacancies made in heaven by the fall of Satan and his angels will be filled by the redeemed of the Lord" (Ibid., vol. 7, p. 949). From these statements one could conclude that heaven and earth will eventually be united as to location, since they will populate both heaven and earth!

40 See Genesis 1:26, 27; Psalm 8:5; and Hebrews 2:7, 9. Note: Christ took upon Him the same flesh as we have.

41 See Matthew 18:1–4; 23:8–12; Mark 9:33–37; and Luke 22:24–27.

42 "To accept the unspeakable gift of God's grace, therefore, is simply to yield ourselves to him, that Christ may dwell in us, and live in us the righteousness of the law as spoken from Sinai, and treasured in the throne of God. From Christ that living stream still flows, so that, receiving him, we shall have in us that well of water spring up unto everlasting life" (E. J. Waggoner, *Waggoner on Romans*, p. 108).

repentance that God has provided for all people and allow themselves to be prepared to be translated or resurrected in the first resurrection when Jesus comes to take them to heaven. Note the reference to the feast we are studying.] …

And if the family of Egypt [an example of the nations that make up the unbelievers, specifically, in Egypt's case, atheists] go not up, and come not [refuse participation in the antitypical Feast of Tabernacles], that have no rain [not partaking of either or both of the early and latter rains]; there shall be the plague [the seven last plagues after the close of probation—similar to the ten plagues of Egypt in Moses' day], wherewith the Lord will smite the heathen that come not up to keep the feast of tabernacles.

This shall be the punishment of Egypt, and the punishment of all nations that come not up to keep the feast of tabernacles. [They *refuse* the repentance so freely provided.] (Zech. 14:16–19)

Today, God is holding back the four winds of strife (the time of trouble) to give His people ample time to allow Him to prepare them for this time of final reckoning. He is not willing that any, including *you*, should be lost. "The Lord is not slack concerning his promise, as some men count slackness; but is longsuffering to us-ward, not willing that any should perish, but that all should come to repentance" (2 Peter 3:9).

Where do *you* stand on these issues? Do you believe God's promise? If you have historically been an unbeliever, either through ignorance or through rebellion, it is not too late. Let God have your heart now and dedicate (or re-dedicate) your life to His service. God will not let you die the second death against your will. He will carry you all the way through.

All this is your heritage, forged out for you by Jesus Christ Himself. Cherish your birthright. Don't throw it away as Esau did.[43] The "rain" has begun to fall, for the latter rain that began in 1888 will soon fall in earnest. As God provided a boat for Noah, so has He provided a "boat" for *you*. As Peter looked to Christ while *he* was walking on the water (Matthew 14), so may *you*, by also looking to Christ, do things every bit as amazing as walking on water.

As we close our study of the feast days, let's consider the following two verses in Leviticus 23:

These are the feasts of the Lord, which ye shall proclaim to be holy convocations, to offer an offering made by fire unto the Lord, a burnt offering, and a meat offering, a sacrifice, and drink offerings, every thing upon his day: *Beside* the sabbaths of the Lord [in addition to the weekly seventh-day Sabbath], and beside your gifts, and beside all your vows, and beside all your freewill offerings, which ye give unto the Lord. (verses 37, 38)

The choice is yours. Let Him have your *own* free will.

---

43 Esau did not appreciate his inheritance as is evident in the biblical account in Genesis 25:19–34.

Epilogue

"It Is Finished"[1]

Christ did not yield up His life till He had accomplished the work which He came to do, and with His parting breath He exclaimed, "It is finished." John 19:30. The battle had been won. His right hand and His holy arm had gotten Him the victory. As a Conqueror He planted His banner on the eternal heights. Was there not joy among the angels? All heaven triumphed in the Saviour's victory. Satan was defeated, and knew that his kingdom was lost.

To the angels and the unfallen worlds the cry, "It is finished," had a deep significance. It was for them as well as for us that the great work of redemption had been accomplished. They with us share the fruits of Christ's victory.

Not until the death of Christ was the character of Satan clearly revealed to the angels or to the unfallen worlds. The archapostate had so clothed himself with deception that even holy beings had not understood his principles. They had not clearly seen the nature of his rebellion.

It was a being of wonderful power and glory that had set himself against God. Of Lucifer the Lord says, "Thou sealest up the sum, full of wisdom, and perfect in beauty." Ezekiel 28:12. Lucifer had been the covering cherub. He had stood in the light of God's presence. He had been the highest of all created beings, and had been foremost in revealing God's purposes to the universe. After he had sinned, his power to deceive was the more deceptive, and the unveiling of his character was the more difficult, because of the exalted position he had held with the Father.

God could have destroyed Satan and his sympathizers as easily as one can cast a pebble to the earth; but He did not do this. Rebellion was not to be overcome by force. Compelling power is found only under Satan's government. The Lord's principles are not of this order. His authority rests upon goodness, mercy, and love; and the presentation of these principles is the means to be used. God's government is moral, and truth and love are to be the prevailing power.

It was God's purpose to place things on an eternal basis of security, and in the councils of heaven it was decided that time must be given for Satan to develop the principles which were the foundation of his system of government. He had claimed that these were superior to God's principles. Time was given for the working of Satan's principles, that they might be seen by the heavenly universe.

Satan led men into sin, and the plan of redemption was put in operation. For four thousand years, Christ was working for man's uplifting, and Satan for his ruin and degradation. And the heavenly universe beheld it all.

---

[1] Ellen G. White, *The Desire of Ages*, pp. 758–764. Chapter 79 of *The Desire of Ages* is reprinted in the epilogue in its entirety.

When Jesus came into the world, Satan's power was turned against Him. From the time when He appeared as a babe in Bethlehem, the usurper worked to bring about His destruction. In every possible way he sought to prevent Jesus from developing a perfect childhood, a faultless manhood, a holy ministry, and an unblemished sacrifice. But he was defeated. He could not lead Jesus into sin. He could not discourage Him, or drive Him from a work He had come on earth to do. From the desert to Calvary, the storm of Satan's wrath beat upon Him, but the more mercilessly it fell, the more firmly did the Son of God cling to the hand of His Father, and press on in the bloodstained path. All the efforts of Satan to oppress and overcome Him only brought out in a purer light His spotless character.

All heaven and the unfallen worlds had been witnesses to the controversy. With what intense interest did they follow the closing scenes of the conflict. They beheld the Saviour enter the garden of Gethsemane, His soul bowed down with the horror of a great darkness. They heard His bitter cry, "Father, if it be possible, let this cup pass from Me." Matthew 26:39. As the Father's presence was withdrawn, they saw Him sorrowful with a bitterness of sorrow exceeding that of the last great struggle with death. The bloody sweat was forced from His pores, and fell in drops upon the ground. Thrice the prayer for deliverance was wrung from His lips. Heaven could no longer endure the sight, and a messenger of comfort was sent to the Son of God.

Heaven beheld the Victim betrayed into the hands of the murderous mob, and with mockery and violence hurried from one tribunal to another. It heard the sneers of His persecutors because of His lowly birth. It heard the denial with cursing and swearing by one of His best-loved disciples. It saw the frenzied work of Satan, and his power over the hearts of men. Oh, fearful scene! the Saviour seized at midnight in Gethsemane, dragged to and fro from palace to judgment hall, arraigned twice before the priests, twice before the Sanhedrin, twice before Pilate, and once before Herod, mocked, scourged, condemned, and led out to be crucified, bearing the heavy burden of the cross, amid the wailing of the daughters of Jerusalem and the jeering of the rabble.

Heaven viewed with grief and amazement Christ hanging upon the cross, blood flowing from His wounded temples, and sweat tinged with blood standing upon His brow. From His hands and feet the blood fell, drop by drop, upon the rock drilled for the foot of the cross. The wounds made by the nails gaped as the weight of His body dragged upon His hands. His labored breath grew quick and deep, as His soul panted under the burden of the sins of the world. All heaven was filled with wonder when the prayer of Christ was offered in the midst of His terrible suffering,—"Father, forgive them; for they know not what they do." Luke 23:34. Yet there stood men, formed in the image of God, joining to crush out the life of His only-begotten Son. What a sight for the heavenly universe!

The principalities and powers of darkness were assembled around the cross, casting the hellish shadow of unbelief into the hearts of men. When the Lord created these beings to stand before His throne, they were beautiful and glorious. Their loveliness and holiness were in accordance with their exalted station. They were enriched with the wisdom of God, and girded with the panoply of heaven. They were Jehovah's ministers. But who could recognize in the fallen angels the glorious seraphim that once ministered in the heavenly courts?

Satanic agencies confederated with evil men in leading the people to believe Christ the chief of sinners, and to make Him the object of detestation. Those who mocked Christ as He hung upon the cross were imbued with the spirit of the first great rebel. He filled them with vile and loathsome speeches. He inspired their taunts. But by all this he gained nothing.

Could one sin have been found in Christ, had He in one particular yielded to Satan to escape the terrible torture, the enemy of God and man would have triumphed. Christ bowed His head and died, but He held fast His faith and His submission to God. "And I heard a loud voice saying in heaven, Now is come salvation, and strength, and the kingdom of our God, and the power of His Christ: for the accuser of our brethren is cast down, which accused them before our God day and night." Revelation 12:10.

Satan saw that his disguise was torn away. His administration was laid open before the unfallen angels and before the heavenly universe. He had revealed himself as a murderer. By shedding the blood of the Son of God, he had uprooted himself from the sympathies of the heavenly beings. Henceforth his work was restricted. Whatever attitude he might assume, he could no longer await the angels as they came from the heavenly courts, and before them accuse Christ's brethren of being clothed with the garments of blackness and the defilement of sin. The last link of sympathy between Satan and the heavenly world was broken.

Yet Satan was not then destroyed. The angels did not even then understand all that was involved in the great controversy. The principles at stake were to be more fully revealed. And for the sake of man, Satan's existence must be continued. Man as well as angels must see the contrast between the Prince of light and the prince of darkness. He must choose whom he will serve.

In the opening of the great controversy, Satan had declared that the law of God could not be obeyed, that justice was inconsistent with mercy, and that, should the law be broken, it would be impossible for the sinner to be pardoned. Every sin must meet its punishment, urged Satan; and if God should remit the punishment of sin, He would not be a God of truth and justice. When men broke the law of God, and defied His will, Satan exulted. It was proved, he declared, that the law could not be obeyed; man could not be forgiven. Because he, after his rebellion, had been banished from heaven, Satan claimed that the human race must be forever shut out from God's favor. God could not be just, he urged, and yet show mercy to the sinner.

But even as a sinner, man was in a different position from that of Satan. Lucifer in heaven had sinned in the light of God's glory. To him as to no other created being was given a revelation of God's love. Understanding the character of God, knowing His goodness, Satan chose to follow his own selfish, independent will. This choice was final. There was no more that God could do to save him. But man was deceived; his mind was darkened by Satan's sophistry. The height and depth of the love of God he did not know. For him there was hope in a knowledge of God's love. By beholding His character he might be drawn back to God.

Through Jesus, God's mercy was manifested to men; but mercy does not set aside justice. The law reveals the attributes of God's character, and not a jot or tittle of it could be changed to meet man in his fallen condition. God did not change His law, but He sacrificed Himself, in Christ, for man's redemption. "God was in Christ, reconciling the world unto Himself." 2 Corinthians 5:19.

The law requires righteousness,—a righteous life, a perfect character; and this man has not to give. He cannot meet the claims of God's holy law. But Christ, coming to the earth as man, lived a holy life, and developed a perfect character. These He offers as a free gift [inheritance] to all who will receive them [into their experience]. His life stands [a heritage, as the representative of the human race] for the life of men. Thus they have remission of sins that are past, through the forbearance of God [in title]. More than this, Christ imbues men with the attributes of God [in experience]. He builds up the human character after the similitude of the divine character, a goodly fabric of spiritual strength and beauty. Thus the very righteousness of the law is fulfilled in the [experience of the] believer in Christ. God can "be just [fair (on paper)], and the justifier of him which believeth in Jesus [the making righteous (in experience) those who believe]." Romans 3:26.

God's love has been expressed in His justice no less than in His mercy. Justice is the foundation of His throne, and the fruit of His love. It had been Satan's purpose to divorce mercy from truth and justice. He sought to prove that the righteousness of God's law is an enemy to peace. But Christ shows that in God's plan they are indissolubly joined together; the one cannot exist without the other. "Mercy and truth are met together; righteousness and peace have kissed each other." Psalm 85:10.

By His life and His death, Christ proved that God's justice did not destroy His mercy, but that sin could be forgiven, and that the law is righteous, and can be perfectly obeyed. Satan's charges were refuted. God had given man unmistakable evidence of His love.

Another deception was now to be brought forward. Satan declared that mercy destroyed justice, that the death of Christ abrogated the Father's law. Had it been possible for the law to be changed or abrogated, then Christ need not have died. But to abrogate the law would be to immortalize transgression, and place the world under Satan's control. It was because the law was changeless, because man [humankind] could be saved only through [(not by)] obedience to its precepts, that Jesus was lifted up on the cross. [Christ obeyed God's law as the representative of the human race, thus saving humanity corporately, and we follow in our experience, by His power, through believing.] Yet the very means by which Christ established the law Satan represented as destroying it. Here will come the last conflict of the great controversy between Christ and Satan.[2]

That the law which was spoken by God's own voice is faulty, that some specification has been set aside, is the claim which Satan now puts forward. It is the last great deception that he will bring upon the world. He needs not to assail the whole law; if he can lead men to disregard one precept, his purpose

---

2   "The Lord in His great mercy sent a most precious message to His people through Elders [E. J.] Waggoner and [A. T.] Jones. This message was to bring more prominently before the world the uplifted Savior, the sacrifice for the sins of the whole world. It presented justification through faith in the Surety; it invited the people to receive the righteousness of Christ, which is made manifest in obedience to all the commandments of God. Many had lost sight of Jesus. They needed to have their eyes directed to His divine person, His merits, and His changeless love for the human family. All power is given into His hands, that He may dispense rich gifts unto men, imparting the priceless gift of His own righteousness to the helpless human agent. This is the message that God commanded to be given to the world. It is the third angel's message, which is to be proclaimed with a loud voice, and attended with the outpouring of His Spirit in a large measure. [This is the latter rain, the loud cry of the third angel.]" (Ellen G. White, *Testimonies to Ministers and Gospel Workers*, pp. 91, 92).

is gained. For "whosoever shall keep the whole law, and yet offend in one point, he is guilty of all." James 2:10. By consenting to break one precept, men are brought under Satan's power. By substituting human law for God's law, Satan will seek to control the world. This work is foretold in prophecy. Of the great apostate power which is the representative of Satan, it is declared, "He shall speak great words against the Most High, and shall wear out the saints of the Most High, and think to change times and laws: and they shall be given into his hand." Daniel 7:25.

Men will surely set up their laws to counterwork the laws of God. They will seek to compel the consciences of others, and in their zeal to enforce these laws they will oppress their fellow men.

The warfare against God's law, which was begun in heaven, will be continued until the end of time. Every man will be tested. Obedience or disobedience is the question to be decided by the whole world. All will be called to choose between the law of God and the laws of men. Here the dividing line will be drawn. There will be but two classes. Every character will be fully developed; and all will show whether they have chosen the side of loyalty or that of rebellion.

Then the end will come. God will vindicate His law and deliver His people. Satan and all who have joined him in rebellion will be cut off. Sin and sinners will perish, root and branch, (Malachi 4:1),—Satan the root, and his followers the branches. The word will be fulfilled to the prince of evil, "Because thou hast set thine heart as the heart of God; … I will destroy thee, O covering cherub, from the midst of the stones of fire…. Thou shalt be a terror, and never shalt thou be any more." Then "the wicked shall not be: yea, thou shalt diligently consider his place, and it shall not be;" "they shall be as though they had not been." Ezekiel 28:6–19; Psalm 37:10; Obadiah 1:16.

This is not an act of arbitrary power on the part of God. The rejecters of His mercy reap that which they have sown. God is the fountain of life; and when one chooses the service of sin, he separates from God, and thus cuts himself off from life. He is "alienated from the life of God." Christ says, "All they that hate Me love death." Ephesians 4:18; Proverbs 8:36. God gives them existence for a time that they may develop their character and reveal their principles. This accomplished, they receive the results of their own choice. By a life of rebellion, Satan and all who unite with him place themselves so out of harmony with God that His very presence is to them a consuming fire. The glory of Him who is love will destroy them.

At the beginning of the great controversy, the angels did not understand this. Had Satan and his host then been left to reap the full result of their sin, they would have perished; but it would not have been apparent to heavenly beings that this was the inevitable result of sin. A doubt of God's goodness would have remained in their minds as evil seed, to produce its deadly fruit of sin and woe.

But not so when the great controversy shall be ended. Then, the plan of redemption having been completed, the character of God is revealed to all created intelligences. The precepts of His law are seen to be perfect and immutable. Then sin has made manifest its nature, Satan his character. Then the extermination of sin will vindicate God's love and establish His honor before a universe of beings who delight to do His will, and in whose heart is His law.

Well, then, might the angels rejoice as they looked upon the Saviour's cross; for though they did not then understand all, they knew that the destruction of sin and Satan was forever made certain, that the redemption of man was assured, and that the universe was made eternally secure. Christ Himself fully comprehended the results of the sacrifice made upon Calvary. To all these He looked forward when upon the cross He cried out, "It is finished."

Dear reader, you are a main character in this story. As such, you have the opportunity to finish this epilogue. What do you want to do? Say "yes" to Jesus Christ right now. The choice is yours. It's not too late. As we close, ponder this quote: "When we acknowledge our life forfeited, and give up all claims to that life, and everything connected with it, that moment we die with Christ."[3]

---

3   E. J. Waggoner, *1891 General Conference Bulletin* #10.

Appendices

The appendices that follow are a collection of articles by Craig Barnes, the author of this book, and such writers as A. T. Jones, E. J. Waggoner, and Ellen G. White. These articles compliment the subject matter covered in the book. If a title has a footnote after it, the entire article is taken from that source, even though quotation marks do not set off the article. May these articles strengthen and deepen your walk with God.

Appendix A

The Loom of Heaven[1]

"Buy of me gold tried in the fire, and white raiment that thou mayest be clothed." [Rev. 3:18] And you remember the description that we have already had of that raiment. The figure is, it is, "that garment that is woven in the loom of heaven, in which there is not a single thread of human making." Brethren, that garment was woven in a human body. The human body—the flesh of Christ—was the loom, was it not? That garment was woven in Jesus; in the same flesh that you and I have, for He took part of the same flesh and blood that we have. That flesh that is yours and mine, that Christ bore in this world—that was the loom in which God wove that garment for you and me to wear in the flesh, and He wants us to wear it now, as well as when the flesh is made immortal in the end!

What was the loom? Christ in His human flesh. What was it that was made there? The garment of righteousness. And it is for all of us. The righteousness of Christ—the life that He lived—for you and for me, that we are considering tonight, that is the garment. God the Father—God was in Christ reconciling the world to Himself. "His name shall be called Immanuel"—that is, "God with us." Now then, He wants that garment to be ours, but does not want us to forget who is the weaver. It is not ourselves, but it is He who is with us. It was God in Christ. Christ is to be in us, just as God was in Him, and His character is to be in us, just as God was in Him, and His character is to be woven and transformed into us through these sufferings and temptations and trials which we meet. And God is the weaver, but not without us. It is the cooperation of the divine and the human—the mystery of God in you and me—the same mystery that was in the gospel and that is the third angel's message. This is the word of the Wonderful Counselor.

---

[1] A. T. Jones, *1893 General Conference Bulletin*, no. 10, p. 207.

Appendix B

Studies in Galatians 2:20[1]

(A discussion of the work of Christ as our representative.)

"I AM crucified with Christ; nevertheless I live; yet not I, but Christ liveth in me: and the life which I now live in the flesh I live by the faith of the Son of God, who loved me, and gave himself for me."

It may not be amiss to emphasize what this scripture *does* say, by noting what it does not say.

It does *not* say, I want to be crucified with Christ. It does *not* say, I wish I were crucified with Christ, that he might live in me. It *does* say, "I am crucified with Christ."

Again: It does *not* say, Paul was crucified with Christ; Christ lived in Paul; and the Son of God loved Paul, and gave himself for Paul. All that is true; but that is *not* what the scripture *says*, nor is that what it means; for it means just what it says. And it *does* say, "*I* am crucified with Christ: nevertheless *I* live; yet not I, but Christ liveth in *me*: and the life which I now live in the flesh I live by the faith of the Son of God, who loved *me*, and gave himself for *me*."

Thus this verse is a beautiful and solid foundation of Christian faith for every soul in the world. Thus it is made possible for every soul to say, in full assurance of Christian faith, "He loved *me*." "He gave himself for *me*." "*I* am crucified with Christ." "Christ liveth in *me*." Read also 1 John 4:15.

For any soul to say, "I am crucified with Christ," is not speaking at a venture. It is not believing something on a guess. It is not saying a thing of which there is no certainty. Every soul in this world can say, in all truth and all sincerity, "I am crucified with Christ." It is but the acceptance of a fact, the acceptance of a thing that is already done; for this word *is* the statement of a fact.

It is a fact that Jesus Christ was crucified. And when he was crucified, *we* also were crucified; for he was one of *us*. His name is Immanuel, which is "God with us"—not God with *him*, but "God with *us*." When his name is *not* God with *him*, but "God with *us*;" and when God with *him* was *not* God with him, but God with *us*, then who was he but "*us*"? He had to be "*us*" in order that God with *him* could be not God with him, but "God with *us*." And when he was crucified, then who was it but "*us*" that was crucified?

This is the mighty truth announced in this text. Jesus Christ was "*us*." He was of the same flesh and blood with us. He was of our very nature. He was in all points like us. "It behooved him to be made in all points like unto his brethren." He emptied himself, and was made in the likeness of men. He was "the last Adam." And precisely as the first Adam was ourselves, so Christ, the last Adam, was ourselves. When the first Adam died, we, being involved in him, died with him. And when the last Adam was crucified,—*he* being ourselves, and we being involved in him,—*we* were crucified *with him*. As the first

---

[1] A. T. Jones, "Studies in Galatians, Galatians 2:20," *Advent Review and Sabbath Herald*, October 24, 1899, emphasis original.

Adam was in himself the whole human race, so the last Adam was in *himself* the whole human race; and so when the last Adam was crucified, the whole human race—the old, sinful, human nature [the fallen sinful human mind]—was crucified with him. And *so* it is written: "Knowing this, that *our old man* [the fallen sinful human mind] IS CRUCIFIED WITH HIM, *that the body of sin* [the fallen sinful human *flesh*] might be *destroyed* [Greek: paralyzed, rendered powerless],[2] that henceforth we should not serve sin."

Thus every soul in this world can truly say, in the perfect triumph of Christian faith, "I am crucified with Christ;" my old sinful human nature [sinful mind] is crucified with him, that this body of sin might be destroyed [again, paralyzed], that henceforth I should not serve sin Romans 6:6. Nevertheless I live; yet not I, but Christ liveth in me. Always bearing about in my body the dying of the Lord Jesus,—the crucifixion of the Lord Jesus, for I am crucified with him,—that *the life also of Jesus* might be made manifest in my body. For I who live am always delivered unto death, for Jesus' sake, that the life also of Jesus might be made manifest in my mortal flesh. 2 Cor. 4:10, 11. And therefore the life which I now live in the flesh I live by the faith of the Son of God, who loved *me*, and gave himself for *me*.

In this blessed fact of the crucifixion of the Lord Jesus, which was accomplished for every human soul, there is not only laid the foundation of faith *for* every soul, but in it there is given *the gift of faith* TO every soul.[3] And thus the cross of Christ is not only the wisdom of God displayed from God to us, but it is the *very power of God* manifested to deliver us from all sin, and bring us to God.

O sinner, brother, sister, believe it. Oh, receive it. Surrender to this mighty truth. *Say* it, say it in full assurance of faith, and say it forever. "I am crucified with Christ: nevertheless I live; yet not I, but Christ liveth in me: and the life which I now live in the flesh I live by the faith of the Son of God, who loved *me*, and gave himself for *me*." Say it; for it is the truth, the very truth and wisdom and power of God, which saves the soul from all sin.

---

2   The fallen sinful human mind is crucified and replaced by the sinless mind of God (Phil. 2:5). The fallen sinful human flesh remains, though in a powerless condition, yet being controlled by the sinless mind of God, and is replaced when Jesus comes to take His people home, and He gives us our new glorious sinless human flesh, as He has now (1 Cor. 15:51–58; 1 Thess. 4:13–17).

3   Romans 12:3.

Appendix C

Every Man Is in Christ When Entering the World[1]

The *whole universe* is given to us in Christ, and the fullness of the power that is in it is ours for the overcoming of sin [righteousness, a spiritual blessing]. God counts each soul as of as much value as all creation. Christ has by grace tasted death for *every man*, so that *every* man in the world has *received the "inexpressible gift."* Hebrews 2:9; 2 Corinthians 9:15. [Every man, therefore, must be "in Christ" at some point.] "The grace of God, and the gift by grace, which is by one Man, Jesus Christ, hath abounded unto many," even to all; for "as by the offense of one judgment came upon all men to condemnation; even so by the righteousness of One the free gift came upon all men unto justification of life." Romans 5:15, 18, KJV.

Christ is given to every man. Therefore each person gets the whole of Him. *The love of God embraces the whole world, but it also singles out each individual.* [Therefore, what is given to the world also accrues to each individual.] A mother's love is not divided among her children, so that each one receives only a third, a fourth, or a fifth of it; each child is the object of all her affection. How much more so with the God whose love is more perfect than any mother's! Isaiah 49:15. Christ is the light of the world, the Sun of Righteousness. But light is not divided among a crowd of people. If a room full of people be brilliantly lighted, each individual gets the benefit of all the light, just as much as though he were alone in the room. [*All* individuals are predestinated to be saved. Ephesians 1:3-8.] So the life of Christ lights *every* man that *comes into the world*. [The inexpressible gift has been given to every man (above).] In every *believing* heart Christ dwells in His *fullness*. [When the individual believes, the inexpressible gift already given begins to be seen in the individual's *experience*.] Sow a seed in the ground and you get many seeds, each one having as much life as the original one sown....

All this deliverance is "according to the will of our God and Father." The will of God is our sanctification. 1 Thessalonians 4:3. He wills that *all* men should be saved and come to the knowledge of the truth. 1 Timothy 2:4. And He "accomplishes all things according the counsel of His will." Ephesians 1:11. "Do you mean to teach universal salvation?" someone may ask. We mean to teach just what the Word of God teaches—that "the grace of God hath appeared, bringing salvation to all men." Titus 2:11, RV. God has wrought out salvation for every man, *and has given it to him*; but the majority spurn it and throw it away. The Judgment will reveal the fact that full salvation was given to every man and that the lost have deliberately thrown away their birthright possession.

---

[1] E. J. Waggoner, *The Glad Tidings*, pp. 11–14.

Appendix D

The Cleansing of the Sanctuary[1]

The service in the earthly sanctuary shows also that in order for the sanctuary to be cleansed and the course of the gospel service there to be finished, it must first be finished in *the people* who have a part in the service. That is to say: In the sanctuary itself, transgression could not be finished, an end of sins and reconciliation for iniquity could not be made, and everlasting righteousness could not be brought in, until all this had been accomplished *in each person* who had a part in the service of the sanctuary. The sanctuary itself could not be cleansed until each of the worshipers had been cleansed. The sanctuary itself could not be cleansed so long as, *by the confessions of the people and the intercessions of the priests*, there was pouring into the sanctuary a stream of iniquities, transgression, and sins. The cleansing of the sanctuary, *as to the sanctuary itself*, was the taking out of and away from the sanctuary all the transgressions of the people which, by the service of the priests, had been taken into the sanctuary during the service of the year. And this stream must be stopped at its fountain in the hearts and lives of the worshipers, before the sanctuary itself could possibly be cleansed.

Therefore the very first work in the cleansing of the sanctuary was the cleansing of the people. That which was preliminary and essential to the cleansing of the sanctuary itself, to the finishing of the transgression and bringing in everlasting righteousness, there, was the finishing of transgression, and the making an end of sins, and making reconciliation for iniquity and bringing in everlasting righteousness *in the heart and life of each one of the people* themselves. When the stream that flowed into the sanctuary was thus stopped at its source, then, and then alone, could the sanctuary itself be cleansed from the sins and transgression which, *from the people, by the intercession of the priests*, had flowed into the sanctuary.

And all that "was a figure for the time then present"—a "figure of the true." Therefore by this we are plainly taught that the service of our great High Priest in the cleansing of the true sanctuary must be preceded by the cleansing of each one of the believers, the cleansing of each one who has a part in that service of the true High Priest in the true sanctuary. It is plain that transgression must be finished, an end of sins and reconciliation for all iniquity must be made, and everlasting righteousness must be brought in, in the heart's experience of every believer in Jesus, before the cleansing of the true sanctuary can be accomplished.

And this is the very object of the true priesthood in the true sanctuary. The sacrifices, the priesthood, and the ministry in the sanctuary which was but a figure for the time then present, could not really take away sin, could not make the comers thereunto perfect, whereas the sacrifice, the priesthood, and the ministry of Christ in the true sanctuary does take away sins forever, does make the comers thereunto *perfect*, does *perfect* "*forever* them that are sanctified."

---

[1] A. T. Jones, *The Consecrated Way to Christian Perfection*, pp. 117–119, emphasis original.

Appendix E

Setting the date of "The End of the World"[1]

TWENTY-THREE HUNDRED DAYS. An abbreviated form of the KJV "two thousand and three hundred days" of Dan. 8:14, literally, "evening morning two thousand and three hundred." The KJV thus considers "evening morning" to refer to the light and dark portions of a 24-hour day. On the basis of the year-day principle, these 2300 prophetic days represent as many literal years. According to Dan. 8:9–14, this was a period at whose close the sanctuary was to be "cleansed." Seventh-day Adventists understand that the 70 weeks (490 literal years) of Dan. 9:24–27 were to be cut off from the 2300 years, and that the two periods of time were to begin simultaneously with "the going forth of the commandment to restore and to build Jerusalem" (v. 25). Three such decrees were issued by the Persian kings Cyrus, Darius, and Artaxerxes, respectively (Ezra 6:14). Because the first two decrees were only partially effective [because they did not empower both civil and religious autonomy] the need for a second and later a third decree indicates—the third decree, issued by Artaxerxes, is taken to be the one specified by Dan 9:25. With 457 B.C. as the beginning date, the 2300 years extend to A.D. 1844. It was this date to which many expositors, including William Miller and Seventh-day Adventists later, pointed as the fulfillment of Dan. 8:14.

Interpretation. The Seventh-day Adventist reckoning of the 2300 days of Dan. 8:14 as 2300 years was inherited directly from the Millerite movement and indirectly from earlier writers of the historical school of prophetic interpretation, which is characterized by the use of the year-day principle. Other schools of interpretation have seen this time period as 2300 literal "evenings and mornings" of desecration of a literal Jewish temple, either by Antiochus in the past or by a personal antichrist in the future.

Many historicist writers on the prophecies in various countries had anticipated William Miller in reckoning the 2300 days as years, beginning at the starting point of the 70 weeks. A number of them had arrived at approximately Miller's dating.

1. *Chronology, From Petri to Miller.* As early as 1768 Johann Petri, a Reformed pastor near Frankfurt, Germany, wrote that the 2300 days, or years, and the 70 weeks (490 years) were to be computed as beginning together. He reckoned the 2300 from 453 years before Christ's birth to 1,847 years after it, and placed the Crucifixion in the middle of the seventieth week (Dan. 9:27) and the Second Advent at the end of the 2300 days, leading to the millennium. A half century later and onward, many expositors dated the period in similar fashion, either 457 B.C. to A.D. 1843 or 1844, or 453 B.C. to A.D. 1847; others

---

[1] The *Seventh-day Adventist Encyclopedia* says this better than I can, so I have reprinted the section about the 2300-day prophecy in its entirety. *The Seventh-day Adventist Encyclopedia,* pp. 1508–1510, used with permission.

used different dates, some ending in 1866 or 1867. The figure 1847 was in many instances (for example, for Petri) virtually equivalent to 1843 because it was reckoned as 1,847 years from the birth of Christ, which was dated in 4 B.C. by the then-popular Ussher's chronology.

In his *Prophetic Faith of Our Fathers*, vol. 4, L. E. Froom lists about 35 writers between 1810 and 1844 who ended the period in 1843 or 1844, most of them in England, but including some in Scotland, Ireland, Germany, and the United States; about 25 who looked to 1847 (five of them using a supposed 2400-year period), writing in England, Germany, India, Canada, the United States, and Mexico. Not all of these began the 70 weeks and the 2300 years together, and a number of those who ended the 2300 years in the 1840s calculated other prophetic periods, such as the 1290 and 1335 years, beyond the 2300 years to such dates as 1877 and 1922. However, for the 2300 years, there was a great vogue for computing the period as ending in the 1840s, and most writers arrived at that dating by computing from the 70 weeks as ending in the time of Christ.

William Miller arrived at his expectation of the Second Advent in 1843 mainly on his computation of the 2300 years. He simply accepted, without question, A.D. 33 (the Crucifixion date as printed in the margin of his KJV Bible) as the end of the 70 weeks, which he took to be the first 490 years of the 2300-year period. Then, he reasoned, the rest of the longer period would extend 1810 years beyond that (2300 - 490 = 1810), and A.D. 33 + 1810 = 1843. Similarly, to count backward from A.D. 33 as the end of the 70 weeks, he calculated that this period of 490 years began in 457 B.C. (he merely subtracted: 490 - 33 = 457). Further, he found the figure "457 B.C." in the margin of Ezra 7 as the date for the return of Ezra to Jerusalem under the decree of Artaxerxes' seventh year, to restore the commonwealth of Judah under Jewish law. This decree Miller equated with "the commandment to restore and to build Jerusalem" (Dan. 9:25), from which the 70 weeks were to begin. Further, he could see that 457 years before Christ plus 1843 years after Christ totals 2300 years.

These two dates (457 B.C. and A.D. 33) in English Bible margins, derived from Archbishop Ussher's chronology and generally accepted as authoritative by theologians of that day, seemed to Miller, as to others before him, to make the computation obvious and inescapable.

Miller's equation 457 + 1843 = 2300, like Petri's similar equation 453 + 1847 = 2300, ignored a one-year difference in computing from B.C. to A.D. dates. This error was to be corrected later by some of Miller's colleagues (see sec. 3 below).

2. *Events at End of 2300 Years.* There was relatively little argument about the beginning date, the decree of the seventh year of Artaxerxes, but there was a variety of expectations among expositors in regard to the cleansing of the sanctuary that was to take place at the end of the 2300 years. This event had been interpreted variously by Miller's predecessors as the purification of the church, the liberation of Palestine from the Muslims, the end of the Papacy or of Islam, the beginning of the millennium, the restoration of true worship, or, in some cases, the return of Christ to set up a kingdom on earth. (Petri, for example, expected the end of the abomination in the church, and the coming of Christ to set up His kingdom and begin the millennium.) Miller held that the cleansing of the sanctuary was the purification of the temple of lively stones—the people of God—through the first resurrection at

the Second Advent; later he included the cleansing of Palestine (the place of God's sanctuary) and of the whole earth in the final fires. This fiery cleansing, he held, would destroy the last trace of sin and purify the earth for the introduction of the divine kingdom, which would last not merely 1,000 years, but throughout eternity.

The Millerite view differed from all the rest in equating the end of the 2300 days with the end of probation, the end of this world and its mortal, sinful inhabitants, and the ushering in of the eternal kingdom of the glorified saints on the renewed earth. [See Millerite Movement.]

3. *Millerite Revision From 1843 to 1844*. Miller came to define his "about 1843" as the "Jewish year 1843," which he thought extended from equinox to equinox, Mar. 21, 1843, to Mar. 21, 1844. However, beginning in 1843, some of his colleagues, especially Hale, Bliss, Litch, and others, began to reckon the "Jewish year 1843" by the Jewish lunar calendar. They ended it (according to the reckoning formerly used by the Karaite Jews) a month later than the modern Jewish calendar with the new moon of April 1844. An editorial, presumably by S. Bliss (in *The Signs of the Times* 5:123, June 21, 1843), discusses this, and also introduces the idea that Miller's 1843 is only the 2300th year (and A.D. 33 the 490th year) from 457 B.C., and that the 70 weeks and the 2300 years actually ended in 34 and 1844, respectively. But it was not until later that it was explained why the computation by straight subtraction (2300 - 457 = 1843) was a year off.

By the spring of 1843 several articles in Millerite journals pointed out that 2300 full years beginning at any time in 457 B.C. would extend to the same point in A.D. 1844, not in 1843. The explanation was that 2300 years would require 457 complete B.C. years plus 1843 complete A.D. years, which if counted from the *beginning* of 457 B.C. would continue to the end of A.D. 1843; therefore, if the period began at any point of time after the beginning of 457, it would not end until that same point of time after the end of 1843, that is, in 1844.

(The reason for this is that in historical dating, the year immediately preceding A.D. 1 is called the year 1 B.C., for there is no zero year between.) [See SDACom 1:178; SDADic "Chronology"; SB, No. 454.]

But already in February 1844 Samuel S. Snow wrote an article using this reckoning of 2300 full years from 457 B.C. (from the autumn, according to his view). Therefore he reached the conclusion that the Second Advent was not to be looked for until the autumn of 1844, and that the sixty-ninth week ended in the autumn of A.D. 27 (*Midnight Cry* 6:243, 244, Feb. 22, 1844). Little attention was given to this new expectation until the summer, by which time he had expanded his explanation and arrived at a definite date, Oct. 22.

4. *Revision of Seventy Weeks*. Miller had ended the 70 weeks with the Crucifixion in A.D. 33, but already by 1843 there was discussion of the idea that the cross was in the "midst" of the seventieth week, and authors were cited for A.D. 31 as the Crucifixion date (see Bliss, in *Signs of the Times* 6:132–136, Dec. 5, 1843).

Now in early 1844 the correction of the subtraction error led not only to the ending of the 2300 days in 1844 instead of 1843 but also to the adopting of several new positions on the 70 weeks:

(1) That the 70 weeks, or 490 years, ended in A.D. 34, not 33;

(2) that the Crucifixion took place, not at the end, but in the midst (Dan. 9:27) of the seventieth week, three and a half years before the end—that is, in A.D. 31 (the date being based on William Hales' *New Analysis of Chronology*), and that the anointing of Christ (at His baptism) at the end of the sixty-ninth week would leave three and a half years for His ministry before the "midst" of the week;

(3) that the seventieth week, ending three and a half years later than the Crucifixion, which occurred in the spring (at Passover time), would therefore have ended in the autumn of A.D. 34;

(4) that consequently the principal points of the seventieth week could be lined up at specific times: autumn 27 (Christ's baptism), spring 31 (the Crucifixion after a three-and-a-half-year ministry), and autumn 34 (the end of the seven years allotted "to confirm the covenant" by Christ and, after Him, by the apostles).

This lent conviction to the final conclusion that the concurrently beginning 2300 years would also end at a specific time—the autumn of 1844. Thus, even after Miller's year of 1843/44 ran out in the spring, the end was still to be looked for.

This autumn ending point came to be assigned to the tenth day of the seventh Jewish month as the proper day for the antitypical cleansing of the sanctuary, and the date was calculated to Oct. 22, fixed according to the former Karaite calendar. The preaching of this date resulted in the "seventh-month movement," which culminated in the expectation of the return of Christ on that day, and in the Great Disappointment [*see* Millerite Movement]. But Miller never set this specific date, and he accepted it only a few weeks before it arrived.

5. *Seventh-day Adventist Interpretation of the Expected Fulfillment.* With the passing of Oct. 22, most of the Adventists concluded that their chronology was in error, and during the next few years progressively later dates for the end of the 2300 days were advanced by one group or another. But a sizable minority held that the error was not in the reckoning of the period but in the interpretation of the closing event to be expected. Among these were a still smaller minority, the little groups who came to form the nucleus of the later Seventh-day Adventist organization [*see* Seventh-day Adventist Church]. Retaining the Millerite chronology of the 2300 years as revised in 1844, that is, as reckoned from autumn 457 B.C. to autumn 1844, they explained the cleansing of the sanctuary, in terms of the antitypical day of atonement, as representing the final phase in Christ's priestly work "in the heavens" as "minister of the sanctuary, and of the true tabernacle" (Heb. 8:1, 2), which phase they came to define as an "investigative judgment."

Appendix F

Will There be a Modern-day Prophet?

"Surely the Lord God will do nothing, but he revealeth his secret unto his servants the prophets" (Amos 3:7). After reading this text, you may be wondering if a prophet will emerge in our day. You may also be wondering who Ellen G. White is since she has been mentioned fairly regularly in this book.

Ellen White was born on November 26, 1827, to Roger and Eunice Gould Harmon just west of Portland, Maine. She grew up to be a writer and lecturer and one of the founders of the Seventh-day Adventist Church. Having been brought up a Methodist, in 1840 she heard the lectures of William Miller, and by 1843, with her family, she accepted his views on the second coming of Christ and was baptized. Because of her Adventist views, she, with her parents and other members of the family, was forced out of the Methodist Church. Three years later she married James Springer White on August 30, 1846. She traveled extensively with her husband, and together they wrote, lectured, and taught. Besides living in the United States, she also spent time living and working in Europe and Australia.

Considered by many, including myself, to possess the prophetic gift as described in the Bible, Ellen White had her first vision in late 1844 regarding the travels of the Adventist people to the city of God. The Adventist group in Portland accepted this vision as light from God. Over the course of her lifetime, she had many other visions regarding various activities of the church and God's people.

However, there have been many people throughout history who have claimed to be a prophet, many of whom have proven to be false prophets. Jesus said there would be many false prophets in the last days before He comes.[1] For these reasons, Ellen White's prophetic gift was, and still is, not without opposition. She is in good company, however, for Daniel, Isaiah, Jeremiah, Elijah, John the Baptist, and many others were all bitterly opposed. Moreover, if the devil is trying to falsify something, one can deduct that the true item must be floating around somewhere. Therefore, the presence of false prophets drives a true Bible scholar to look expectantly for a true prophet. The Bible indicates that there *will* be the true prophetic gift in the last days.[2] Therefore, all who claim to have the prophetic gift[3] must be tested according to the biblical tests of a prophet.

> Beloved, believe not every spirit, but try the spirits whether they are of God: because many false prophets are gone out into the world. (1 John 4:1)

---

1 Matthew 24:5, 11, 14, 23–27
2 A good study on the prophetic gift in the last days is found in Joel 2 and Matthew 24.
3 Not to be confused, the *generic* definition of "prophet" means a teacher or preacher of God's message. The *specific* prophetic gift is accompanied by all the spiritual manifestations of a "prophet," particularly that of receiving true visions from Jehovah.

And I took the little book out of the angel's hand, and ate it up; and it was in my mouth sweet as honey: and as soon as I had eaten it, my belly was bitter. And he said unto me, Thou must prophesy again before many peoples, and nations, and tongues, and kings. And there was given me a reed like unto a rod: and the angel stood, saying, Rise, and measure the temple of God, and the altar, and them that worship therein [that is, measure those who claim to be God's people, which is what is called "the investigative judgment"—"Shall he find faith on the earth?" (Luke 18:8)]. (Rev. 10:10–11:1)

And the dragon was wroth with the woman [God's church], and went to make war with the remnant of her seed, which keep the commandments of God, and *have the testimony of Jesus Christ*. (Rev. 12:17)

And I fell at his feet to worship him. And he said unto me, See thou do it not: I am thy fellowservant, and of thy brethren that have the testimony of Jesus: worship God: for *the testimony of Jesus is the spirit of prophecy*. (Rev. 19:10)

And it shall come to pass afterward [literally, "the hinder extremity," that is, the last days of earth's history as we know it], that I will pour out my spirit upon all flesh; and your sons and your daughters shall prophesy, your old men shall dream dreams, your young men shall see visions: And also upon the servants and upon the handmaids in those days will I pour out my spirit. And I will shew wonders in the heavens and in the earth, blood, and fire, and pillars of smoke. The sun shall be turned into darkness, and the moon into blood [1780[4]], before the great and terrible day of the LORD come. And it shall come to pass, that whosoever shall call on the name of the LORD shall be delivered: for in mount Zion and in Jerusalem shall be deliverance, as the LORD hath said, and in the remnant whom the LORD shall call. (Joel 2:28–32)

There are several tests of the prophetic gift as outlined below with supporting scriptures for each point:
1. A true prophet never prophecies in his own name, always in the name of Jehovah (the "God of Abraham, Isaac, and Jacob"). In addition, true prophets never give their own interpretation, but only what God tells them. Their statements will not contradict predecessors who wrote Scripture.

    "Knowing this first, that no prophecy of the scripture is of any private interpretation. For the prophecy came not in old time by the will of man: but holy men of God spake as they were

---

[4] This prophecy was fulfilled on May 19, 1780. Check out the Wikipedia article titled *New England's Dark Day*.

moved by the Holy Ghost" (2 Peter 1:20, 21).

"To the law and to the testimony: if they speak not according to this word, it is because there is no light in them [literally, they don't have the light of dawn]" (Isa. 8:20).

2. A true prophet's predictions always come to pass—a 100 percent success rate.

"The prophet which prophesieth of peace, when the word of the prophet shall come to pass, then shall the prophet be known, that the LORD hath truly sent him" (Jer. 28:9).

"When a prophet speaketh in the name of the LORD , if the thing follow *not*, nor come to pass, that is the thing which the LORD hath *not* spoken, but the prophet hath spoken it presumptuously: thou shalt not be afraid of [pay attention to] him" (Deut. 18:22).

3. A true prophet stresses that Jesus took upon Himself *fallen sinful human flesh.*

"Beloved, believe not every spirit, but try the spirits whether they are of God: because many false prophets are gone out into the world. Hereby know ye the Spirit of God: Every spirit that confesseth that Jesus Christ is come in the flesh is of God: And every spirit that confesseth not that Jesus Christ is come in the flesh is not of God: and this is that spirit of antichrist, whereof ye have heard that it should come; and even now already is it in the world" (1 John 4:1–3).

"For what the law could not do, in that it was weak through the flesh, God sending his own Son in the likeness of *sinful* flesh, and for sin, condemned sin in the flesh" (Rom. 8:3).

4. A true prophet will bring messages from God to individuals and institutions regarding their personal and corporate lives. These messages will build up the church and bring counsel regarding sacred issues.

"Cry aloud, spare not, lift up thy voice like a trumpet, and shew my people their transgression, and the house of Jacob their sins" (Isa. 58:1).

"But he that prophesieth speaketh unto men to edification, and exhortation, and comfort. He that speaketh in an unknown tongue edifieth himself; but he that prophesieth edifieth the church" (1 Cor. 14:3, 4).

5. A true prophet will bring messages regarding present truth. In these days just before the coming of Christ, there will be messages regarding the coming judgment. (See Joel 2:28–32.)

"The earth shall reel to and fro like a drunkard, and shall be removed like a cottage; and the transgression thereof shall be heavy upon it; and it shall fall, and not rise again" (Isa. 24:20).

"And I saw another angel fly in the midst of heaven, having the everlasting gospel to preach unto them that dwell on the earth, and to every nation, and kindred, and tongue, and people, Saying with a loud voice, Fear God, and give glory to him; for the hour of his judgment is come: and worship him that made heaven, and earth, and the sea, and the fountains of waters" (Rev. 14:6, 7).

"Immediately after the tribulation of those days shall the sun be darkened, and the moon shall not give her light [see the above note about 1780], and the stars shall fall from heaven, and the powers of the heavens shall be shaken [which occurred on November 12, 13, 1833]:[5] And then shall appear the sign of the Son of man in heaven [still future]: and then shall all the tribes of the earth mourn, and they shall see the Son of man coming in the clouds of heaven with power and great glory. And he shall send his angels with a great sound of a trumpet, and they shall gather together his elect from the four winds, from one end of heaven to the other. Now learn a parable of the fig tree; When his branch is yet tender, and putteth forth leaves, ye know that summer is nigh: So likewise ye, when ye shall see all these things, know that it is near, even at the doors" (Matt. 24:29–33).

6. Finally, what are the results? Has the "prophet's" life been an influence for good and consistent with the cause of God?

"Beware of false prophets, which come to you in sheep's clothing, but inwardly they are ravening wolves. Ye shall know them by their fruits. Do men gather grapes of thorns, or figs of thistles? Even so every good tree bringeth forth good fruit; but a corrupt tree bringeth forth evil fruit. A good tree cannot bring forth evil fruit, neither can a corrupt tree bring forth good fruit. Every tree that bringeth not forth good fruit is hewn down, and cast into the fire. Wherefore by their fruits ye shall know them" (Matt. 7:15–20).

"Thou shalt not learn to do after the abominations of those nations. There shall not be found among you any one that … useth divination,[6] or an observer of times [astrology], or an enchanter,[7] or a witch.[8] Or a charmer,[9] or a consulter with familiar spirits,[10] or a wizard,[11] or a necromancer.[12] For all that do these things are an abomination unto the LORD: … [But] Thou shalt be perfect with the LORD thy God" (Deut. 18:9–13).

"I will raise them up a [true] Prophet from among their brethren, like unto thee, and will put my words in his [or her[13]] mouth; and he shall speak unto them all that I shall command him. And it shall come to pass, that whosoever will not hearken unto my words which he shall speak in my name, I will require it of him. But the prophet, which shall presume to speak a word in my name, which I have not commanded him to speak, or that shall speak in the name of other gods, even that prophet shall die. And if thou say in thine heart, How shall we know the word which the LORD hath not spoken? When a prophet speaketh in the name of the

---

5 God sent a prophet after 1833.
6 The act of foreseeing or foretelling future events; the pretended art of discovering secrets, answering questions, or gaining information about the future by preternatural means.
7 One who enchants; a sorcerer or magician; also, one who delights, as by an enchantment.
8 One who practices witchcraft or sorcery, the female version of an "enchanter."
9 A dealer in spells, especially one who, by binding certain knots, was supposedly thereby binding a curse or a blessing on its object.
10 Demons can reproduce the image of any deceased human character and make him or her look and sound real to us, thus they would appear familiar to us. (See 1 Samuel 28 and Ecclesiastes 9.)
11 One devoted to the black art; a magician; a conjurer; a sorcerer; an enchanter.
12 "One who interrogates the dead," as the word literally means, with the view of discovering the secrets of the future.
13 There have been female prophets in the Bible: Deborah is an example (Judges 4:4).

Lord,[14] if the thing follow not, nor come to pass, that is the thing which the Lord hath not spoken, but the prophet hath spoken it presumptuously: thou shalt not be afraid of [i.e., don't pay attention to] him" (Deut. 18:18–22).

As a parenthetical note, let's backtrack a little and talk about the term "familiar spirit" (Deut. 18:11) because this is a vitally important subject. The *common* meaning of "familiar spirit" is a disembodied "soul"; in other words, the human soul (mind) after it has "left the body." An example of a familiar spirit would be a demon who is impersonating someone's "mind," sometimes accompanied by a facial or bodily "form" of a deceased person we have known in the past and is familiar to us (your parent or maybe your spouse—anyone you know or recognize). This "person" knows us and comes to visit us, perhaps in a dream, either as a voice or through all of our senses, including touch. This "person" appears convincingly real, as if he or she has been resurrected from the dead. This is what a familiar spirit is. These manifestations cannot be true because of what the Bible says in Ecclesiastes 9:5, 6: "For the living know that they shall die: but the dead know not any thing, neither have they any more a reward; for the memory of them is forgotten. Also their love, and their hatred, and their envy, is now perished; neither have they any more a portion for ever in any thing that is done under the sun." The devil and his demons can reproduce the image of any deceased human character and make him or her look and sound real to us, thus they would appear familiar to us. This is the actual, *true* meaning of this term "familiar spirit" (see 1 Sam. 28 and Eccles. 9). Let's look at Genesis 2:7: "And the Lord God formed man of the dust of the ground, and breathed into his nostrils the breath of life; and man became a living soul." The human entity is made up of the *body* ("*dust* of the ground") and the *spirit* ("*breath* of life"), and then he or she becomes a living *mind* ("a living *soul*"). The word in the Bible that is translated "spirit" means "breath"; this is that part of a person's mind that communicates with God—the seat of one's character.[15] When a person dies (the first death), the *body* returns to the ground as *dust*; the *breath* (*spirit,* character) returns to God,[16] thus He remembers who you are and all about you, and the soul (*mind*) goes back to what it was before conception, a non-existent, unconscious state. It can be said that the mind "dies,"[17] yet God still holds your character. In the resurrection, your character will be revived intact. Therefore, it is not the *soul* that goes back to God, but the *character* that goes back to Him to be returned again. Most people have never experienced such manifestations. If you are one of these, count your blessings. However, if you ever have someone who is dead come talk to you, run!

---

14 "Lord" in small capitals, as is used here, refers to Jesus Christ's official name, "Jehovah." This is the name in whom all true prophets work.

15 In Isaiah 42:5, the words "spirit" and "breath" are used in parallel.

16 "And when Jesus had cried with a loud voice, he said, Father, *into thy hands* I commend my *spirit* [movement of air, breath (seat of the character)]: and having said thus, he gave up the *ghost* [to breathe out, as in His last breath]" (Luke 23:46). Jesus tells us here where the spirit goes upon death.

17 The Bible talks about the death of the *soul* in the following passages: Psalm 33:19; 56:13; 78:50; 89:48; 116:8; Proverbs 8:36; Isaiah 53:12; Matthew 26:38; Mark 14:34; and James 5:20. These can refer to either the first death or the second death.

Now let's get back to our subject. A true prophet of God will not say anything against what Scripture says because God has a special relationship with His prophet. The true prophet of God will understand the true nature of human beings and the true (unconscious) state of those who have died. The devil will (and does) try to counterfeit the true prophetic gift by trying to get us to believe that the dead are still alive in a conscious state and that we can talk to them and, thereby, receive a "better" understanding of what God wants through them than what He has already told us in scripture. The truth is that God never changes. He is the same today as He has always been, and He will never contradict Himself (Heb. 13:8). If anyone, even your best friend, tries to tell you that God is setting a new order of things and that any part of the Bible no longer applies, find a new friend!

Accompanying the work of a true prophet of God will often be physical manifestations of a supernatural nature. Daniel was placed in a trance-like condition on some occasions, and though in the company of others, only he could see the vision. He would be without physical strength and had to be strengthened by God to receive the vision (Dan. 8:15–19; 10:7–11, 15–19). Sometimes Daniel's visions came in the form of dreams at night (Dan. 7:1, 2; 2:19). Zacharias was rendered unable to speak because of his vision (Luke 1:11–13, 18–22, 57–66.) John fell at the feet of Christ and appeared as though dead (Rev. 1:17.) Ezekiel saw things that were many miles away from where he was (Ezek. 8). Saul, who, after this vision, became the apostle Paul, was knocked from his horse, saw a great light (while the men around him heard a voice, but saw no one), and was rendered blind (Acts 9:3–7). On another occasion Paul writes (in the third person) about being "caught up into paradise," that is, the very presence of God Himself (2 Cor. 12:1–4).

A partial list of supernatural physical manifestations that may accompany the prophetic work can be summarized as follows:

- communication with a supernatural being,
- often accompanied by a loss of strength and/or falling to the ground in a deep sleep (or even given *superhuman* strength),
- capable of seeing things far away as if actually there while unaware of their immediate earthly surroundings even though their eyes are open,
- sometimes can't speak until their lips are touched,
- often do not breathe, and after the vision ends will resume normal vision, normal voice, and normal breathing while sometimes accompanied by some sort of physical trauma.

Not all of these manifestations accompany every vision, but generally, one or more will be present.

Physical manifestations are not to be trifled with. Though they are not the only indication of a true prophet, and by themselves cannot prove anything, they can separate self-made "prophets" from one who has a special communication from Jehovah. All the other criteria, as listed above, must also be met. Even though a person may bring fire down from the sky (as God did for Elijah), if the person does not meet all the criteria, he or she is not a genuine prophet of Jehovah. The highest test of all is the test of whether the message itself is true to the Bible. Even though all the other above criteria may be met, if the message does not square up with the Bible, "there is no light in them" (Isa. 8:20). Remember from above, there is no light of dawn. Therefore, the message is not from Jehovah, for He is the One who said, "Let there be light."

So what does all this have to do with Ellen White? The purpose of this book is not to try to prove that she is a prophet. There are books listed in the bibliography that cover that subject. I do want you to have a good understanding of who she was and how God used her to bring His message to the world. After all, her work has affected the lives of millions of people throughout the years, and all of her writings bear review. I present to you samples of what she wrote. This is what she says about her own work: "The Lord has sent his people much instruction, line upon line, precept upon precept, here a little, and there a little. Little heed is given to the Bible, and the Lord has given a lesser light to lead men and women to the greater light" (*Colporteur Evangelism*, p. 37).

Her writings are to introduce people to the Bible, that we might understand how to better understand Scripture. If we studied the Bible as we should, we would not need her writings. Her work satisfies criteria number 1, which states that a genuine prophet of God always prophesies in His name and is consistent with Scripture.

Regarding predictions, among other manifestations, she had a vision where she saw beforehand the destruction of San Francisco in the earthquake of 1906. This vision was given to her two days before the earthquake happened. None of her predictions have failed, although some are yet to be fulfilled.

> While at Loma Linda, the second night after the dedication of the sanitarium, there passed before me a most wonderful representation. During a vision of the night, I stood on an eminence, from which I could see houses shaken like a reed in the wind. Buildings, great and small, were falling to the ground. Pleasure resorts, theaters, hotels, and the homes of the wealthy were shaken and shattered. Many lives were blotted out of existence, and the air was filled with the shrieks of the injured and the terrified.
>
> The destroying angels of God were at work. One touch, and buildings so thoroughly constructed that men regarded them as secure against every danger, quickly became heaps of rubbish. There was no assurance of safety in any place. I did not feel in any special peril, but the awfulness of the scenes that passed before me I can not find words to describe. It seemed that the forbearance of God was exhausted, and that the Judgment day had come.
>
> The angel that stood by my side then instructed me that but few have any conception of the wickedness existing in our world today, and especially the wickedness in the large cities. He declared that the Lord has appointed a time when he will visit transgressors in wrath for persistent disregard of his law....
>
> We went to Glendale, near Los Angeles, and the following night, April 17, further representations passed before me. I seemed to be in an assembly, setting before the people the requirements of God's law. I read the scriptures regarding the

institution of the Sabbath in Eden at the close of the creation week, and regarding the giving of the law at Sinai; and then I showed that the Sabbath was to be observed "for a perpetual covenant," as a sign between God and his people forever, that they may know that they are sanctified by the Lord, their Creator....

Wednesday morning, April 18, I was to speak in the church at Los Angeles, where the Southern California Conference was assembled. As we neared the church, we heard the newsboys crying, "San Francisco destroyed by an earthquake!" With a heavy heart I read the first hastily printed news of the terrible disaster. ("The San Francisco Earthquake," *Review and Herald*, May 24, 1906)

Here is prophecy that came before research backed it up: "Tobacco is a slow, insidious, but most malignant poison. In whatever form it is used, it tells upon the constitution; it is all the more dangerous because its effects are slow and at first hardly perceptible. It excites and then paralyzes the nerves. It weakens and clouds the brain. Often it affects the nerves in a more powerful manner than does intoxicating drink. It is more subtle, and its effects are difficult to eradicate from the system. Its use excites a thirst for strong drink and in many cases lays the foundation for the liquor habit" (*The Ministry of Healing*, p. 328).

Regarding the humanity that Christ took, she wrote, "For four thousand years the race had been decreasing in physical strength, in mental power, and in moral worth; and Christ took upon Him the infirmities of degenerate humanity. Only thus could He rescue man from the lowest depths of his degradation" (*The Desire of Ages*, p. 117).

I close with this incredible story from her own pen, which includes an eyewitness report of one of her visions:

> "By invitation of Brother and Sister Nichols, my sister and myself again went to Massachusetts, and made their house our home. There was in Boston and vicinity a company of fanatical persons, who held that it was a sin to labor. Their principal message was, 'Sell that ye have, and give alms.' They said they were in the jubilee, the land should rest, and the poor must be supported without labor. Sargent, Robbins, and some others, were leaders. They denounced my visions as being of the devil, because I had been shown their errors. They were severe upon all who did not believe with them. While we were visiting at the house of Brother S. Nichols, Sargent and Robbins came from Boston to obtain a favor of Brother Nichols, and said they had come to have a visit, and tarry over night with him. Brother Nichols replied that he was glad they had come, for Sisters Sarah and Ellen were in the house, and he wished them to become acquainted with us. They changed their minds at once, and could not be persuaded to come into the house. Brother Nichols asked if I could relate my message in Boston, and if they would

hear, and then judge. 'Yes,' said they, 'Come into Boston next Sabbath, we would like the privilege of hearing her.'

"We accordingly designed to visit Boston, but in the evening, at the commencement of the Sabbath, while engaged in prayer, I was shown in vision that we must not go into Boston, but in an opposite direction to Randolph; that the Lord had a work for us to do there. We went to Randolph, and found a large room full collected, and among them those who said they would be pleased to hear my message in Boston. As we entered, Robbins and Sargent looked at each other in surprise and began to groan. They had promised to meet me in Boston, but thought they would disappoint us by going to Randolph, and while we were in Boston, warn the brethren against us. They did not have much freedom. During intermission one of their number remarked that good matter would be brought out in the afternoon. Robbins told my sister that I could not have a vision where he was.

"In the afternoon while we were pleading with God in prayer, the blessing of the Lord rested upon me, and I was taken off in vision. I was again shown the errors of these wicked men and others united with them. I saw that they could not prosper, their errors would confuse and distract; some would be deceived by them; but that truth would triumph in the end, and error be brought down. I was shown that they were not honest, and then I was carried into the future and shown that they would continue to despise the teachings of the Lord, to despise reproof, and that they would be left in total darkness, to resist God's Spirit until their folly should be made manifest to all. A chain of truth was presented to me from the Scriptures, in contrast with their errors. When I came out of vision, candles were burning. I had been in vision nearly four hours.

"As I was unconscious to all that transpired around me while in vision, I will copy from Brother Nichols' description of that meeting.

"'Sister Ellen was taken off in vision with extraordinary manifestations, and continued talking in vision with a clear voice, which could be distinctly understood by all present, until about sundown. The opposition was much exasperated, as well as excited, to hear Sister E. talk in vision, which they declared was of the devil; they exhausted all their influence and bodily strength, to destroy the effect of the vision. They would unite in singing very loud, and then alternately would talk and read from the Bible in a loud voice, in order that she might not be heard, until their strength was exhausted, and their hands would shake so they could not read from the Bible. But amidst all this confusion and noise, Sister Ellen's clear and shrill voice, as she talked in vision, was distinctly heard by all present. The opposition of these men continued as long as they could talk and sing, notwithstanding some of their own friends rebuked them, and requested them to stop. But Robbins said, "You are bowed to an idol; you are worshiping a golden calf."

"'Mr. Thayer, the owner of the house, was not fully satisfied that her vision was of the devil, as Robbins declared it to be. He wanted it tested in some way. He had heard that visions of Satanic power were arrested by opening the Bible and laying it on the person in vision, and asked Sargent if he would test it in this way, which he declined to do. Then Thayer took a heavy, large quarto family Bible which was lying on the table, and seldom used, opened it, and laid it upon Sister Ellen while in vision, as she was then inclined backward against the wall in the corner of the room. Immediately after the Bible was laid upon her, she arose upon her feet, and walked into the middle of the room, with the Bible open in one hand, and lifted as high as she could reach, and with her eyes steadily looking upward, declared in a solemn manner, "The inspired testimony from God," or words of the same import. While the Bible was thus extended in one hand, and her eyes looking upwards, and not on the Bible, she continued for a long time, to turn over the leaves with her other hand, and place her finger upon certain passages, and correctly repeat their words with a solemn voice. Many present looked at the passages where her finger was pointed, to see if she repeated them correctly, for her eyes at the same time were looking upwards. Some of the passages referred to were judgments against the wicked and blasphemers, and others were admonitions and instructions relative to our present condition.

"'In this state she continued all the afternoon until near sunset, when she came out of vision. When she arose in vision upon her feet, with the heavy open Bible in her hand, and walked the room, uttering the passages of scripture, these men were silenced. For the remainder of the time they were troubled, with many others; but they shut their eyes and braved it out without making any acknowledgment of their feelings.'" (*Life Sketches of James White and Ellen G. White 1880*, pp. 231–234)

Please study and decide for yourself. Each Christian, as a true Bible student, must become conversant with the biblical teaching on spiritual gifts and particularly the gift of prophecy. We each have a responsibility to not only reject false prophets and false manifestations, but also to cling to the teachings of true prophets. Please take advantage of the resources in the bibliography.

Appendix G

Health

There are eight basic principles regarding health and natural remedies that will help you reach your full physical potential. Ellen White outlines these principles in *The Ministry of Healing*:

> Pure air, sunlight, abstemiousness, rest, exercise, proper diet, the use of water, trust in divine power—these are the true remedies. Every person should have a knowledge of nature's remedial agencies and how to apply them. It is essential both to understand the principles involved in the treatment of the sick and to have a practical training that will enable one rightly to use this knowledge.
>
> The use of natural remedies requires an amount of care and effort that many are not willing to give. Nature's process of healing and upbuilding is gradual, and to the impatient it seems slow. The surrender of hurtful indulgences requires sacrifice. But in the end it will be found that nature, untrammeled, does her work wisely and well. Those who persevere in obedience to her laws will reap the reward in health of body and health of mind.
>
> Too little attention is generally given to the preservation of health. It is far better to prevent disease than to know how to treat it when contracted. It is the duty of every person, for his own sake, and for the sake of humanity, to inform himself in regard to the laws of life and conscientiously to obey them. All need to become acquainted with that most wonderful of all organisms, the human body. They should understand the functions of the various organs and the dependence of one upon another for the healthy action of all. They should study the influence of the mind upon the body, and of the body upon the mind, and the laws by which they are governed. (pp. 127, 128).

To practice these will give many people a new start in life. To help us remember what they are, these eight principles can be arranged to form the acronym "NEW START":

Nutrition (proper diet)	Sunlight
Exercise	Temperance (abstemiousness)[1]
Water	Air (pure)
	Rest
	Trust in divine power[2]

You, too, can have a NEW START in life. If you would like to improve your health, contact a healthcare provider who practices these eight principles of health and begin reaping the joy of the best possible health for the rest of your life.

The following comments are not intended to be scientific but introductory in nature. They are the results of years of experience and conversations with healthcare professionals rather than detailed perusal of scientific studies, even though some scientific studies may be referenced. These comments are designed to point you in the right direction, not to establish a health program for you, for all good health programs will have these principles as a basis. You should consult a healthcare professional regarding a program specific for you and your health needs.

It is important to remember that practicing these health principles will not save you—Jesus has already given you salvation. Your main concern with following these health principles is a general feeling of healthy well-being within your mind and body. In these last days, good health will allow God to communicate with your mind so that He can better bring you through the closing events of earth's history and use you in His final work of preparing a people to be translated without seeing death. With your salvation fully secure and your health in as optimum state as possible (given the circumstances), you can go forth each day knowing that God is using you according to His purposes.

Nutrition (proper diet)

Probably the second hottest subject in society today is diet. What shall we eat? We are very opinionated on this subject, as well as on dress, and many people have their own ideas regarding what they want to do. The level of disease in society today, with its resultant cost to those who pay insurance premiums, is staggering. This does not even touch the untold sorrow of the loss of loved ones and the loss of quality of life to those who manage to "survive." The situation is very nearly to the point of becoming unmanageable to society. God cares about what we eat and has given us guidelines regarding this subject. The other seven principles of health are not nearly as volatile as this subject of diet. Satan hates this principle. And why shouldn't he? After all, proper diet is the first line of defense against disease.

The original diet that God gave to the human race was fruits, nuts, and grains. Even the animals

---

1   Abstemiousness is the complete abstinence from anything harmful and the moderation of anything good. Abstemiousness expresses a greater degree of *abstinence* than does the word, "temperance," the latter of which is merely moderation in all things. Temperance is good, and it works in our acronym, but abstemiousness is the operative word.

2   Trust is not to be confused with *faith*, which is a heartfelt appreciation of the price God paid for our salvation—even to the cost of His own eternal life, and results in dependence upon God's word only to do what it says. Thus, "trust" pertains to trusting God to heal our diseases and descends from this idea of faith.

were vegetarians: "And God said, Behold, I have given you every herb bearing seed, which is upon the face of all the earth, and every tree, in the which is the fruit of a tree yielding seed; to you it shall be for meat [food]. And to every beast of the earth, and to every fowl of the air, and to every thing that creepeth upon the earth, wherein there is life, I have given every green herb for meat: and it was so. And God saw every thing that he had made, and, behold, it was very good. And the evening and the morning were the sixth day" (Gen. 1:29–31).

This diet was the original diet given by God, who ought to know what we need, because He made us. This diet did not include flesh, dairy, or poultry products. In addition, Adam and Eve were told that their diet did not include fruit from the tree of the knowledge of good and evil. Also, note that the animals ate vegetables (green herbs), but humans did not. Humans did not begin eating vegetables until after the fall, when sin entered, at the time they took it upon themselves to add the forbidden tree to their diet. Until Adam and Eve ate of the tree of the knowledge of good and evil, they knew only good. After this, they began to learn evil, and because humanity now had fallen flesh, they needed an extra boost in their diet. So God added vegetables in Genesis 3:17–19: "And unto Adam he said, Because thou hast hearkened unto the voice of thy wife, and hast eaten of the tree, of which I commanded thee, saying, Thou shalt not eat of it: cursed is the ground for thy sake; in sorrow shalt thou eat of it all the days of thy life; Thorns also and thistles shall it bring forth to thee; and thou shalt eat the herb of the field; In the sweat of thy face shalt thou eat bread, till thou return unto the ground; for out of it wast thou taken: for dust thou art, and unto dust shalt thou return."

Anything that is not according to God's original plan for us only gives us knowledge of evil, sorrow, and *pain!*

There is hope, however. Some of these diseases that we have caused through ignorantly practicing poor habits can be slowed, stopped, or even, in some cases, reversed[3] through a change in lifestyle. The evidence in favor of a total vegetarian diet is beginning to be proclaimed by many healthcare professionals.

Many Christians in the last days before Jesus comes will need to *learn* about God's desire for health reform. This is not something that is commonly taught to our children, and it is not commonly understood or practiced. We need not be surprised that this is true, however, because this state of affairs in the last days was predicted in the Bible. Isaiah 4:1 says, "And in that day [the last days before Jesus comes[4]] seven women [all churches] shall take hold of one man [Jesus Christ], saying, We will eat our *own* bread, and wear our *own* apparel: only let us be *called* by thy name [Christian], to take away our reproach."

I would encourage all brave souls to become proactive in preserving their own health. I would love to see all people enjoying the fullness of life here on earth and also in the kingdom to come. I feel confident in wishing this upon you because God desires the same for you: "Beloved, I wish above all

---

3   Heart disease is one example. See Dr. Nedley's comments below.
4   The context of chapter 4 is taken from chapter 3, especially verse 13, referring to the day of judgment.

things that thou mayest prosper and be in health, even as thy soul prospereth" (3 John 1:2). May we allow our pride to be leveled to the dust of the ground and in humility allow Jesus to show us His ways. I recommend to all a total vegetarian diet:

From the pen of Dr. Neil Nedley[5]:

> In Resnicow's own research, as well as in nine other studies that he analyzed, total vegetarians generally had lower cholesterol, lower LDL levels, *and* lower triglyceride levels—all with equally good HDL levels.[6]

When Dr. Ornish analyzed his data to find the most important part of his diet in reversing heart disease, he found it was its low cholesterol content rather than its low fat content.[7] It implies that the absence of animal products in the diet (which ensures that a diet will have no cholesterol) is more important than dramatic reductions in fat content.

From the pen of Ellen G. White:

> Concerning flesh meat we can all say, Let it alone. And all should bear clear testimony against tea and coffee, never using them. They are narcotics, injurious alike to the brain and to the other organs of the body. The time has not yet[8] come when I say that the use of milk and eggs should be wholly discontinued. Milk and eggs should not be classed with flesh meats. In some ailments the use of eggs is very beneficial.
>
> Let the members of our churches deny every selfish appetite. Every penny expended for tea, coffee, and flesh meat is worse than wasted; for these things hinder the best development of the physical, mental, and spiritual powers.[9]
>
> The diet reform should be progressive. As disease in animals increases, the use of milk and eggs will become more and more unsafe. An effort should be made to supply their place with other things that are healthful and inexpensive. The people everywhere should be taught how to cook without milk and eggs so far as possible, and yet have their food wholesome and palatable.[10]

---

5   Neil Nedley, M.D., *Proof Positive: How to Reliably Combat Disease and Achieve Optimal Health through Nutrition and Lifestyle,* p. 100.
6   K. Resnicow, J. Barone, et al., "Diet and serum lipids in vegan vegetarians: a model for risk reduction," *J Am Diet Assoc*, pp. 447–53.
7   D. Ornish, "Reversing heart disease through diet, exercise, and stress management: an interview with Dean Ornish [interview by Elaine R Monsen]," *J Am Diet Assoc,* pp. 162–65.
8   The statement "not *yet*" implies that there is a day that will come when it is time to discontinue wholly the use of milk and eggs. Check the research regarding salmonella, e-coli, "mad cow disease," etc., to see whether that time has come *yet*.
9   Ellen G. White, *Counsels on Diet and Foods,* p. 402.
10 Ellen G. White, *Counsels on Diet and Foods,* p. 469.

Exercise

The best possible exercise, and the simplest to perform, is walking. Yes, just walking. It is the least financially burdening of all forms of exercise. For the most rewarding of all activities, walking on a warm sunny day accomplishes three of these eight principles of health and natural healing all at one time, for fresh air and sunshine are both provided with this exercise free of charge. This is not to mention the peace and quiet time that one can spend with God. At least 30 minutes a day of brisk walking, at least four days a week, is the minimum, although more is better.

If you can't get outside, there are several options. An exercise ball you bounce and roll on is a good second option. It will help your circulation of the blood and the lymph system (very important) and build muscle tone, but this exercise lacks fresh air or sunshine. Therefore, I feel that this is a good rainy-day option. A good third option is a passive exercise machine. It will help your circulation of the blood and the lymph system, as well as helping with some back issues, but it does little for muscle tone or fresh air or sunshine. If using a walking exercise machine, look at a tread "climber" rather than a treadmill because of the climbing aspect. A walking exercise machine will add muscle tone to the other benefits already mentioned.

Exercise in the gym can assist specific goals, such as weight-loss programs or sports training, which also carry the added benefit of access to professional trainers, but for most people, a simple walk in the park is a blockbuster. Walking is also better than jogging because the bouncing of the latter can place unnecessary stress on the knees, hips, ankles, and feet.

In summary, thirty minutes of "something moving," at least four times a week, is what matters. Even two minutes on an exercise machine per day, if consistent, is better than nothing at all. Walking, as we mentioned earlier, is best. Other options not mentioned may include carefully lifting weights, swimming, playing light outdoor-type games, etc.—even parking at the far end of the parking lot. These can all be helpful. The important thing to remember is to pick something fun so that you will be consistent!

Water

Good clear water is the lubricant of the entire human system. It is very important that your body get plenty of it. If you don't get enough water, your cells will not be able to perform their functions of accepting nutrients or expelling wastes efficiently. A good rule of thumb is to drink at least eight, eight-ounce glasses of good clear water every day. Notice that I said at least. Each person is different. Larger people and those who exercise more or perspire more need to drink even more water than that. (Generally no more than a gallon.) Moreover, this 64-ounce per day minimum does not count any other beverages you may drink during the day, so don't count any orange juice or soup you may partake of. One good way to know whether you are getting enough water is to check your urine. If it is nearly clear, you are probably getting enough water. If it is dark yellow, you probably need to increase your water intake.

Soft water is best for drinking and cooking, but the water that is made soft with salt is not. I prefer distilled water because distilled water is as pure as you can get. One has better control of one's salt and sugar intake with distilled water, not to mention the taste. A good trace mineral tablet is recommended if you solely drink distilled water. A routine that includes plenty of good clear water will reduce headaches and increase your energy level. See if you can notice the difference.

Sunlight

Sunlight provides the best source of absorption of vitamin D, which helps in the prevention of many diseases. However, sunlight should be received in moderation. For most people exposing 6 to 10 percent of the body two to three times per week for five to sixty minutes per session will generally provide adequate vitamin D levels without increasing risk of contracting skin cancer. And if you get adequate exposure during the spring, summer, and fall, it will generally last you through the winter.[11] All these variables depend on your age, weight, pigmentation, the presence of chronic disease, and latitude on the planet. These variables give one quite a range to work with. Experimentation is good; just avoid being burned. If you need more specifics regarding your personal needs, please consult a healthcare professional.

Sunscreens add confusion to the mix. "In both human and animal research there is a worrisome lack of protection—or even increase in melanoma risk with sunscreen use. As expressed by the U.S. Preventive Services Task Force, 'It is possible that sunscreens may increase skin cancer risk by encouraging susceptible persons to prolong exposure of greater skin surface areas to solar rays that are not blocked by most currently used sunscreens.'"[12]

Opening the blinds in your house every day allows the precious sunlight to kill mold spores, etc., that might get into your house. In addition, the warm, bright feeling that comes with the sunlight will sooth your spirit. God provided sunlight for our use. It is the least expensive healer we know, and it ranks high with walking and drinking water.

Temperance (Abstemiousness)

Too much of any *good* thing is *still too much* and *any* amount of *any bad* thing is *always* too much.

You want to abstain from anything that is going to affect your judgment, even for a short period of time. You also want to abstain from anything that is insidious, such as tobacco, tea, coffee, and the flesh of dead animals. The long-term use of alcohol, caffeine, nicotine, narcotics, phosphates (as found in soda pop), trans-fats, etc., will eventually destroy your health, and you will not realize the full extent of the joy your heavenly Father has for you, both in this world and in the world to come.

I encourage you to study the ingredients found on products sold in the grocery store. Check the Internet to find out what these ingredients really are. "Natural flavorings" may not necessarily be either natural or flavorings. Research this for yourself. You may be surprised at the results.

Eat moderately. Overeating affects the power of the mind since excess blood from the heart is diverted from the brain to the stomach for digestion. Overeating also often leads to obesity, which

---

11 Mike Adams, ed., "Every Person Needs Sunlight Exposure to Create Vitamin D, Obesity Impairs Vitamin D Absorption," NaturalNews.com, January 1, 2005.
12 Neil Nedley, M.D., *Proof Positive: How to Reliably Combat Disease and Achieve Optimal Health through Nutrition and Lifestyle*, p. 32.

is a killer in its own right and it leads to many diseases, including such maladies as heart disease and diabetes.

Eating too often or too late in the day causes your stomach to fail to digest your food properly, which will then putrefy and release poisons into the system. It is best to give your stomach at least four hours to digest after finishing the last meal before burdening it again with another meal because that causes your stomach to stop what it is doing and start the digestive process all over again, leaving the old food to putrefy. This means scheduling meals at least five hours apart. It is also a good policy to allow at least four full hours between finishing the last meal of the day before retiring for the night. If your stomach is working while you are trying to sleep, the stomach's activity is not all that will be impaired, but your sleep will be also. What does this say about snacking between meals? Snacking between meals gives your stomach no rest at all, while releasing poisons constantly, thus overburdening your body's "sanitation" system of which your liver is the head. I'm sure this is not the way you want to treat your body.

If you do some math, you will discover that your daily schedule can be rather rigid. If you want to eat three meals a day and retire at 10:00 p.m., to get all this in at the suggested intervals, you would have to eat at 7:00 a.m., 12:00 p.m., and 5:00 p.m. with little room for variation. Some days are not going to work out according to this schedule. However, most adults can do quite well on two meals a day. This will give your schedule some wiggle room. If your work or school schedule does not allow for this, do the best you can in your circumstances. Personally, my wife and I like the two-meal schedule, eating breakfast about 8:00 or 9:00 a.m. and dinner about 3:00 or 4:00 p.m. For children, a light third meal is generally required. If your family is gone to various places during the day and comes home for the evening, a light supper may be just the bonding your family needs at the end of the day. A light supper is not burdensome to prepare and gives your family a chance to be together. Ask God to show you what is best for your family. If you choose the three-meal plan, remember this general rule of thumb—breakfast like a king, dinner like a prince, and supper like a pauper—as much as possible.

Having said all this, depending on your circumstances, it may be impossible to have a "perfect" diet or a perfect schedule until your situation improves. (For example, some people live where fresh fruits and vegetables are not available.) I believe the best possible posture is to do the best you can in the circumstances you find yourself while continuing to seek improvements in your diet and in your situation. Then leave the results in God's hands. He will honor your desires and bless you in your health. Let Him have the final word and be ready to let Him make changes in your life as He presents them to you. In this, you will find joy. Remember, it really is a true statement that "an ounce of prevention is worth a pound of cure."

Air

The fresher you can get your air, the better. Spending time outside is a good thing, as we already discussed when talking about exercise. Living in the clear air of the country beats city smog any day, so relocate if you can. Opening your windows for a few minutes during the day to air out your house, even in cold weather (even for only 15 minutes), has a positive effect on your health. Believe it or not, this will not kill your heating budget, for this amount of time will not cool your walls. (It is the heating and cooling of your *walls* that uses so much energy.) Crack the window next to your bed at night, or even better, sleep on the *porch* if that's feasible. I know people who have slept on their porch even in 30-degree weather! *That* will clear your lungs!

One winter it was so cold that I didn't want to open the house. However, the house became so stuffy that I had trouble breathing, so in 15-degree weather I opened the house for 15 minutes. Although there was a breeze that day, I opened all the windows and doors I could. That set up a stiff breeze going through the whole house. I was afraid I might freeze my wife's plants, for they were right in the line of the breeze, so I kept a close watch on the temperature of the plant room. After 15 minutes, the house (plant room) air temperature dropped 20 degrees from 70 to 50. I proceeded to close all the doors and windows, and the house quickly returned to a normal temperature. I was invigorated! I could breathe again! The plants are still blooming profusely, and I never noticed anything strange with the heating bill that month. I have never again let the house get that stuffy! Try it. You might be as surprised as I was.

Rest

Many people believe that to "get the work done," one simply does it, and if there is more work to do, just keep doing it. The same would apply for play, but the difference between "work" and "play" is very subjective. This temptation is a particular problem for students who feel that they must stay up all night to study for an important examination. Nevertheless, after a certain amount of time spent working, the body begins to break down and becomes less efficient. Our "production" begins to wane, and we eventually find ourselves unable to do anything at all. This could seriously impair how well you perform on the test! However, even worse than this, our internal bodily functions begin to break down and our overall health suffers, making it even more difficult to work. Many people feel tired all the time. Could this be one reason? As I write this, I'm writing to myself, because I know I have had this problem. If this is your problem also, you are definitely not alone. The issue of rest may very well be the most difficult of all the health principles to accomplish.

To avoid long-term physical exhaustion and diminished interest in work, one must take a break regularly. These breaks can include anything from taking a two-minute nap to a full blown three-month vacation, even if it only means doing something different for awhile. It is best to take these breaks regularly before you burn out so that your body can stay healthy and function at a steady pace. We really do our best work when we are fresh and otherwise healthy, following all the health principles we are discussing.

What kinds of breaks can we take? Sometimes the best thing we can do on our "day off" is to go to the park, the arboretum, or the botanical gardens and sit. That's it. Just sit! If you want to, look around, talk to your spouse, take a walk, or enjoy a picnic. In my younger days when this idea was first suggested to me, I thought, "How can I do that? There are too many other things to do!" Now that I am older, I realize that this kind of break makes it easier to do all the other things that we tend to think are so important, but generally can wait. Even now, this can be a struggle for me. Moreover, the quiet time associated with this type of break makes it easier to do the last item on our list, place our faith and trust in God, which we will cover in the next section.

Don't forget regular church attendance, although even that, especially for pastors, can require a day off from responsibilities such as teaching, leading in worship, or preaching the sermon, etc.

Finally, think about breaks you can take every day throughout the day, even every couple of hours. A short nap might be beneficial, as can placing your mind on something else for a few minutes. Don't forget to take a long weekend mini-trip every few weeks or months, and, of course, the standard two-week vacation. Use your imagination. Just don't forget—there is always prayer. You can do that at any moment.

Another very important break that we must not forget about is sleep. We are told that we need eight hours of sleep each night, but I understand that when one gets older, many times as little as six hours of sleep is enough for *some* people. However, if the statement is true that two hours of sleep before midnight is worth more than four hours of sleep after midnight,[13] then it behooves one to be in bed with the lights out by 10:00 p.m.[14] In that case, if you consider that we get the *equivalent* of at least four hours sleep *before* midnight, and, coupled with four hours of actual sleep *after* midnight, that adds up to the equivalent of eight "hours" of sleep! Bingo! We have it! So, one *could* conclude that 10:00 p.m. to 4:00 a.m. is enough sleep. You could try this and see how it works for you. However, don't make any assumptions. You may need at least the full eight hours, anyway.

My conclusion is that sleep should include at least the time from 10:00 p.m. to 4:00 a.m. every night—more on either side is a good thing. The National Sleep Foundation has concluded that most adults need seven to nine hours of sleep each night.

I'm sure someone will ask, "What should I do if I wake up too early?" This happens a lot, and you can help reduce the number of occurrences by drinking all of your 64+ ounces of water before 6:00 p.m. Here is my suggestion—it just might work for you. If you wake up before you have slept seven hours, and it is at least 3:30 a.m., wait fifteen minutes before getting up and starting your day. Make a note of the time you try to go back to sleep, and then don't think about it. (If you watch the clock, you will have a more difficult time going back to sleep; and don't set an alarm, for that will just wake you up!) If you do not fall back asleep, and it is at least fifteen minutes since you noted the time, then get up and start your day. Sometimes reading a psalm and praying helps you to relax before starting the 15-minute "countdown." It works great for me! Having your Bible on your cell phone helps, too, because then you don't have to turn on the light. During the fifteen-minute countdown, or any time you are awake, take inventory of your body. Choose a body part—a forearm, leg, shoulder, or whatever—and concentrate on relaxing it. Actually feel it relax. Then do another body part and feel it relax. There is a good chance you will never get through your whole body.

These eight principles of health should alleviate most cases of insomnia. If you have been practicing

---

13 "Two hours' good sleep before twelve o'clock is worth more than four hours after twelve o'clock" (Ellen G. White, *Manuscript Releases*, vol. 7, p. 224).

14 From this, I conclude that no meeting should ever last past 9:00 p.m., and it should end even earlier if possible. Of course, emergencies happen.

these eight principles of health for several months and you have a regular habit of not being able to go to sleep for, say, two hours after going to bed, or not being able to go back to sleep after waking up at, say, 1:00 or 2:00 a.m., you should consider seeking the assistance of a healthcare professional. There are many causes for insomnia, including sleep apnea, parasites, nutritional deficiency, and eating late at night. If you seek the help of a healthcare professional, I recommend finding someone who understands the eight principles of health.

The thrust of this principal is to get enough rest and don't burn the "midnight oil." If you work the night shift, I encourage you to pray for divine wisdom and maybe even a miracle to find a job that allows you to work during the day or otherwise to be able to cope. Your biological clock needs to be reversed, somehow, which may require a sleep chamber that has no windows.

Dr. Neil Nedley teaches the following seven ways to improve sleep quality:[15]

- "Sleep in a cool, dark, comfortable, tidy, and quiet room
- "Set anxieties and worries aside as you get into bed [Reading a little before turning the light out, especially your Bible, can help.]
- "Daily exercise and a clear conscience will help
- "Eliminate 'sleep robbers three': alcohol, tobacco, and caffeine
- "Check medications that could interfere with sleep
- "Maintain a regular bedtime and do not eat at least four hours before
- "Provide fresh air in your sleeping room"

The two-hours-of-sleep-before-midnight concept seems to be plausible regarding melatonin[16] production. Since the optimum conditions for producing melatonin is darkness, it would appear that production time would be from sunset to dawn. However, because melatonin levels peak between the hours of 2:00 and 3:00 a.m., it would appear that melatonin production stops or slows significantly about that time. With a dramatic increase in the rate of the rise in melatonin levels beginning about 10:00 p.m., you can see that it is best to turn the lights out[17] by 10:00 p.m. or earlier since our melatonin levels are set to rapidly rise about that time. Because melatonin levels begin to rapidly drop off after 2:00 or 3:00 a.m.—suggesting that production has stopped or slowed significantly—rising at 4:00 a.m. will not significantly detract from melatonin production.[18]

Getting up at 4:00 or 5:00 a.m. is a very good way to start the day.[19] It is quiet, and your daily devotionals will go uninterrupted. For me, those early hours are also the best time of the day I can write. It is the time I prepare my sermons for Sabbath. The telephone is off (except for family and emergencies) and my family honors this special time for me. For me, those hours of quiet time each morning seem to

---

15   Neil Nedley, M.D., *Proof Positive: How to Reliably Combat Disease and Achieve Optimal Health through Nutrition and Lifestyle*, p. 503.
16   One of the advantages of a good melatonin level is to promote sound sleep.
17   If you keep a light on in your room, it should be no brighter than the moonlight.
18   Neil Nedley, M.D., *Depression—The Way Out*, pp. 201–203.
19   If you get up at 4:00 a.m., it means you have to be in bed by 9:00 p.m. the night before to get seven hours of sleep. If you need eight hours of sleep, bedtime should be at 8:00 p.m.

be just as much "rest" as is sleeping (especially on those days that I physically "oversleep", which, believe it or not, does actually happen occasionally[20]). Then add in the Sabbath "rest" from our own labors to save ourselves, and we have a God-given recipe for the foundation of good health, which brings us to our final health principle.

Trust in God

"Trust" in God is not to be confused with "faith," the latter of which is a heartfelt appreciation for the cost of salvation and results in dependence upon God's word only to do what it says. The cost to God for our salvation is the infinite price of Jesus' death on the cross when He took our second death on our behalf, that He might save us from our sins and from receiving the second death ourselves. "Trust" is simply that confidence in God that relies upon His word *only* to bless us and provide for our needs—spiritual, mental, emotional, and temporal.

The final principle of these eight remedial tenets of good health is that you ask God to give these treatments of the eight natural remedies the efficiency they need to accomplish His purposes for you, giving your heart to Him, yielding to His control, and then relaxing and resting in His care. When you know you are resting in His hands, you can stop worrying, for nothing can happen to you without His permission. When you believe this, even those events that happen to us that we might otherwise think are "bad" for us will be *good* for us instead, and we can say with Job, "Though he [God] slay me [Himself], yet will I trust in him" (Job 13:15).

When you stop worrying about your own salvation, realizing that your salvation is safe in God's hands, resting your soul in the pillow of His love, you will realize for your life the true meaning of the Sabbath day, and your life's experience will flourish with all the good things of "heaven on earth."

In closing, remember that "all things work together for good to them that love God, to them who are [being[21]] called according to his purpose" (Rom. 8:28). Furthermore, "beloved, I wish above all things that thou mayest prosper and be in health, even as thy soul prospereth" (3 John 1:2). That is God's wish for you!

---

20 Did you know that God promises to wake us up? That eliminates the need for that jarring enemy—the *alarm clock!* It takes away the guilt that otherwise might be associated with "sleeping in," unless, of course, you say no to God and roll over. One time I asked Him to wake me at 3:00 a.m. so we could leave early on a trip. Do you want to know what happened? At precisely 3:00 on the dot, my eyes gently opened. I rejoiced in the goodness of God. I then knew beyond a shadow of doubt that God wanted me to wake at 3:00 a.m. I decided to let God wake me up again. For many years I have enjoyed my daily gentle awakening. Since there is nothing special about me more so than anyone else, I know *you* can enjoy God's gentle "alarm clock" too. (Check out Isaiah 50:4.)

21 "Being" is the original language of this passage of scripture.

Appendix H

Apparel

Probably the hottest subject in society today is sex, which is also related to the subject of dress and what we should wear. We are very opinionated on this subject, and many people have their own ideas regarding what they want to do. As a result, every business has a dress code for their employees and also (although generally unwritten) for their customers. The dress question is not the *entire* problem of society with its loss of commitment, and the sadness of broken families, resulting in sorrow that lasts for generations, thus threatening the fabric of society. However, how we appear to others tells them about ourselves and affects everyone around us. God cares about how we dress and how we look to others, so He has given us guidelines regarding this volatile subject in 1 Timothy and 1 Peter.

> In like manner also, that women adorn[1] themselves in modest[2] apparel, with shamefacedness[3] and sobriety;[4] not with broided[5] hair, or gold, or pearls, or costly array.[6] (1 Tim. 2:9)

> Likewise, ye wives, be in subjection to your own husbands; that, if any obey not the word, they also may without the word be won by the conversation of the wives; While they behold your chaste conversation coupled with fear. Whose adorning let it not be that outward adorning of plaiting the hair, and of wearing of gold, or of putting on of apparel;[7] But let it be the hidden man of the heart, in that which is not

---

1 Adorn means adding to the beauty of something or dressing with ornaments.
2 Modest means decent, proper, moderate, and not showy (*not* sensual, luxurious, voluptuous, lewd, libidinous, lascivious, forward, bold, excessive, vain, egoistic, boastful, pretentious, extravagant, ostentatious, or irreverent).
3 Shamefacedness (English) is being bashful and respectful from modest reserve. The original Greek means a sense of shame, modesty, reverence—having the effect of preventing the shameful act. Some translators focus on the modesty and humility aspect to avoid any confusion that the "shame" connotation may engender in this context.
4 Sobriety is a calm, cool, disposition displaying self-control and moderation.
5 Broided means embroidered or braided—what is woven, plaited, or twisted together; a web, plait, or braid. This would represent excessive effort, time, or money spent on our grooming. Keep it simple, for simple is generally easy to understand.
6 This would be costly or expensive-looking jewelry of all types; jewel-like (and metallic looking) buttons, barrettes, pins, snaps, etc., as well as metallic fabric would also apply. Watches, being hard to avoid functionally, can be an exception if not gaudy and expensive. It is sometimes hard to think of such beautiful things as "ornaments" as appropriate only for Christmas trees, but we are to realize that true treasures come from God and He considers our physical bodies are beautiful without artificial ornamentation. After all, He created us. He knows what He likes. Allow Him to decorate you on the inside through an indwelling of His mind, for such attitude results in the true treasure of righteous behavior. That is how He wants to decorate you.
7 Do not consider that your *clothing* is what makes you beautiful; it may make you presentable and good looking, yes, but not *beautiful*. Never forget, your *real* beauty comes from that which God has placed within you.

corruptible, even the ornament of a meek and quiet spirit, which is in the sight of God of great price. For after this manner in the old time the holy women also, who trusted in God, adorned themselves, being in subjection unto their own husbands: Even as Sara obeyed Abraham, calling him lord: whose daughters ye are, as long as ye do well, and are not afraid with any amazement. (1 Peter 3:1–6)

These verses point out that we are not to give excessive consideration to our clothing.

What is the purpose of dress reform? Let's consider the exodus. While leading His people to the Promised Land of the *earthly* Canaan, God instituted a style of dress to keep the thought before the Israelites of who they were and what He was doing with them. The dress reform of today is to remind God's people that they are preparing to enter the *heavenly* Canaan—the new earth. Their dress distinguishes them as belonging to God.

Many Christians in the last days before Jesus comes will need to *learn* about God's desire for dress reform. This is not something that is commonly taught to our children, and it is not commonly understood or practiced. We need not be surprised that this situation exists, however, because this very state of affairs in these last days was predicted in the Bible. Isaiah 4:1 says, "And in that day [the last days before Jesus comes[8]] seven women [*all* churches] shall take hold of one man [Jesus Christ], saying, We will eat our *own* bread, and wear our *own* apparel: only let us be *called* by thy name [Christian], to take away our reproach."

I am not on a campaign to have everyone change the way they dress, although that would be ideal. I present God's perspective only for those who feel called to present God's last-day message to the world. God cares how His people look to others, how they carry themselves, and how they represent Him to the world. May all of us allow our pride to be leveled to the dust of the ground and in humility allow Jesus to show us His ways.

Perhaps the following will help to clarify the idea. There are seven basic principles regarding dress that God's last-day prophet, Ellen G. White, wrote about. Her counsel follows in the next few pages.

Dress Should Distinguish God's Commandment Keeping People From the World

The very dress will be a recommendation of the truth to unbelievers. It will be a sermon in itself. (*The Review and Herald*, May 30, 1871)

I was referred to Numbers 15:38-41: "Speak unto the children of Israel, and bid them that they make them fringes in the borders of their garments throughout their generations, and that they put upon the fringe of the borders a ribband of blue: and it shall be unto you for a fringe, that ye may look upon it, and remember all the commandments

---

[8] The context of chapter 4 is taken from chapter 3, especially verse 13.

of the Lord, and do them; and that ye seek not after your own heart and your own eyes, after which ye use to go a whoring: that ye may remember, and do all My commandments, and be holy unto your God. I am the Lord your God, which brought you out of the land of Egypt, to be your God: I am the Lord your God." Here God expressly commanded a very simple arrangement of dress for the children of Israel *for the purpose of distinguishing them from the idolatrous nations around them.* As they looked upon their peculiarity of dress, they were to remember that they were God's commandment-keeping people, and that He had *wrought in a miraculous manner to bring them from Egyptian bondage to serve Him, to be a holy people unto Him.* They were not to serve their own desires, or to imitate the idolatrous nations around them, but to remain a *distinct, separate people*, that all who looked upon them might say: These are they whom God brought out of the land of Egypt, who keep the law of Ten Commandments. An Israelite was known to be such as soon as seen, for God through simple means distinguished him as His. (*Testimonies for the Church*, vol. 1, p. 524)

Even the style of the apparel will express the truth of the gospel. Their dress bears its testimony to their own family, to the church and the world, that they are being purified from vanity and selfishness. They demonstrate that they are not idolaters. (*Manuscript Releases*, vol. 6, p. 161)

Our Dress Should Not be a Stumbling Block to Others

No occasion should be given to unbelievers to reproach our faith. We are [already] considered odd and singular, and should not take a course to lead unbelievers to think us more so than our faith requires us to be. Some who believe the truth may think that it would be more healthful for the sisters to adopt the American costume [more information to follow], yet if that mode of dress would cripple our influence among unbelievers so that we could not so readily gain access to them, we should by no means adopt it, though we suffered much in consequence. But some are deceived in thinking there is so much benefit to be received from this costume. While it may prove a benefit to some, it is an injury to others. (*Testimonies for the Church*, vol. 1, pp. 456, 457)

God Has an Opinion on "Modest" Dress

The form [bodice] should not be compressed in the least with corsets and whalebones. The dress should be perfectly easy that the lungs and heart may have healthy action. The dress should reach somewhat below the top of the boot [ladies' ankle-length boot, not men's knee-length boot], but should be short enough to clear the filth of the sidewalk and street without being raised by the hand. A still shorter dress than this would be proper, convenient, and healthful for women when doing their housework, and especially for those who are obliged to perform more or less out-of-door labor. With this style of dress, one light skirt, or two at most, is all that is necessary, and this should be buttoned on to a waist, or suspended by straps.... Whatever may be the length of the dress, [for cold weather] their limbs should be clothed as thoroughly as are the men's. This may be done by wearing lined pants [of the same material as the dress], gathered into a band and fastened about the ankle, or made full and tapering at the bottom; and these should come down long enough to meet the shoe. The limbs and ankles thus clothed are protected against a current of air. If the feet and limbs are kept comfortable with warm clothing, the circulation will be equalized, and the blood will remain pure and healthy because it is not chilled or hindered in its natural passage through the system.

The principal difficulty in the minds of many is in regard to the length of the dress. Some insist that "the top of the boot," has reference to the top of such boots as are usually worn by men, which reach nearly to the knee. If it were the custom of women to wear such boots, then these persons should not be blamed for professing to understand the matter as they have; but as women generally do not wear such boots, these persons have no right to understand me as they have pretended....

In regard to my wearing the short dress, I would say, I have but one short dress, which is not more than a finger's length shorter than the dresses I usually wear. I have worn this short dress occasionally. In the winter I rose early, and putting on my short dress, which did not require to be raised by my hands to keep it from draggling in the snow, I walked briskly from one to two miles before breakfast. I have worn it several times to the office, when obliged to walk through light snow, or when it was very wet or muddy. Four or five sisters of the Battle Creek church have prepared for themselves a short dress to wear while doing their washing and house cleaning. A short dress has not been worn in the streets of the city of Battle Creek, and has never been worn to meeting. My views were calculated to correct the present fashion, the extreme long dress, trailing upon the ground, and also to correct the extreme short dress, reaching about to the knees, which is worn by a certain class. I was shown that we should shun both extremes. By wearing the dress reaching about to the top of a woman's gaiter boot we shall escape the evils of the extreme long dress, and shall also shun the evils and notoriety of the extreme short dress. (*Testimonies for the Church*, vol. 1, p. 460–464)

What Is the "American Costume"?

In wide contrast with this [God's] modest dress is the so-called American costume, resembling very nearly the dress worn by men. It consists of a vest, pants, and a dress resembling a coat and reaching about halfway from the hip to the knee.[9] This dress I have opposed, from what has been shown me as in harmony with the word of God; while the other I have recommended as modest, comfortable, convenient, and healthful. (*Testimonies for the Church*, vol. 1, p. 465)

What Was Wrong With the "American Costume"?

… [They] had gone to that extreme in the short dress as to disgust and prejudice good people, and destroy in a great measure their own influence. This is the style and influence of the "American Costume," taught and worn by many at "Our Home," Dansville, N.Y.[10] It does not reach to the knee. I need not say that this style of dress was shown me to be too short.[11] (*Selected Messages*, book 3, p. 278)

I saw that God's order has been reversed, and His special directions disregarded, by those who adopt the American costume. I was referred to Deuteronomy 22:5: "The woman shall not wear that which pertaineth unto a man, neither shall a man put on a woman's garment: for all that do so are abomination unto the Lord thy God." God would not have His people adopt the so-called reform dress. It is immodest apparel, wholly unfitted for the modest, humble followers of Christ. (*Testimonies for the Church*, vol. 1, p. 457)

What About Unisex Clothing?

There is an increasing tendency to have women in their dress and appearance as near like the other sex as possible, and to fashion their dress very much like that of men, but God pronounces it abomination [Deut. 22:5]. 'In like manner also, that women adorn themselves in modest apparel, with shamefacedness and sobriety.' 1 Timothy 2:9. (*Testimonies for the Church*, vol. 1, p. 457)

---

9   This would appear to resemble the modern-day pantsuit.
10   For more information, do a web search titled "American costume Dansville New York."
11   If God feels *this* is too short, how must He feel about wearing the pants *without* the dress?

Dressing Like the Opposite Sex Deadens Our Influence as Christians

Those who feel called out to join the movement in favor of woman's rights and the so-called dress reform [the woman's rights version of it—*e.g.*, the American Costume] might as well sever all connection with the third angel's message [the 1888 message[12]]. The spirit which attends the one cannot be in harmony with the other. The Scriptures are plain upon the relations and rights of men and women. Spiritualists have, to quite an extent, adopted this singular mode of dress. Seventh-day Adventists, who believe in the restoration of the gifts, are often branded as spiritualists. Let them adopt this costume, and their influence is dead. The people would place them on a level with spiritualists and would refuse to listen to them.

With the so-called dress reform there goes a spirit of levity and boldness just in keeping with the dress. Modesty and reserve seem to depart from many as they adopt that style of dress. I was shown that God would have us take a course consistent and explainable. Let the sisters adopt the American costume and they would destroy their own influence and that of their husbands. They would become a byword and a derision. Our Saviour says: 'Ye are the light of the world.' 'Let your light so shine before men, that they may see your good works, and glorify your Father which is in heaven.' There is a great work for us to do in the world, and God would not have us take a course to lessen or destroy our influence with the world. (*Testimonies for the Church*, vol. 1, pp. 457, 458)

Those among Sabbathkeepers who have yielded to the influence of the world are to be tested. The perils of *the last days* are upon us, and a trial is before the professed people of God which many have not anticipated. The genuineness of their faith will be proved. Many have united with worldlings in pride, vanity, and pleasure seeking, flattering themselves that they could do this and still be Christians. But it is such indulgences that separate them from God and make them children of the world. Christ has given us no such example. Those only who deny self, and live a life of sobriety, humility, and holiness, are true followers of Jesus; and such cannot enjoy the society of the lovers of the world.

Many dress like the world in order to have an influence over unbelievers, but here they make a sad mistake. If they would have a true and saving influence, let them live out their profession, show their faith by their righteous works, and make the distinction plain between the Christian and the worldling. The words, the dress, the actions, should tell for God. Then a holy influence will be shed upon all around them, and

---

[12] Ellen G. White, *Testimonies to Ministers and Gospel Workers*, pp. 91, 92.

even unbelievers will take knowledge of them that they have been with Jesus. If any wish to have their influence tell in favor of truth, let them live out their profession and thus imitate the humble Pattern. (*Testimonies for the Church*, vol. 4, p. 633, 634)

The following is a testimony from Beth Williams, who is serving in a country that is unfriendly to evangelism. Thus, the names of people and places have been changed.

"I knew you were a good woman the moment I saw you, and I really wanted to be friends with you!" This is how the wife of one of my husband's friends began the first conversation we ever had together. Curious, I asked her what made her feel that way.

"Well, I noticed you dress similar to conservative women here, so I knew right away that you have good morals. Most of the Western women I've seen don't dress very modestly, but you're different."

My new friend's words started me thinking. When we first went overseas, I knew the way I chose to dress would make a big difference in what people thought of me. So, out of deference to local tradition and out of a genuine desire to be modest, I chose to wear the same clothing as local conservative women—long skirts with leggings underneath and long-sleeve shirts. You might think only conservatives would appreciate my choice of clothes, but even the most secular of our friends have told me they think my clothes are in good taste.

I often wonder how much most Westerners think about the impression their clothes give to those around them. For example, last year while we were in the States, I found myself seated a couple rows behind a young woman who was wearing a strapless shirt. Because the seatback was higher than the back of her shirt, she appeared to be naked from my vantage point. I can't remember what the speaker said that day, but I clearly remember the distraction. I'm pretty sure that when the young woman dressed that morning she probably never guessed at the impression it would give to those behind her. Actions speak louder than words, and I will always dress accordingly as I seek to make my life a witness.[13]

---

13   *Adventist Frontiers*, June 2010, p. 14. Reprinted by permission. Adventist Frontier Missions seeks to establish Seventh-day Adventist church-planting movements among unreached people groups (AFMonline.org).

Appendix I

The Daniel 8 and 9 Timeline

Following is the timeline of the 2300-day prophecy in Daniel 8:
- 457 BC, Autumn – the command to rebuild Jerusalem
- 408 BC, Autumn (seventh week or forty-nine years) – the completion of the rebuilding of Jerusalem
- 4 BC, Autumn – Christ was born[1]
- AD 27, Autumn (no year zero; sixty-ninth week or 483 years) – Christ was baptized at age 30[2]
- AD 31, Spring (*midst* of seventieth week or three and a half years) – Christ was crucified
- AD 34, Autumn (seventieth week or 490 years) – the time for Israel ended at the stoning of Stephen[3]
- AD 1844, Autumn (2300 days[4] or 2300 years) – the cleansing of the heavenly sanctuary began

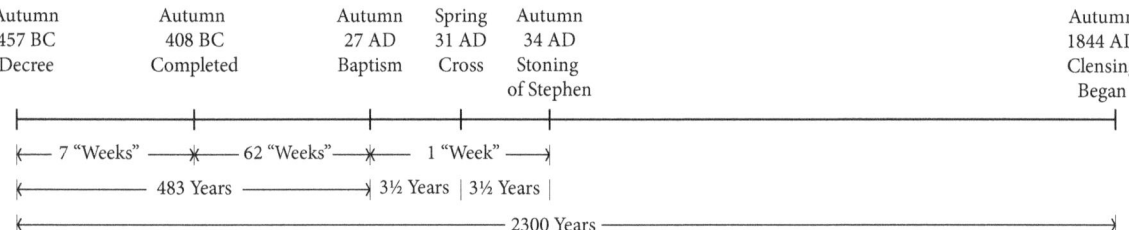

Daniel 9:24 says, "Seventy weeks are determined [This word in the original language is used several times in this passage, and the specific meaning comes from the context. In the original language it means to cut or to divide, hence to decree, to determine—also "decreed," "cut," or "cut off"—in this case it is cut from the 2300-year prophecy of Daniel 8.] upon thy people and upon thy holy city, to finish the transgression, and to make an end of sins, and to make reconciliation for iniquity, and to bring in everlasting righteousness [This is the removal of sin, which was done for all people corporately by Christ in His day and is being brought, in our day, to experiential fulfillment for all who believe, which

---

1   Not prophesied in Daniel 9, but provided here for reference only.
2   See Luke 3:21–23; 4:1–3. This is when Jesus began His ministry. It was common for priests to begin their official ministry at age 30, which action confirms that Christ was a priest, though after the order of Melchizedek and not after the order of the "official" Levitical priesthood. Directly after His baptism, He spent forty days in the wilderness where He conquered Satan's attempts to cause Him to sin.
3   See Acts 6-8, especially 7:51–60, where Stephen has his vision at his trial before the high priest. This was the formal rejection of the gospel of Christ by the highest of Jewish authorities—the Sanhedrin. After this, the gospel began to be taken to the Gentiles.
4   In the original language a day is referred to as "evening morning" because each day starts with the evening (sunset) and continues (after the sleep break) with the morning.

is the subject of this book.], and to seal up [establish] the vision and prophecy [the 2300-year prophecy of Daniel 8], and to anoint the most Holy [that is, to prepare the heavenly sanctuary for cleansing, which is done in the Most Holy Place of the same and which takes place beginning with the end of the 2300-year prophecy]."

Remember the principle of a day for a year in Bible prophecy found in Numbers 14:34 and also in Ezekiel 4:6? One day of Bible prophecy is the same as one year of real time. This prophecy of Daniel 9 covers a period of 490 literal years (seventy weeks times seven prophetic days). And by the end of this time all of these things—to finish the transgression, to make an end of sins, to make reconciliation for iniquity, to bring in everlasting righteousness, to seal up the vision and prophecy, and to anoint the most Holy—were accomplished by, in, and through Jesus Christ corporately for *all* people. (At the *end* of the 2300 years, the process to accomplish the cleansing from sin for all who choose to believe would, and actually did, begin.)

Daniel 9:25 states, "Know therefore and understand, that from the going forth of the commandment to restore and to build Jerusalem unto the Messiah the Prince shall be seven weeks, and threescore and two weeks: the street shall be built again, and the wall, even in troublous times."

There were actually three commands to restore and rebuild Jerusalem, but the last one was the one that actually worked, for it established a civil government. It was given in 457 BC (see Ezra 7). There was a fourth order after this date and after the beginning of the work. This was when Nehemiah was commissioned to assist with the work already underway (Neh. 2), so we can't use this command as a starting point for the prophecy.

Seven times seven is forty-nine. Forty-nine years after the command to restore and rebuild Jerusalem, the task was completed, but it was indeed carried out in troublous times, which is the reason the king had to send Nehemiah to complete the job.[5] The last act of restoration was completed in 408 BC. (Note: The historical records do indeed manifest the success of the day-year prophetic principle.)

Now let's turn to Daniel 9:26, 27: "And after threescore and two weeks shall Messiah be cut off [or determined/decreed—His official ministry was determined at His baptism, at age 30, which was the age that priests generally began their ministry], but not for himself [literally, no one for/with Him]: and the people of the prince that shall come [the Roman army] shall destroy the city and the sanctuary [i.e., the destruction of Jerusalem in AD 66–70]; and the [its] end thereof shall be with a flood [the battle will be overwhelming], and unto [until] the [an] end of the war [the "the" is not in the original so it would actually be referring to *all* war, including the war of Satan against Christ, also known as the "Battle of Armageddon"—which ends at the lake of fire] desolations are determined [cut, decreed].

"And he shall confirm the covenant [God's promise to us through Abraham (and Adam)] with

---

5   See Nehemiah 2 and 13.

[the] [6] many [i.e., the whole human race] for one week: and in the midst [middle, three and a half years] of the week he shall cause the sacrifice and the oblation to cease [The sacrificial services in the earthly sanctuary ended at Christ's death, as indicated by God tearing the veil to the Most Holy Place of the earthly sanctuary at the point of death.], and for [upon] the overspreading [literally, "wing," that is, the *tip* of the wing; or *extremity*, pinnacle] of abominations he shall make it desolate, even until the consummation [until an utter end—the consummation of earth's history when Jesus comes the second time, culminating with the lake of fire after the 1000 years of desolation (Rev. 20)], and that [which was] determined [decreed] shall be poured upon the desolate [literally, the one who desolates, that is, the "*desolator*," Satan, will be consumed in the lake of fire].

I suggest the following paraphrase of Daniel 9:24–27:

> Four hundred and ninety years are cut off from the 2300-year prophecy of Daniel 8 for God's people and the city of Jerusalem to receive the finishing of the transgression that began with Adam (i.e., the making of an end of sins), to receive the reconciliation for iniquity, and to receive the bringing in of everlasting righteousness. (This refers to the removal of sin, which was accomplished by Christ for the whole human race corporately and is the subject of this book. Also, this removal of sin is accomplished in the experience of each believer individually, constantly throughout the history of earth, because God gave it to the race corporately.) This seals up the 2300-year prophecy of Daniel 8 and prepares the heavenly sanctuary for cleansing. This is done in the Most Holy Place of the heavenly sanctuary and will take place starting with the end of the 2300-year period (in the autumn of AD 1844).
>
> Know therefore and understand, that from the going forth of the commandment to restore and rebuild Jerusalem (in the autumn of 457 BC) until the time of the Messiah the Prince shall be 483 years (to the autumn of AD 27).
>
> After forty-nine years (in the autumn of 408 BC), the rebuilding of the street and the wall shall be completed, even through troublous times. And after another 434 years (in the autumn of AD 27), the Messiah shall be baptized and begin His official ministry, but He will be unpopular with the authorities. The Roman army shall destroy Jerusalem and the temple therein (in AD 70) and its end thereof shall be the result of an overwhelming battle. And until the end of *all* war, desolations are decreed.
>
> And he shall *confirm* (or *ratify*) God's covenant promise made to Adam and renewed through Abraham of salvation for, and with, the whole human race for the

---

6   The "the" is in the original. This phrase, "the many," refers to all people ever created on the face of this planet. It does not refer to "a lot" of people, as in "many," but *the* many—all people. In Romans 5:18, 19, the "the" is in the original also (in verse 19), making the same point as Daniel 9:27. An interesting comparison is found between the KJV and the NIV in both of these passages, the NIV being correct to the original language in Romans, but does not follow through in Daniel 9:27, even though that "the" is present in the original.

next seven years, until the autumn of AD 34, and after three and a half years (in the spring of AD 31), through His sacrificial death for all people, he shall cause the sacrificial services in the earthly sanctuary to come to an end (because those sacrificial services pointed to His death as their fulfillment). Upon the pinnacle of abominations is Satan who desolates, even until the consummation of earth's history, when all those desolations which are decreed shall be poured out upon Satan himself, because he is causing all this desolation.

Seven weeks plus sixty-two weeks, or sixty-nine weeks, brought about the baptism of Christ, the beginning of the ministry of the Messiah. This happened in AD 27. And in the *midst* of the *final week*, the final seven-day period, He died and brought the sacrificial system to an end, for *He* was the lamb, *He* was the sacrifice to which the sacrificial system was pointing.

In the ninth chapter of Daniel, the Lord completes the vision He gave to Daniel in chapter 8, which states, "And the vision of the evening and the morning which was told is true: wherefore shut thou up the vision; for it shall be for many days. And I Daniel fainted, and was sick certain days; afterward I rose up, and did the king's business; and I was astonished at the vision, but none understood it" (verses 26, 27).

The completion appears in Daniel 9: "And whiles I was speaking, and praying, and confessing my sin and the sin of my people Israel, and presenting my supplication before the Lord my God for the holy mountain of my God; Yea, whiles I was speaking in prayer, even the man Gabriel, whom I had seen in the vision at the beginning, being caused to fly swiftly, touched me about the time of the evening oblation. And he informed me, and talked with me, and said, O Daniel, I am now come forth to give thee skill and understanding. At the beginning of thy supplications the commandment came forth, and I am come to shew thee; for thou art greatly beloved: therefore understand the matter, and consider the vision" (verses 20–23).

The vision referred to is the vision that Daniel had been so confused about before—the vision of the 2300 days in chapter 8. So let's go back to that vision in Daniel 8:14: " And he said unto me, Unto two thousand and three hundred days; then shall the sanctuary be cleansed."

If you add 2300 years to 457 BC, which means you actually subtract 457 from 2300, you get 1843. Then you add back in 1 because there is no year zero in our calendar reckoning. That brings us to 1844—this is the date that the cleansing of the sanctuary began.

When the *earthly* sanctuary was cleansed, once each year, the high priest went into the Most Holy Place, the second apartment. While the high priest was there, through the sprinkling of blood onto the mercy seat (representing the death of Christ and forgiveness of sin), he symbolically removed the sins of the people that had gathered all year long, having been brought into the first apartment through the sacrifices of the daily services. These were then placed on the scape ("escape") goat and sent into the wilderness to die, representing Satan bound in chains of darkness for 1000 years (see Rev. 20; Lev. 16; and 2 Peter 2:4).

During the cleansing of the *heavenly* sanctuary, which will only happen once in the history of the universe (and is happening right now), the heavenly High Priest is working in the Most Holy Place, the second apartment, of the heavenly sanctuary. He is applying the sprinkling of blood on the seat of mercy (applying His own death and forgiveness of sin) and is removing the sins of the people that have gathered throughout all history, since sin began. These sins will be placed on Satan when Jesus comes the second time and takes His people to heaven for 1000 years (see Rev. 20).

This is what Jesus, the antitypical High Priest, is doing in the heavenly sanctuary right now. Will you consent to be included in that ministry?

Appendix J

The Hebrew Religious Calendar

Feasts 1 through 4 (Months 1 through 3)						
(Leviticus 23; Exodus 12; Leviticus 8,9; Acts 1,2)						
1st day (Sunday)	2nd day (Monday)	3rd Day (Tuesday)	4th Day (Wednesday)	5th Day (Thursday)	6th Day (Friday)	7th Day (Sabbath)
2 The month of Nisan	3	4	5	6	7 Christ arrives at Bethany (before sunset).	8 Christ anointed for His death by Mary. (This could have happened on Friday.)
9 Christ's triumphal entry into Jerusalem means that He now officially accepts the title of King of Israel. (Palm Sunday)	10 Selection of the Passover lamb. The process of Christ being set aside to die was completed at the cleansing of the temple on Monday. (Then He teaches in the temple.) The priests, having previously decided to take Christ after the feast when the people have gone home, now escalate it to ASAP.	11 Christ teaches in the temple: the fig tree withers, the authority of Jesus is questioned, the parable of the tenants, the parable of the wedding banquet, paying taxes to Caesar, marriage and the resurrection, the greatest commandment, Seven woes to the teachers and Pharisees, signs of the end of the age. (This could have continued through Thursday.)	12	13 Passover [1] begins at even (sunset). (The Passover meal was eaten with unleavened bread.) Christ ate the Passover meal with His disciples on Thursday night. Today this meal is called "The Last Supper". (Then He goes to Gethsemane and is taken by the "authorities" there.)	14 Passover ends at even (sunset). The Passover is the sacrifice of the Lamb at the evening sacrifice (3:00 PM). Christ died at 3:00 PM and was placed in the tomb by sunset. Day 1. (Martyrs are thrown out of their tombs at the 3:00 earthquake.) The Feast of Unleavened Bread [2] begins at even (sunset) (lasts 7 days). Note: the Passover meal was eaten with unleavened bread also, making a total of 8 days of unleavened bread.	15 Christ rests in the tomb all day. Day 2. (The corpses of the martyrs rest on the ground all day.) This day is a holy convocation.

1st day (Sunday)	2nd day (Monday)	3rd Day (Tuesday)	4th Day (Wednesday)	5th Day (Thursday)	6th Day (Friday)	7th Day (Sabbath)
16 The Feast of Firstfruits [3] Christ lays in the tomb until resurrected at dawn. (The martyrs come to life, also.) Day 3.	17	18	19	20	21 The Last day of the Feast of Unleavened Bread (ends at even). This day is a holy convocation.	22 (7 Since Firstfruits)
23	24	25	26	27	28	29 (14)
30	1 The month of Iyar	2	3	4	5	6 (21)
7	8	9	10	11	12	13 (28)
14	15	16	17	18	19	20 (35)
21	22	23	24	25 (40) Christ's Ascension. (The martyrs ascend with Him.) The time of tarrying for the disciples begins.	26 Day 1 after the ascension (Acts 1:4)	27 (42) Day 2 after the ascension
28 Day 3 after the ascension. Christ's inauguration into the heavenly Sanctuary begins. Time of separation for the priest begins-Day 1 of the ceremony. (Lev 8:33-9:1)	29 Day 4 after the ascension, Day 2 of the ceremony	1 The month of Sivan Day 5 after the ascension, Day 3 of the ceremony	2 Day 6 after the ascension, Day 4 of the ceremony	3 Day 7 after the ascension, Day 5 of the ceremony	4 Day 8 after the ascension, Day 6 of the ceremony	5 (49) Day 9 after the ascension, Day 7 of the ceremony. The Feast of Weeks begins at even (sunset).
6 (50) The Feast of Weeks (Pentecost) [4] Day 10 after the ascension, the final day of Christ's inauguration. The Holy Spirit comes down upon the disciples as tongues of fire. (Acts 2:3) Day 8 of the ceremony, Fire comes down upon the sacrifice from God Himself. (Lev 9:24,25) "Shavuot"	7	8	9	10	11	12
	[1] Feast #1	[2] Feast #2	[3] Feast #3	[4] Feast #4		

The Hebrew Religious Calendar

Feasts 5 through 8 (Months 3 through 7)

(Leviticus 23)

1st day (Sunday)	2nd day (Monday)	3rd Day (Tuesday)	4th Day (Wednesday)	5th Day (Thursday)	6th Day (Friday)	7th Day (Sabbath)
13 (Sivan Continued)	14	15	16	17	18	19
20	21	22	23	24	25	26
27	28	29	30	1 The month of Tammuz	2	3
4	5	6	7	8	9	10
11	12	13	14	15	16	17
18	19	20	21	22	23	24
25	26	27	28	29	1 The month of Av	2
3	4	5	6	7	8	9
10	11	12	13	14	15	16
17	18	19	20	21	22	23
24	25	26	27	28	29	30
1 The month of Elul	2	3	4	5	6	7
8	9	10	11	12	13	14
15	16	17	18	19	20	21
22	23	24	25	26	27	28
29	1 The month of Tishri The Feast of Trumpets [5] The Great Awakening of the 1800s led by William Miller. A sabbath of rest. "Rosh Hashanah"	2	3	4	5	6
7	8	9	10 The Day of Atonement [6] The time of heart searching and preparation. A sabbath of rest. A holy convocation. "Yom Kippur"	11	12	13
14	15 The Feast of Tabernacles [7] Christ comes. It is a time of celebration. (Lasts 7 days) Day 1. A sabbath of rest. A holy convocation. "Sukkot"	16 Day 2.	17 Day 3.	18 Day 4.	19 Day 5.	20 Day 6.

1st day (Sunday)	2nd day (Monday)	3rd Day (Tuesday)	4th Day (Wednesday)	5th Day (Thursday)	6th Day (Friday)	7th Day (Sabbath)
21 Day 7.	22 Day 8. A sabbath of rest. A holy convocation. "Shemini Atzeret"	23	24	25	26	27
	[5] Feast #5	[6] Feast #6	[7] Feast #7			

Appendix K

The Godhead

How many Gods do Christians worship? Is there one? Are there three? Or are there only *two*? The subject can be confusing to some who may be encountering this for the first time. However, it does not have to be confusing if we ask God to show us the logic. It is assumed that if you have read this far, you understand some of the concepts that we will be using in our discussion here.

The New Testament translators used the word "Godhead" to describe God. This term includes (1) the Father, the Ancient of Days,[1] sometimes called simply God; (2) the Son, Jehovah (Yahweh),[2] also called Michael (the Archangel)[3] and Jesus Christ (the Messiah, the "Anointed")[4]; and (3) the Holy Spirit, sometimes called the Holy Ghost, the Comforter, or the Counselor. Godhead implies one God in plurality; that is, three separate, distinct, individual beings acting harmoniously as one unit, a *trio*—all singing harmoniously the same tune. Our modern-day corporation is an example of the *many* acting as *one unit*. This subject is closely related to the representative concept we have been discussing elsewhere in this book, for it is the representative concept in practical application. In the representative concept,

---

1 In Daniel 7:9-14 the "Son of man" comes to the "Ancient of days." They are not the same person.
2 The terms "Yahweh" and "Jehovah" refer to Jesus Christ. These are transliterations of "YHWH," Christ's proper name. It means "the one who is: i.e. the absolute and unchangeable one, … the existing, ever-living [one], … the one ever coming into manifestation as the God of redemption" (*Brown-Driver-Briggs Hebrew and English Lexicon*, p. 218). (Some have said, perhaps at least partially in response to this latter phrase regarding manifestation, that this word also means "the one bringing into being, lifegiver, … giver of existence, creator … he who brings to pass … performer of his promises" (Ibid.). Jesus Christ is all of these. Specifically, He was the active agent in creation (John 1:3; Col. 1:10–17; Eph. 3:9). He is God *manifested* in human flesh. Jesus used the primitive form of this word in referring to Himself in His conversation with Moses at the bush in Exodus 3:14 (and the later version of the name in verse 15) and also claimed this same name in John 8:58 (the Greek version of the word) when He said, "Before Abraham was, I am." In the Bible, you may see it in all capitals, "LORD" or Lord." This word is singular and should not be confused with *Elohiym*, the plural name for the Godhead corporate. Because of a misinterpretation of the third commandment (Exod. 20:7; see also Lev. 24:10–16), or, possibly, by some other superstition, the Jewish people considered this word to be too holy to pronounce, although sometimes it was read as "Adonai." Isaiah 12:2–4 tells us, "Behold, God [Hebrew: the Almighty, all-knowing, everlasting, God of glory] is my salvation; I will trust, and not be afraid: for the LORD JEHOVAH [Jesus Christ] is my strength and my song; he also *is* become my salvation. Therefore with joy shall ye draw water out of the wells of salvation. And in that day shall ye say, Praise the LORD, call upon his name, declare his *doings among the people*, make mention that his name is exalted." Christ *became* our salvation at His incarnation (in that He represents the human race) and *completed* that metaphor in the perfect life He *lived among the people* as our heritage and in the price He paid on the cross. There He took the death that we deserve (again as our representative), and now He is in heaven as High Priest, removing the sins of His people—all because He is our righteousness. (See also Exodus 20:11; John 1:3, 14.)
3 Not that Jesus *is* an angel, but He is *creator* of all the angels (seraphim and cherubim) and has *charge* over them.
4 There are other names for Christ such as "Immanuel" or "Emmanuel" (God with/in us), the Lamb of God (slain from the foundation of the world); the Lion of the tribe of Judah; "Reverend" (worthy of being revered or worshipped [Ps. 111:9]) the Root (Branch) of Jesse (referring to Christ's humanity that He took, that is, of the seed of David, the seed of Abraham, and the seed of the woman, Eve); the Son of God; and the Son of man. For a discussion of these last two, see later in this chapter.

one person acts as the whole. In the corporation, the group acts as one unit through the basic three representative officers they elect (president, secretary, and treasurer, each having their own individual functions that can sometimes overlap). Let's look at some scriptures that reference the Godhead:

- "Forasmuch then as we are the offspring of God, we ought not to think that the *Godhead* is like unto gold, or silver, or stone, graven by art and man's device" (Acts 17:29).
- "For the invisible things of him from the creation of the world are clearly seen, being understood by the things that are made, even his eternal power and *Godhead*; so that they are without excuse" (Rom. 1:20).
- "For in him dwelleth all the fulness of the *Godhead* bodily" (Col. 2:9).

The word for God in the Old Testament Hebrew is *Elohiym*. It means "Gods" in the plural.[5] God refers to Himself in the plural in the following texts, stating explicitly that there is more than one divine being.

- "And God [plural, *Elohiym*] said, Let *us* make man [also plural, men, "humankind," the one whole human race] in *our* image, after *our* likeness" (Gen. 1:26).
- "And the LORD[6] [Jesus Christ] said, Behold, the people is one, and they have all one language; and this they begin to do: and now nothing will be restrained from them, which they have imagined to do. Go to, let *us* go down, and there confound their language, that they may not understand one another's speech" (Gen. 11:6, 7).
- "Also I heard the voice of the Lord,[7] saying, Whom shall I send, and who will go for *us*?" (Isa. 6:8).

What can seem confusing is that God sometimes refers to Himself in the singular. For example, Genesis 1:27 (right after Genesis 1:26, above) refers to *Elohiym* in both the plural and the singular *in the same sentence*: "So God [plural, *Elohiym*] created man [also plural, "men" or "mankind"] in *his* [singular] own image, in the image of God [plural, *Elohiym*] created *he* him; male and female created *he* them."

Although this may seem confusing, it doesn't have to be. This duality of the use of the plural Elohiym indicates multiple beings (verse 26) that make up one God, or "Godhead" (verse 27), a corporate entity. This mixing of the plural and singular pronouns is typical of the ancient Hebrew writers because they thought in terms of the proverbial "group" as one unit. For example, the whole human race is one man, Adam (which means "mankind," by the way[8]). This is the thinking of the Eastern

---

5   The -iym -im (ם׳) suffix indicates plural in the Hebrew, as in cherub versus cherubim, for example.
6   This is the Hebrew word "YHWH" (יהוה), *Yahweh*, or, later, "Jehovah" (see the footnote above about Jesus' titles). This is the *proper* name for the second person of the Godhead, Jesus Christ. It is singular and should not be confused with *Elohiym*, the plural name for the Godhead corporate. In this case, Jesus is speaking to the other two members of the Godhead.
7   The lowercase version, Lord, refers to a master, a teacher, or other authority of rank and sometimes, but not necessarily, to God. In this case, "Lord" is referring to the Godhead corporate.
8   The Hebrew word translated "Adam" means "of the ground, firm; red, ruddy (referring to blood); man, a human being, mankind, the human race;" it is also used as the proper name of the first man as well as a city in the Jordan valley (Joshua 3:16).

Hemisphere. In the West, particularly in America, the thinking is far more individualistic. For example, the United States was built on rugged individualism, having forged a new nation out of the wilderness. It is harder for those in the West to conceptualize the way the Bible writers thought. An example of Eastern thought can be found in Genesis 25:23, "And the LORD said unto her [Rebekah], Two *nations* are in thy womb, and two manner of people shall be separated from thy bowels."

Here are some Bible texts that refer to each of the three members of the Godhead:
- "Go ye therefore, and teach all nations, baptizing them in the name of the Father, and of the Son, and of the Holy Ghost" (Matt. 28:19).
- "And Jesus, when he was baptized, went up straightway out of the water: and, lo, the heavens were opened unto him, and he saw the Spirit of God [the Holy Spirit] descending like a dove, and lighting upon him: And lo a voice from heaven [the Father], saying, This is my beloved Son, in whom I am well pleased" (Matt. 3:16, 17).
- "For there are three that bear record in heaven, the Father, the Word [Christ], and the Holy Ghost: and these three are one" (1 John 5:7). [The "three *are* one" (in *unity*), not "three *in* one," (*i.e.*, not three *in* one *substance;* not three *in* one *being.*)]

Following are some texts that refer to different aspects of the heavenly trio:

The Father – the first person of the Godhead
- "I beheld till the thrones were cast down, and the Ancient of days did sit, whose garment was white as snow, and the hair of his head like the pure wool: his throne was like the fiery flame, and his wheels as burning fire. A fiery stream issued and came forth from before him: thousand thousands ministered unto him, and ten thousand times ten thousand stood before him: the judgment was set, and the books were opened. I beheld then because of the voice of the great words which the horn spake: I beheld even till the beast was slain, and his body destroyed, and given to the burning flame. As concerning the rest of the beasts, they had their dominion taken away: yet their lives were prolonged for a season and time. I saw in the night visions, and, behold, one like the Son of man [Christ] came with the clouds of heaven, and came to the Ancient of days, and they brought him near before him. And there was given him dominion, and glory, and a kingdom, that all people, nations, and languages, should serve him: his dominion is an everlasting dominion, which shall not pass away, and his kingdom that which shall not be destroyed" (Dan. 7:9-14).

The Son – the second person of the Godhead
- "Blessed be the LORD God of Israel from everlasting [no beginning] to everlasting [no end]: and let all the people say, Amen" (Ps. 106:48).
- "Let this mind be in you, which was also in Christ Jesus: Who, being in the *form* of God, thought it not robbery to be equal with God" (Phil. 2:5, 6).
- "Then said the Jews unto him, Thou art not yet fifty years old, and hast thou seen Abraham?

Jesus said unto them, Verily, verily, I say unto you, Before Abraham was, I am [Jesus here claims to be self-existent God]" (John 8:57, 58).
- "Behold, a virgin shall be with child, and shall bring forth a son, and they shall call his name Emmanuel, which being interpreted is, God with [Greek: with or *in*] us" (Matt. 1:23).
- "But thou, Bethlehem Ephratah, though thou be little among the thousands of Judah, yet out of thee shall he [Christ] come forth unto me that is to be ruler in Israel; whose goings forth have been from of old, from everlasting" (Micah 5:2).

Here is a quiz for you. To which of the three persons of the Godhead is the following text referring? "Now unto the King eternal [no beginning and no end], immortal [cannot die], invisible, the only wise God [Greek: *theos*, a deity], be honour and glory for ever and ever. Amen" (1 Tim. 1:17).

On the surface, we cannot tell. Some people believe it refers to the Father. But, if you place it in its context and read verses 12 through 16, you will find that it is referring to Jesus Christ. Jesus (being God, in the form of God, and as part of the Godhead) is eternal, having no beginning and no end, yet He was born in Bethlehem.

Another term for Jesus Christ is "the only begotten Son of God," which was used by Him to refer to Himself in John 3:18. (See also John 1:18; 3:16; Hebrews 11:17; and 1 John 4:9.) As the only begotten, Christ was commissioned for His work at His incarnation: "Yet have I set my king upon my holy hill of Zion. I will declare the decree: the Lord hath said unto me, Thou art my Son; *this day* have I begotten thee. Ask of me [this day], and I shall give thee the heathen [Hebrew: nations] for thine inheritance, and the uttermost parts of the earth for thy possession. Thou shalt break them with a rod of iron; thou shalt dash them in pieces like a potter's vessel" (Ps. 2:6–9).[9]

The Holy Spirit and the Father both acted in the incarnation of Christ: "Then said Mary unto the angel, How shall this be, seeing I know not a man? And the angel answered and said unto her, The Holy Ghost [the Holy Spirit] shall come upon thee, and the power of the Highest [the Father] shall overshadow thee: therefore also that holy thing which shall be born of thee shall be called the Son of God" (Luke 1:34, 35).

Jesus is called the Son of God with reference to His incarnation.[10] I maintain that this is the primary if not the only meaning of this term. This concept does not preclude Christ being *called* the Son of God, only begotten, or even only begotten Son of God *prior* to His incarnation (see Dan. 3:25). This is because such an eternal application of terms could apply to Christ in *anticipation* and expectation of what He *would* do in the future, as Revelation 13:8 calls Christ the "Lamb slain from the foundation of the world" at least 4,000 years prior to the physical event. I find no biblical reference of Christ as the "only begotten" outside of the context of His incarnation or existence as a human being.[11]

---

9   When the Bible mentions the Son as being "begotten," it refers to His *birth* as a human being for the purpose of dwelling on the earth (as the reference to the earth and the heathen indicates). His *resurrection* as a glorified human being is the fulfillment thereof. The Bible here uses the figure of speech of personification to have Jesus (as God) speaking to Jesus (as man).
10 This is on his Father's side. On His mother's side, He is known as the Son of man (see Matt. 8:20).
11 Compare with Psalm 2:7; John 1:14, 18; 3:16, 18; Acts 13:33; Hebrews 1:5, 6; 5:5; 1 John 4:9; and Revelation 1:5.

Christ's commission was fulfilled when He arose from the dead: "But God raised him from the dead: And he was seen many days of them which came up with him from Galilee to Jerusalem, who are his witnesses unto the people. And we declare unto you glad tidings, how that the *promise* which was made unto the fathers, God hath *fulfilled* the same unto us their children, in that he hath *raised up* Jesus *again*; as it is also written in the second psalm, Thou art my Son, this day have I *begotten* thee [Ps. 2:7]" (Acts 13:30–33).

Jesus Christ is fully God, eternal and self-existent. "Begotten" refers to His incarnation in becoming human and being brought into the world (the *first* "raising") for the purpose of ministering to the fallen human race,[12] which is the *purpose* of and the reason for Jesus saying He "proceeded forth and came from God" (John 8:42). It also refers indirectly to His resurrection in that He was raised *again* ("proceeded forth and came from," this time from the dead,[13] the *second* "raising") at His resurrection.

Hebrews 1:1–14 provides us a wealth of insight into this subject:

> God [the Father], who at sundry times and in divers manners spake in time past unto the fathers [human ancestors] by the prophets,[14] Hath in these last days spoken unto us by his *Son*, whom he hath appointed heir of all things, by whom also he made the worlds;
>
> Who being [*is*,[15] not "reflects"] the brightness [in the original: to radiate, to emit (in His own right) radiance, brightness] of his [the Father's] glory [character], and the express image [the original word means carved engraving (three-dimensional), an impression, an exact representation, a precise reproduction in every respect] of his [the Father's] person [the original word means substance, essence[16]], and upholding all things by the word of his power [Christ sustains all things constantly through His creative word], when he had by himself purged our sins [He buried our sins in the grave and nailed to the cross our debt to the law[17]], sat down on the right hand[18] of the Majesty [the Father] on high:

---

12 Read all of Psalm 2.
13 This is also for the purpose of ministering to the fallen human race.
14 Note: This indicates that the Old Testament is inspired by God.
15 This is the same word that Jesus uses to refer to Himself as eternal and self-existent in John 8:58.
16 This does *not* say that the Father and Son are one person, but that being a *carved* engraving, an *impression*, an exact *representation*, a precise *reproduction*, Christ had, before His incarnation into *human* form, the same type of three-dimensional sinless *godly* form as the Father, the same radiant, perfect character as the Father, and the same spiritual nature as the Father. That means that Jesus Christ was omniscient (all-knowing), omnipotent (all-powerful), and omnipresent (capable of being everywhere at once), and immortal (cannot die) just as the Father. (All of this applies to the Holy Spirit as well. Why should the nature(s) of the Three be any different? They are of one nature, in the same sense as you and I are of the same fallen, sinful human flesh.)
17 See Colossians 2:14. The word translated "handwriting of ordinances" means "debt instruments," such as mortgage papers, for we had mortgaged ourselves to the law by our transgression.
18 For most people, the right hand is the hand of action. This phrase means that Jesus Christ is formally established (functionally) as the active agent in creation and the other affairs of the universe (Heb. 1:2, 10).

Being made so much better than the angels, as he hath by inheritance [by His nature as a *member* of the *family* of God] obtained a more excellent name than they.

For unto which of the angels said he [the Father] at any time, Thou art my Son, this day have I begotten thee? [Jesus had become human.] And again, I will be to him a Father, and he shall be to me a Son?[19]

And again, when he bringeth in the firstbegotten *into the world* [Greek, *the inhabited earth*. Jesus is born as a baby.], he saith, And let all the angels of God worship him. [Prior to His incarnation, the angels worshipped Christ as God. Now that He has become human, are the angels to continue their worship of Him? The Father answers the question unequivocally, "Yes!"]

And of the angels he saith, Who maketh his angels spirits, and his ministers a flame of fire. But unto the Son he saith, Thy throne, O God, is for ever and ever: a sceptre of righteousness is the sceptre of thy kingdom. [The Father here is addressing the *Son* as God of the Father. He states that Christ is King of the universe and that His reign will last for all eternity.]

Thou hast loved righteousness, and hated iniquity; therefore God, even thy God, hath anointed thee with the oil of gladness above thy fellows. [The Father here is addressing the Son and referring to *Himself* as God of the Son.]

And, Thou, Lord, [Again, the Father here is addressing the *Son* as "Lord," *His* "Lord." These statements of the Father to the Son indicate that God the Father does not consider that God the Son is inferior in any respect. They are individually and mutually self-existent and equal, yet willing to be subservient to each other.[20]] in the beginning hast laid the foundation of the earth; and the heavens are the works of thine hands: [Christ was the active agent in creation.]

They shall perish; but thou remainest; and they all shall wax old as doth a garment; And as a vesture shalt thou fold them up, and they shall be changed: but thou art the same, and thy years shall not fail. [Christ is eternal.]

But to which of the angels said he at any time, Sit on my right hand, until I make thine enemies thy footstool? Are they not all ministering spirits, sent forth to minister for them who shall be heirs of salvation? [You and I are the heirs of salvation. Angels are commissioned to meet our daily needs at the command of Jesus. We have much to be thankful for.]

Isaiah 49 is a very interesting conversation between the Father and Son. In this passage they discuss Christ's birth (the meaning of "begotten") and the purpose of Him becoming a human being to

---

19 After His incarnation, Jesus, as the begotten Son of God, relied entirely upon the Father for what He did (John 5:30).
20 "Let nothing be done through strife or vainglory; but in lowliness of mind let each esteem other better than themselves" (Phil. 2:3).

bring the human race, particularly His own people, back to God, along with some of the related events and problems. It mentions what Christ is to accomplish, including His covenant (promise) to humanity. They even mention activity of normal human beings begetting children with respect to giving birth in the metaphorical context of God's "children" (His people) feeling discontent and finally being replaced by the Gentiles. It is not necessary to quote the chapter here, but you will find it useful reading, for it speaks to several concepts regarding the Godhead.

To explore the meaning of only begotten, let's examine John 1:1-4, 14: "In the beginning [Greek: *arche*, meaning origin, the absolute beginning of all things. Therefore, Jesus Christ is eternal, self-existing, and possesses life underived.] was the Word, and the Word was with God [with the Godhead], and the Word [Christ] was God. The same *was* [already] in the beginning with God [with the Godhead]. All things were made by him; and without him was not any thing made that was made. In him was life [underived]; and the life was the light of men.... And the Word was *made* flesh [fallen sinful human flesh, something He was *not* before the incarnation], and dwelt among us, (and we beheld his glory, the glory as of the *only begotten* of the Father,) [He was made flesh by being born as a baby. *This is the context.*] full of grace and truth.

The "Word" is Jesus Christ. Although Jesus, in His godly prerogatives, is eternal, immortal, self-existing, and possesses life underived,[21] when He became human, He laid aside His godly prerogatives, some temporarily, and some for all eternity. He temporarily took mortality upon Himself when He took fallen sinful human flesh. That means He could have committed sin. He was fully exposed! He was right where Satan wanted Him, for the devil was trying to get Christ to sin. *Had Jesus committed any sin while possessing fallen sinful human flesh, He would have ceased to exist, even as God!* Thankfully (*while* He was fully exposed), by faith *alone*, He relied completely upon the Father to hold Him in righteousness (John 5:30). He never took His eyes off the Father. When He died, He thought He had lost His eternal life, for He had no assurance that His gift was accepted of the Father, which is why He cried out, "My God, my God, why hast thou forsaken me?" (Ps. 22:1; see also Matt. 27:46; Mark 15:34). Even after His resurrection, He had to go to the Father to receive personal assurance that His gift was accepted (John 20:17). When He was resurrected (in the same glorified immortal human body that *His people* will posses upon being resurrected or translated), He re-assumed immortality.

The human race is now *safe* from destruction! Oh God! My God! How *supreme* the gift! Human words cannot express it. We are safe! You and I are safe, in Christ, our representative.

The Holy Spirit – the third person of the Godhead

- The Holy Spirit is God. "But Peter said, Ananias, why hath Satan filled thine heart to lie to the Holy Ghost, and to keep back part of the price of the land? … why hast thou conceived this thing in thine heart? thou hast not lied unto men, but unto *God*" (Acts 5:3, 4).
- The Holy Spirit is eternal. "How much more shall the blood of Christ, who through the *eternal*

---

21 See John 5:26.

[Holy] Spirit offered himself without spot to God, purge your conscience from dead works to serve the living God?" (Heb. 9:14).
- The Holy Spirit has feelings. "And *grieve not* the holy Spirit of God, whereby ye are sealed unto the day of redemption" (Eph. 4:30).
- The Holy Spirit acts on our behalf. "For it seemed good to the Holy Ghost, and to us, to lay upon you no greater burden than these necessary things" (Acts 15:28).

I believe this is as succinct as is possible to state it: "The Holy Spirit is a *PERSON* because He has attributes of a real person. He exercises a personal ministry through convicting and convincing sinners to repent. He gives new life to the repentant sinner; He guides us to all truth; He empowers us for service. When the Bible tells us of His activities, it indicates that He does them directly by His own initiative. The Bible makes it clear that the Holy Spirit is capable of being related to personally, such as when Ananias and Sapphira lied to Him. Paul admonishes us not to grieve Him. You can't lie to or grieve a 'power' or 'influence.'"[22]

The Holy Spirit, being God (as part of the Godhead), is eternal and self-existent, possessing life underived, having no beginning and no end.

The Godhead

The Godhead is composed of three separate, distinct, eternal, self-existent beings: the Father, the Son, and the Holy Spirit, each with their own unique, primary functions.

Note that all three were present at Jesus' baptism: "And Jesus, when he was baptized, went up straightway out of the water: and, lo, the heavens were opened unto him, and he saw the Spirit of God descending like a dove, and lighting upon him: And lo a voice from heaven [the Father], saying, This is my beloved Son, in whom I am well pleased" (Matt. 3:16, 17).

You see, all three were present at Jesus' baptism: Jesus on the earth itself, in the water; the Holy Spirit in the sky above the earth, descending; and the Father in heaven above both the earth and sky, speaking.

Let's look at the various roles of each member of the Godhead. "Now there are diversities of *gifts*, but the same *Spirit* [the Holy Spirit]. And there are differences of *administrations*, but the same Lord [the Father]. And there are diversities of *operations*, but it is the same God [Jesus] which worketh all in all" (1 Cor. 12:4–6).

Each of the three divine Beings have their own individual official work, or function, even though they sometimes can, and do, overlap. The Father does things that the Son and the Holy Spirit generally do not do. His work can be considered administrative and can be compared to that of the "chief executive officer."

The Son is the active agent in creation and all things in the operational realm, sometimes shared by the others. Currently, He is the High Priest in the Most Holy Place of the heavenly sanctuary,

---

[22] This comment was made by Ann Walper, avid Bible student, Bible instructor, and author, in an e-mail conversation among friends. Used with permission.

removing the sins from God's people on earth and preparing to come and take them back to heaven with Him. His work can be compared to that of the "chief operations officer." His work can also be compared to that of the "chief legal officer" as humanity's legal representative before the throne of God (1 John 2:1).

Finally, the Holy Spirit does things that neither the Father nor the Son generally do. His function is to comfort, convict, convert, and empower.[23] His work can be generally compared to that of the "chief financial officer," for the CFO administers means (power) for operations. The Holy Spirit also carries the function of "divine psychiatrist." Yet all three are in one accord, working for the same end. All are working together for our salvation. Each One is capable of performing all the functions of the others, but the Son and the Holy Spirit, by their own free will, choose to be subordinate to the Father.

Isaiah 48:16 demonstrates the presence of all three: "Come ye near unto me [Jesus], hear ye this; I have not spoken in secret from the beginning; from the time that it was, there am I: and now the Lord God [the Father], and his Spirit [the Holy Spirit], hath sent me."

We have other verses indicating the presence and workings of all three:
- "The grace of the Lord Jesus Christ, and the love of God, and the communion of the Holy Ghost, be with you all. Amen" (2 Cor. 13:14).
- "Elect according to the foreknowledge of God the Father, through sanctification of the Spirit, unto obedience and sprinkling of the blood of Jesus Christ: Grace unto you, and peace, be multiplied" (1 Peter 1:2).
- "Grace be unto you, and peace, from him which is, and which was, and which is to come [the eternal Father]; and from the seven Spirits[24] [the Holy Spirit] which are before his throne; And from Jesus Christ, who is the faithful witness, and the first begotten of the dead [representing the human race in the resurrection], and the prince of the kings of the earth [as "begotten" (of the Father), human King of kings]" (Rev. 1:4, 5).
- "Go ye therefore, and teach all nations, baptizing them in the name of the Father, and of the Son, and of the Holy Ghost" (Matt. 28:19).

A more modern gospel writer refers to all three beings as the Godhead, possessing the divine nature:
- "The Godhead was stirred with pity for the race, and the Father, the Son, and the Holy Spirit gave Themselves to the working out of the plan of redemption."[25]
- "The salvation of human beings is a vast enterprise, that calls into action every attribute of the divine nature. The Father, the Son, and the Holy Spirit have pledged themselves to make God's children more than conquerors through him that has loved them."[26]
- "There are three living persons of the heavenly trio; in the name of these three great powers—the

---

23   See John 16:7, 8; Romans 15:13; Luke 1:35; and Acts 10:38.
24   The number seven in Bible prophecy indicates completeness, not necessarily a specific quantity.
25   Ellen G. White, *Counsels on Health*, p. 222.
26   Ellen White, *The Review and Herald*, January 27, 1903.

Father, the Son, and the Holy Spirit—those who receive Christ by living faith are baptized."[27]

All three Beings make up the Godhead, each possessing every attribute of the divine nature. I know of nothing in the scriptures that would indicate that any of the Beings of the Godhead should possess a nature any different from the others.

There is another theory regarding the Godhead that you may have heard about. It is called the "Trinity" or, sometimes, the "Triune God." The Athanasian Creed states as follows regarding the Trinity:

> … we worship one God in Trinity, and Trinity in Unity; Neither confounding the Persons; nor dividing the Essence [substance[28]]. For there is one Person of the Father; another of the Son; and another of the Holy Ghost. But the Godhead of the Father, of the Son, and of the Holy Ghost, is all one; the Glory equal, the Majesty coeternal.[29] … And yet they are not three eternals; but one eternal. As also there are not three uncreated; nor three infinites, but one uncreated; and one infinite.… The Father is made of none; neither created, nor begotten. The Son is of the Father alone; not made, nor created; but begotten. The Holy Ghost is of the Father and of the Son; neither made, nor created, nor begotten; but proceeding.… And in this Trinity none is before, or after another; none is greater, or less than another. But the whole three Persons are coeternal, and coequal.

"Coeternal" means that the eternalness of one or more of those under consideration depends on the eternal attributes of one or more of the others. "Coequal" means that the equal qualities of the members depend on the equal attributes of the others. In other words, They depend upon each other for Their existence. According to the concept of the Trinity, only the Father is self-existent, but the Son is constantly "begotten," or brought forth, of the Father alone. The Holy Spirit is constantly "proceeding" from the combination of the Father and the Son through their mutual love and delight in each other. Since all three make up *one essence* or *one substance* ("nor dividing the Essence"), each is a different *aspect* or *manifestation* of the *one* substance, different *personalities* of *one being*. This is subtly different than the biblical concept of who God is. Because it misrepresents the nature of God, we receive a false impression of the character of God that diminishes the work of both Jesus Christ and the Holy Spirit in removing the sin from our lives, particularly as we live in the last days before Jesus comes. Under this "Trinitarian" scenario, Jesus Christ, rather than honored as a being in His own right, is relegated to an "aspect" or "manifestation" of a single entity (as would also be the Holy Spirit). Jesus, as begotten

---

27 Ellen G. White, *Evangelism*, p. 615.
28 According to Louis LaRavoire Morrow. [Author's note: The concept being expressed here is that God is three persons in *one being* (essence, substance) with three aspects or expressions (rather than three separate and distinct beings working as one unit).]
29 The prefix "co-" means together, joint, jointly, mutually. The existence of one or more members depends upon the existence of one or more of the others.

of the Father only, without the human input, could never be considered human without receiving from humanity the human genetic substance (DNA), such as that which came through Mary. Additionally, having no existence or substance outside of the Father (as a mere "manifestation" or aspect), Jesus could not be in a position to receive this human input. It would take a legitimate "card carrying" (and, in this case, divine) being in His own right to receive the substance of the human genetic makeup. Jesus could not be a personal being understanding human woe by firsthand experience, but merely a force to be reckoned with. Many people today think of God in just such a manner. The doctrine of Docetism, for example, would be a logical result of this "Trinitarian" concept of God. Docetism is the teaching that Jesus Christ was a mere phenomenon and that His existence was a semblance without reality. Under this belief, Christ's ability to represent the human race before the Father would be compromised, if not downright impossible (not to mention the impossibility of His sacrificial "death"). How could an impersonal "phenomenon" represent real people with real problems? How does one relate to "may the Force be with you" as a personal Savior? How does one connect vitally to a God who is little more than a hologram? Humanity needs a Savior who is a real person and has real feelings, who can get down in the "trenches" with us and feel what we feel, whose strength we can connect with. Such a person is a true leader. Jesus Christ is that man. Jesus Christ is that kind of God. Because of this confusion, I discourage the use of the term, "Trinity" and also the term, "Triune God" to describe God. Instead, I suggest the biblical term "Godhead" for this purpose. Even the term "heavenly trio" would more accurately describe who God is. The final issue before Jesus comes is understanding who God is. That question will be answered by God's witnesses in His trial as you and I represent Him in our daily lives. Then Jesus will come. Are you on board? The "train" is still at the "station." Now is the time to get on.

Summary

Jesus has always been the Son of God, even the "(only) begotten" Son of God. The term "begotten" refers to the *fact* of His incarnation, both *before* and *after* the fact of His birth, in the same sense as Christ is *called* the Lamb slain from the foundation of the world, even *before* the fact of His death. In addition, the title Son of God can be thought of in that same sense. To say that Jesus is called the Son of God because He was of the same nature as the Father would appear to leave the Holy Spirit out in the cold, so to speak, because there is no indication anywhere that the Holy Spirit is of any different nature than either the Father or the Son. It would appear that Christ has always been referred to as the "Son" (and concurrently, the Father is called "Father"). First, because there is a need to differentiate between the two; second, because Christ chose to be subservient to the Father; and third, since He was *going* to be incarnated, the Father-Son comparison had a dual application, both relational in heaven and physical on earth, as Jesus became the God-man. This physical aspect of His incarnation is a "new sense" of being called the "Son of God."[30]

In the same line of thought, the Holy Spirit is called "Holy Spirit" because He was *not* going to be

---

30   Compare with Ellen G. White, *Selected Messages,* book 1, p. 226.

incarnated and His function with the human race was *going* to be *spiritual only, without adding any of the physical aspects*. In addition, it appears that the Holy Spirit, in choosing to be subservient to both the Father and the Son, also chose not to be worshiped[31]—*not* that He is not *worthy* of worship, but logically, that *His work is to lead people to Christ,* the remedy for sin. He does not want to distract from the issue of His own work of leading people to Christ by diverting attention to Himself. What a lesson in humility *that* is!

These names are just names. They describe Their function and also Their relationship to each other, the exception (to the latter) being the "new sense" of Christ becoming a human being, actually *experiencing* the human role He was to take. It is a mistake to try to tie these names to what our finite minds might want to speculate as to what their nature(s) might be.

The Bible teaches that the Godhead is composed of three separate, distinct, self-existent, eternal Beings acting harmoniously as one unit. Although each Being is truly God in His own right, the corporate unit form is called "God (Elohiym)." All this differs from the pagan concept of "gods" who each have their own agendas and sometimes even *war* against each other. The *creator* God who made the universe[32] and re-makes you and me into righteous beings after Their own image[33] is the one true God of the universe. He is worthy of our worship. The proper way to address Him in prayer is "Our Father" while praying "in the name of Jesus Christ" who represents us in heaven. There is no need to address the "Holy Spirit" directly[34] because *He* receives our prayers first. He interprets and edits our prayers, perfecting them, and then delivers them to the Father,[35] who *then* communicates with the Son, who *then*, in turn, takes action through the Holy Spirit. Thus, it is best to address the Father directly.

It is crucial that we believe the *words* and *actions* of the functional Godhead, in addition to believing *in* them and who they claim to be. Believe in Them for who They are—one harmonious corporate unit—that is, one God. "The grace of the Lord Jesus Christ, and the love of God, and the communion of the Holy Ghost, be with you all. Amen" (2 Cor. 13:14).

---

31 Nowhere in the Scriptures do I see a command to worship the Holy Spirit directly; the Father, yes, the Son, yes, but never the Holy Spirit.

32 The second person of the Godhead, Jesus Christ, the Son, is the *active* agent in the creation and sustenance of the world, but all three participated.

33 That is, *character,* not *nature.* The third person of the Godhead, the Holy Spirit, is the active agent in the re-creation of His people into righteous and holy beings. Each member of the Godhead has His own individual function in our salvation.

34 In fact, since He does not seem to want our worship, it appears He prefers to work in the background, behind the Father and the Son. All three persons of the Godhead are willingly subservient to each other, the Father taking the administrative role.

35 Sometimes Jesus will do this. Each of the three are capable of performing across function lines.

Appendix L

Are the Feasts to be Observed Literally Today?

This is a logical question and deserves a logical and thoughtful answer. Many thoughtful people are wondering whether there is a benefit in keeping the biblical feast days today. I don't want anyone to come up short in the spiritual blessings that God has for us, so we will look at this question and see what God has to say. As a background to our discussion in this appendix, let's briefly review each feast with its individual antitypical fulfillment:

- **The Feast of the Passover** – This feast is manifested in four different ways. The *literal* Passover happened when the angel of death passed over those who applied the blood of the sacrifice that represented Christ's death the night the Hebrews were delivered from Egypt and began their journey to the Promised Land. (It is worthy of note that God will do whatever it takes to accomplish His purposes in us, if we let Him, for twice God parted the waters for His people, first at the Red Sea and then, later, at the Jordan River.) The *ceremonial* (or *typical*) Passover was observed every year. It pointed forward to Jesus' death on the cross, at which point the ceremony was not needed anymore. Jesus' sacrificial *death* was the *antitypical fulfillment* of the Feast of the Passover. When Jesus died He died as the Passover Lamb. In doing this, He sealed His promise of deliverance to the human race and personally became our Passover by *taking our penalty*. He is our Passover because the gift of His *blood* (representing His eternal *life*) is the forfeit price for our salvation. The Passover feast is the flagship feast, not only because it is the first one, but because it represents the blood (the life) of Christ and His death on the cross, the completion of God's oath to save the human race. (For the oath, see Genesis 22:15–18.) "Christ *our passover* is sacrificed for us" (1 Cor. 5:7). His eternal *life* is to be applied to the doorposts of our hearts (Exod. 12:7). This is the contemporary manifestation of this feast.
- **The Feast of Unleavened Bread** – The eating of bread without the leaven of sin was fulfilled antitypically in the eternal, sinless life of Jesus Christ given to the human race as an heritage. We are to observe this feast today in our hearts by allowing God to make us sincere and truthful. First Corinthians 5:7, 8 tells us to "purge out therefore the old leaven, that ye may be a new lump, as ye are unleavened. For even Christ our passover is sacrificed for us: Therefore let us keep the feast, not with old leaven, neither with the leaven of malice and wickedness; but with the unleavened bread of sincerity and truth."
- **The Feast of Firstfruits** – This feast has a dual antitypical fulfillment. First, the firstfruits being a representative of the whole, Jesus Christ is the firstfruits representative of the entire human

race, which has its antitypical fulfillment at His incarnation when He became a human being and, as "one of us," conquered Satan.

Because Jesus is the representative of the entire human race, the second antitypical fulfillment actually branches off of the first. Literally, the firstfruits wave sheaf represented the entire harvest of grain; antitypically, it represents Christ's resurrection from the dead, which in turn represents the harvest of the end of the world. (This harvest of the end of the world has to encompass both the first and second resurrections in order to represent the entire human race.) Jesus Christ represents us in both His death and His resurrection[1] and covers the entire human race, all the way to the final harvest of the race, and on through eternity. There is an ancillary aspect to this harvest and that is the end of death. The end of death is still to happen in the future at the lake of fire (Rev. 20:14).

"But now is Christ risen from the dead, and become the firstfruits of them that slept. For since by man came death, by man came also the resurrection of the dead. For as in Adam all die, even so in Christ shall all be made alive. But every man in his own order: Christ the firstfruits; afterward they that are Christ's at his coming. Then cometh the end, when he shall have delivered up the kingdom to God, even the Father; when he shall have put down all rule and all authority and power. For he must reign, till he hath put all enemies under his feet. The last enemy that shall be destroyed is death" (1 Cor. 15:20–26).

- **The Feast of Weeks, or Pentecost** – The antitypical fulfillment of this feast was the beginning of the work of the former rain of the Holy Spirit, which ushered in the beginning of the Christian era and the Christian church and was symbolized by the tongues of fire resting upon Christ's followers on Pentecost: "And when the day of Pentecost was fully come, they were all with one accord in one place. And suddenly there came a sound from heaven as of a rushing mighty wind, and it filled all the house where they were sitting. And there appeared unto them cloven tongues like as of fire, and it sat upon each of them. And they were all filled with the Holy Ghost" (Acts 2:1–4).
- **The Feast of Trumpets** – This feast was fulfilled antitypically by the worldwide warning of the anticipated beginning of the "cleansing of the sanctuary." Though at first thought to be the "sanctuary" of this *earth*, it was soon understood to be referring to the cleansing of the sanctuary in *heaven*.
- **The Feast of the Day of Atonement** – The cleansing of the sanctuary in heaven must first begin in the hearts of the people. When the sins of God's people stop flowing into His sanctuary, Christ can close the work of cleansing the sanctuary from sin. The antitypical fulfillment of this feast began in 1844 and is ongoing. You can join this movement by telling God you want Him to take your sin away and by letting Him cleanse your heart from all sin.
- **The Feast of Tabernacles** – The antitypical fulfillment of this feast takes place when Jesus

---

[1] He also represents us in His birth, life, ascension, priesthood, and throne.

Christ comes as King to take His people home. This is the only feast whose entire antitypical fulfillment is still in the future. It is closely related to the final fulfillment of the Feast of Firstfruits.

We learned from the chapter on the Passover feast that Christ's death covers the entire feast day system, fulfilling the whole system corporately and each feast individually in the same sense that His death gave salvation to the entire human race, thus providing salvation to each individual. Quoting from that chapter:

> The Passover is the kingpin feast in the Hebrew system. All the other feasts in the spiritual economy of this sacrificial system have this feast as their foundational support. Being the first of the seven feasts, the Passover is the opening statement made by God that, by itself, has all the elements needed to give us, corporately and individually, salvation from our sins as well as deliverance from the condemnation of God's broken law. Every subsequent feast has, as part of its ceremony, the sacrifice of animal(s), thus pointing back to the Passover as its basis. Each subsequent feast adds details regarding the overview of God's grand plan of salvation. They reveal to us the methods and plan of action on God's part in bringing an end to sin on this planet and eradicating sin for all eternity from the whole universe. They also reveal the unfolding of history, especially the final unfolding of events in earth's history and the ushering in of the new earth and a new era of government for the universe.
>
> Furthermore, the Passover is the kingpin feast not only because it is the first one but because it represents the blood of Christ and His death on the cross, the completion of God's oath to save the human race. The Passover is the representative of the entire feast system, and Christ's death is the antitypical fulfillment of this feast. Therefore, while different aspects of Christ's ministry fulfill each feast individually (as the rest of this book will show), His death covers and fulfills the entire feast system corporately.

There are four great types of laws in the Bible: the moral law, the health law, the ceremonial law, and the civil law. All of these are first articulated in the books of Moses.

The moral law is the Ten Commandments.[2] This law is God's character in written form. It represents who God is and what He does. These ten promises are what God will do in your life if you consent; thus, you become like Him in character. It is to establish this law in our hearts that Jesus became a human being, lived a perfect life in fallen sinful human flesh, and died the second death, the penalty for sin, so that you do not have to die that eternal death. This action on the part of God established the immutability of God's moral law. It can never be changed. This law will be kept for today and for all eternity.

---

2   The Ten Commandments are recorded in Exodus 20 and Deuteronomy 5.

The *health* law is the "operators manual," if you will, that God uses to show us how to take care of our bodies. As long as our bodies continue to work the same as they did in Moses' day, the principles of this law will not go away. Specific applications may change as we discover new technologies, but the principles stay the same. This law is still in effect today.

The CEREMONIAL laws are the main subject of this book. They are primarily the feast days plus, and including, the entire system of ceremonial rites,[3] temple sacrifices, and priestly order.

The veil of the earthly sanctuary was torn from top to bottom at the exact moment of Christ's death (Matt. 27:50–53; Mark 15:37–39). This veil would have been the one at the entrance to the Most Holy Place (Luke 23:44–46[4]), thus opening to view the part of the sanctuary that was to be seen by the high priest only (and then only once a year). The tearing of the veil at the precise moment of Christ's death announced the end of the significance of the temple and priestly system because the One to whom all the ceremonies pointed had come and fulfilled the antitypical purpose of the ceremonial services.[5] This work is laid out in Daniel 9:27, which reads, "And he shall confirm the covenant with many for one week: and in the midst of the week he shall cause the sacrifice and the oblation to cease." (See chapter 9 in this book titled "Feast of Trumpets: The Prophecy.")

The *civil* laws were the laws needed to govern a country or a city. These laws change as needs change. We are not required to keep the civil laws of the Bible, although sometimes the principles expressed can carry a significant spiritual application, as studies of the "cities of refuge" (Num. 35), the "kinsman redeemer" (illustrated in the book of Ruth), and the "year of jubilee" (Lev. 25, 27) will bear out. These civil laws all represent a different aspect of the work of Jesus Christ, and they all give us a very good picture of who God is. They make good object lessons. However, unless our own governments choose to adopt any of these laws, we are not enjoined by God to keep them today.

In summary, the moral law will be kept for all eternity. The health laws (including the law of heredity) will be kept as long as human beings have fallen sinful human flesh. Civil laws are kept as long as they are needed, for they will change with the circumstances. The ceremonial laws (including the

---

3 Circumcision (Gen. 17) and the Nazarite vow (Num. 6) are two examples.
4 Luke 23:45 says, "And the sun was darkened, and the veil of the temple was rent in the midst." In my opinion, the word "midst" probably refers to the middle of the temple, that is, the second (central) veil—the one between the two apartments at the entrance to the Most Holy Place. (There was another veil at the entrance of the holy place, the first apartment.) It can't refer to the place on the veil that the tear started (e.g., the center, or midsection) because Matthew 27:51 and Mark 15:38 plainly indicate that the veil was torn from top to bottom. Additionally, Matthew and Mark specifically use the phrase "into two" and not "midst." A plausible alternative interpretation could be that "in the midst" may mean "in the middle from top to bottom," thus logically separating the veil into two parts. I can truly accept that interpretation, for it does not negate the central veil. However, I believe that if Luke had wanted to express such a separation (as Matthew and Mark describe), he would most likely have used the same specific language that Matthew and Mark used.
5 Exposing the Most Holy Place in such a fashion would symbolically end its significance. Since the Bible specifically mentions the way it was torn, it must be important. Logically, the second veil, covering the entrance to the Most Holy Place, is the only veil that carries such a level of importance. This treatment of the veil could not have been done by any human being unless (1) he had a ladder (there was none mentioned), (2) he knew the exact moment of Christ's death (hand signals would not have been fast enough), or (3) he knew that the veil was supposed to be rent at that moment (yet, the priests were actually trying to disparage Christ, not exalt Him, so they would not want the veil torn). Only an angel or God Himself could have torn that veil.

animal sacrifices, the feast days, circumcision, etc.) were fulfilled at the death of Jesus Christ. They are no longer required services.

Having said all this, one might wonder if it is a sin to participate in the biblical feast services today.

Since circumcision is a ceremonial rite, a related question would be, "Is it a sin to be *circumcised* today?" After all, there was a huge discussion about rite of circumcision in Paul's writings. The entire book of Galatians was written in response to this topic.[6] The opening statement in this discussion is made in Acts 15:1: "And certain men which came down from Judaea taught the brethren, and said, Except ye be circumcised after the manner of Moses, ye cannot be saved." However, Paul lays down the following principle in Romans 2: "For he is not a Jew, which is one outwardly; neither is that circumcision, which is outward in the flesh: But he is a Jew, which is one inwardly; and circumcision is that of the heart, in the spirit, and not in the letter; whose praise is not of men, but of God" (verses 28, 29).

What Paul is saying here is that the true substance is more important than the form it takes. Following are some examples that speak to this principle:

- How many of you have opened a *huge* Christmas present only to discover successively smaller but beautifully wrapped packages inside that eventually led to something really small such as a watch or a check? Thus proving that small things really do come in big packages.
- How about those horrid April Fools' "jokes" where the salt and sugar get switched? They *look* alike, don't they?
- Lumberjacks sometimes cut into a great looking tree only to find it hollow inside and wholly unusable.
- As an auditor I looked for business contracts that had the form of a lease agreement (say for an automobile) but had a clause buried in it that allowed the lessor to purchase the object at the end of the time period for an insignificant amount of cash. Such an agreement, though it *looked* like a lease in *form*, really was an installment purchase in *substance* and should be accounted as such.
- Docetism is the heretical doctrine (associated with the Gnostics) that Jesus had no real human body and His sufferings and death on the cross were apparent rather than real. In other words, He may have had some sort of a *form*, but there was no *substance*, either to *what* He was, *who* He was, or what He *did*.
- Some unfortunate people know to their sorrow that it is possible to go to church every Sabbath, return a faithful tithe, give offerings, feed the homeless and disaster refugees, be kind and friendly to people at work, do lots of faithful "good works" that people can see, and still be unkind and tyrannical at home.
- Although, there are many good and beneficial clubs helping society today, when I was a child, my father warned me to never think that church was merely another form of those clubs. Yes, the church does many good deeds to help people, but church is much more than that. Church

---

6   Romans 14, regarding eating food offered to idols, deals with a related topic also.

is where we go to meet with *God*. Yes, church is a good opportunity to meet and work with people, but thinking of the church in *that* fashion is one of the ways to "have a *form* of godliness, but denying the *power* thereof" (2 Tim. 3:5).

Israel reached a place in their religious experience that the feasts and sacrifices were a means to be saved. If you sinned, you could just take a sacrifice to the sanctuary, give it to the priest, and then God would change His mind about you and you would be back in God's "good graces." The rite of circumcision was the same way. If you were circumcised, you were "saved." An extension of this line of thinking is that if you are an official member of a church you are saved.

This is truly a *form* of religion, but do you have the *substance*? Do you know God's *power* in your experience? That power is power for obedience; it is power to make the sacrifices obsolete and unnecessary because God's people are no longer committing sins..

The rite of circumcision is simply the acknowledgment that it is not through the fallen sinful human *flesh* that God's will is accomplished but through the *cutting off* of that flesh that His will is accomplished in your life. Check out 1 Samuel 15:22: "And Samuel said, Hath the LORD as great delight in burnt offerings and sacrifices, as in obeying [Hebrew: listen attentively to] the voice of the LORD? Behold, to obey [Hebrew: pay attention] is better than sacrifice, and to *hearken* than the fat of rams."[7]

All of this is wrapped up in Acts 15:

> When therefore Paul and Barnabas had no small dissension and disputation with them, they determined that Paul and Barnabas, and certain other of them, should go up to Jerusalem unto the apostles and elders about this question. And being brought on their way by the church, they passed through Phenice and Samaria, declaring the conversion of the Gentiles: and they caused great joy unto all the brethren. And when they were come to Jerusalem, they were received of the church, and of the apostles and elders, and they declared all things that God had done with them. But there rose up certain of the sect of the Pharisees which believed, saying, That it was needful to circumcise them, and to command them to keep the law of Moses. And the apostles and elders came together for to consider of this matter. (verses 2–6)

Thus, the stage is set. This is a very important meeting. It could be said that this is the first recorded "General Conference" session after Jesus formed His new church. The apostolic delegation is all present, and they are discussing a most important topic regarding the doctrine of "righteousness by faith" as it applies to ecclesiastical belief and practice. This decision will reverberate down through the ages.

> And when there had been much disputing, Peter rose up, and said unto them, Men

---

7 Also, check out Genesis 16, 17, and 21 where God institutes the rite of circumcision to show Abraham that it is not through his own efforts to accomplish God's promise of a child but through God's own miracle. Thus, in this rite, Abraham's flesh is cut off.

> and brethren, ye know how that a good while ago God made choice among us, that the Gentiles by my mouth should hear [Greek: listen attentively] the word of the gospel, and believe.[8] And God, which knoweth the hearts, bare them witness, giving them the Holy Ghost, even as he did unto us; And put no difference between us and them, purifying their hearts by faith. Now therefore why tempt[9] ye God, to put a yoke upon the neck of the disciples, which neither our fathers nor we were able to bear? But we believe that through the *grace*[10] of the LORD Jesus Christ we shall be saved, even as they. (verses 7–11)

Peter is referring to all of the traditions of the Jews, particularly the ceremonial law that included the feast days and the sacrifices, which had added to them all the myriads of manmade "enhancements." The whole system had become a works-oriented attempt at salvation and, thus, an intolerable mess.

It is interesting to note the amount of discussion that takes place over this subject. It is mentioned twice: in verse two, and also in verse seven. Apparently, from the intensity of these discussions, the apostles are still observing these feast days. After all, they did observe Pentecost at Christ's command after His death and resurrection. Of course, we know what they probably had not heard yet, that this particular "observance" of Pentecost was actually the antitypical fulfillment of that feast. It was only when the Gentiles began joining the church that the issue of the feast days came to the forefront.

If the apostles were keeping the feasts, they were doing so because that was their habit. After all, it was in their heritage. They probably even kept time by them, as we also sometimes reckon time by our holidays. As long as no one objected to observing them, why not? However, the Gentiles had no reason to keep them. Therefore, Paul wondered why they had to carry that burden. And, to continue the logic, if the Gentiles didn't need to keep them, why did the disciples, or anyone else for that matter, have to keep them?

The closing argument and a decision made through the power of the Holy Spirit is recorded in verses 12–21:

> Then all the multitude kept silence, and gave audience to Barnabas and Paul, declaring what miracles and wonders God had wrought among the Gentiles by them. And after they had held their peace, James answered, saying, Men and brethren, hearken unto me: Simeon hath declared how God at the first did visit the Gentiles, to take out of them a people for his name.[11] And to this agree the words of the prophets; as it is written, After this I will return, *and* will build again the tabernacle of David, which is fallen down; and I will build again the ruins thereof, and I will set it up: That the

---

8   See Acts 10.
9   God was "tempted" because He had already made His will known regarding the salvation of the Gentiles.
10 Grace is God's free dual gift: first, unmerited favor in giving us *pardon* and salvation and second, *power* to do His will. It cannot be anything that *we* do.
11 See Luke 2:25–35.

residue of men might seek after the Lord, and all the Gentiles, upon whom my name is called, saith the Lord, who doeth all these things.¹² Known unto God are all his works from the beginning of the world. Wherefore my sentence is, that we trouble not them, which from among the Gentiles are turned to God: *But that we write unto them, that they abstain from pollutions of idols, and from fornication, and from things strangled, and from blood.* For Moses of old time hath in every city them that preach him, being read in the synagogues every sabbath day.

Since these four "rules," which I have italicized in the text, are taken from the various laws of God as given through Moses, we can apply the principle of representation.¹³ Abstaining from the pollutions of idols comes from the second commandment, in the *first* table of the moral law, which addresses love to God. Abstaining from fornication comes from the seventh commandment, in the *second* table of the moral law, which addresses love to humankind. This representation from both tables of the moral law of Ten Commandments indicates all ten, for if one commandment is broken, all ten are broken (James 2:10). Thus, the *moral* law is represented.

Abstaining from things strangled and from blood refer to the health laws of Moses, thus representing the principles that apply to our health, the diet being the first line of defense against disease (see Appendix G). What we put into our bodies will affect everything we think, say, and do. So the apostles used diet to represent the *health* laws.

I find it fascinating that only two of the four great types of laws are represented in the decision revealed at this meeting of the disciples. There are two others that are not mentioned. They are the civil laws and the ceremonial laws. The *civil* laws will apply to the specific situations any civil group of people encounter while trying to live and work together. These laws change as needs change. But it is the *ceremonial* laws that are actually the laws in question. It is what this meeting of the apostles is all about: that is, is it necessary to continue to practice the ceremonial laws, such as the sacrificial system, including the feast days and circumcision? The answer is no. The moral and health laws were kept. The civil and ceremonial laws were discarded. Let's read the rest of Acts 15:

---

12   Quoting from Amos 9:11, 12.

13   The principle of representation is the concept on which this book opened (see chapter 1). In Matthew 22:36–40, Jesus tells us that love to God and love to humanity are the two great principles upon which all the law and prophets hang. Thus, they represent all the law and prophets. If you examine the Ten Commandments, you will find two tables, or two sides. Commandments one through four express love to God: no other Gods, no worship of graven images, use of God's name with reverence and respect, and remembering the Sabbath day. Commandments five to ten express love to humankind: honor to parents, respect for the life of others, respect for others' property, sexual propriety, truthfulness, and contentment with what you have. So the law of the Ten Commandments comes in two parts. In Zechariah 5:1–4 we are shown a flying roll (or scroll) with two sides. One side talks about swearing (misusing God's name) and the other side talks about stealing (respect for others' property). It is plain to see that these two statements about swearing and stealing, one from each side, represent all ten precepts of God's law, both love to God and love to humankind. It is the same statement that Jesus made regarding the two main principles of God's law, upon which all the law and prophets hang. Therefore, we can apply this same principle of representation to other passages in Scripture.

Then pleased it the apostles and elders with the whole church, to send chosen men of their own company to Antioch with Paul and Barnabas; namely, Judas surnamed Barsabas and Silas, chief men among the brethren: And they wrote letters by them after this manner; The apostles and elders and brethren send greeting unto the brethren which are of the Gentiles in Antioch and Syria and Cilicia. Forasmuch as we have heard, that certain which went out from us have troubled you with words, subverting your souls, saying, Ye must be circumcised, and keep the law [referring to the ceremonial laws]: to whom we gave no such commandment: It seemed good unto us, being assembled with one accord, to send chosen men unto you with our beloved Barnabas and Paul, Men that have hazarded their lives for the name of our Lord Jesus Christ. We have sent therefore Judas and Silas, who shall also tell you the same things by mouth. For it seemed good to the Holy Ghost, and to us, to lay upon you no greater burden than these necessary things; That ye abstain from meats offered to idols, and from blood, and from things strangled, and from fornication: from which if ye keep yourselves, ye shall do well. Fare ye well. So when they were dismissed, they came to Antioch: and when they had gathered the multitude together, they delivered the epistle: Which when they had read, they rejoiced for the consolation. And Judas and Silas, being prophets also themselves, exhorted the brethren with many words, and confirmed them. (verses 22–32)

Thus, they made it official.

Circumcision actually carries with it some minor health benefits. If you apply the health principles to the subject of circumcision, it may actually be a good thing to do. However, what the apostle Paul is trying to tell us is that if you tell people that the rite of circumcision is *required to be saved*, you are denying the sacrifice of Christ to have accomplished His purpose, for you now must *do* something to be saved and the free gift aspect of salvation is voided.

To practice or observe the feasts for purposes of illustration or education, or even as an act of worship, is not forbidden in Scripture. However, if one believes that these services are *necessary for salvation*, or *necessary as acts of worship*, the one who believes this also denies the sacrifice of Christ that sealed the gift of salvation to the entire human race corporately and individually. Because of Christ's death, the only way we can be lost is by rejecting this gift already given as Esau threw away his birthright (Gen. 25:27–34). In Romans 14 Paul tells us it is best, if possible, to avoid practicing in public anything that may be confusing to others and possibly cause someone to stumble in their Christian experience. This is the case even though the practice, by *itself,* may not be immoral, illegal, or unethical. Therefore, I have concluded that the *private* practice of these rites, including the feasts, is not forbidden in Scripture if the principles are thoroughly understood, but to practice them in public (or for public worship) would be misunderstood by many and would likely result in the stumbling of some.

So, is it a sin to practice the feasts? Not necessarily. Is it a sin to tell others they *need* to do it to be saved or as an act of worship? Yes.

Paul sums it up quite nicely in Hebrews 10. Why continue to require a practice that could not do in substance what it pointed to in principle after the Substance has already been fully realized and effective? See what he says:

> For the [levitical, ceremonial] law having a *shadow* of good things to come, and not [even] the very image of the things, can never with those sacrifices which they offered year by year continually make the comers thereunto perfect. For then [if they actually *did* make people perfect] would they not have ceased to be offered? because that the worshippers once purged should have had no more [guilty] conscience of sins. But in those sacrifices there is a remembrance again made of sins every year [at the Day of Atonement]. For it is not possible that the blood of bulls and of goats should take away sins.
>
> Wherefore when he cometh into the world, he saith, Sacrifice and offering thou wouldest not, but a body hast thou prepared me [a body was prepared for Jesus Christ—fallen sinful human flesh—that *He* would be the *true sacrifice* that would take away sins]: In burnt offerings and sacrifices for sin thou hast had no pleasure. Then said I, Lo, I come (in the volume of the book it is written of me,) to do thy will, O God. Above when he said, Sacrifice and offering and burnt offerings and offering for sin thou wouldest not, neither hadst pleasure therein; which are offered by the law; Then said he, Lo, I come to do thy will, O God. He taketh away the first [the earthly tabernacle, sacrifices, and priesthood], that he may establish the second [the *heavenly* temple, Christ's *true* sacrifice, and the *heavenly priesthood*]. By the which will we are sanctified [set aside for holy use and given the experience of Christ's perfect righteousness[14]] through the offering of the body of Jesus Christ [in title; before we even knew Him or accepted Him] once for all [people].
>
> And every priest standeth daily ministering and offering oftentimes the same sacrifices, which can never take away sins: But this man, after he had offered one sacrifice for sins for ever, sat down [a formal ceremony] on the right hand of God [as heavenly High Priest]; From henceforth expecting till his enemies be made his footstool. For by *one offering* he hath perfected for ever [as long as they believe] them that are [Greek: being] sanctified [that is, those who are allowing God to have control of their lives are perfected in experience forever as long as they allow Him control].
>
> Whereof the Holy Ghost also is a witness to us: for after that he had said before, This is the [new] covenant that I will make with them after those days, saith the Lord,

---

14 Note: Jesus Christ, through His death, delivered us from *all sin*, not just from the ceremonial law.

I will put my laws into their hearts, and in their minds will I write them; And their sins and iniquities will I remember no more. Now where remission of these is, there is no more offering for sin. [Jesus does not need to die a second time (verse 10).]

Having therefore, brethren, boldness [confidence] to enter into the holiest [the heavenly sanctuary; in Christ who represents us there (both apartments are intimated by the Greek)] by the blood of Jesus [through His death (only)], By a new and living way, which he hath consecrated [inaugurated, initiated] for us, through the veil [Most Holy Place connotations], that is to say, his flesh [by taking our flesh and conquering Satan in that flesh, He became our representative in the heavenly sanctuary]; And having an [heavenly] high priest over the house of God; Let us draw near with a true heart in full assurance of faith, having our hearts sprinkled [with Christ's blood; that is, through His death] from an evil conscience, and our bodies washed with pure water.[15] Let us hold fast the profession of our faith [Greek: hope, expectation] without wavering; (for he is faithful that promised [the new covenant[16]];). (Heb. 10:1–23)

Keep your eyes firmly fixed upon Christ. Understand with a heartfelt appreciation what He has done for you, especially the price of His own eternal life that He paid for your salvation. Understand and appreciate who He is to you today and what He is about to do for the universe in the near future and you cannot go astray. He will not *let* you go astray!

Let's close by reviewing the promise of Christ in Daniel 9:27: "And he shall confirm the covenant with many for one week: and in the midst of the week he shall cause the sacrifice and the oblation to cease."

Thank you, Lord, for saving my soul.
Thank you, Lord, for making me whole.
Thank you, Lord, for giving to me
Thy great salvation so full and free.

---

15 The priests had to wash every time they entered the sanctuary. This washing was figurative of purification of sin.
16 See Jeremiah 31:31–33 and Ezekiel 36:26–28.

Appendix M

Christ, Our Representative: Treatise Relating to Arminianism/Calvinism

Jacobus Arminius[1] (1560–1609) was, among other appointments, a professor of theology at the University of Leiden (twice) and also a pastor in Amsterdam. He was a Dutch Reformed theologian who objected to the Calvinistic idea that humans have no free will in their salvation (e.g., one is either predestined to be saved or predestined to be lost, and there is nothing that can be done about it). Arminius' response was an alternative, now called "Arminianism." John Wesley accepted the term for his theological position and published the Arminian Magazine. Admittedly, Calvinism was bearing very bad fruit, for if we have no say in our own salvation then we can believe or do anything we want without affecting the consequences.

The basic concept of Arminianism is the idea that human beings do have a say in their own salvation. In other words, Jesus Christ gave us an *offer* of salvation, that is, what Christ did on the cross can be activated on our behalf if we do something ourselves. For example, the washing machine at the laundromat is ready for us but nothing happens until you put a coin in the slot, hence the idea that we do have a choice. However, Arminianism also teaches that we are born in a *lost* condition and we *remain* in that condition until we "accept Christ." *We* must somehow "find" Him, and when we take that first step, He will hold His arms open wide and accept us. This idea comes out in language that says Christ made "provision *for*" our salvation (instead of "Christ *provided* to us a complete[2] salvation"), thus implying that there is something more that must be done on *our* part and that Christ's sacrifice alone does not provide a complete atonement.

Although this is far better than Calvinism, Arminianism does not provide anything in the way of assurance of our own salvation. Arminianism implies questions such as: What is *our* part in being saved? What can *we* do to help God? Or, to say it another way, what can we do with God's "help"? This alludes to a subsidy religion. Because of our sinful natures, we know intrinsically that we can never do anything good. So will God accept our best efforts? In Arminianism, we are never really sure. Actually, the Bible says that our best efforts are like *filthy rags* that God cannot accept (Isa. 64:6). Even if all we have to do is to make a decision to "accept Christ" that in itself is something *we* have to do, thus the

---

1   His given name was actually Jakob Hermanszoon.
2   It is not a *completed* salvation, for there is still much more work for God to do before He can finish cleansing the earth of sin.

initiative of our salvation falls upon us. As a result, we can be lost by default, by accident, or by misunderstanding, for we can "fall through the cracks." What if the missionaries don't make it all the way to my town and I never hear the name of Jesus? Unless we can do or believe something that will "make God happy" with us, we are still lost! The result of this is that we lose hope in the idea that one can be made sinless before translation and vindicate the character of God in the face of Satan's charge that it is impossible to keep God's law. This vindication of God in His hour of trial is the very purpose that God raised up the Laodicean church ("a people judged"). Therefore, Arminianism cannot be the judgment hour message. (Read Revelation chapters 3 and 12.)

To summarize, Calvinism teaches that some people are predestined to be saved eternally in God's kingdom and all others are predestined to be eternally lost, and there is no crossing over. Arminianism teaches that all people are predestined to be lost, but God made an *offer* of salvation so that those who are saved must take the initiative to accept, or they will be lost by default. (There is another system of belief, called universalism that claims that all are predestined to be *saved*.) However, the Bible teaches that all were predestined to be lost when Adam sinned, but Christ stepped in and *completely reversed* what Adam did, and now all are predestined to be *saved*—unless they take the initiative to *choose* to be lost by discarding their birthright while knowing the light of God's truth revealed to them through the Holy Spirit, even at a very young age.

We need to learn that God is completely reconciled to us. He does not condemn us (2 Cor. 5:19; John 3:17, 18). Can we believe this? We don't have to "find" Him, for He has already found us. He has already provided acquittal for all of us on the cross (Rom 5:18). This is our birthright. We are all born in a saved condition, and we keep that condition unless we actively decide we do not want it and throw it away. God has predestined each of us to be saved from all aspects of sin (Eph. 1:5; 2:10). If we end up being lost in the end it is because we actively chose *not* to *keep* God's gift already given to us at the cross, on which He took our penalty, our condemnation, the second death, upon Himself as our representative, and so, we were there, also, in Him. And in the end God will still not condemn us, but if we throw away His gift to us, we will condemn ourselves (John 3:17–19).

God is not looking for people who try to keep His law. God is looking for people who are humble enough to allow Him to keep His own law in them! Therefore, the pressure is off! It is all on Him.

What happens when we believe this? For those who choose to believe, this is overwhelmingly good news (the gospel). Their hearts respond with gratitude and heartfelt appreciation, so much so that, suddenly, they are willing to do anything for the Lord, perhaps for the very first time. When we believe God's Word, Christ (through the Holy Spirit) can then enter the heart and live His life in us, causing us to do His will (Ezek. 36:26, 27). And while Christ has *full control*, the *only* thing we can do is His will. This is because the power of God is infinitely stronger than the power of Satan (Matt. 28:18; Gal. 5:16, 17). God does the "willing,"[3] and God does the "doing" in us (Phil. 2:13). We simply say, "Thank You." Indeed, our *whole life* and our *whole being* says "Thank You" constantly! However, we *still* can choose

---

3   Yes, it is true; He will control your thoughts and He will control your desires so that when He is doing His will in you, you are in a state of highest delight!

unbelief and go the way of perdition. And, if so, perdition is the *only* way we can go, for, intrinsically, humans have no strength to do God's will alone, and God will allow us to suffer the consequences of our decisions.

Let's look at some Bible texts:

Ephesians 1:11 says that Christ "worketh all things after the counsel of his own will." God does not fail. He *succeeds* at everything He attempts. He did not just *try* to save us; He *did indeed* save us.

There are many Bible passages on this topic, some of which are presented here. Please do not take my word for this, but study these passages (and others) for yourself.

First John 2:2 says, "He is the *propitiation* [atoning sacrifice] for our sins: *and not for ours only, but also for the sins of the whole world.*"

In Scripture a part of something is often used to represent the whole population. In auditing, this is called sampling. An auditor draws an opinion on the whole company based on tests performed on a representative sample. In many ways, God uses this method to teach important lessons on spiritual subjects, including ownership (spiritual trusts) and stewardship (care of the property of others). Some examples are time (Sabbath), money (tithe), humility (footwashing), salvation of the human race (the life and death of Christ), and provision (dispensation). This "portion," or sample is called in the Bible, "firstfruits." We will discuss these last two in the following paragraphs.

Let's continue reading four texts from the New Testament:

- "If the *firstfruit* be holy, the *lump* is also holy: and if the root be holy, so are the branches" (Rom. 11:16). Jesus, as the representative of the human race, made the whole human race holy.
- "For the love of Christ constraineth [compels] us; because we thus judge, that if one died for all, then were all dead" (2 Cor. 5:14). Because Jesus Christ is our representative, when He died, He died *as* us, and *we* died also, corporately, *in Him.*
- "But now is Christ risen from the dead, and become the *firstfruits* [representing us] of them that slept. For since by man came death, by man [100 percent man] came also the resurrection of the dead. For *as in Adam all die,* even so *in Christ shall all be made alive.* But every man in his own order: Christ the firstfruits; afterward they that are Christs' [believers in Him] at his coming" (1 Cor. 15:20–23).
- "For therefore we both labour and suffer reproach, because we trust in the living God, who *is* the Saviour of *all* men, *specially* of those that *believe*" (1 Tim. 4:9, 10).

Please notice that *unbelief* can make the fullness of this universal gift of grace in vain, for we truly throw it away, as Esau threw away his birthright, for this salvation *is our* birthright. God's word has inherent within it the power to create what it says. Therefore, He cannot lie, for while He is saying it, it happens!

Romans 5:6 says, "For when we were yet *without strength,* in due time Christ died for the *ungodly.*" How many people are without strength and ungodly? *They* are atoned (justified, or made right with God). Isaiah 53:6 says, "*All* we like sheep have gone astray; we have turned *every one* to his own way; and the Lord hath laid on him the iniquity of us *all.*" This means that *all* of us have been given righteousness, salvation, and eternal life.

Romans 5:10 states, "For if, when we were *enemies*, we were reconciled to God [By what? Our *acceptance* of Him? No. Keep reading.] *by the death of his son*, much more, *being* [already] reconciled, we shall be saved by his life." We are not saved by *our* initiative, but by *God's*. Not by anything *we* do, but by God's *gift*.

Romans 5:18 says, "Therefore as by the offence of one [Adam] judgment *came* [past tense] upon *all men* to condemnation; *even so* by the righteousness of one [Christ] the *free gift came* [past tense] upon *all men* unto justification of life [made right with God, that is to say, made *righteous*, because that is the only way we can be *made* right with God]." (The New English Bible uses the word "acquittal" for the "free gift.")

Satan condemns everyone because of Adam's sin (who passed fallen sinful human flesh on to everyone). The devil wants you to think that you are lost, that you have to dig your way out of a huge hole, and that your situation is hopeless. However, the Bible teaches us that Christ brought *acquittal* to *everyone* by, and because of, His *death* (not our decision), wherein He took our penalty for sin. If Christ took our penalty for sin, then everything else being the same, where does that leave *us* in the judgment day? Jesus will be fine, for although He took our sin, His perfect life lived in the same fallen sinful human flesh that *we* have covers Him fully. He completely undid the effects of our sin *as our representative*, both in His life (experience) and in His death (taking our penalty).

Notice that this is a *FREE* gift. This means that there are no conditions, no qualifications, and no prerequisites. If there were any of these things, it could not be a *FREE GIFT*. Think about it; since this gift was provided by Christ's *death*, how can we add anything to it? Why would we need to? The gift is free to *ALL* people, whether they know it, or not; whether they feel it, or not; whether they want it, or not; whether they believe it, or not. Those who do not want it are free to throw it away. In the end, it will be revealed to them just exactly *when* they threw it away. Those who appreciate the gift and the price paid for the gift will receive the experience of Christ's perfect life in their own lives.

We are reminded in Romans 3:23, 24 that we "*all* sinned [in Adam, when Adam sinned] and [Greek: continue to] come short of the glory of God, [all] being justified [made right with God (including the gift of righteousness)] as a FREE gift by His grace through the redemption in Christ Jesus."[4]

Second Corinthians 5:19 says, "God was reconciling *the world* to Himself *in Christ*, not counting [any] people's sins against them" (NIV). Where does that leave you? Can you believe it? Is this news too good to be true? The gift is real. Cherish it!

Hebrews 2:9 reads, "But we see Jesus, who [also, as mankind[5]] was made a little lower than the angels for the suffering of death [the *second* death], crowned with glory and honour; that he by the grace of God should *taste death for every man* [i.e., every human being]." If He tasted death for you, then you don't have to die. However, this can't be the first death that we all have to taste (unless we are translated and taken to heaven). This must be the second death, the penalty for sin. And if we don't have to taste

---

4 J. P. Green, Sr., *A Literal Translation of the Holy Bible*, Romans 3:23, 24.
5 See Hebrews 2:6–8.

the second death, then it is clear that our final destination is heaven and the new earth. This is a tremendous gift. Let me remind you again to cherish it! Don't throw it away.

Paul wrote in Titus 2:11, 12, "For the grace of God that brings salvation has appeared to all men. It teaches us to say 'No' to ungodliness and worldly passions, and to live self-controlled, upright and godly lives in this present age" (NIV). Another translation of verse 11 is as follows: "The grace of God hath appeared, brining salvation to all men" (RV). The original Greek states as follows for verse 11, "*epiphaino gar charis theos soterion pas anthropos*," or in English (reordering the words for clarity), "For the grace of God appeared to all human beings saving." This is saying that salvation has already been brought to you. It is yours in *title*. You may receive the *experience* of it through believing God's new covenant promise.

Peter wrote, "Praise be to the God and Father of our Lord Jesus Christ! In his great mercy he *has given* us *new birth* [past tense] into a living hope [when?] *through the resurrection of Jesus Christ from the dead*" (1 Peter 1:3, NIV). Jesus' resurrection, not *our decision*, gave us new birth (in Christ) and thus saved us from sin (1 John 3:9). This rebirth becomes our *experience* as we believe, which was what Nicodemus needed to do (John 3).[6]

Romans 12:3 says, "… according as God *has dealt* to *every man* the measure of faith," and Romans 1:19, 20 says that God has revealed Himself to *all men* through nature, so that nobody has any excuse.

From the pen of Ellen G. White, we read:

> Desponding soul, take courage, even though you have done wickedly. Do not think that *perhaps* God will pardon your transgressions and permit you to come into His presence. God has made the first advance. While you were in rebellion against Him, He went forth to seek you. With the tender heart of the shepherd He left the ninety and nine and went out into the wilderness to find that which was lost.[7] The soul, bruised and wounded and ready to perish, He encircles in His arms of love and joyfully bears it to the fold of safety.
>
> It was taught by the Jews that before God's love is extended to the sinner, he must first repent. In their view, repentance is a work by which men earn the favor of Heaven. And it was this thought that led the Pharisees to exclaim in astonishment and anger. "This man receiveth sinners." According to their ideas He should permit none to approach Him but those who had repented. But in the parable of the lost sheep, Christ teaches that salvation does not come through our seeking after God

---

[6] By the way, we need to be careful about claiming to be "born-again Christians" because of what it says in 1 John 3:9: "Whosoever is born of God doth not commit sin; for his seed remaineth in him: and he cannot sin, because he is born of God." No Christian can claim sinlessness for himself, even if it *may* be true, mainly because God's people will never know this *for sure* until Jesus comes to take them home. Only one who is God can make such a claim, as Jesus did (John 8:46; 1 John 1:8–10).

[7] Note: Those who are in a state of conscious and deliberate rebellion against God are the ones who are in a lost condition.

but through God's seeking after us. "There is none that understandeth, there is none that seeketh after God. They are all gone out of the way." Romans 3:11, 12. We do not repent in order that God may love us, but He reveals to us His love in order that we may repent.[8]

Notice that, according to this, we do not need to "find" God because God has already found us. Bible texts that admonish us to seek for God, such as Isaiah 55:6, "Seek ye the LORD while he may be found, call ye upon him while he is near," are telling us to seek Him in the sense of to resort to, to rub over, efface, investigate, scrutinize, or tread, as in reading repeatedly or to study. He wants you to acknowledge Him while He is near and take advantage of the delicacies He has for you. He is not hiding from you.

Think about it this way: "With His own blood He has signed the emancipation papers of the race."[9] All of this can be compared to when President Lincoln signed the emancipation papers for the slaves. When were the slaves set free? When the president signed the emancipation papers. They were then free to go, were they not? Why did not all of the slaves leave the plantations? They had to *hear* about it first, didn't they? Then they had to *believe* it, right? If they did not believe, they would not go, would they? Once they heard and *believed*, they could leave or they could stay; it was their choice. Those who believed and chose to leave realized freedom in their *experience*. God's message to us today is that we are free from sin. Christ's life, death, and resurrection has *freed* us *all*, which includes *you*, from all sin through His infinite power (Rom. 6:11, 14). Do we *believe* it? If we do, then God's power (grace) will cause us to keep His statutes (in our experience) out of appreciation for what He has done for us (Ezek. 36).

"Before the foundations of the earth were laid, the Father and the Son had united in a covenant to redeem *man* if he should be overcome by Satan. They had clasped Their hands in a solemn pledge that Christ should become the surety for the *human race*. This pledge Christ has fulfilled. When upon the cross He cried out, 'It is finished,' He addressed the Father. *The compact had been fully carried out*. Now He declares: Father, *it is finished*. I have done Thy will, O My God. *I have completed the work of redemption*. If Thy justice is satisfied, 'I will that they also, whom Thou hast given Me, be with Me where I am.' John 19:30; 17:24."[10]

As Jesus died, He said, "It is finished." What is it that was finished? "The compact had been fully carried out." He had "completed the work of redemption." The only way this could be true at the cross is if Jesus died as the representative of the human race. Christ's death, in that small *part* of the whole world, could speak for the *entirety* of the whole world because Jesus died *as* the human race, for He was representing all of us on the cross. When He died, we died also *in Him* (see Rom. 11:16, above; 6:3–8; 1 Cor. 15:12–23). For God to say "It is finished" would *have* to include the salvation of *every* member, for

---

8   Ellen G. White, *Christ's Object Lessons*, pp. 188, 189. Therefore, repentance is a *gift!* See Acts 5:31 and 2 Timothy 2:25.
9   Ellen G. White, *The Ministry of Healing*, p. 90.
10 Ellen G. White, *The Desire of Ages*, p. 834.

God does not fail in accomplishing His purposes (see Eph. 1:11). This salvation has already been given to *you*. Will you believe it? Will you receive it?

The word "finished" applies to the completion of the work of redeeming humankind, the first major stepping stone in the whole process of the plan of salvation. This process was started before the world was made (Eph. 1:3–7). Christ's death as firstfruits represents the whole human race (see 2 Cor. 5:14). The preceding statement about the process serves to illustrate the representative principle regarding the compact, for even though Christ said "It is finished," He is still looking for the completion of a future event—the gathering of His people and the establishing of His throne. The covenant, the compact, was "to redeem man." The method was by Christ becoming "surety for the human race." (A surety is one who cosigns on a loan; if the borrower does not pay, the surety pays in the borrower's place.) The compact will be consummated at the gathering of God's people from all ages, and it will be completed when sin and death is destroyed in the lake of fire. Note that this is about the human race corporate. There is no exception and no individual is excluded. Christ became the surety for the *whole* human race, including *everyone* who is a member. No one needs to go to the lake of fire unless they choose to cling to the sin that is being destroyed.

> There are thousands today who need to learn the same truth that was taught to Nicodemus by the uplifted serpent [Num. 21]. They depend on *their* obedience to the law of God [*their* initiative] to commend them to His favor. When they are bidden to *look* to Jesus, and *believe* that He saves them *solely through His grace* [on *His* initiative], they exclaim, 'How can these things be?'…
>
> *How, then, are we to be saved?* 'As Moses lifted up the serpent in the wilderness,' so the Son of man *has been lifted up*, and everyone who has been deceived and bitten by the serpent may *look* and live. '*Behold* the Lamb of God, which taketh *away* the sin of *the world*.' John 1:29. [See also John 3:14, 15.] The light shining from the cross reveals the love of God. His love is drawing us to Himself [John 12:31, 32]. *If we do not resist* this drawing, we shall be *led* to the foot of the cross in repentance for the sins that have crucified the Saviour. Then the Spirit of God through faith produces a new life in the soul. The *thoughts* and *desires* are *brought* into obedience to the will of Christ. The heart, the mind, are *created anew* in the image of Him who works *in* us to subdue all things to Himself. Then the law of God is written in the mind and heart, and we can say with Christ, '*I delight* to do Thy will, O my God.' Psalm 40:8.[11]

There is one thing, and only one thing, that we can do on our part, and that is to *yield* to the Word[12] who has all power.[13] Who draws? Who leads? Who produces? Who brings? Who creates? Who

---

[11] Ibid., pp. 175, 176.
[12] John 1:1–3.
[13] Compare with Ellen G. White, *Christ's Object Lessons*, p. 61; Matthew 28:18.

subdues? Who works? Galatians 5:6 tells us that faith [Greek: believing, yielding] *works* [Greek: energizes] by God's love [Greek: agape]. God does it all. We simply say "Thank You" and receive at His gracious hand. When we appreciate what God did for us at the cross and the fact that He has given everything He has to save humankind (Heb. 6:13–18; Gen. 22:16), we then will be energized to good works by His self-sacrificing love. For each of us who believe, our whole *life* will say "thank You" because of what He does in us.

Paul wrote the following in Romans 2:4: "Or despisest thou the riches of his goodness and forbearance and longsuffering; not knowing that the goodness of God *leadeth* thee to repentance?"

God's goodness does not *hope* to lead us, nor does it *try* to lead us, to repentance. God's goodness *does* lead us all the way to the gift of repentance. We can be lost only by resisting the love of God and calling Him a liar.

> Although Jesus Christ has passed into the heavens, there is still a living chain binding His believing ones to His own heart of infinite love. The most lowly and weak are bound by a chain of sympathy closely to His heart. He never forgets that He is our representative, that He bears our nature.
>
> … But exalted "to be a Prince and a Saviour, to *give* repentance to Israel, and remission of sins," will Christ, our representative and head, close His heart, or withdraw His hand, or falsify His promise? No; never, never.[14]

---

14 Ellen G. White, *Testimonies to Ministers and Gospel Workers,* pp. 19, 20.

Appendix N

When All Earthly Hope Is Gone

"Then will I sprinkle clean water upon you, and ye shall be clean: from all your filthiness, and from all your idols, will I cleanse you. A new heart also will I give you, and a new spirit will I put within you: and I will take away the stony heart out of your flesh, and I will give you an heart of flesh. And I will put my spirit within you, and cause you to walk in my statutes, and ye shall keep my judgments, and do them. And ye shall dwell in the land that I gave to your fathers; and ye shall be my people, and I will be your God" (Ezek. 36:25–28).

Faith is the dependence on the word of God only. So long as there is any dependence on himself, so long as there is any conceivable ground of hope for any dependence upon anything in or about himself, there can be no faith, since faith is dependence on "the word only."

"But when every dependence on anything in or about himself is *gone*, and it is acknowledged to be gone; when everything is against any hope of justification, *then* it is that throwing himself on the promise of God, upon the word only, hoping against hope, faith enters. And by faith he finds justification full and free, all ungodly though he be."[1]

When we acknowledge our life forfeited, and give up all claims to that life, and everything that is connected with it, that very moment we die with Christ."[2]

---

1 A. T. Jones, *Give Us This Day Our Daily Good News,* vol. 2, no. 161.
2 E. J. Waggoner, *Bible Studies on the Book of Romans*, p. 39.

Bibliography

Adams, Mike, ed. "Every Person Needs Sunlight Exposure to Create Vitamin D, Obesity Impairs Vitamin D Absorption." NaturalNews.com, January 1, 2005.

Brown, Francis, Charles A. Briggs, and S. R. Driver. *The Brown-Driver-Briggs Hebrew and English Lexicon.* 13th edition. Peabody, MA: Hendrickson Publishers, Inc., 2010.

Green, J. P., Sr., trans. *The Literal Translation of the Holy Bible.* Sovereign Grace Publishers, 1985.

Johnson, Harry. *The Humanity of the Saviour.* London: Epworth Press, 1962.

Jones, A. T. *1893 General Conference Bulletin.* Payson, AZ: Leaves-of-Autumn Books, Inc., 1989.

_____. *The Consecrated Way to Christian Perfection.* Dodge Center, MN: The Upward Way, 1988.

_____. *Give Us This Day Our Daily Good News.* Vol. 2. Paris, OH: Glad Tidings Publishers, 1994.

_____. "Studies in Galatians, Galatians 2:20." *Advent Review and Sabbath Herald.* October 24, 1899.

Nedley, Neil, M.D. *Depression—The Way Out.* Ardmore, OK: Nedley Publishing, 2001.

_____. *Proof Positive: How to Reliably Combat Disease and Achieve Optimal Health through Nutrition and Lifestyle.* Ardmore, OK: Nedley Publishing, 1999.

Nichol, F. D., ed. *The Seventh-day Adventist Bible Commentary.* 12 vols. Washington, DC: Review and Herald Publishing Assn., 1957.

Ornish, D. "Reversing heart disease through diet, exercise, and stress management: an interview with Dean Ornish [interview by Elaine R Monsen]." *J Am Diet Assoc* 91, no. 2 (February 1991).

Prideaux, Humphrey. *The Old and New Testament Connected in the History of the Jews.* Vol. I. New York: Harper & Brothers, 1845.

Resnicow, K. and J. Barone, et al. "Diet and serum lipids in vegan vegetarians: a model for risk reduction." *J Am Diet Assoc* 91, no. 4 (April 1991).

Seventh-day Adventist Encyclopedia. Second revised edition. Hagerstown, MD: Review and Herald Publishing Association, 2002.

Smith, Uriah. *The Prophecies of Daniel and the Revelation.* Nashville, TN: Southern Publishing Association, 1944.

Waggoner, E. J. *1891 General Conference Bulletin #10.* On "Ellen G. White Writings Comprehensive Research Edition 2008" CD-ROM.

_____. *Bible Studies on the Book of Romans.* Queensland, Australia: Destiny Press, 1981.

_____. *The Glad Tidings: Studies in Galatians.* 1900. Reprint, Paris, OH: The 1888 Message Study Committee, 1988.

_____. *Gospel in Creation.* 1899. Reprint, Ringgold, GA: TEACH Services, Inc. 1995.

_____. *Waggoner on Romans.* Paris, OH: Glad Tidings Publishers.

Webster's Seventh New Collegiate Dictionary. G. & G. Merriam Co., 1967.

White, Ellen G. *Christ's Object Lessons.* Washington, DC: Review and Herald Publishing Assn., 1900.

_____. *Colporteur Evangelism.* Mountain View, CA: Pacific Press Publishing Assn., 1953.

_____. *Counsels on Diet and Foods.* Washington, DC: Review and Herald Publishing Assn., 1938.

_____. *Counsels on Health.* Mountain View, CA: Pacific Press Publishing Assn., 1923.

_____. *The Desire of Ages.* Mountain View, CA: Pacific Press Publishing Assn., 1898.

_____. *Early Writings.* Washington, DC: Review and Herald Publishing Assn., 1882.

_____. *Evangelism.* Washington, DC: Review and Herald Publishing Assn., 1946.

_____. *Fundamentals of Christian Education.* Nashville, TN: Southern Publishing Association, 1923.

_____. *The Great Controversy.* Mountain View, CA: Pacific Press Publishing Assn., 1911.

_____. *Life Sketches of James White and Ellen G. White 1880.* Battle Creek, MI: Seventh-day Adventist Publishing Assn., 1880.

_____. *Manuscript Releases.* Vol. 6. Silver Spring, MD: Ellen G. White Estate, 1990.

_____. *Manuscript Releases.* Vol. 7. Silver Spring, MD: Ellen G. White Estate, 1990.

_____. *Maranatha.* Washington, DC: Review and Herald Publishing Assn., 1976.

_____. *The Ministry of Healing.* Mountain View, CA: Pacific Press Publishing Assn., 1905.

_____. *Patriarchs and Prophets.* Washington, DC: Review and Herald Publishing Assn., 1890.

_____. *Selected Messages.* Book 1. Washington, DC: Review and Herald Publishing Assn., 1958.

_____. *Selected Messages.* Book 2. Washington, DC: Review and Herald Publishing Assn., 1958.

_____. *Selected Messages.* Book 3. Washington, DC: Review and Herald Publishing Assn., 1980.

_____. *Testimonies for the Church.* Vol. 1. Mountain View, CA: Pacific Press Publishing Assn., 1868.

_____. *Testimonies for the Church.* Vol. 4. Mountain View, CA: Pacific Press Publishing Assn., 1881.

_____. *Testimonies for the Church.* Vol. 5. Mountain View, CA: Pacific Press Publishing Assn., 1889.

_____. *Testimonies to Ministers and Gospel Workers.* Mountain View, CA: Pacific Press Publishing Assn., 1923.

_____. *Thoughts from the Mount of Blessing.* Mountain View, CA: Pacific Press Publishing Assn., 1896.

Williams, Beth. *Adventist Frontiers.* June 2010.

Further References for Study

This book has only begun to tap the many blessings that God has for us regarding the broad meanings of the feast days that He gave to the Israelites. This subject is vast and still largely untapped.

In preparing this book for publication, I found the insights in the following books helpful as I researched the subject matter. I quoted from some of the sources below, which are listed in the bibliography for this book. The other books listed in this section contain valuable background information that you may find of interest as you study this topic.

Some of the opinions expressed in the following books and web pages may not necessarily reflect the opinion(s) of the author of this book, so please compare everything you read (including this book) to the Bible.

There are many other excellent sources I could have listed, but these readings will give you a solid start. I believe they will assist you in your understanding and pursuit of mental, physical, and spiritual health and happiness. May God bless you as you study.

Books on Theology

The Acts of the Apostles, Ellen G. White
Christ and His Righteousness, E. J. Waggoner
Christ's Object Lessons, Ellen G. White
The Consecrated Way to Christian Perfection, A. T. Jones
The Cross and Its Shadow, Stephen N. Haskell
Daniel and Revelation, Uriah Smith
The Desire of Ages, Ellen G. White
Feast Days: Shadows of Our Faith, Herbert E. Douglass
The Feasts of the Lord, Howard & Rosenthal
Give us this Day our Daily Good News, Vol. 1 and 2, A. T. Jones and E. J. Waggoner
The Glad Tidings, E. J. Waggoner (edited by Robert J. Wieland)
The Gospel in Daniel, Robert J. Wieland
The Gospel in Revelation, Robert J. Wieland
The Great Controversy, Ellen G. White
Lessons on Faith, A. T. Jones and E. J. Waggoner
The Mystery of the Daily: An Exegesis of Daniel 8:9-14, John W. Peters
The Path to the Throne of God: The Sanctuary, Sarah E. Peck
Patriarchs and Prophets, Ellen G. White
Pillars of the Gospel, Craig Martin Barnes
Prophets and Kings, Ellen G. White
The Story of Daniel the Prophet, Stephen N. Haskell
The Story of the Seer of Patmos, Stephen N. Haskell

Testimonies for the Church, Vol. 1–9, Ellen G. White
Testimony to Ministers and Gospel Workers, Ellen G. White
The Third Angel's Message 1893, A. T. Jones
The Third Angel's Message 1895, A. T. Jones
Waggoner on Romans, E. J. Waggoner

Books on Health

Back to Eden, Jethro Kloss
Depression: The Way Out, Neil Nedley, MD
The Lost Art of Thinking: How to Improve Emotional Intelligence and Achieve Peak Mental Performance, Neil Nedley, MD
Proof Positive: How to Reliably Combat Disease and Achieve Optimal Health through Nutrition and Lifestyle, Neil Nedley, MD
Your Heart's Desire, Good Health, Calvin G. Dence, ND

Other Books of Interest

Ellen G. White: Prophet of Destiny, Rene Noorbergen
Messenger of the Lord: The Prophetic Ministry of Ellen G. White, Herbert E. Douglass
Stories of My Grandmother, Happy Memories About Ellen G. White, Ella M. Robinson

Websites

1888 Message – http:/www.1888message.org
1888 Most Precious Message – http://www.1888mpm.org
1888 Message Study Committee – http://www.1888msc.org
EGW Writings – http://www.egwwritings.org
Gospel Herald, Lancaster Seventh-day Adventist Church – http://www.gospel-herald.com
Glory Light Ministries – http://www.glorylight.org
Moving Toward Modesty – http://www.movingtowardmodesty.com
Remnant Raiment – http://www.remnantraiment.com (Check out the article, "History of Women's Dress in Pictures," http://remnantraiment.com/subpages/history.htm)

Index

A

Aaron, 39, 116-118

Abhor, 76, 135

Abide, 73, 133, 152

Abraham, 37-39, 65, 73-74, 109, 116, 118, 135, 142, 153, 155, 184, 209, 230, 237-238, 245, 247, 262

Abram, 37-38

Accept, 16, 50-51, 65, 99, 135, 150, 168-169, 187, 190, 260, 268-269

Acknowledge, 15-16, 27, 64, 74, 79, 114, 125, 128, 167, 197, 273, 276

Acquittal, 21, 269, 271

Acts, 8, 16, 22, 29, 45, 87, 89, 91, 143-144, 158-159, 165-166, 188, 213, 236, 241-242, 246, 248-249, 251-253, 258, 261-265, 273, 279

Adam(s), 8, 20-21, 23-30, 33-34, 37, 47, 51, 64, 66, 75, 77, 81, 109, 130, 136, 200-201, 219-220, 222, 237-238, 246, 258, 269-271, 277

Adonai, 245

Adopt(etc.), 21-23, 50, 73, 80, 84, 125-126, 206, 231, 233-234, 260

Adorn, 126, 229, 233

Adultery, 61, 67-68, 143, 158

Advent, 95-100, 102-103, 200, 204-206, 277

Afraid, 25, 57, 59, 88, 91, 210, 212, 224, 230, 245

Ananias, 251-252

Antichrist, 204, 210

Antitype(ical), 9, 19-20, 41-42, 44, 77-79, 81-83, 87, 89, 91-93, 98, 100, 105, 112, 115-116, 118-120, 123, 127, 129, 159, 175-176, 178, 182-183, 186-188, 191, 207, 240, 257-260, 263

Antitypically, 9, 45, 81-82, 173, 184, 257-258

Apostles, 20, 45, 151, 187, 207, 262-265, 279

Apparel, 5, 121, 123-127, 180, 220, 229-231, 233

Appetite, 63, 66, 221

Archangel, 49, 71, 85, 245

Armageddon, 24, 82, 176-177, 237

Arminianism, 5, 23, 28, 51, 268-269

Ascension, 22, 29, 98, 119, 242, 258

Ashes, 35-36, 65, 70, 83, 119, 134

Auditor(s, ing), 7, 20-21, 261, 270

Author(s), 2-3, 7-8, 10, 19, 60, 118, 122, 167, 174, 198, 206, 252, 254, 279

Autumn, 91, 98-100, 108, 206-207, 236, 238-239, 277

Av, 243

Awakening, 94, 96, 227, 243

B

Baal, 139-140, 184

Babylon, 98, 107, 129, 143-145, 157-158

Baptism, 79-81, 109, 207, 236-237, 239, 252

Begotten, 11, 13, 55, 69, 75, 150, 193, 248-251, 253-255

Being(s), 41, 63, 71, 228, 249, 252, 254, 256, 259

Belief(s), 68, 88, 95-96, 140, 142, 188, 255, 262, 269

Birthright, 22, 179-180, 191, 202, 265, 269-270

Bondage, 44, 50, 73, 99, 125, 166, 231

Booths, 173-175, 177-178, 183, 186

Bridegroom, 102, 122, 185-187, 189

Brimstone, 35, 82, 139, 143, 158

C

Calvary, 109, 193, 197

Calvinism, 5, 23, 28, 51, 268-269

Canaan, 37-39, 230

Candlestick, 59, 118

Captain, 94

Carmel, 119, 140, 147, 184

Celebration(s), 86, 146, 161, 165, 174, 243

Censer, 118, 178-179

Circumcise(d), 156, 261-262, 265

Circumcision, 156, 260-262, 264-265

Coequal, 254

Coeternal, 254

Comfort, 49-50, 53, 85, 90, 138-141, 193, 210, 253

Comforter, 49, 88, 90, 245

Commandment(s), 26, 45, 59, 70, 124-125, 144, 149, 155, 159-160, 166, 182, 195, 209, 230-231, 259, 264

Communion, 42, 253, 256

Compact, 273-274

Corporate, 21-22, 29, 45, 48, 50, 63, 86, 91, 136, 149, 153, 185-186, 188, 210, 245-246, 256, 274

Corporately, 8, 40-42, 66, 78-80, 86, 173, 188, 195, 236-238, 259, 265, 270

Counselor, 11, 199, 245

Count(ed), 33, 40, 44, 87, 99, 191, 205-206, 212, 222

Court, 151, 175

Courtroom, 70

Courts, 14, 174, 183, 189, 193-194

Covenants, 24, 140

Crucifixion, 80, 185, 201, 204-207

Curse, 53, 58, 134, 146, 211

D

Debt, 249

Decrease, 53

Deliverance, 18, 37-38, 41-42, 44, 47, 58, 69, 89-90, 92, 123, 125, 127-128, 135, 141-142, 144, 187, 193, 202, 209, 257, 259

Destroyer, 15, 41

Dispensation, 22, 68, 79, 270

Docetism, 255, 261

E

Earthquake(s), 24, 113, 178, 181, 184, 214-215

East(ern), 71, 106, 145, 154, 176-177, 183, 246-247

Egypt, 37, 39, 41-44, 75, 117, 124, 136, 158, 167, 174, 176-177, 190-191, 231, 257

Elijah(elias), 134, 136-141, 143-144, 147, 159, 170-172, 175, 184, 208, 213

Elul, 243

Emmanuel, 245, 248

Estate, 38, 53, 73, 278

Eternals, 254

Extremity, 109, 167, 209, 238

F

Fallen sinful human flesh, 24, 32-33, 47, 50, 54-55, 62, 65-66, 72, 80, 140, 143, 156, 159, 190, 210, 251, 259-260, 266, 271

Faultless, 117, 193

Fear, 17, 25, 62, 64, 91, 129, 131, 133-134, 139, 143-144, 152, 157, 159-160, 169, 180, 210, 229

Firstborn, 39, 41, 65

Firstfruit(s), 5, 8-9, 19-20, 33, 40, 44-46, 51, 63, 77, 86-87, 142-143, 173, 242, 257-259, 270, 274

Force, 16-17, 23, 35, 61, 119, 137, 150, 166, 178, 192, 223, 255

Forehead, 62, 142-143, 158
Forever, 17, 35, 70, 73, 120, 144, 148-149, 153, 158, 167-168, 174, 194, 196, 201, 203, 215, 266
Forfeit(ed, ing), 160, 197, 257, 276
Forged, 26, 51, 55, 66, 79-80, 191, 247
Forgive(en, es, ing, ness), 16, 22, 27, 51-52, 55, 114, 193-195, 239-240
Fornication, 73, 143, 158, 264-265
Fortress, 47
Frontal, 62, 142, 155
Fruit(s), 5, 17, 42, 48, 53, 57, 76-77, 91-92, 130-132, 138, 169, 173-174, 192, 195-196, 211, 219, 224, 268
Fund(trust), 23, 63, 79

G

Gabriel, 71, 107, 239
Godhead, 5, 23, 30, 45, 87, 139, 153, 189, 245-248, 251-256
Grace, 21-22, 33, 50, 57, 62, 75, 79, 186, 188, 190, 202, 251, 253, 256, 263, 270-274, 277
Grass, 54, 90, 92, 128, 138, 140, 154, 187
Grave, 34-36, 49, 80, 89, 249
Guile, 142
Guilt, 33-34, 50-51, 55-56, 227
Gunslinger, 6

H

Heir(s), 38-39, 73, 80, 84, 146, 189, 249-250
Hell, 35, 48, 60-61, 70-71, 83, 89, 139
Herbs, 41, 129, 219
Heritage, 8, 26, 28-29, 38, 51, 60, 63, 86, 161, 164, 166, 173, 191, 195, 245, 257, 263
Holies, 8, 98-100, 118-120
Holiest, 118-119, 267
Holiness, 32, 50, 62, 193, 234
Human(ity, kind), 21, 23-27, 29-32, 37, 56, 62, 69, 89, 109, 130, 136, 143, 145-146, 157, 159, 173, 176, 186, 195, 215, 218, 220, 245-246, 250, 253-255, 264, 274-275, 277
Inaugurat(ed, tion), 119, 242, 267
Incarnate, 73, 245, 248-251, 255, 258
Increase, 53, 76, 131, 222-223, 227
Individual, 22, 29, 68, 79, 87,

I

Idols(atry), 32, 135, 261, 264-265, 276
Ignorance, 23, 188, 191
Immanuel, 199-200, 245
Immature, 78
Immortality, 103, 145, 251
Immutable(ity), 17, 39, 196, 259
Impart, 151, 187
Impersonating, 212
Implications, 101, 155
Impossible, 39, 60, 72, 132, 149, 153, 155, 171, 194, 224, 255, 269
Impregnable, 47
Imput(ed, ing), 139, 156
Infallibility, 73, 75
Infinite, 11-13, 15, 17, 68, 227, 254, 273, 275
Infinites, 254
Infirmities, 33, 215
Influence, 13, 16-17, 27, 61, 94, 125-126, 178, 211, 216, 218, 231, 233-235, 252
Inherent, 37, 45, 52, 55, 58, 60, 68, 74, 90, 116, 128, 140, 159, 166, 169, 187-188, 190, 270
Inheritance, 22-23, 29, 40, 51, 62, 66, 72, 79, 90, 119, 176, 191, 195, 248-249
Iniquity, 12, 18, 33-34, 36, 51, 55, 70, 83, 88, 90, 93, 107, 109, 123, 135-136, 138, 148, 156, 181, 187, 203, 236-238, 250, 270
Initiative, 252, 269, 271, 274
Isaac, 38-39, 65, 118, 135, 184, 209
Ishmael, 65, 118

Iyar, 242

J

Jehovah, 11, 17, 39, 72, 101, 140, 153, 155, 157, 159, 175, 193, 208-209, 212-214, 245-246
Jewelry, 121-122, 124, 229

K

Katargeo, 80

L

Lamb, 20-21, 40-41, 77, 100, 109, 113-114, 142-143, 146-147, 155, 158, 239, 241, 245, 248, 255, 257, 274
Laodiceans, 188-189, 269
Latter rain, 20, 29, 91-92, 151, 184, 186-188, 191, 195
Laws, 14, 17, 48, 72, 117, 134, 141, 144-145, 166, 196, 218, 259-260, 264-265, 267
Leaven, 43-44, 46, 87, 257
Leavened(eth), 43-44
Legalism, 24, 136, 145, 159, 166, 168, 170
Levi, 133, 141, 152
Liar(s), 26, 31, 60, 73-74, 139, 275
Lifestyle, 131, 151, 187, 220, 223, 226, 277, 280
Lion, 33, 49, 101, 111, 245
Lisbon, 184
Listen, 8, 123, 139, 145-146, 149, 177, 187-188, 190, 234, 262-263
Locust, 91, 138
Loins, 24, 41, 62, 138

M

Manna, 118, 129, 164, 175
Martyrs, 241
Mary, 241, 248, 254
Melchisedec(k), 40, 116-117, 236

Memorial, 39, 41, 93, 167, 172, 174, 190
Messiah, 108-109, 137, 185, 237-239, 245
Michael, 71-72, 127, 176, 245
Millennium, 34-35, 96-97, 100, 103, 112, 120, 159, 204-205
Millerism, 94, 103-104
Mystery, 8, 16-17, 22, 101-102, 111, 141, 177, 199, 279

N

Nailed, 249
Nebuchadnezzar, 129-130
Nicodemus, 272, 274
Nisan, 241
North(ern), 71, 94, 158-159, 176-177
Numbers, 16, 41, 45, 51, 93, 107, 124, 131, 142, 230, 237

O

Obedience, 12, 17, 140, 149-150, 167, 195-196, 218, 253, 262, 274
Obey, 79, 145-146, 160, 167, 218, 229, 262
Offer, 20, 43, 60, 77, 87, 93, 117, 120, 133, 152-153, 173, 178, 191, 268-269
Ornaments, 122, 124, 229

P

Paralyze, 69, 80
Pardon, 139, 186, 263, 272
Penalty, 17, 33, 40, 69, 90, 134, 136, 141, 144, 257, 259, 269, 271
Perfection, 45-46, 68, 116, 141-142, 147, 177, 203, 277, 279
Pilate, 163, 193
Plaintiff, 70, 149, 153
Policy, 16, 106, 223
Postmillennialism, 96
Powers, 12, 42, 158, 184, 193, 211, 221, 253

Premillennialism, 94, 96, 103
Preparation, 40, 114, 134-135, 163-164, 169, 173, 186, 243
Prevent, 17, 25, 49, 84, 167, 193, 218
Price, 22, 57
Price, 7, 42, 50, 61, 68, 78, 159, 218, 227, 230, 245, 251, 257, 267, 271
Pride, 13, 15-16, 63-66, 71, 220, 230, 234
Probation, 103, 109, 178, 191, 206
Prophet, 5, 35, 82, 134, 136-138, 182-184, 208-214, 217, 230
Psychiatrist, 90, 253
Punishment, 28, 40, 135, 139-140, 159-160, 191, 194
Purge, 44, 119, 133, 141, 152, 251, 257
Purged, 32, 120, 249, 266
Purification, 21, 92, 97, 141, 149, 152-153, 186, 205, 267
Purify(ed, er, ies, ing), 89-90, 92, 119-120, 133-134, 141, 149, 152, 186, 206, 231, 263
Purity, 149, 189

Q

Qualify, 21, 24, 26, 29-30

R

Rebellion, 11, 13-17, 191-192, 194, 196, 272
Rebirth, 272
Redeem(ed), 27, 29, 33, 142, 190, 273-274
Redeemer, 8, 157, 260
Redemption, 22, 26, 99, 119, 192, 194, 196-197, 245, 252-253, 271, 273
Refines(er,i ng, ment), 89, 108, 119, 133-136, 141, 152
Reflect(s, ing), 2, 7, 12, 57, 82, 128, 174, 186, 249, 279
Reform(s,ed), 121, 126, 131, 133, 147, 149, 152-154, 180, 204, 220-221, 230, 233-234, 268
Refreshing, 186
Refuge, 40, 65, 260
Reins, 62
Reject(ed, ers, ing, tion), 15-16, 22, 51, 103, 108, 144, 150, 185, 196, 217, 236, 265
Relationship, 106, 213, 256
Raiment, 54, 123, 137-138, 188-189, 199, 280
Rains, 9, 19-20, 29, 90-92, 151, 173-175, 184, 186-188, 191, 195, 258
Raised, 6, 79, 81, 90, 137, 149, 170, 232, 248-249, 269
Ratify(ed,es,cation), 22-23, 38, 118, 238
Realm, 45, 52, 130, 252
Remit(sion), 31, 114, 120, 194-195, 267, 275
Remnant, 92, 209, 280
Repent, 16, 47-48, 116, 135-136, 188-189, 252, 272-273
Repentance, 31, 47-48, 50, 136-137, 142-144, 149, 152-153, 159, 186, 190-191, 272-275
Representation, 5, 20, 29, 71, 77, 83, 158, 214, 249, 264
Representative, 5, 8, 19, 21-24, 26-31, 33, 38, 40, 42, 45-46, 51, 62-64, 66, 77-81, 84, 90, 173, 195-196, 200, 245-246, 251, 253, 257-259, 267-271, 273-275
Reputation, 58
Resist, 123, 133, 152, 216, 274
Respect, 10, 29, 66, 80, 164, 249-251, 264
Respond, 76, 131, 135, 139, 180, 269
Response, 27-28, 50, 65, 80-81, 147, 166, 188, 245, 261, 268
Reverence, 10, 14, 229, 264
Reverend, 245
Reversed, 21, 28, 66, 125, 220, 226, 233, 269
Revival, 96
Reward, 49, 58, 159-160, 180, 212, 218
Ribband, 124, 230

Rich, 23, 123, 128, 149, 174, 177, 189, 195

Ride, 146-147, 161, 164, 166

Righteous, 15, 21, 46-48, 60, 79, 113, 122-124, 144, 146, 177, 187-188, 190, 195, 229, 234, 256, 271

Righteousness by faith, 101,143-145, 152-153, 159, 190, 262

Rise, 25, 39, 49, 72, 81, 85, 94, 97-98, 116, 139, 179, 181, 190, 209-210, 227

Risen, 81, 137, 258, 270

Rosh hashanah, 243

Royal(ty), 51, 189

S

Sabbatismos, 170

Sacred, 13, 16, 19, 114, 143, 164-165, 168, 174, 182, 210

Sacredness, 114, 143

Saints, 35, 82, 97, 103, 113, 144, 146, 159, 175, 178, 186, 196, 206

Salt(ed, iness), 59, 160, 222, 261

Sanctification, 202, 253

Sanctify, 75, 119, 121, 148, 156, 163, 203, 215, 266

Sanctuaries, 36, 70, 83, 112

Sand, 35, 38, 68, 82

Sapphira, 252

Savior(saviour), 7, 10, 27, 31, 34, 40, 47, 50, 52, 68, 86, 94-95, 125, 149, 151, 157, 192-193, 195-196, 234, 255, 270, 274-275, 277

Scapegoat, 120

Scepter(re), 12, 179, 250

Schoolmaster, 186

Seal, 34, 40, 82, 101, 107, 109, 111, 144-145, 154-157, 159-160, 176, 178, 184, 186, 237

Sealed(est), 12, 38-39, 42, 46, 145, 151, 154-155, 160, 192, 252, 257, 265

Sealing, 37, 55, 111, 146, 154-155, 160

Secular, 164, 168-169, 235

Secure, 12, 14, 16, 90, 197, 214, 219

Security, 192

Seed(s), 25-26, 36-38, 71, 73, 91-92, 129-130, 196, 202, 209, 219, 245, 272

Seek, 2, 13, 16, 25, 54, 67, 69, 73-74, 94, 96, 122, 124, 133, 141, 151, 177, 196, 224, 226, 231, 235, 264, 272-273

Selfishness, 54, 231

Selfsame, 20, 43-44, 77, 87

Sensual, 229

Seraph(s, im), 71, 193, 245

Serious, 19, 98, 159-160

Serpent, 25-26, 34, 48, 69, 72, 82, 150, 274

Servant, 65, 73, 122, 134, 157, 180, 184

Service, 12, 17, 42, 114, 116-120, 147-148, 174, 191, 196, 203, 252

Servile, 43, 87, 93, 173

Shaking, 84

Shamefacedness, 126, 229, 233

Shavuot, 242

Shewbread, 71, 118

Showdown, 140, 159, 184

Shower(s), 90, 92, 187

Sick, 22, 106, 189, 218, 239

Sight, 36, 53, 70, 76, 83, 105-106, 121, 133, 136-137, 149, 157, 170, 186, 193, 195, 230

Sign(s), 97, 143-144, 156-160, 181, 183-184, 206, 211, 215, 241

Signal, 92-93, 169

Sinai, 38, 55, 121-122, 134, 190, 215

Sinlessness, 272

Sivan, 242-243

Slain, 84, 114, 245, 247-248, 255

Slaves(ery), 15, 30, 273

Slumbered, 185

Snakebites, 69

Sobriety, 126, 229, 233-234

Solemn(ity), 93-94, 96, 109, 126, 173, 175, 217, 273
Solomon, 54, 189
Song, 62, 142, 174-175, 189, 245
South(ern), 106, 149, 158, 215, 277-278
Speak, 6, 8, 20, 25, 28, 30, 40, 72-73, 77, 87-90, 93, 95, 113, 116, 118, 121, 124, 126, 138, 156, 169, 173, 177, 179, 187, 196, 210-211, 213, 215, 230, 235, 255, 261, 273
Specially, 270
Spiritual(ist(s)), 2, 19, 21, 23, 41, 50, 53, 63, 77-79, 91, 96, 103, 143, 145, 158, 166-167, 169, 182, 185, 188-189, 195, 202, 208, 217, 221, 228, 234, 249, 255, 257, 259-260, 270, 279
Spirituality, 19
Spiritualizers, 103
Spiritually, 77, 80, 147, 188-189
Spotless, 186, 193
Spouse, 212, 225
Standard(s), 3, 46, 155, 182, 225
Star(s), 8, 12, 38, 71, 106, 158, 176, 179, 184, 189, 210
Statute(s), 15, 17, 20, 52, 57, 76-77, 84, 87, 121-122, 134-135, 144, 154, 172-173, 273, 276
Steadfast(stedfast), 40, 172
Stealing, 264
Stephen, 109, 185, 236, 279
Stewardship, 270
Stiffnecked, 122
Strangled, 264-265
Street(s), 93, 108, 174, 232, 237-238
Strength, 6, 11-12, 65, 72, 91, 119, 128, 166, 169, 175, 194-195, 213, 215-216, 245, 255, 270
Stress, 220, 222, 277
Strife, 39, 45, 145, 154, 191, 250

Strong, 11, 16, 39-40, 59, 65, 105, 215
Struggle, 47, 56, 193, 225
Struggling, 13, 56, 166
Stubble, 35-36, 83, 89, 134, 139, 144, 158
Stumble(ing), 231, 265
Style, 230-234
Submission, 17, 127, 194
Submit, 15-16, 129, 176, 186
Subordinate, 253
Subservience, 24
Subservient, 250, 255-256
Subsidy, 268
Substance, 164, 247, 249, 254-255, 261-262, 266
Substitute, 28, 33-34, 65, 159
Substitution, 27
Success, 10, 210, 237
Suffer(ed, ing(s), ers), 15, 17, 28-29, 33, 35, 40-41, 48, 53, 73, 120, 137, 168, 175-176, 180-181, 193, 199, 225, 231, 261, 270-271
Sufficient(iency), 14, 27, 45, 54, 71, 143, 158
Sukkot, 243
Sunday, 40, 44, 77, 79, 81, 113, 163, 171, 241-244
Sunlight, 218, 222-223, 277
Sunset(sundown), 40, 43-44, 154, 162-163, 168, 171, 177, 216-217, 227, 236, 241-242
Sunshine, 132, 221
Superficial, 186
Superhuman, 90, 213
Supernatural, 113, 213
Superstition, 245
Supper, 224, 241
Surety, 33, 149, 195, 273-274
Surrender, 59, 170, 186, 201, 218
Sustain, 13, 140, 175, 249, 256
Swear(sware), 38-39, 101, 111, 116, 170
Swears(ers, eth, ing), 38, 47-48, 133, 152, 193,

264
Sweet, 20, 77, 87, 102, 111-112, 124, 138, 209
Sword, 59, 93, 124, 175, 183-184
Symbol(s, ic, ically, ism, ized), 38, 45, 103, 107, 114, 119, 122, 125, 147, 155, 166, 182, 239, 258, 260
Sympathy, 31, 50, 56, 62, 144, 194, 275
Synagogue(s), 162, 165, 264
System, 7-8, 19, 32, 41-42, 118, 142, 188, 192, 215, 221-223, 232, 239, 259-260, 263-264, 269

T

Tabernacle(s), 5, 7, 9, 19, 82-83, 99, 112, 114, 116-120, 122, 165, 173-175, 178, 182-183, 186, 188, 190-191, 207, 243, 258, 263, 266
Table(s), 5, 38, 71, 75-76, 91, 118, 175, 217, 264
Tablet(s), 124, 132, 222
Tammuz, 243
Tares, 78, 88
Taste, 33, 74, 222, 235, 271
Taxes, 241
Teaching(s), 10, 62, 90, 92, 94, 103, 171, 179-180, 187, 216-217, 225, 255
Tears, 52, 83, 147, 171
Temperance, 132, 218, 223
Temple, 24, 41, 46, 63, 67, 69, 71, 75, 112-115, 119, 133, 141, 143, 145-147, 151, 165, 174-175, 181, 204-205, 209, 238, 241, 260, 266
Temporal, 54-55, 63, 78, 91, 137, 149, 153, 166-167, 169, 175, 228
Tendency, 16, 126, 233
Tenth, 20, 40-41, 77, 87, 98-100, 120, 133, 153, 176, 207
Terrible, 15, 17, 33-34, 91, 193-194, 209, 215
Territory, 45, 182
Terror, 70, 94, 196
Test, 58, 65, 182-183, 189-190, 213, 217, 225
Testament(s), 8, 35, 39, 44-45, 59, 80, 108, 119-120, 127, 135, 245-246, 249, 270, 277
Testator, 119
Tested, 196, 208, 217, 234
Testified, 17, 72, 81, 116, 151, 156
Testing, 100
Tests, 208-209, 270
Thankfulness, 55, 78
Thanksgiving, 128, 146, 174
Theology(ical), 268, 279
Theoretical, 27-28
Theory, 254
Theos, 248, 272
Thistles, 26, 130, 211, 220
Thorns, 26, 130, 146, 211, 220
Thoughtful, 257
Thousand, 13, 34-36, 44, 82, 95, 99, 106, 134, 142, 145, 154, 192, 204, 215, 239, 247
Threat(en(ed,ing)), 150, 178, 229
Thrilled, 13, 72
Throne(s), 11-13, 15, 18, 34-35, 39, 46, 71, 82-83, 117, 137, 142, 146-147, 158, 176, 178-179, 189-190, 193, 195, 247, 250, 253, 258, 274, 279
Thunder(s, ings), 101, 111, 142, 178
Tidings, 122, 202, 249, 277, 279
Timeline, 5, 40, 109, 236
Tishri, 243
Tithe(s, ing), 46, 78, 261, 270
Title, 8, 69, 90, 155, 157, 173, 179, 195, 198, 241, 255, 266, 272
Tomb(s), 34, 241-242
Tongue(s), 87-89, 92, 102, 112, 129, 143, 146, 157, 188, 209-210, 242, 258
Torment(ed), 25, 35, 82, 143, 158-159
Torn, 112-114, 194, 260

Torture, 53, 56, 89, 159, 194
Touch, 48, 183, 212, 214, 219
Touched, 33, 105, 107, 163, 213, 239
Toward, 22, 53, 71, 90, 105-106, 177, 184, 187, 280
Toxic, 138
Trace(d), 94, 132, 206, 222
Tradition(s), 136, 235, 263
Traffic(k), 36, 45, 70, 83
Traitors, 47
Trample(ing), 160
Trance, 213
Tranquil, 10
Transaction, 21, 24-28, 63
Transcript, 70, 155
Transfer, 114
Transfiguration, 184
Transform, 188
Transgression, 15, 17, 51, 55, 106-107, 109, 148, 182, 195, 203, 210, 236-238, 249
Transgressions, 119, 148, 203, 272
Transgressor(s), 33, 106, 176-177, 214
Transition, 5, 29, 86-87, 89, 91, 177
Translated, 33-35, 69, 79-80, 105-106, 108, 138, 147, 149, 163, 170, 190, 212, 219, 246, 249, 251, 271
Translation, 80, 109, 119-120, 122, 179, 269, 271-272, 277
Translators, 119, 229, 245
Transparent, 142
Trauma, 213
Tread(ing), 134, 161, 164, 175, 221, 273
Treasure(s), 54-55, 129, 229
Treasury, 69
Treat, 143, 164, 218, 223
Treatise, 5, 28, 51, 268
Treatment(s), 218, 228, 260
Tree(s), 23, 25-26, 30, 32, 48, 76, 91, 130, 138, 145, 154, 173, 184, 211, 219-220, 229, 241, 261
Trembling, 64
Trespass(ed, er, es), 114, 135, 139
Trial(s), 31, 46, 48-49, 52, 58, 70, 72, 90, 133, 143, 149, 153, 155, 157, 183, 188-189, 199, 234, 236, 255, 269
Tribe(s), 45, 145, 154, 184, 211, 245
Tribulation, 147, 155, 183-184, 210
Tried, 30, 61, 89, 95, 115, 123, 128, 133, 163, 166, 188-189, 199
Tries, 58, 64, 150, 213
Trinity, 254-255
Trio, 45, 245, 247, 253, 255
Triumph, 96, 146, 190, 201, 216
Triumph(al,ed,antly), 146, 174, 192, 194, 241
Triune, 254-255
Trodden, 59, 106, 174, 183
Trouble, 124, 127, 145, 147, 154-155, 175-178, 182-184, 186, 188, 191, 224, 264
Troubled, 57, 181, 217, 265
Troublous, 108, 237-238
Trump(et(s)), 5, 8-9, 19, 49, 72, 85, 93, 99, 103, 105, 111, 113, 173, 175, 178, 184, 210-211, 243, 258, 260
Trust(s), 14, 23, 26, 29, 51, 63, 75-76, 79, 90, 132, 167-169, 175, 218, 225, 227-228, 245, 270
Trustee, 29, 68, 79
Truths, 49, 65, 149
Twelve, 45, 71, 113, 132, 137, 145, 170, 225
Type(s), 19, 77, 90, 94, 98-100, 112, 115-116, 119, 158, 222, 225, 229, 249, 259, 264
Typical, 19, 42, 99, 151, 182-183, 246, 257
Typically, 50, 81, 184
Typified, 99
Tyrannical, 261

U

Ultimate, 24, 83, 150, 178
Ultimately, 22, 70, 78, 125, 134, 145, 157
Unable, 30, 213, 225
Unaccountable, 15
Unaided, 24
Unanswered, 27-28
Unappetizing, 188
Unavoidably, 188
Unbelief, 26, 31, 52, 56, 66, 145, 153, 166, 169-170, 193, 270
Unbeliever(s, ing), 56, 139, 170, 176, 190-191, 230-231, 234-235
Unblemished, 193
Unchangeable, 245
Unchanging, 11, 13
Uncircumcised, 135, 156
Unclean, 48, 119, 122, 125, 130
Uncleannesses, 57, 76
Uncommitted, 16
Unconditional, 183
Unconscious, 163, 212-213, 216
Uncreated, 254
Unction, 117
Undefiled, 12
Underived, 251-252
Unequivocally, 250
Unethical, 265
Unfair, 155
Unfallen, 192-194
Unfitted, 126, 233
Ungodly(ness), 62, 139, 270, 272, 276
Unguarded, 13
Union, 143, 158-159, 182
Unisex, 233
Unit, 245-246, 254, 256
Unite(d), 3, 16, 97, 146, 155, 171, 174, 182, 190, 196, 205, 208, 216, 234, 247, 273

Unity, 45, 247, 254
Universal, 146, 174, 202, 270
Universalism, 269
Unjust, 15, 46
Unleavened, 5, 8, 19, 41, 43-44, 46, 53, 60, 63, 67, 75-76, 79, 83, 86, 142, 173, 241-242, 257
Unlocked, 110
Unmanageable, 219
Unmasked, 17
Unmercifully, 159
Unmerited, 263
Unmistakable, 195
Unnumbered, 13
Unpardonable, 22
Unpopular, 137, 140, 238
Unpopulated, 101, 154
Unprepared, 17, 94
Unquenchable, 94
Unreached, 235
Unreasonable, 72
Unrestricted, 16
Unrighteous, 56
Unrighteousness, 118, 139
Unsanctified, 64-65
Unsealed, 111
Unsearchable, 14
Unseen, 107, 112, 149
Unselfish, 12, 56
Unspeakable, 9, 190
Untapped, 279
Untold, 219
Untrammeled, 218
Unusable, 261
Unutterable, 13
Unveiling, 192
Unwillingness, 150, 187
Unwritten, 229

V

Vain, 81, 229, 270
Value, 54, 164, 182, 202
Vanity, 49, 231, 234
Vegan, 220, 277
Vegetables, 129-132, 219-220, 224
Vegetarian(s), 131-132, 219-220, 277
Vengeance, 53
Vessels, 120, 129, 143, 185-186
Victory, 21, 23, 27-29, 39, 46, 66, 131, 192
Vindicate(d, tion), 46, 58, 73, 196, 269
Vine, 42, 91, 169, 174
Vineyard, 123
Violence, 70, 137, 193
Virgin(s), 142, 185, 187, 248
Virtue, 69
Vision(s), 91, 105-107, 109, 130, 208-209, 213-217, 236-237, 239, 247

W

Wages, 29, 33, 133, 152
Waggoner, 149, 151, 168, 187, 190, 195, 197-198, 202, 276-277, 279-280
Warfare, 138-139, 196
Warning, 8, 13, 16, 19, 46, 93, 123, 139, 179, 188, 258
Wars, 181
Wash(ed), 121, 147, 267
Washing, 121, 131, 153, 168, 232, 267-268
Watch, 146, 180, 190, 224, 226, 261
Watchmen, 93
Wave, 20-21, 77-78, 87, 100, 258
Weak, 31, 118, 128, 210, 275
Wear, 124-125, 127, 137, 146, 180, 196, 199, 220, 229-230, 232-233, 235
Weather, 224, 232
Wedding, 185-186, 241

Week, 46, 77-78, 96, 109, 132, 160-165, 167, 169, 177, 185, 204, 206-207, 215, 221-222, 225, 236, 238-239, 260, 267
Weekend, 79, 171, 225
Weeks, 5, 9, 19, 86-87, 89-92, 98, 100, 107-109, 129, 186, 204-207, 225, 236-237, 239, 242, 258
Weep(ing), 50, 53, 180
Weight, 34, 193, 222
Welfare, 73, 127
West(ern), 105, 183, 208, 235, 247
Westerners, 235
Wheat, 88, 91
Whosoever, 35, 43, 55, 59-61, 69, 73, 75, 83, 92, 137, 144, 150, 154, 159, 170, 196, 209, 211, 272
Wicked, 17, 36, 48, 89, 128, 134, 140-141, 146, 196, 216-217
Wickedness, 24, 44, 62, 214, 257
Widow, 56, 78, 133, 152
Wife, 6, 25-26, 49, 130, 161, 220, 224, 235
Wilderness, 63-64, 69, 91, 120, 137-140, 150, 169-170, 174-175, 177-178, 183, 236, 239, 247, 272, 274
Willing, 15, 39, 47, 53, 58, 65, 76, 84, 86, 122, 180, 188, 191, 218, 250, 269
Willpower, 58
Wind, 68, 84, 87, 122, 125, 128, 137, 145, 154, 214, 258
Winds, 45, 84, 105, 145, 154, 184, 191, 211
Wine, 20, 49, 77, 91, 129-130, 143, 158, 174-175
Wing, 12, 238
Winter, 183, 222, 224, 232
Wisdom, 12-17, 22, 45, 49, 57, 62, 70, 129-130, 146, 192-193, 201, 226
Wise, 6, 48, 53, 59, 107-108, 170, 176, 180, 185, 187-188, 248

Wish, 200, 220, 228, 235
Withdraw(n, al), 31, 34, 193, 275
Wither(s, ed, eth), 138, 140, 165-166, 241
Withheld, 38
Witness, 8, 27, 34, 46, 59, 69, 82, 99, 113, 133, 146, 152, 156, 182, 185, 188, 235, 253, 263, 266
Witnesses, 31, 70, 72, 74, 81, 151, 157, 193, 249, 255
Witnessing, 59
Wives, 229
Woman, 25-26, 30, 36, 48, 61, 67-68, 117, 124-126, 130, 142, 185, 190, 209, 232-235, 245
Womb, 29, 247
Women, 124-127, 137, 142, 179-180, 185-186, 188, 214, 220, 229-230, 232-235, 280
Wonder, 125, 193, 235, 261
Wonderful, 11, 167, 192, 199, 214, 218
Wonders, 91, 183, 209, 263
Wood, 124, 143, 184
Wool, 120, 247
Word, 11, 69, 75, 80, 144, 159, 169, 202, 247, 251, 269, 274
Worldliness, 140
Worldly, 19, 62, 118, 272
Worlds, 14, 16-17, 192-193, 249
Worldwide, 3, 24, 258
Worn, 124-125, 232-233
Worry(ies, ing), 166, 169, 180, 227-228
Worse, 34, 93, 129, 221, 225
Worship, 19, 63-65, 127-128, 139, 143-144, 157-161, 168-169, 172, 177, 182, 190, 205, 209-210, 225, 245, 250, 254, 256, 264-266
Worth, 7, 19, 61, 132, 179, 215, 224-225
Worthless, 31
Worthy, 56, 71, 136, 151, 245, 256-257
Wounded, 27, 50, 193, 272
Woven, 199, 229
Wrapped, 7, 53, 152, 261-262
Wrath, 34, 53, 61, 139, 143, 158, 170, 193, 214
Wretched, 33, 123, 189
Wrong, 7, 15, 33, 64, 93, 100, 123, 164, 179-180, 233
Wrote, 63, 67-68, 94-95, 97, 114, 149, 169, 175, 204, 206, 208-209, 214-215, 230, 265, 272, 275
Wroth, 209
Wrung, 33-34, 193

Y

Yahweh, 72, 245-246
Yeshua, 153, 170
Yhwh, 245-246
Yield, 15, 58, 91, 97, 132, 150, 186-187, 190, 192, 274
Yoke, 139, 169, 263
Yom kippur, 19, 243

We invite you to view the complete
selection of titles we publish at:

www.TEACHServices.com

Scan with your mobile
device to go directly
to our website.

Please write or email us your praises, reactions, or
thoughts about this or any other book we publish at:

P.O. Box 954
Ringgold, GA 30736

info@TEACHServices.com

TEACH Services, Inc., titles may be purchased in bulk for
educational, business, fund-raising, or sales promotional use.
For information, please e-mail:

BulkSales@TEACHServices.com

Finally, if you are interested in seeing
your own book in print, please contact us at

publishing@TEACHServices.com

We would be happy to review your manuscript for free.